SOCIAL AND MORAL VALUES

Individual and Societal Perspectives

SOCIAL AND MORAL VALUES

Individual and Societal Perspectives

Edited by

NANCY EISENBERG
Arizona State University

JANUSZ REYKOWSKI
Polish Academy of Sciences

ERVIN STAUB
University of Massachusetts at Amherst

LEA LAWRENCE ERLBAUM ASSOCIATES, PUBLISHERS
1989 Hillsdale, New Jersey Hove and London

Lawrence Erlbaum Associates, Inc., Publishers
365 Broadway
Hillsdale, New Jersey 07642

Library of Congress Cataloging-in-Publication Data

Social and moral values: individual and societal perspectives/
edited by Nancy Eisenberg, Janusz Reykowski, Ervin Staub.
p. cm.
Bibliography: p.
Includes index.
ISBN 0-89859-956-3
1. Social values. 2. Values. I. Eisenberg, Nancy.
II. Reykowski, Janusz. III. Staub, Ervin.
HM216.S549 1989
303.3'72–dc19 88-37456
CIP

Contents

Introduction

For many decades psychologists were preoccupied with studying behavior and the stimulus conditions that control it. Gradually, however, they turned their attention to the role of internal factors in the regulation of behavior – first of all, to the regulatory role of cognitive processes. In recent years, however, there has been a growing interest in other kinds of regulatory mechanisms of behavior, namely in values and related phenomena. True, studies on values have a rather long history; for example, more than 50 years ago Allport and Vernon tried to develop an instrument for measuring value orientations. But the history of research on values is not a very elaborated one; in fact, until recently the real significance of values was appreciated primarily by sociologists and philosophers. In recent years, however, there have been various attempts to construct general theoretical models that integrate the term into the broader network of psychological concepts, analyze the role of values in the regulation of various forms of social behavior, and delineate the development of values.

In spite of this surge of interests in values, the crucial concept – the term *value* – is still somewhat ambigious. Some authors adhere to the definition proposed by Rokeach (1973) in his widely cited book: "A value is an enduring belief that a specific mode of conduct or end state is personally or socially preferable relative to an opposite or converse mode of conduct or end state of existence" (p. 5).

There are problems with this definition. First, the formulation that a value is a "belief that (something) is preferable to" seems to imply that a value can be interpreted as a kind of descriptive knowledge. Its formal structure is similar to the structure of statements that define the descriptive concepts such as, for example, "Heliocentrism is the belief that sun is the center of the planetary system" or "Spiritualism it is the belief that spirits of the dead communicate with the living." It should be stressed, however, that in both these examples, the belief has some objective referent – it refers to the location of the sun and planets against one another or to the (alleged) communication with the dead. Thus, the question arises, what is the referent of the belief in the statement that a value is a "belief that (something) is preferable"?; that is, what is the basis of the view that the given end state *X* is preferable to the end state *Y*? Aren't we saying that something is preferable because it has greater value than something else? If this is the case, we run into a kind of circularity: Values are beliefs about preferences and preferences originate from values.

Of course, we can also assume that values and preferences are not as just described and that an individual can have correct or incorrect beliefs about preferences. However, acceptance of this assumption means that we must face a new problem: What is the nature of preferences? If values do not determine preferences – what does?

Assuming that the concept of value refers to preferences (whatever their nature), we are confronted with yet another ambiguity. In some contexts the term *preference* implies that the person likes (or dislikes) a given object (event, situation) more than other ones because it better (or worse) suits his or her needs. An example is the case when an individual prefers a well-done steak to a rare one. There is another context, however, in which an object, event, or situation has nothing to do with a person's needs or even with the person himself or herself. For example, if some people say that they are against slavery, they do not necessarily mean that they do not want to be slaves; usually they intend to say that they object to slavery for all human beings. Sometimes such a preference means much more – it implies that people would be ready to fight against slavery and even to risk their lives to preclude or eradicate it. A real life example of such a reaction is the behavior of persons who risked their lives rescuing people persecuted by Nazis during the second world war.

There is the major difference between the two aforementioned meanings of the term *prefer*. Although we can say "I prefer freedom over slavery" and "I prefer well-done to rare steak," the psychological prerequisites of these two statements are very different. One may argue that in the first case, special mental organizations have to be formed as the basis for both making such a statement and for determining appropriate actions – actions aimed at protection, maintenance and/or enhancement of well being of objects (concrete or abstract) that have nothing to do with satisfaction of our personal needs. These organizations are qualititively different from those that are necessary for choosing steaks. Most often the term value is used to refer to the former rather than to the latter type of situation.

One may argue that the meaning of a concept is a question of convention. In other words, we may use the term values to refer to all situations involving orderings on the basis of preferences or use it to refer to a more limited range of contexts. One of these contexts is in reference to social relationships that are of upmost importance, an importance that might be greater than the needs and interests of the individual himself or herself.

The focus of this book is on values in the more narrow and more restricted sense. Although none of the authors says it explicitly and few of the authors are concerned with the distinction that was made here, most of the chapters in the volume deal with psychological factors that make people attend to the well-being of others and of society.

Specifically, this volume is organized into five sections. In the first, various theoretical perspectives on the nature of values are presented. Seymour Epstein discusses the various definitions of values and the role of values within his cognitive-experiential self-theory. Janusz Reykowski focuses on moral values and their origins. Ervin Staub also discusses moral values, but in the context of exploring their role in benevolent and aggressive behavior.

In the second section, the contributors focus specifically on the development of positive values. Nancy Eisenberg uses work concerning the development of moral reasoning within various cultures as a basis for her discussion. Martin Hoffman focuses on the development of political activism in relation to empathy and related moral principles. Adam Niemczynski and Agnieszka Kisiel also deal with the development of moral reasoning but focus specifically on changes with age in moral relativism (that is, the negation of unconditional and universal principles and rules). In the next chapter, Martin Kaplan deals with the issue of differentiating values and moral reasoning when studying moral development.

In the third section of this volume, authors consider the place of values in various types of decisions and explore relevant decision-making processes. Morton Deutsch focuses on the issue of the oft assumed incompatibility of egalitarian and economic efficiency. His conclusions are highly relevant for decisions regarding the structuring of work environments. Krystyna Skarżyńska, like Deutsch, deals with issues related to distributive justice and considers how evaluations of justice are affected by the evaluator's perspectives. In the third chapter, Tadeusz Tyszka discusses processes involved in decision making, and various possible strategies for making choices. In the last chapter, John Levine and Richard Moreland focus on people's use of comparison processes in the context of formulating social values.

The topic of the fourth section is values in the regulation of behaviors. In this section, the relation of values to behavioral outcomes is explicitly examined. C. Daniel Batson and Jane Piliavin both examine values in relation to prosocial, helping behavior. Batson explores the role of egoistic versus altruistic values in the performance of prosocial actions whereas Piliavin analyzes the way in which behaviors affect the development of altruistic values and commitment to the performance of subsequent altruistic actions. In contrast, Wojciszke focuses on the role of idealism in moderating the relation between personal value preferences and value-relevent behavior.

In the final section of the volume, sociopolitical, socioeconomic, and historical perspectives on values are considered. Aleksandra Jasińska-Kania analyzes the relations among moral reasoning (and values), perceptions of justice, and the tendency to accept or deny the legitimacy of the political order. This work was conducted in 1984 in Poland, a time when values and political legitimacy were no doubt salient issues in the society. Krzysztof Korzeniowski also deals with people's feeling of autonomy alientation and their processing of and reactions to aspects of the political system. Duane Alwin focuses on a somewhat different set of issues: the effects of the work environment and socioeconomic factors on parent's socialization values. He argues that aspects of the work environment may play a mediational role in the relation between educational and occupational status and parenting values. Finally, E. Ann Kaplan takes a historical perspective on views related to gender-related conceptions of morality. She uses literature as well as psychological works to illustrate her points.

ACKNOWLEDGMENTS

This book was prepared as a joint venture of a group of American and Polish psychologists. The two groups met in November, 1984 in Zaborow (Poland) to compare their approaches to the problems of values. There are good reasons to believe that science is an international endeavor and that scientific truth does not vary as a function of state boundaries. Nonetheless, one can expect that cultural differences and differences in societal problems that various societies face must have some bearing on the way that scientific problems are approached, especially in social sciences. This is why it seemed worthwhile to compare the somewhat different perspectives of psychologists working in different social contexts.

One may wonder how much these two perspectives do in fact differ from each other. After all, in the last few decades there has been an observable trend towards the development of a global psychology – social, cultural, and political differences notwithstanding. But in spite of this trend towards unification, some differences remain. We hope that the present book illustrates both the similarities that exist between different approaches and some culture-bound differences.

The preparation of the book (as well as the previously mentioned conference) was sponsored by two institutions: The Polish Academy of Sciences and IREX (International Research and Exchange Board). We are very grateful for their assistance. While working on this project, Nancy Eisenberg also received support from a Career Development Award from the National Institute of Child Health and Development (KO4 HD00717), the National Science Foundation (BNS-8509223), and the Max Planck Institute (Director, Paul Baltes) and Technical University in Berlin. The contributions of these institutions were substantial. In addition, we would like to acknowledge the contributions and cooperation of our collegagues, Duane Alwin, Martin Hoffman, Krystyna Skarżyńska, and Marek Ziółkowski, who helped with the preparation of the volume. Finally, we thank our spouses, Jerry Harris, Maria ZuzannaSmoleńska, and Sylwia Staub, for their support throughout.

REFERENCE

Rokeach, M. (1973). *The nature of human values.* New York: MacMillan.

Part 1

VALUES: GENERAL THEORETICAL PERSPECTIVES

1 Values from the Perspective of Cognitive-Experiential Self-Theory

Seymour Epstein
University Massachusetts at Amherst

For over a decade I have been working on the development of a unified theory of personality that I refer to as Cognitive-experiential Self-theory (e.g., Epstein, 1973, 1976, 1979a, 1980, 1981, 1983a, 1985, in press a, in press b; Epstein & Erskine, 1983). The theory integrates various aspects of different theories of personality, including psychoanalytic theories, behavioral theories, phenomenological theories, existential theories, and cognitive theories, at least insofar as they can be combined without doing violence to the coherence of the overall theory. As my aim is to construct a complete theory, it became an interesting challenge to determine how well it could account for phenomena referred to by constructs that do not appear in my own theory. Values is one such construct. Although values occupy a position of central importance in social psychology, they are not often referred to in personality theories. This state of affairs suggests either an important omission in most personality theories, my own included, or that the phenomena that social psychologists use values to explain are explained otherwise by personality theorists. An examination of values from the perspective of Cognitive-experiential Self-theory has the potential of both extending the theory and contributing something of significance to an understanding of values.

This article is divided into three sections. The first consists of an analysis of the nature of values, the second of a review of relevant aspects of Cognitive-experiential Self-theory, and the third of an exploration of the implications of the latter for the former.

THE NATURE OF VALUES

Values are beliefs about desirability that organize experience and direct behavior with respect to certain broad classes of events. Thus, if I value achievement, I believe achievement is desirable, and I therefore attend to events related to achievement, remember events related to achievement, and behave in ways related to achievement. Concepts somewhat similiar to values are goals and motives. A goal is the object of a motive, and, because it is desired, is also something that is valued. Thus, in a broad sense, goals, values, and motives account for similar phenomena and, within limits, are interchangeable. Motives imply goals and goals imply motives. Neither can exist without the other. Motives emphasize the person part of the person-situation interaction, whereas goals emphasize the situation part of the interaction. Values, like goals, usually emphasize situational characteristics, but they also imply attributes of the person with reference to the situations.

Personality psychologists are concerned primarily with motives and social psychologists with values. Is there a need for both concepts, or is the use of the terms simply a matter of preference? Typically, values refer to broad, socially significant constructs, such as freedom and equality, and motives to more narrowly defined realms, such as sex and aggression, which may or may not have a physical basis. However, there is a middle ground in which the two overlap. Included are constructs such as achievement, power, and affiliation. One can speak of achievement, power, and affiliative motives as well as of valuing achievement, power, and affiliation. There is no theoretical significance in the consideration that values generally refer to wider ranging phenomena than motives, as there is no reason why one could not extend motives to include broader variables and values to include narrower variables. Values, no less than motives, are often operationalized by tests of preference. Thus, if in a free choice situation, an animal or person consistently selected a sex object over a food object, it would be as meaningful to say that the person or animal valued sex more than food as it would be to say that he, she, or it had a stronger sex than hunger motive. By the same token, one could say that a person who values freedom or equality is motivated to support the cause of freedom or equality. Thus far, no theoretically meaningful distinction has been found between motives and values. Yet there is an important distinction, one that points to a serious limitation in the concept of values, at least as it has been traditionally employed.

Consider the following example. If I am motivated to be aggressive, does it necessarily mean that I place a positive value on aggression? Clearly it does not, for a person who detects aggressive tendencies in his or her behavior may be disturbed by the observation precisely because he or she places a negative valuation on aggression. What is the explanation of why the two concepts, value and motivation, diverge in this case, whereas they converged in the other examples? The answer is that in the present example different levels of the response are involved. At one level the person is *motivated* to be aggressive, whereas at another the person is oppositely motivated. Alternatively, it could be said that at one level the person positively *values* aggression, but at another level the person negatively values aggression. This may appear awkward, because social psychologists have tended to assume that values are all of a piece. Thus, when verbal reports and behavioral inferences diverge, social psychologists are prone to assume that the two indexes depart from a single true value because of error of measurement, rather than considering the possibility that different conceptual systems exist at different levels, each with its own values. To the extent that the assumption of two systems is correct, it has important implications for the prediction of behavior from values, for the systems may be differentially related to behavior. As will be seen shortly, one of the systems is assumed to be more closely associated with behavioral and emotional responses and the other with verbal responses.

It might be argued that the problem can be resolved by defining values as existing solely within the verbal system. In support of such a solution is the consideration that values are usually measured in social psychological research by self-report measures. The problem with such a solution, although theoretically defensible, is that the usefulness of values for predicting behavior would then be very limited, and, further, it would not be very convincing, as indicated by the following example. Consider a person who devotes his or her life to accumulating great wealth, freely choosing to engage in this pursuit, and then using the wealth for no purpose other than to hoard it. How meaningful would it be to conclude that such a person does not value wealth if he or she does not admit to valuing it? Clearly, values are important mainly for what they imply about a person's behavior, not for predicting his or her verbal statements.

Let us examine the same issue from another perspective. Consider that values include components of thought, behavior, and emotion. In the realm of thought, values are experienced in terms of desirable or undesirable, of how things should or should not be, of what is important or unimportant, and of the overall worth or "value" of an event or outcome. Because values are beliefs about desirability, they necessarily imply affect. Thus, when a value is upheld, it often produces feelings of joy and/or pride, and if another person is considered responsible, it often produces feelings of appreciation and/or admiration. Likewise, the assessment that a value has been violated is associated with feelings of dejection, shame, or guilt if the self is assumed to be responsible, and with feelings of anger if someone else is deemed responsible. In the realm of behavior, values are indicated either by preference in a free choice situation, or by how much an individual is willing to pay or sacrifice for the valued object, or, relatedly, by the amount of effort he or she is willing to exert to achieve the valued outcome.

Given that values are revealed by thoughts, emotions, and behavior, this raises the question of how to interpret results when the different indexes do not correspond. For example, what does it signify when a person reports that he or she values achievement but exhibits this not a whit in his or her daily behavior and is emotionally unresponsive to issues involving achievement? Because a great deal of research on values is based on direct self-report, which neither assesses emotions nor behavior, this issue is one of considerable importance. A common interpretation is that each index has its virtues and limitations, but all are manifestations of the same underlying construct, that is, there is presumably a true degree to which the person in the aforementioned has a latent value of achievement, which is but imperfectly reflected in each of the indexes, thereby accounting for differences in the obtained results. An alternative interpretation is that different values exist in different conceptual systems, and that the differences are therefore meaningful. We return to this issue when we discuss the implications of Cognitive-experiential Self-theory for an understanding of values.

Values clearly exist at various levels of generality. Although the word "value" is generally restricted to concepts referring to broad social interests, as already noted, there is no good theoretical reason why the concept should not be extended to include more narrowly defined variables. A complete theory of values should be able to outline the domain of values and to hierarchically arrange them with the broader values subsuming the narrower ones. As a beginning, it would be helpful to determine whether there exists a limited set of basic values that are common to all people. This would be analogous to the attempt in trait theory to identify basic traits, which, according to Eysenck (1970) consist of neuroticism, extroversion, and psychoticism, or egostrength. In factor-analytic terms, the basic traits correspond to higher order factors. It would be interesting to determine if there is some theoretical basis for establishing basic values. As becomes evident shortly, Cognitive-experiential Self-theory provides a hypothesis along these lines. Of course, if values exist within two different conceptual systems, the possibility must be considered that basic values may exist in one system and not in the other, or that they may differ in the two systems.

In summary, I am proposing that there is no fundamental difference between values and motives, and that once this is realized, it follows that, like motives, values can exist at different levels of awareness and can conflict with each other, not only within the same conceptual system but across different conceptual systems within the same individual.

COGNITIVE-EXPERIENTIAL SELF-THEORY

For present purposes, a brief summary of Cognitive-experiential Self-theory will suffice. For the reader who wishes to learn more about the theory, a number of additional sources, some of which present a general summary

(Epstein, 1973, 1983a) and others of which present specific aspects of the theory (Epstein, 1976, 1979a, 1980, 1981, in press a, in press b; Epstein & Erskine, 1983), can be consulted.

It is assumed that in order to function in the complex world of reality, humans must organize their experiences within an implicit, or preconscious, theory of reality that contains subdivisions of a self-theory and a world theory. An individual's implicit theory of reality is not a conscious theory that a person can report if asked to do so. It is a subconscious, or implicit theory that the individual unwittingly constructs in the course of living his or her life. The theory, like any other theory, consists of a hierarchical arrangement of higher and lower order beliefs, or schemas. The most fundamental beliefs in a personal theory of reality are referred to as postulates. Some of the postulates are descriptive beliefs about the self and the world. Other postulates are motivational beliefs that indicate what one should do to gain what one wishes and to avoid what one fears. An example of a descriptive postulate is "Authority figures are cruel and domineering." An example of a motivational postulate is "You can avoid being hurt by authority figures if you placate them."

The basic beliefs in a person's implicit theory of reality consist, for the most part, of generalizations inductively derived from emotionally significant experiences. The strength of such beliefs is a function of the intensity and frequency of the experiences from which the beliefs were derived, and the position of the beliefs in the hierarchy of the conceptual system. The greater the number and intensity of the experiences on which they are based and the more they are interrelated with other beliefs, the more the beliefs are resistant to modification. Postulates such as the ones described earlier could readily be derived from emotionally significant interactions with a father figure. Beliefs formed early in life are particularly important, as they become higher order postulates that influence the assimilation of new experiences and the development of new beliefs. This is not to deny that later experiences in life can have a profound influence on personality.

A person's preconscious theory of reality is a very significant part of a person's personality, but it is not the whole of personality, for personality also consists of biologically determined reactions and conscious beliefs that are intellectually derived. A personal theory of reality determines how a person automatically makes sense of experience and automatically reacts to the world. If a person's beliefs were to change at the preconscious level about what he or she and the world are like and how he or she should behave in it, the person would perceive differently, remember differently, feel differently, and behave differently. In other words, the person would be a different person. In order to cope with the world and preserve their identity, people must maintain the stability of their theories of reality. It can be expected, therefore, that people will do almost anything in their power to maintain the integrity of their conceptual systems, for the disorganization of a conceptual system is equivalent to the death of a personality.

The Four Basic Functions of a Personal Theory of Reality. The construction of a personal theory of reality is not an exercise undertaken for its own sake. Rather, the theory is a conceptual tool for fulfilling life's most basic psychological functions, namely, assimilating the data of reality within a relatively stable, coherent conceptual system; maintaining a favorable pleasure-pain balance over the anticipated future; maintaining relationships with significant others and maintaining a favorable level of self-esteem. These four functions are not completely independent but overlap and interact with each other. Although some developmentally precede the others, once developed, they are equally important. Which function, if any, is dominant varies among individuals and within individuals over time. One individual may be predominantly characterized by a need to enhance self-esteem and another by a need to maintain the stability of his or her conceptual system. The former will be driven by a quest for prestige and the latter by an attempt to establish a secure and predictable environment. Under appropriate circumstances, each could shift to the position of the other. For example, should the stability of the former individual's conceptualization of self and world be seriously threatened, the need to maintain stability would likely become prepotent over the need to enhance self-esteem. In order to be well adjusted, a person must maintain a balanced position among the four functions.

Behavior can be viewed as a compromise among the four basic functions. Each exerts its influence in proportion to its significance for the individual under the circumstances. Such a process is adaptive, as it provides a series of checks and balances, reducing the likelihood that any one motive will exert a disproportionate influence. For example, the motive to enhance self-esteem is limited by the motives to realistically assimilate the data of reality, to avoid the pain of disappointment, and to maintain favorable relationships with others. Accordingly, delusions of grandeur are a rare occurrence, and when they occur are regarded as abnormal.

The Structure of a Personal Theory of Reality. Acording to Cognitive-experiential Self-theory, there are not one, but three conceptual systems that are differentially accessible to conscious awareness. The three conceptual systems are the rational conceptual system, the experiential conceptual system, and the associationistic conceptual system. It is the first two conceptual systems that mainly concern us in what follows.

A personal theory of reality consists of an organization of constructs within the experiential conceptual system, which is intimately associated with the experience of emotions and operates predominantly at the preconscious level of consciousness. The preconscious level of awareness differs from conscious and unconscious levels of awereness in that it is less accessible than the former, which consists of material that can readily be accessed, and more accessible than the latter, which is highly resistant to access. The preconscious level includes background thoughts and images of which people are normally unaware, but of which they can become aware by attending to their stream of consciousness. As the experiential conceptual system is intimately associated with the experience of emotions, the examination of thoughts that occur immediately preceding and during emotional experience is particularly useful in uncovering beliefs in the experiential conceptual system.

TABLE 1.1.

Comparative Features of the Experiential and Rational Conceptual Systems

Experiential Conceptual System	*Rational Conceptual System*
1. Tied more closely to immediate, affective experience.	1. More abstract and removed from direct experience.
2. Mediated by preconscious thought and imagery associated with past emotional experience.	2. Mediated by conscious use of conventional words, symbols, and rules of logic.
3. Action oriented.	3. Thought oriented, analytic, contemplative.
4. Exhibits partial dissociation between emotional states that function somewhat as self-contained conceptual systems, or modules.	4. More integrated and internally consistent.
5. Judgments apt to be categorical and represent the extreme ends of dimensions. All-or-none decisions rather than qualified judgments.	5. Judgments more apt to be dimensional, differentiated, and qualified.
6. Broad generalization gradient. The more intense the emotional experience, the broader the generalization gradient.	6. Narrower generalization gradient.
7. Experienced passively, as if the belief is automatically triggered by events.	7. Experienced as under volitional control.
8. Self-evident validity. "Experiencing is believing."	8. Beliefs require validation in the form of evidence and logic.

In Table 1.1 the characteristics of the experiential conceptual system are contrasted with those of the rational conceptual system. Table 1.1 was constructed from an informal analysis of thinking during highly emotionally arousing events. The items in Table 1.1 are tentative and can best be regarded as hypotheses that require verification. The essence of the experiential conceptual system is that it is a system adapted to immediate action, in contrast to the rational conceptual system, which is better suited for analysis where delayed action is appropriate.

The rational conceptual system is a system characterized by conscious, logical thinking. The associationistic conceptual system, in contrast to both the rational and experiential conceptual systems, is characterized by unconscious processes and creativity and consists of an altered state of consciousness. It is manifested in dreams and in states of delirium, when cortical control is reduced. The three conceptual systems are analogous to three computer programs, each with its own data banks and rules of logic. Each has its advantages and disadvantages as tools for adapting to reality. Because the systems overlap, and the rational system can become aware of the content in the other systems, it is possible for individuals to coordinate the three systems. In the absence of integration, the three conceptual systems can be a source of conflict and stress, as the same organism cannot effectively respond to opposite messages at the same time.

People tend to consciously identify themselves with their rational conceptual system, as this is the system they are aware of and the one that makes sense to them, because it is "rational". They tend not to be aware of the extent to which their behavior is determined by their experiential conceptual system, which operates automatically, in the background of consciousness. Moreover, behavior that is determined by the experiential conceptual system can often be rationalized so that it appears to be consciously and rationally determined. In reality, however, behavior is far more often determined by what "feels" right and is therefore determined by motives in the experiential-conceptual system, than by what is judged to be reasonable, and is therefore determined by motives in the rational conceptual sytem. Psychologists, no less than lay people, tend to underestimate the extent to which this is true. They tend to attribute behavior to either conscious or deeply unconscious factors and fail to appreciate the degree to which their behavior is automatically controlled by preconscious cognitions.

A personal theory of reality is both integrated and differentiated. There is an overall unity, or organization, to the system, and within the system there are subunits that themselves are integrated and differentiated. Unity is less than complete, however, and conflict may exist within as well as between systems. The organization of a personal theory of reality consists of an organization of schemas. A schema, as used here, is a personal construct that organizes the data of experience and/or other schemas. Schemas can be descriptive, they can direct action, or they can do both. They consist of images, verbal thoughts, and implicit meanings. They exist at different levels of complexity, including, in decreasing order of complexity, identities (real and imagined), roles, and scripts. Other schemas consist of concepts and descriptive and motivational beliefs, which also exist at different levels of generality and complexity.

The basic postulates in a personal theory of reality can be inferred from repetitive behavior patterns and from emotions. Although any one instance of behavior is likely to be determined primarily by situational influences, by aggregating behavior over many situations and occasions, specific situational influences can be cancelled out, and broad, stable dispositions detected (Epstain, 1979b, 1983b, 1984). Not all important implicit beliefs in a personal theory of reality are broadly cross situational. Some are specific to particular kinds of situations. How are these to be detected? They, too, can be inferred from appropriate aggregation, but here the aggregation must be accomplished within an appropriately narrow range of stimulus variation that is confined to the class of stimuli over which one wishes to generalize (Epstein & O'Brien, 1985).

As to inferring preconscious schemas from emotions, this is accomplished through the recognition that associated with almost all emotions are implicit cognitions. Thus, with the knowledge of the nature of an emotion and/or of an emotion-eliciting situation, it is possible to infer the underlying belief. For example, because the cognitions associated with anger often consist of judgments that one has been treated badly by someone who, therefore, deserves to be punished, it can be inferred if a person is often angry that he or she probably believes that people often behave badly and deserve to be punished (see Epstein, 1983b, for discussion and research on the cognitions associated with different emotions). Also, if a particular kind of situation repeatedly elicits an emotional reaction from a person, it can be assumed that the situation is related to a significant belief in the person's implicit theory of reality.

The Development of Personal Theories of Reality. Personal theories of reality are assumed to develop through assimilation and accommodation, i.e., through interpreting experience within the context of the extant conceptual system, and through modifying, or accommodating, the conceptual system so that it becomes able to interpret a new experience (Piaget, 1954). Expressed otherwise, like a theory in science, an individual's conceptual system becomes increasingly differentiated and integrated through a continuous interaction between conceptualization and empirical experience. Following Kuhn (1962), it is assumed that accommodation takes place in two ways, one of which corresponds to what Kuhn refers to as normal science, and consists of small incremental changes that do not upset the overall organization of the conceptual system. The other, which corresponds to what Kuhn refers to as scientific revolutions, involves major reorganizations of the conceptual system. The latter occurs when an individual encounters new demands in life with which the old conceptual system is unable to cope. Adolescence is often such a period. Unlike Kuhn, I assume that the revolutions need not involve major reorganizations but can consist of minor ones that do not seriously destabilize the personality.

It is important to recognize that personality development occurs in the context of a dialectic between growth and stability. Assimilation is associated with pleasurable affect, which provides an intrinsic source of motivation for individuals to expand their assimilitive capacity by differentiating their conceptual systems. Emotionally significant experiences that are too far beyond an individual's assimilative capacity produce anxiety and destabilize the conceptual system, to which the person often reacts by defensive retrenchment. Thus, new experience, up to a point, is pleasurable, and beyond it is aversive. Accordingly, a balance is established in which novelty is sought up to a point, and beyond which it is avoided. The less the stress that is acting on an individual, the more the balance within the individual is likely to shift toward growth. By the same token, the more the stress that is acting on an individual, the more the balance is likely to shift toward maintaining stability. Thus, individuals who are experiencing a great deal of stress will tend to value the familiar, to react to new experiences with fear and/or hostility, and, accordingly, to exhibit little personality growth. If the stress continues to mount and cannot be defended against, disorganization will ultimately occur. It is assumed that disorganization arose in the course of evolution as an emergency reaction for correcting a maladaptive conceptual system and facilitating, thereby, the emergence of a new organization. (For further treatment of disorganization as a natural corrective process, see Epstein, 1979a. For further elaboration of the development of a personal theory of reality as analogous to the development of a theory in science, see Epstein & Erskine, 1983).

Although Cognitive-experiential Self-theory has not, up to now, considered the topic of values, it has considered motives. As already noted, it is assumed there are four basic functions of a personal theory of reality. These functions can be translated into four basic motives, namely (a) to maintain a favorable pleasure-pain balance, (b) to maintain the stability and integrity of one's conceptual system for assimilating the data of reality, (c) to maintain a favorable level of self-esteem, and (d) to maintain favorable relationships with significant others. It is particularly important to note that these motives exist within the preconscious conceptual system and therefore are not necessarily available to conscious verbal report. It is possible for conflicting motives to exist between and within the different conceptual systems. Having concluded that there is no fundamental distinction between motives and values, what has been said about motives can readily be translated into statements about values, a topic to which we turn next.

VALUES FROM THE PERSPECTIVE OF COGNITIVE-EXPERIENTIAL SELF-THEORY

Having considered the nature of values and having presented a review of the most relevant aspects of Cognitive-experiential Self-theory, we are now in a position to examine the implications of the latter for the former.

Values and the Experiential Conceptual System. Perhaps the most important implication of Cognitive-experiential Self-theory for an understanding of values is that values exist at two levels, a conscious, verbal level and a preconscious, experiential level. The values at the two levels can differ in content and degree, as they are embedded within different conceptual systems that not only differ in content but also operate by different rules. This does not mean that the two systems never correspond; they often do, but it is important to note that they need not correspond, and, when they do not, self-reported values are often poor predictors of emotions and behavior.

In discussing "guiding attitudes," which correspond to implicit values as defined here, Allport (1935) make the following statement:

> Without guiding attitudes the individual is confused and baffled. Some kind of preparation is essential before he can make a satisfactory observation, pass suitable judgment, or make any but the most primitive reflex type of response. Attitudes determine for each individual what he will see and hear, what he will think and what he will do. To borrow a phrase from William James, they "engender meaning upon the world"; they draw lines about and segregate an otherwise chaotic environment; they are our methods for finding our way about in an ambiguous universe. (p. 806)

It is clear from this statement that Allport is referring to cognitions that reside within the experiential conceptual system, as they automatically structure experience and direct behavior and are not necessarily accessible to direct verbal report.

Lest there remain any doubt that there are two conceptual sysems, each with its own values, consider the following examples. The first concerns a fellow student with whom I used to have political discussions when we were graduate students. His political orientation was rightist, in contrast to my own, which was liberal. He made it clear that he valued extreme individualism, in which each person fends for himself or herself and assumes no responsibility for others, including those in need, for such well-meaning behavior, he argued, only encourages weakness and fosters a destructive welfare-state mentality. From his viewpoint, only a sentimental fool would sacrifice his or her welfare for another. Later, I learned that during the war he had been a navigator in a bomber that was hit by enemy flak. It began to lose altitude over France, and the men were ordered to bail out. When it turned out that one of them did not have a parachute, my friend volunteered to have the fellow ride down with him piggyback. He had no idea whether either could make it under the circumstances. The question I wish to raise for the reader is which was his "true" value, the one that he glibly stated in argument, or the one that he demonstrated at the risk of his life? The second example concerns my daughter, who, when she was 4 years old, came home from a party with the following penetrating insight: "You know all those kids who are always telling everyone how they should share? I watched them, and they were the ones who grabbed the cookies first." The third example is of someone who had just been raped. Although she knew full well that a single rapist cannot be representative of men in general, she developed an aversion to being touched by any man. The intellectual part of her mind recognized that the experiential part of her mind was generalizing inappropriately. Accordingly, she made a deliberate point of going out with a gentle, sympathetic man. She was aware that she could not intellectually talk herself out of her maladaptive belief but needed a corrective experience to counter her experientially derived maladaptive belief.

Given the assumption that values in the experiential conceptual system are important determinants of behavior, this raises the question of how they can best be measured. It will be recalled that the experiential conceptual system is assumed to be inimately associated with the experience of emotions, and that it determines what "feels" right as distinguished from what is intellectually judged to be right. To illustrate the issues involved in attempting to predict behavior from an assessment of values in the experiential, as contrasted with the rational, conceptual system, consider the prediction of voting behavior. If one were to construct an inventory based on the rational conceptual system to predict how people will vote in an upcoming election, one would proceed by listing the important issues in the campaign and determining to what extent individuals agreed with the positions of the different candidates on these issues. Presumably, a person would vote for the candidate who came closest to sharing the voter's views on issues he or she regarded as important. In contrast, if one were to construct an inventory on the basis of the experiential conceptual system, one would include questions about how the voter "feels" about the candidate, which might have little to do with the candidate's political beliefs. Questions would be asked about how much the voter likes the candidate as a human being, how much he or she feels the candidate is a decent, trustworthy person, makes decisions well, has leadership qualities, inspires confidence, and makes the voter feel good about himself or herself and proud of his or her country.

Does it follow from the aforementioned analysis that System 2, the experiential conceptual system, always provides a better basis for prediction than System 1, the rational conceptual system? The answer is no, both systems are important. Their degree of importance can be expected to vary according to the behavior that is predicted and the personalities of the people for whom the predictions are made. Some issues are apt to be less associated with emotions that others, and some people are apt to be more intellectual and react less according to their intuitions and spontaneous feelings than others. To complicate matters further, decisions made on the basis of System 2 are apt to be rationalized and attributed to System 1, in which case people will tend to revise their stated views about issues to make them congruent with their feelings about the candidate.

It is an interesting challenge for future research to develop ways of assessing values in System 2 and use them in conjunction with assessment of values in System 1 for determining how much each contributes individually and in combination to particular kinds of behavior. An interesting parameter to include in the equation is a measure of individual differences in tendency to react in terms of System 1 relative to System 2.

In some cases, it seems reasonable to have people report their emotional reactions to specific situations or people, as in the previous example. In other cases there may be no specific target, such as a political candidate, on whom emotions can be focused. Under such circumstances, a procedure worth exploring is to present vignettes describing real or imaginary experiences that are exemplars of the value in question. Subjects can respond by indicating how they believe they would react based on how they have reacted to similar situations in the past. Presenting items within situational contexts is more likely to remind people of emotions abstract, situationally disembodied items.

In addition to inferring values in System 2 from the kinds of situations that arouse emotions, values can be inferred from repetitive behavior patterns. There are several possibilities to be considered here. The most direct procedure would be to obtain samples of actual behavior through direct observation. Alternatively, people who know the subjects can rate the subjects' typical behavior. Finally, subjects can be asked to keep records of their own ongoing behavior or to retrospectively report such behavior. Although the last procedure is the most convenient, depending on the nature of the behavior, people may or may not be able or willing to report accurately. Nevertheless, it is likely that people can report more accurately on concrete behaviors from which values can be inferred than on their more ambiguous and abstract values, which are likely to reflect only their System 1 beliefs.

Basic Values in the Experiential Conceptual System. Whatever is of significance to an individual will be valued by the individual, either positively or negatively. It follows that the four basic functions of a personal theory of reality generate four basic values. These values are assumed to exist in all human beings because they arise out of common biological structures and common conditions in living. Thus, all humans have pleasure and pain centers, all experience distress when they cannot assimilate experience, all are cared for by parent-figures and raised in social groups, thereby fostering a need for belonging or relatedness, and all feel good when successful or approved of by others and bad when they fail or are disapproved of by others, which fosters the development of self-esteem. As a result, all individuals implicitly value (a) maximizing pleasure and minimizing pain; (b) assimilating the data of reality, which requires maintaining the stability and coherence of their implicit conceptual systems; (c) belonging or relatedness; and (d) positive self-evaluation. Behavior can be viewed as a compromise among these four values. One does not normally think of these implicit values as values because values have usually been treated as self-reported, socially oriented beliefs, and these values are implicit and have to be inferred. As noted earlier, the emphasis on direct self-reported values is considered an important limiting factor both in theory development and empirical research.

The view that there are four basic values has interesting implications for theory and research. With respect to theory, the basic values should be capable of subsuming other, more specific values and should therefore provide a basis for a hierarchical organization of values. Consideration of the four basic values can also indicate whether an important value has been ignored when attempting to account for a particular kind of behavior. There is one value that is most likely to be overlooked because it appears in behavior mainly as a background factor; that is, one looks out from it as a vantage point, and not reflexively back on it as an object of perception, and therefore one is not normally aware of its existence. One must implicitly value the maintenance of the stability of one's conceptual system, for when it is threatened, anxiety necessarily follows. The importance of this value is most apt to become evident in extreme circumstances when an individual's conceptual system is under threat of disorganization. The individual will then experience confusion and anxiety and will be desperately motivated to impose order on experience. Threats to this value continuously influence behavior in less apparent ways, which, because they are subtle, tend to be attributed to other sources.

What are the implications for research of assuming the existence of four basic values? The assumption can be tested by confirmatory factor analysis. Research can also investigate whether the values postulated by other theoretical approaches can be subsumed under the four basic values. The four basic values have direct implications for predicting behavior. To the extent that behavior is a result of the four values, it should be possible to predict behavior by a regression equation in which they are included as predictor variables. It is important to consider, in this respect, that the four basic values can only predict the degree to which a particular kind of behavior is desired, and that to predict actual behavior, it is necessary to take into account both what is perceived as, and what actually is, feasible (Ajzen, 1987).

Let us take, as an example, the prediction of dieting behavior. To predict from the proposed model, it would be necessary to obtain the following measures: (a) the anticipated net gain in the pleasure-pain balance that the person believes would result from dieting, which would include the anticipated displeasure that would be experienced from dieting and the anticipated pleasure that would be gained from a successful outcome; (b) the degree to which the person's conceptualization of self as a successful dieter and as a thinner person is congruent with the person's self- and world theory, which could be inferred, in part, from the person's past experience with dieting and other attempts at self-discipline (i.e., does remaining on a diet correspond more to the individual's implicit self-image than quitting?); (c) the degree to which self-esteem is implicated in successfully dieting (i.e., how will dieting versus the consequences of failing to diet affect one's self-esteem); and (d) the influence that success or failure in dieting will have on anticipated relatedness to significant others. It is noteworthy that there is considerable overlap between the model just proposed and a model proposed by Ajzen (1985, 1987; Ajzen & Madden, 1985; Schifter & Ajzen, 1985) for predicting behavior from attitudes. The predictor variables in Ajzen's model are (a) attitude toward the behavior, which refers to its desirability; (b) subjective norm, which refers to the degree of perceived social pressure from others to perform the behavior, measured by the subject's judgments of how significant others would react to the behavior; (c) perceived behavioral control, measured by perceived feasibility, as judged from past experiences in performing the behavior under similar circumstances, and (d) actual control, which corresponds to real feasibility in carrying out the behavior. The Ajzen model is a modification of a similar model by Ajzen & Fishbein (1980, Fishbein & Ajzen, 1975, 1981). A considerable amount of research has provided support for both versions of the model (see review by Ajzen, 1987), The major difference between the Ajzen model and the one derived from Cognitive-experiential Self-theory is that the latter model contains an additional variable, self-esteem, which may be included in desirability in the Ajzen model. Other differences would possibly relate to emphases in the wording of the items that are to be rated by the subjects. Both models emphasize judgments of emotional as opposed to intellectual reactions. Of course, to the extent that the two models, derived from different theoretical sources, converge, some degree of support for the validity of both is implied.

When assessing the basic values, it is important to make a distinction between assessing values within the rational and experiential conceptual systems. The former are revealed by a person's straightforward assessment of his or her beliefs, whereas the latter must be inferred from observations of emotions and/or behavior, or, when this is not feasible, from statements about emotions and/or behavior if it can be assumed under the circumstances that they are reasonably accurate. It would be interesting to obtain measures from both rational and emotional perspectives and compare their ability to predict different kinds of behavior. As suggested previously, it would be particularly interesting to determine how much they supplement each other and whether their relative contributions differ for predominantly intellectual (System 1) and affectively responsive (System 2) individuals.

VALUES AT THE LEVEL OF THE SOCIAL GROUP

It is interesting to apply the concepts of Cognitive-experiential Self-theory to the behavior of social groups. It is, of course, dangerous to assume that relationships that hold for individuals necessarily apply to groups. A case must be made that the relationships in question are compelling, in their own right, for elucidating group processes. Undoubtedly some relationships can and others cannot be transferred from the individual to the group. What reasonable parallels are there in Cognitive-experiential Self-theory that would seem to apply as well to social groups as to individuals? It is assumed that nations, like individuals, have theories of reality, explicit and implicit belief systems, basic values, and that they adapt to reality through assimilation and accommodation. Let us briefly examine each of these in turn.

Theories of Reality in Nations. Nations, no less than individuals, require theories of reality to organize the data of their experience and direct their behavior. Like individuals, they do not view their construction of reality as a construction, but as reality itself. They therefore tend to view other nations with radically different views as unrealistic and as either violating the laws of nature or of God. Capitalist nations, for example, regard it as a law of human nature that people are basically competitive and individualistic. To violate this law is to court disaster. They thus view communism as espousing an unrealistic and dangerous belief system. Communist nations, on the other hand, hold opposite views of human nature. The theories of reality of nations include self-theories and world theories. Each nation has a view of what it is like and of what the rest of the world is like, and each nation has a vested interest in defending its own view, for apart from whether it is a source of well-being or anxiety, it at least provides a way of organizing the world and of purposefully directing behavior in it.

The Basic Values of Nations. It is hypothesized that nations have four basic implicit values analogous to those of individuals. Corresponding to maximizing pleasure and minimizing pain in individuals, nations strive to maximize economic gain and to minimize exonomic loss. Marx believed this was the one major value that moves social events. According to Cognitive-experiential Self-theory, there are three other equally basic values, which are to enhance national pride, to enhance group belongingness, and to maintain the nation's implicit belief system for organizing the data of reality and directing behavior.

War provides a critical test of whether societies consider certain values important enought to die for. It is obvious that nations go to war for economic reasons, including seizing land and materials from other nations and defending their own land and materials from seizure by other nations. Relatedly, countries go to war to destroy or weaken the economies of competing nations. Thus, maximizing economic gain and minimizing economic loss clearly qualifies as a basic value for nations.

National pride corresponds to self-esteem in individuals. Nations go to war not only for economic reasons but also to enhance or defend their pride. Individuals, in the service of nations, are willing to die to defend the honor of their countries. Soldiers are often proud to go to war. Not only do nations defend their honor against assaults to their dignity from other nations, but successful nations throughout history have sought to increase their glory through conquests. History is replete with examples of nations that have attempted to conquer the world, only to destroy themselves in the process. When a nation wins a war, the mood of the nation is one of jubilation and elevated pride, even if the cost in life and economic consequences makes the victory a poor bargain. When a nation loses a war, the national mood tends to be one of demoralization and depression. For reasons of pride, the United States found it difficult to acknowledge that the war in Vietnam was a mistake, and therefore was resistant to withdraw, even when it became apparent that little good could come out of continuing the war. President Johnson made pride explicit as the motivation for continuing the war when he stated that he did not want to be the first American president to lose a war. Following withdrawal from Vietnam, recognized as a defeat by most, demoralization was widespread in the United States, and it was widely believed that there was an increase in cases of depression.

Belongingness is clearly valued by societies. People desire to be together with others who look and dress like them, talk like them, have similar customs, and share similar values and beliefs. Wars are fought to join together people of similar cultures and races and to throw off the yoke of rulers from different cultures or races, despite the actual economic hardship this may bring. Scapegoating and violence directed toward those outside the mainstream of a society have, as one of their functions, separating the outgroup from the ingroup and increasing feelings of similarity and belongingness among the latter.

Differences in belief systems are perhaps the most common sources of conflict among social groups. Nations, no less than individuals, are motivated to maintain their theories of reality, and they tend to view the existence of other belief systems as an implicit threat to the validity of their own belief systems. The history of humankind provides endless examples of groups that have slaughtered each other because of relatively trivial differences in belief systems. An exemple is the annihilation of Christian sects by other Christian sects because of different beliefs about the Trinity. In his satire on warfare, Jonathan Swift gave as the reason for the conflict between the Lilliputians and their enemies, one nation's belief in opening their eggs on the larger end and the other nation's belief in opening their eggs on the smaller end of the egg. If there is anything that attests to the importance in human behavior of maintaining personal and national theories of reality, it is the violence with which people throughout the course of history have reacted to those with different beliefs.

Two Belief Systems. Like individuals, nations have explicit and implicit belief systems. Anthropologists refer to an overt culture, manifested in what people say and write about how one should behave, and a covert culture, the rules of which must be inferred from how people actually behave. The written constitution of nations often proclaim equality and justice for all, whereas their implicit values usually condone special privileges for the wealthy. Consistent with the viewpoint of Cognitive-experiential Self-theory, it is recognized by anthropologists that if one wishes to predict behavior in a society, one must study the covert culture and not be misled by verbally stated beliefs and values.

Assimilation and Accommodation. Adjustment in nations, no less than in individuals, requires a continuous interaction between experience and conceptualization. Through assimilation and accommodation, the belief system of a nation becomes increasingly differentiated and integrated. The result is that the nation is able to engage in effective action over a widening range of situations. What are the obstacles to such growth of a national conceptual system? Growth is impeded primarily in two ways, through insufficient and excessive stability. The former can occur if a nation lacks well-established, implicit beliefs inductively derived from historical experience with governing itself. As a result, it has an insecure foundation and is susceptible to disorganization under stress, or, in political terms, revolution (Kuhn, 1962). Revolutions can be a source of a new and more effective organization, but they are a costly way for growth to occur.

A nation can also suffer because its basic postulates have become so rigidified that the nation can no longer adapt to new experiences. This occurs when nations view their identities as being seriously threatened. They, like individuals, then "batten down the hatches." They reduce the assimilative demands on their conceptual systems by reducing environmental demands, by refusing to tolerate dissent, and by staunchly and rigidly defending their most basic values. A second way that rigidity can occur is through overvaluing certain basic postulates and considering it unpatriotic to question them. Abstract principles that are basically sound and that have contributed to a nation's greatness can become rigidified in slogans that lack the flexibility of the initial abstraction. Moreover, times may have changed and other principles have to be taken into account in order to effectively cope with current circumstances. As a result, an espoused principle that worked under previous conditions, although not incorrect, may become counterproductive.

It is important to recognize that the rigidification of basic postulates does not arise only through the imposition of an autocratic system. It can develop within a democratic system, as no external force is required to influence people to think in a certain way. Under circumstances where assimilative demands increase to the point that they threaten a nation's identity, a politically flexible system will tend to adjust by becoming more conservative. Under such circumstances, a nation will normally shift back to a more growth-oriented approach when the crisis has passed. However, there is the danger that an overvalued principle, overvalued in the sense that it overshadows other equally important principles, will, over time, exert an increasingly biased influence on the interpretation of reality and behavioral reactions to that reality. The nation will then assimilate without accommodating. The result is that the belief will increasingly usurp the entire conceptual system, until it ultimately reshapes it into a caricature of itself. It follows that nations, like individuals, must establish a reasonable balance between assimilation and accommodation if they are to effectively adjust to reality and not endanger themselves and each other.

ACKNOWLEDGMENTS

The writing of this article was supported by NIMH Research Grant MHO1293 and by NIMH Research Scientist Award 1KO5 MH00363.

I wish to express my appreciation for the helpful comments of Alice Epstein, George Levinger, Carol Shadoian, and Laurie Teraspulsky.

REFERENCES

Ajzen, I. (1985). From intentions to actions: A theory of planned behavior. In J. Kuhl & J. Beckman (Eds.), *Action control: From cognition to behavior.* Heidelberg: Springer.

Ajzen, J. (1987). *Attitudes traits, and actions: Dispositional prediction of behavior in personality and social psychology.* In L. Berkowitz (Ed.), *Advances in experimental social psychology.* New York: Academic.

Ajzen, I., & Fishbein, M. (1980). *Understanding attitudes and predicting social behavior.* Englewood-Clifs, NJ: Prentice-Hall.

Ajzen, I., & Madden, T. (1985). *Prediction of social behavior: The role of intention, perceived control, and prior behavior.* Unpublished manuscript. University of Massachusetts at Amherst.

Allport, G. (1935). Attitudes. In G. Murchison (Ed.), *Handbook of social psychology.* Worcester, MA: Clark University Press.

Epstein, S. (1973). The self-concept revisited, or a theory of a theory. *American Psychologist, 28,* 404–416.

Epstein, S. (1976). Anxiety, arousal, and the self-concept. In I. G. Sarason & C. D. Spielberger (Eds.), *Stress and anxiety* (Vol. 3). Washington, DC: Hemisphere.

Epstein, S. (1979a). Natural healing processes of the mind:. I. Acute schizophrenic disorganization. *Schizophrenia Bulletin*, National Institute of Mental Health, *5*, 313–321.

Epstein, S. (1979b). The stability of behavior: I. On predicting most of the people much of the time. *Journal of Personality and Social Psychology*, 37, 1097–1126.

Epstein, S. (1980). The self-concept: A review and the proposal of an integrated theory of personality. In E. Staub (Ed.), *Personality: Basic issues and current research.* Englewood Cliffs, NJ: Prentice-Hall.

Epstein, S. (1981). The unity principle versus the reality and pleasure principles, or the tale of the scorpion and the frog. In M. D. Lynch, A. A. Norem-Hebeisen, & K. J. Gergen (Eds.), *Self-concept: Advances in theory and research.* Cambridge, MA: Ballinger.

Epstein, S. (1983a). The unconscious, the preconscious, and the self-concept. In J. Suls & A. Greenwald (Eds.), *Psychological perspectives on the self* (Vol. 2). Hillsdale, NJ: Lawrence Erlbaum Associates.

Epstein, S. (1983b). Aggregation and beyond: Some basic issues on the prediction of behavior. *Journal of Personality, 51*, 360–392.

Epstein, S. (1984). The stability of behavior across time and situations. In R. Zucker, J. Aronoff, & A. I. Rabin (Eds.), *Personality and the prediction of behavior.* San Diego, CA: Academic Press.

Epstein, S. (1985). Implications of cognitive-experiential self-theory for research in personality and social psychology. *Journal for the Theory of Social Behaviour, 15*, 283–310.

Epstein, S. (in press a). Implications of cognitive self-theory for psychopathology and psychotherapy. In N. Cheshire & H. Thoma (Eds.), *Self esteem and psychotherapy.* New York: Wiley.

Epstein, S. (in press b). *The self-concept, the traumatic neurosis, and the structure of personality.*

Epstein, S., & Erskine, N. (1983). The development of personal theories of reality. In D. Magnusson & V. Allen (Eds.), *Human development: An interactional perspective.* New York: Academic Press.

Epstein, S., & O'Brien, E. J. (1985). The person-situation debate in historical and current perspective. *Psychological Bulletin, 98*, 513–537.

Eysenck, H. J. (1970). The structure of human personality (3rd ed.), London: Methuen & Co., Inc.

Fishbein, M., & Ajzen, I. (1975). *Belief, attitude, intention, and behavior: An introduction to theory and research.* Reading, MA: Addison-Wesley.

Fishbein, M., & Ajzen, U. (1981). Attitudes and voting behavior: An application of the theory of reasoned action. In G. M. Stephenson & J. M. Davis (Eds.), *Progress in applied social psychology* (Vol. 1). London: Wiley.

Kuhn, T. S. (1962). *The structure of scientific revolutions.* Chicago, IL: University of Chicago Press.

Piaget, J. (1954). *The construction of reality in the child.* New York: Basic Books. (originally published, 1937)

Schifter, D. B., & Ajzen, I. (1985). Intention, perceived control, and weight loss: An application of the theory of planned behavior. *Journal of Personality and Social Psychology, 49*, 843–851.

2 Dimensions of Development in Moral Values

Janusz Reykowski
Polish Academy of Sciences

TWO APPROACHES TO THE DEVELOPMENT OF MORALITY

Students of contemporary approaches to moral development may be struck by the apparent similarity of views espoused by different schools. The proposition that seems to be shared by different theoretical orientations implies that one of the major dimensions of developmental change in morality is the transition from heteronomy to autonomy. It was Jean Piaget who for the first time in psychology systematically described changes in moral reasoning in these terms (Piaget, 1932). The best articulated and most extensively tested theory of moral development that was formulated by Kohlberg contains the same assumption: as an individual moves from preconventional through conventional to postconventional levels he or she loses his or her moral dependency on superior power and societal requirements and becomes instead a self-governing individual (Kohlberg, 1964).

Although it is not surprising that Kohlberg takes a similar view to that of Piaget (because his theory was derived from the Piagetian one), there are other authors with different backgrounds who make the same assumptions. The Russian author Drobnitsky (cited by Jacobson, 1981) contends that there exist two kinds of morality. One is based on custom and tradition (obytchno-traditsyonnaya orientatsya) that implies conformity to commonly accepted rules; the criteria of good and bad are contained in the existing norms and nonconformity is, ex definitione, morally reprehensible. The second kind of morality based on moral principles (moralno nravstviennaya orientatsya) is determined by concepts of value and duty. A person's moral convictions are derived from his or her moral views and become a source of criteria of good or bad (right or wrong). Obviously, the two kinds of morality Drobnitsky describes refer to the same aforementioned dichotomy of heteronomy versus autonomy. And it should be emphasised that the author, apparently, implies that the second kind of morality (autonomy) is developmentally higher than the first one.

If we now turn to empirical studies on the development of morality by authors who do not belong to the Piaget–Kohlberg school, we continue to find a similar view on the nature of the change. For example, Eisenberg, who studied the development of prosocial reasoning, describes five main stages: the first stage (Hedonistic, pragmatic orientation) resembles Piaget's premoral stage; the third stage (approval and interpersonal orientation) is similar to the heteronomous (conventional) level of Piaget and Kohlberg; and the fifth stage (values, norms, responsibilities) seems to be the same as the postconventional (autonomous) level of the two aforementioned authors (Eisenberg, 1982).

Noticing that the same basic idea of moral development is shared by authors of very different cultural origin, we may wonder about the source of this apparent similarity; why does the attainment of moral autonomy become the criterion of moral advancement? Is it because there is an universal law governing the structural transformations of the human mind or is it rather an abstract formulation of normative principles developed by contemporary economically advanced societies in America and Europe?

Structuralists (e.g., Kohlberg) claim that the former is the case. But there are others who provide arguments for the proposition that the concept of moral development is culturebound. This means that the previously described developmental differences can only be meaningfully applied to certain cultures or even to certain segments of society.

Strong support for such a view comes from the research of Melvin Kohn and his colleagues. Although recognizing the importance of the autonomy-heteronomy dimension, Kohn argues that one's position on the dimension is not a developmental issue but is determined by an individual's life conditions, first of all by his or her work experience (Kohn, 1969). Work conditions of factory workers and professionals differ with respect to the kind of demands they have to meet; whereas the role of a worker requires, basically, conformity to group expectations, the role of a professional requires, in most cases, self-reliance and self-directedness. Although it has been recently demonstrated by Alwin (1984) that there is a gradual shift in value orientations from obedience (conformity) to self-directedness in some groups of American society, and that the shift is connected with a rise in the level of education, it can be interpreted as the consequence of a change in job requirements and, possibly, in way of life.

There are some other data consistent with the idea that a culture might determine the character of morality. It has been found that young people at the age of 16, if assessed by Kohlberg's method, reach the fifth stage in the United States, the third stage in Mexico, and the first stage in Turkey. One could argue that the observed differences are due to the moral "backwardness" of whole societies. On the other hand, however, the observed differences can be interpreted as resulting from differences in dominant institutions in the given society. Hence, societies in which democratic institutions play an important role in life might be more prone to use reasoning characteristic for stage 5; if authority institutions are dominant, prevailing morality would be at stage 4; in societies where family influences are salient, the third stage might be the most common one (Taylor 1978).

The idea that form of morality depends on characteristics of a social system, most of all on its institutions developed in a historical process, implies that moral development consists of the attainment of an appropriate level of correspondence (kind of fit) between individual morality and morality as defined in society. The concept of correspondence, however, is rather vague. Moreover, it is likely to be interpreted as a kind of conformity to social institutions. But it does not have to be the case; one can argue that it is not conformity to existing institutions but, rather, to some ideal (or prototypical) ones.

We have, therefore, two competing approaches to the concept of moral development: one that assumes that there is one major path of developmental change determined by the structural characteristics of the human mind, and the second that assumes that moral development is determined by cultural requirements. This second approach implies that there are several possible ways or paths of developmental change in this respect.

MORALITY AS PART OF THE EVALUATIVE SYSTEM

The previously mentioned approaches to morality tend to consider it as a "self-contained" phenomenon, i.e., as a separate area of psychological functioning (although moral reasoning is regarded as a cognitive process but possessing a high degree of "sovereignty"). There is another possible perspective on the issue stemming from the fact that the elementary act of morality, a moral judgment, can be considered as an act of evaluation. Evaluation is meant here, as a process of attaching or attributing positivity or negativity to objects, events, situations, etc. In the case of morality, it is an evaluation of social phenomena.

Of course, morality is not constituted by an object of evaluation but by its criteria. In other words, only certain kinds of criteria of evaluation can be regarded as moral ones. Nevertheless, it seems feasible to look at the process of evaluation and its development as the point of departure for the analysis of moral development.

The analysis can begin with the proposition that the most basic form of mental functioning consists in an ordering of phenomena (stimuli, objects, events) in terms of their positivity and negativity, that is, in terms of their valence. This is what we call an evaluative process. The evaluative process can have two basic forms, affective response and evaluative judgment. We concentrate in this chapter on the latter phenomenon only.

An evaluative judgment is conceptualized as an internal covert process that should not be confused with an overt verbal act of making public statements (allegedly about one's own judgments). An evaluative judgment is a kind of cognitive process. It presupposes that in the cognitive system of an individual there are appropriate "instruments of evaluation," namely evaluative standards. Evaluative standards can be conceptualized as cognitive schemata charged with valence.

The idea that cognitive schemata can possess evaluative content is espoused by various authors. For example, Fiske suggested that some categories stored in memory may be charged with affect (Fiske, 1982); the stimuli that activate such categories evoke affective states. Hoffman discusses two kinds of schemata: charged schema and neutral schema (Hoffman, in press).

Both of the previously mentioned authors focus on affective phenomena. In the present chapter I want to make a distinction between an affective response and an evaluative judgment. Though in both cases the process of conferring positivity and negativity on a stimulus object takes place, in the former some degree of automonic arousal is necessarily involved (Mandler, 1976), whereas in the latter such arousal is absent. It can be added that under certain conditions the activation of evaluative standards can produce an autonomic arrousal. In such a case we must say that judgemental processes are accompanied by affective ones.

Now, assuming that the precondition for making an evaluative judgment is an evaluative standard (schema with valence), we face the question: Where do evaluative standards come from,in other words, what is the origin of positivity and negativity in certain cognitive schema?

And as a follow-up question we should also ask: How do evaluative standards develop?

I want to argue that there exist three independent sources of evaluative standards:

1. The organismic source: there exists an inborn affective sensitivity to certain sensory stimuli and perceptual patterns (i.e., to unconditional affective stimuli). Schemata that comprise representations of such stimuli or patterns possess the characteristics of eveluative standards (hedonic standards).
2. The societal source: social interaction "installs" in a cognitive system criteria of positivity and negativity (conformity standards).
3. The cognitive source: cognitive representations of objects, systems of

objects or any other entities (i.e., cognitive structures) form a state of equilibrium (Piaget, 1981). The incoming information can either support the equilibrium or disturb it producing positive or negative affective states, respectively. Thus, the criteria of positivity and negativity are embedded in the content of cognitive structures (conceptual standards).

In the remaining part of the chapter I want to concentrate on the problem of the development of evaluative standards and to discuss the implication of this analysis for the problem of moral development.

ORGANISMIC SOURCES OF EVALUATIVE PROCESSES: THE DEVELOPMENT OF HEDONIC STANDARDS

The major precondition of evaluative processes is the capability of an organism to experience affective reactions in response to various kinds of stimuli. It is based on an inborn, phylogenetically determined mechanism. Thus, such events as strong or gentle stimulation (Schneirla, 1959), sudden change in stimulation (Mowrer, 1960), deficit or excess of stimulation (Strelau, 1983, Zuckerman, 1980), interruption of ongoing activity (Dollard, Doob, et al., 1947, Mandler, 1976), and successful completion of activity (White, 1960) produce affective states of various intensities. It has been demonstrated that stimuli that differ with respect to modality, intensity, and distribution in time produce affective states of different content (Tomkins, 1984).

The affective states produced by stimuli of this kind, that is by unconditional stimuli, are more or less transient phenomena because they depend, almost completely, on momentary stimulus situations. But in the course of development of more complex and stable representations of objects and activities (images, concepts, scripts, dimensions), affective states are likely to become associated with them. Henceforth cognitive organizations acquire some affective qualities; in other words, they become charged with valence.

There are several ways of associating cognitive representations with affect. One possible way is conditioning. A good example of this process as applied to social interaction can be taken from the study of Aronfreed and Pascal (Aronfreed, 1970). They are believed to have demonstrated that children can learn positive reactions to another person's expression of joy if they have previously been rewarded for that; they can also learn negative reactions to signs of distress emitted by another person by means of aversive conditioning (see Rushton, 1982). Thus, one could contend that the cognitive schema of another person's facial expression acquires the characteristics of evaluative standards due to the fact that some association has been made between memory traces of this event (facial expression) and affect produced by the unconditional stimulation. It can be conjectured that the effects of conditioning are especially powerful if strong affective processes are evoked during the first encounter with the given object (or, more precisely, in the stage when its representation is being formed).

A specific but very important instance of affective conditioning concerns the acquisition of affective meaning by words and sentences. Due to the semantic connections between linguistic elements, affective meaning is likely to be transmitted from one element to another. A very simple illustration of this process comes from early studies made in Russian laboratories on the functioning of the semantic system. In one of the experiments with pupils, Volkova used a salivatory response to sweet cranberries as an unconditional (autonomic) reaction making the word "good" the conditioned stimulus and the word "bad" the conditioned inhibitor. She found, first, that sentences that contained the respective words influenced the salivary reactions of the children. But she also observed that a similar effect could be obtained when sentences with positive or negative meaning were applied; for example, she could instigate a salivary reaction by such sentences as "The Red Army won" and an inhibitory reaction with sentences as "A pupil did not prepare his homerowk," "The Nazis destroyed many towns" (Volkova, 1953).

In the previously described experiment, the word ("good") acquired the capability to evoke the salivary reaction that can be regarded as analogous to affective response and this capability was transmitted through the semantic system to more complex structures (also see Lacey, Smith, & Green, 1964). In other words, some areas of the linguistic system became for a certain time (probably rather short) associated with a salivary reaction to sweet cranberries, that is, they acquired a specific connotative meaning. In natural conditions such an experience can be much stronger and have more enduring consequences. Thus, words and sentences become charged with valence, i.e., they can operate as evaluative standards of a specific, hedonic kind.

It seems feasible to assume that objects as well as other complex stimuli (including linguistic ones), which became associated with affect in the stage when their cognitive representations were formed, possess a specific functional characteristic. They act as affective prototypes.

It can be conjectured, however, that there also are other mechanisms of formation of affective prototypes. One such mechanism consists of the inclusion into an object's representation of some sensory patterns, which have affect generating qualities. An example of such a pattern is the "babyishness" of certain facial features. It has been demonstrated that such features tend to evoke some affective reactions (Ullrich, 1976). For example, McArthur found that the judgment of a profile of a human face changes systematically with head shape maturity; the mature profile is perceived as older (the descriptive judgment) and also as less lovable, less kind, more sexy, more threatening (the evaluative judgment "mixed" with the descriptive one) (McArthur, 1984).

On the basis of the previous reasoning, it can be concluded that there exist cognitive schemata possessing affective content. Such content is the consequence of three processes: conditioning, incorporation into the object's representation a perceptual pattern that can generate affective states (under appropriate stimulation), and generalization (especially semantic generalization). Such schemata can be called the hedonic standards of evaluation.

Further developmental changes in hedonic standards result from the fact that they become organized into systems that belong to the cognitive network. It is the precondition of coordination of evaluative judgments made on the basis of different standards. A clear-cut example of such coordination is the ability to delay gratification. This ability implies a certain "trade off" between an immediate smaller reward and a remote bigger one (or between immediate gratification coupled with some pain and remote gratification with no pain). It can be assumed that the precondition for making such a trade off is a some degree of development of operational thinking – in this case an individual performs operations on his or her evaluative standards.

A more advanced stage in the same process is expressed in the form of social exchange. The exchange with another person is a kind of "hedonic detour"; an individual performs an action that does not satisfy him or her but satisfies someone else expecting that an action of the other will in turn satisfy him or her. Such an exchange requires some level of development of cognitive operations (operations on evaluative standards).

The exchange arrangement is an elementary form of prudence. The prudent person evaluates the present state of affairs, taking into account more or less remote consequences of his or her action. To have more pleasure (or less pain) in the future one sacrifices various smaller pleasures in the present and is able to withstand the minor pains.

Generalization of a mental attitude of this kind might lead a person to the position of "generalized reciprocity" that is based on expectation that good deeds will be eventually repaid. Some authors, e.g., Bar-Tal and Raviv (1982), regard generalized reciprocity as an advanced stage in the development of prosocial behavior. An expectation of eternal happiness in heaven for good behavior on earth seems to represent the same way of thinking.

At this stage it can be concluded that developmental processes concerning hedonic standards can result in evaluative functioning that takes into account interests of other people and society at large, and it can, under certain conditions, instigate behavior having apparently some moral quality. As a matter of fact, how many people would question the morality of a saint who makes self-sacrifices having in mind the rewards that God is preparing for him or her in a heaven?

SOCIETAL SOURCES OF EVALUATIVE PROCESSES: THE DEVELOPMENT OF CONFORMITY STANDARDS

Many psychologists, especially those reared in the tradition of learning theory, seem to make the implicit assumption that value attributed by an individual to objects and events is related, directly or indirectly, to affective processes stemming from organismic sources. The social world is regarded as providing the information when, where, and under what conditions a given outcome is likely to occur. In addition, the social environment creates rules and contingencies that determine various kinds of outcome (Magnusson & Allen, 1983). An example of such rules is the norm of proper behavior that determines which forms of behavior are rewarded and which punished.

This approach implies that the rules and norms an individual acquires in the course of socialization are the product of "sign learning" (Mowrer, 1960); sign learning is the precondition of cognitive control over reinforcement. It can be challenged, however, on the ground that consequences of a social impact on the individual are much deeper than that. A society provides an individual not only with information about reinforcement but also with "criteria of reinforcement." In other words, a society can establish within an individual an "internal frame of reference" that determines what is regarded as positive and what negative.

In the paradigm of neo-behaviorism such a "frame of reference" is explained in terms of secondary reinforcement. But we can argue that this does not give a full account of the consequences of social influence because people can acquire from a social environment criteria of evaluation (evaluative standards). Such criteria are not dependent on organismic affect. In other words, some products of the social impact are functionally independent of a primary reinforcement (which does not seem to be true of secondary reinforcement – see Mowrer, 1960). Evaluative standards of this kind develop as the result of specific forms of social interaction[1].

Two forms of social interaction seem to play the major role in the formation of evaluative standards: modelling and power execution. As far as modelling is concerned, it has been shown that an individual (especially a child) who witnesses an action of another individual (a model) tends, under certain conditions, to imitate such an action. Imitations include the tendency to select the objects that were selected by the model and reject those rejected by the model. The same type of behavior can be displayed verbally when an individual is exposed to opinions of another person (a model).

A model can have a lasting effect on an individual. Even short exposure to

---

1 The standards based on organismic affect can emerge as a product of any interaction with the outer world that evokes affective states; the societal standards emerge as the result of social interaction only.

a model in laboratory conditions can have consequences detectable after weeks (Bandura, 1969). It is reasonable to assume, therefore, that interactions with a model in natural conditions can have an enduring impact on a child. Such an impact is, supposedly, encoded in memory as a schema that possesses a sign and the sign depends on the behavior of the model.

We may leave aside, here, the issue as to the conditions of such an impact, that is who can become a model for a given person, and why. The issue has been extensively studied by Bandura (1977)[2]. We want only to emphasize that there is a specific form of social relation – the relation of modelling, which produces enduring effect on the human mind.

Another source of "schemata with evaluative content" is power execution (Hoffman, 1970). This refers to the situation where an expression of will by an agent possessing superior power over an individual defines for that individual what is positive and what is negative. This kind of impact is the most pronounced with immature individuals and also in conditions of "induced immaturity," as in the case of deep regressive states produced by extreme situations. (A dramatic example of a situation of this kind was provided by Bettelheim in his description of behavior of prisoners in Nazi concentration camps; Bettelheim, 1958).

Superior power can be executed by a particular person (e.g., a parent), by an institution (e.g., a state), or by a peer group. Such power can have different bases such as physical strength, competence, a potential for granting or denying rights (especially rights to belong to a group). An agent of superior power – that is, an authority – provides an individual with criteria of positivity and negativity; the positive valence is acquired by objects and activities that are approved by authority and negative by those disapproved. Hence, approval and disapproval become the major factors controlling the evaluative functioning of an individual.

It should be noted that execution of power by an authority very rarely requires the direct application of physical or political force; expulsion from a group, total rejection, withdrawing most of the rights of an individual, or physically overpowering him or her are very infrequent cases. The major mediating role is played by various forms of expression of approval and disapproval, which communicate to the person whether he or she is following the will of authority or not. Thus, in the case of standards of societal origin, social approval becomes the criterion of positivity and negativity. We may call them, therefore, conformity standards.

[2] The good example of the process of acquisition of standards through modelling is the experiment of Bandura and Kupers (Bandura, 1969) who demonstrated that standards can be acquired on the basis of observational learning; they found that children apply standards presented to them for self-rewarding in absense of external control. Though Bandura claims that observational learning requires some reinforcement, it seems possible to present data showing that it does not have to be the case (Gelfand & Hartmann, 1979; Grusec, 1982).

Developmental changes in conformity standards can take two basic paths. One consists in the gradual internalization of external requirements (of authority) and patterns of activity provided by models. Whereas initially standards produced by societal impact can operate only under the direct control of external agents (i.e., when a model is present or when an authority oversees the behavior), after repeated exposure to such situations the standards are able to function without an external support. In other words, in the early stage of the development of conformity an individual employs standards mainly if they are practiced by others or controlled by authority. At the other end of the developmental cycle the standards become fully internalized, that is, independent of external support.

It seems rather unlikely that the process of internalization can occur as the result of single or few encounters with a model or with a requirement. Frequent exposure and broad external support seem to be the major preconditions for internalization. Such conditions are met, primarily, by requirements and forms of behavior that are fairly common in a given social environment, i.e., those that are established as social norms. We may say, therefore, that internalization mainly concerns the norms that function in a given society.

There are several indicators of internalization. According to Hoffman (1984), in case of internalization "the cognitive dimension of the norm, the associated affect (guilt), and the disposition to act in accord with the norm are experienced as self-generated. The original source of the norm, for example the parent, has lost most or all its motive power and may be forgotten" (p. 119).

The analysis of the process of internalization made by Hoffman indicates those hypothetical processes that are responsible for the fact that the respective evaluative standards "lose" their original ties with sources of norms. There is no need to repeat it here. We should point out, however, that the cognitive growth of an individual leads to further developmental changes in his or her evaluative standards. As Russian authors have pointed out, the major role in the stabilization and organization of evaluative standards is played by an elaborated system of beliefs that provides justification for the norms. In other words, the development of a person's worldview (ideology) is one of the main preconditions of integrity of the standards (Bozovitch, 1968).

Another line of development of conformity standards concerns change in the sources of authority. In the early stages of development an authority is perceived by an individual as someone with superior physical power and superior competence. Such an authority exerts complete control over an individual. It is represented in the mind of a child as overpowering. But the concept of authority changes. There are indications that change can have stage-like characteristic (Damon, 1977). At the initial stage (Stage O according to Damon), children tend not to differentiate what they want and what the authority expects from them; the authority is perceived as a psychical power over others.

At the next stage, authority is related to special talents and skills; these justify obedience (unilateral authority). At the last stage, the authoritarian relationship of leader to follower is supplanted by the conception of bilateral relation, and authority can be seen as a consensual relation among people that is adopted temporarily (Shantz, 1983).

The previously mentioned description of developmental changes in the concept of authority probably gives only a partial account of the process. In fact, we may conjecture that there are other processes involved here as well. For example, we can observe that the concept of an agent of authority undergoes change from a personal authority to an institutional one, from an overall (or total) authority to a partial one (one that can operate only in certain areas; e.g., the authority of the physician who can influence a judgment concerning health but on no other issue).

There is, also, another major change in this sphere that is related to the transition from "vertical" authority of "elders" to "horizontal" authority of peers. These two sources of authority compete with each other from a very early age. In childhood the authority of elders tends to prevail, whereas in adolescence there is a shift in the opposite direction. This shift appears to be a very broad, transcultural phenomenon and is described by West (Andersson, 1969) and East European authors (Bozowitch, 1968), as well as by American ones (Hartup, 1983). There are, however, some data showing that in late adolescence the conflict between standards of peers and parents decreases (Hartup, 1983).

And, of course, the concept of peers undergoes change as well. Although initially peers are age mates in the immediate surrounding, later on they comprise a large group: professional opinion, community, youth culture, etc. This implies major changes in the forms of communication between peers and in the ways that peer opinion is expressed and executed.

All these processes contribute to changes in evaluative standards. In the case of standards of societal origin, the conformity standards (that are sensitive to information concerning approval), developmental changes result first in changes in sources of approval and in the degree of immediacy of external control over evaluative judgment. In the advanced stage of development of these standards, the person can become relatively independent of external control because a well-established conceptual organization, grounded in the person's ideology, can have a high degree of selectivity: It will reject demands that are inconsistent with the well-established system. In other words, developmental processes result in changes in susceptibility to external influences on an individual's evaluative judgment.

COGNITIVE SOURCES OF EVALUATIVE PROCESSES: THE DEVELOPMENT OF CONCEPTUAL STANDARDS

The two previously described sources of evaluative standards emerge as the result of input of evaluative content into cognitive schemata. The schemata can obtain such input either from affective arousal (evoked by physical stimulation, changes in homeostasis, physical activity) or from societal influences. In a sense, in both cases the valence comes from "outside" the cognitive system. But it is also possible that the valence originates from "inside" the system. This is because the fact that cognitive processing is an intrinsic source of affective states.

This fact was discovered long ago (Hebb, 1949; J. McV. Hunt, 1963; Lewin, 1935; Pavlov, 1952). Further theoretical analysis and empirical studies (e.g., Berlyne, 1967; Festinger, 1957; Mandler, 1976; Zajonc, 1968) have since confirmed it. Thus it may be concluded that specific states are evoked whenever a well-established cognitive organization undergoes some changes resulting from an inconsistent input.

Later studies have shown that the valence and the intensity of affect, which is evoked in cognitive structures, is a rather complex function of many factors. But nevertheless it is possible to formulate the general conclusion that events, which foster the preservation of integrity of a given representation of an object in a cognitive system, usually have a positive valence, and events that might threaten such integrity are likely to acquire a negative one. The same can be said about the representation of an action; conditions that contribute to the smooth execution of an action become positive and conditions that interfere with an action – negative. We can say that cognitive schemata, which represent such events or conditions, possess the characteristics of evaluative standards. Their evaluative content originates in the affective processes generated in cognitive structures. We may call them conceptual standards.

This reasoning suggests that any object – social or physical – can be a source of evaluative standards and that the major criterion of evaluation in these cases is the integrity of a particular object or smooth functioning of action program. For example, a positive evaluation of nonleaded gasoline may stem from the fact that it saves trees and flowers, and a negative evaluation of the earthquake in Mexico is due to the destruction that was brought to the city. The precondition for such evaluative judgments is the existence of well-developed representations of the respective objects[3] (tree, flowers, Mexico City) and some understanding of the needs of these objects. In fact, we may surmise that the better developed the representations, the stronger the evaluative reaction to their fate.

The assumption that each cognitive representation can generate criteria of positivity or negativity (evaluative standards) implies that an individual possesses an infinite number of such criteria. But representations differ with respect to their position in the meaning system of the individual (i.e., in their importance); such a difference has some bearing on the regulatory role of the respective standards.

---

3 In his analysis of sources of prosocial behavior, Staub contends that one of the major preconditions of such behavior is "a well-developed sense of other people" (Staub, 1984).

Typically, the representation of an individual's own person, the self, holds a very high position in the system. It is a representation of great complexity, which is able to generate many different standards (*ipsocentric standards*). There are other important representations in the system as well: (a) representations of other persons (the preconditions for *allocentric standards*); (b) representations of groups of people and institutions (the basis for *sociocentric standards*); (c) representations of symbolic entities and systems (such as objects of arts, holy places, ideology, world view, etc.). The standards generated by these representations refer to conditions of preservation, well-being and/or growth of the respective objects.

The thesis that standards can originate from cognitive representations of objects and actions has some bearing on the problem of the formation of standards concerning a well being of other people or some social entities. Formation of these standards is likely to be facilitat by socializing procedures that contribute to the cognitive growth of the respective representations. Some support for such a view comes from authors who argue that so called induction plays an important role in formation of prosocial values (Hoffman, 1970; Staub, 1984). Moreover, in our laboratory there were some studies that have shown that the mere concentration of attention of children on the fate of another person can enhance the regulatory role of allocentric standards as manifested in helping (Kochańska, 1980) and that extensive use of induction in early stages of socialization results in an increasing role of allocentric standards in adolescence (Karyłowski, 1984).

The origin of conceptual standards indicates that their evaluative meaning depends on the content of representations; in other words, a person's concept of the given object determines what he or she regards as positive or negative for the given object. For example, parents' view of their child (his or her needs and interests) is the major factor in the evaluation of events whenever the child is considered. As the concept of the child changes over time, the criteria of good and bad must change as well. The same applies to other objects (friends, patients, neighbors, associates, self, etc.).

Conceptual standards undergo developmental changes that are related to gradual transformation of the respective concepts. As far as the concept of a person is concerned its development can be described as a gradual change in an individual's "cognitive apprehension" of the other, as M. Hoffman put it. According to this author, it is a three stage process: (a) the formation of person permanence (a sense of the other as a physical entity), (b) the formation of role-taking ability (that presupposes an acquisition of a sense of others as psychological entities), and (c) the formation of the conception of others as continuous persons ("with their own histories and identities") that is the precondition for seeing another person – as well as onself – as having stable, long-ranging interests. The latter is viewed as the basis of differentiation between the interests of different people (Hoffman, 1976, p. 132 and ff.).

Hoffman contends that the individual who progresses through these stages becomes capable of sympathetic responses to another person's distress. One may add that it should have another effect as well, namely, the individual might also be sensitive to opportunities for growth and expansion of the person. In other words, the development of the "cognitive apprehension" of another person accounts for the formation of allocentric standards.

Changes in "cognitive apprehension" must cause ensuing changes in the content of these standards: As individuals move from a physical to psychological interpretation of a person, their criteria of the well-being of the other will change accordingly. Thus we can argue that less developed individuals will make their judgment concerning the well-being of another person primarily in physical terms, whereas more developed individuals will consider psychological criteria as well.

As an example of this phenomenon I might mention one study from our laboratory. Andrzejczyk (Reykowski, 1979) found that socially less developed boys (from penitentiary school) tended to perceive other people mainly in physical terms (their needs for food, discomfort related to cold, fear of physical threat), whereas their peers from a vocational school were more able to recognize the psychological needs of others (need to achieve, to be accepted, to have power); there was no difference in the level of intelligence between these two groups that could explain this difference in perception of needs.

Conceptual allocentric standards also change as a function of increasing generality of the concept of a person. As the generality of the concept increases, the range of applicability of standards becomes broader (Staub, 1979). This accounts for the fact that standards of well-being of a person that originally are applied only to people from the immediate surrounding can be extended to include broader classes of people; one can react to the fate of people from the neighborhood, from the whole town, from the whole country; one can apply the standards to one's own colleagues, to people from the same school, to all youth, etc. Such an extension of the range or application of standards is the precondition of reactions to the fate of people who are very remote (geographically, culturally, etc.) from the self.

Developmental change in conceptual standards also is related to the formation of new forms of representation of social objects. A person can become capable of developing representations of some "aggregations" of social objects. A dyad is a simple form of aggregation (e.g., a marriage). More complex forms include small groups (extended family, school class, institutions in which an individual is employed, etc.) and larger organizations (church, political party, social class, state, etc.), Ability to perceive such a large whole as a separate entity (instead of a sum of individuals) is the precondition for treating the interests of the whole as the criterion for evaluative judgments. As an illustration of the previously described phenomenon of aggregation, we may refer to the study of Trzebińska. She compared the modes of communication of marriage partners who differed with respect to an elaboration of three different concepts: the concept of the self, the concept of the partner, and the concept of the marriage. It was found that those subjects who had a well-developed concept of marriage as compared to those who had developed, primarily, concepts of the self or the partner tended to use the so called egalitarian style of communication; that is, they tried to respect the rights of both partners (to protect marriage instead to protect interests of a particular person) (Trzebińska, 1978).

It seems feasible to conjecture that there is some analogy between the development of the "cognitive apprehension" of a person and the cognitive apprehension of a social organization. In other words, one can expect that initially an individual forms the representation of a group as a separate entity. Next he or she must acquire the ability to differentiate between the needs of individual members of the organization and needs of the whole (that seems to be a special case of perspective taking – the perspective of organization), and finally, the advanced concept of organization as having a stable identity must be developed. A person who attains the advanced concept of a social organization becomes capable a making evaluative judgments in terms of interests of the given organization. In other words, sociocentric standards are being formed.

The development of allocentric and sociocentric standards form the basis for a special kind of a moral judgment; it is a judgment in which the interests of another person or social organization are used as the criterion of positivity and negativity.

INTEGRATION OF EVALUATIVE PROCESSES: THE DEVELOPMENT OF AXIOLOGICAL STANDARDS

In the previous sections we have argued that evaluative standards originate from three different sources. These sources reflect the different aspects of human life: Hedonic standards represent "interests" of the human organism and human species; conformity standards represent interests of the particular form of interconnections (or bonds) between people; and conceptual standards represent interests of concrete individuals (people including oneself and, in many cases, other living creatures as well) or some forms of social organizations.

It goes without saying that judgments based on different standards can enter, quite often, into conflict one with another. It is a situation that can easily lead to a kind of stalemate in the evaluation process. There are, however, some ways of dealing with the problem. One possible way is to select evaluative standards by means of centration; due to centration an individual is able to take only one perspective, eliminating all others. Such a solution seems to be typical for small children and for instances when one has a very strong involvement in the issue. But it is a solution that can, quite likely, result in major harm to important interests of the individual or his or her social surrounding.

Some forms of safeguards against such harm are embedded in each type of standard. For hedonic standards there is a kind of hierarchy of urgency; the more urgent needs produce, typically, more extreme judgment. In the case of conformity standards there is the hierarchy of norms and authorities; in most cases the demands of higher authority exert a greater influence on evaluative judgment than demands of the lower one. As for conceptual standards, the hierarchy is determined by the position of the given concept in the meaning system of individual. Thus, in cases of conflict, people whose own selves have the highest position in their meaning system will tend to make egocentric judgements and choices. The more advanced form of dealing with such situations consists in coordination of different perspectives.

Prerequisite to the coordination of evaluative standards is the development of meta-rules that determine the way in which various standards should be integrated. Such rules can be developed due to the capability of the cognitive system to form higher order organizations. One example of such meta-rules is the concept of justice. This is the concept that defines the way of dealing with situations when different partners (social objects having their representations in the person's mind) have conflicting claims.

The concept of justice has its own developmental logic. Damon (1976) who conducted extensive studies on this issue described the early stages of development of the concept of justice. He found that at the very beginning of this process a child becomes capable of making allocations of some goods on the basis of some external, objective characteristics of competing parties (Level O-B). Judgment at this level tends to be primarily self-serving but it contains at least a minimal awareness that evaluation should respect some objective criteria.

The next level, one which for the first time represents a real consideration for justice (that is, a attempt at coordination of conflicting claims), introduces the notion of strict equality. The child requires that everyone should get the same (Level 1-1). Damon suggests that it has a major adaptive role in reducing ingroup fighting. One may add that it also can contribute to protection of basic interests of all members of a group. At the more advanced sublevel the idea of deserving and merit begins to emerge (Level 1-B). It assumes some recognition of previous actions of the individual as a factor that has to be taken into consideration in formulating judgment about justice.

The next step forward in the development of the concept of justice occurs when an individual manifests an awareness that different persons can have different needs and different justifications for their claims; in other words, an individual begins to realize that there is more to justice than the mere assessment of an input (Level 2). Such an awareness is the precondition of the coordination of interests of various kinds.

The most advanced stage described by Damon (Level 2-B) reflects the capability to coordinate two different principles of justice: equity and equality (Damon, 1981).

Note that the previously described stages or levels of development of the concept of justice are related, to some extent, to the developmental changes in cognitive apprehension of another as described by Hoffman. Although the formation of person permanence appears to be the necessary condition for attaining Level 0-B (that requires on ability to take into account some characteristics of the people involved), the formation of role-taking ability seems to presuppose an appreciation of the rules of strict equality (Level 1). Finally, an apprehension of individuality seems to be the precondition for the consideration of particular needs and claims of others (Level 2).

The aforementioned transformations in the concept of justice possibly account for only part of the developmental changes concerning this concept. We may observe that there are major changes with respect to the range of application of the concept. The answer to the question, "who are those others who are entitled to justice," is different at different stages of life. It can be conjectured that initially justice operates for those in the immediate presence. Developmental changes result in the gradual extension of this range.

Some interpretation of these changes can be derived from the recent works of Kohlberg (1976). We can argue that definitions of stages provided by this author describe the changing range of application of justice principles. At the third stage, people respect claims of members of small groups they belong to; at the fourth stage, the range of application of justice is defined by the institution, group, society that has established the given rules of justice; at the fifth stage the rights to justice are extended beyond the scope of the given institution (or broader, beyond the given society); and at the sixth stage, justice becomes a universal principle.

There is one more important developmental dimension that concerns changes in the regulatory role of the concept of justice. This role can differ depending on the situation of an individual. In the situation of an observer, an individual can use more advanced forms of judgement about justice than in the situation of a participant. In the situation of a participant, there is a strong tendency for centration; in many cases it is centration on interests of the self (egocentrism), but there are also instances of centration of the interests of others. The development can be described in terms of the increasing role of justice in the situation of participant.

MULTIDIMENSIONAL DEVELOPMENT OF MORALITY

The main implication of the argument presented in the previous sections seems to point to the fact that moral development is a multidimensional process. If we accept the view that the core issue of morality is justice (Lickona, 1976), we may conclude that people can make judgments about justice within the framework of different evaluative modalities.

People can use rules of justice as the most prudent choice in the given situation. Obviously, their understanding of the meaning of the rule will change developmentally. The rule of justice also can be interpreted by the individual as a social requirement that he or she must follow. The meaning of the justice is defined by authority. Developmental changes in justice appear to be the consequences of transformations of the concept of authority and the content of requirements that are set by it.

It should be worthwhile to note, however, that the content of the concept of justice[4] in a person's mind does not have to be the exact copy of its social definition. One cause of the difference between justice as practiced in a given society and justice as interpreted by a particular person is his or her ability for cognitive processing of acquired knowledge. Such processing may result in the formation of a concept of justice that reflects its prototypic meaning rather than its everyday use. This possibility is suggested by research on concept formation; it has been found by Posner and his associates (see Wessells, 1982) that subjects who are exposed to series of patterns consisting in distortions of certain prototypical pattern (not exposed) can develop a concept of the original with a remarkable accuracy. We can conjecture therefore, that people who observe various "distorted" forms of justice can, nevertheless, formulate the concept of justice that reflects its original meaning as embedded in the given culture.

The rule of justice can also evolve as the result of an active process of construction of a higher level conceptual (axiological) system in order to deal with conflicting standards originating in person's own representations of social objects. Such a system seems to be the product of an advanced level of cognitive development.

The three previously described ways of interpreting justice (as prudent choice, as compliance to social authority, and as the creation of abstract principles for coordination of conflicting standards) seem to correspond, in certain ways, to Kohlberg's three levels of moral development (preconventional, conventional, postconventional). They also resemble three stages described by Eisenberg, 1982 (the first, third, and fifth). But this similarity notwithstanding, the theoretical framework proposed here is, apparently, a different one and this difference has some bearing on the interpretation of the nature of moral development.

---

4 It has been shown that the concept of justice can have great variety of meanings. The extensive analysis of the concept is provided by Deutsch in his recent book (1985).

First of all, as far as the attainment of moral autonomy is concerned, there seems to be not one but three different forms of such:

– the autonomy of persons who have achieved enough independence from their urges and desires to appreciate own interest in respecting other people's needs and goals;

– the autonomy of persons who have deeply internalized external demands and act without any external control and guidance whatsoever;

– the autonomy of persons who have developed moral principles as a part of their axiological system. The ability to coordinate conflicting standards protects the person against centration on the interests of any specific object[5].

The aforementioned analysis suggests that, as far as moral development is concerned, autonomy is in fact the major developmental outcome. One can practice justice in autonomous ways but for different psychological reasons. Thus, we postulate that there are different tracks (or pathways) or moral development. Because it is rather unlikely that people with normal brains are lacking in any of the aforementioned evaluative modalities, we should expect that within any given personality all of them are present and all of them may have some impact on moral judgment. This might explain the fact that the same person is capable of, and tends to make, moral judgments using different criteria. Such a picture, apparently, emerges from the data presented by Eisenberg (1982). It is, however, possible that a given modality can achieve a dominant position in a person, or even more so, in a given culture. In other words, it seems quite likely that the cultural impact can determine what kind of evaluative modality (and the respective kind of morality) will prevail in a given society.

It can be noted that each kind of morality can achieve the criterion of universality postulated by Kohlberg. One can, for all practical reasons, espouse the universal law of justice if one perceives one's own interests in a universal context, especially in the eschatological perspective. One can also act in universal ways if one's moral standards have originated from universal authority. And, of course, a universality can be an attribute of a highly developed axiological system. Such an approach poses, however, a problem of assessment. If we accept the view that there are different kinds of justice and different kinds of autonomy, we are confronted with the question: How do these differences become manifest in the moral discourse? Are there some clear indicators of different evaluative modalities in publicly expressed moral reasoning? Can we distinguish whether the reason a given person offers for

---

5 It does protect, however, against centration on a particular principle. The ability to coordinate different principles in an axiological system is a different developmental issue.

a given moral act represents justice originating in the axiological system, in his or her internalized and cognitively developed societal standards, or, in his or her firm grasp of what is socially rewarded (what is prudent behavior in the given situation)?

It seems that such a distinction can be easily obtained in case of the less developed forms of moral judgment, i.e., in a period when a given person has not yet reached the ability to understand what is the prudent response in the given situation or if he or she has not reached an advanced level of internalization. But we can not, at all, be sure that procedures that are used currently are sensitive enough to differentiate between advanced forms of development of evaluative modalities. We would like to conclude, therefore, that the full account of a psychological meaning of moral autonomy is, as yet, an open issue.

REFERENCES

Alwin, D.F. (1984). *Education, occupation and parental values.* Unpublished paper, University of Michigan.

Anderson, B. E. (1969). *Studies in adolescent behaviour.* Stockholm: Almquist & Wiksell.

Aronfreed, J. (1970). The socialization of altruistic and sympathetic behavior: Some theoretical and experimental analyses. In J. Macaulay & D. L. Berkowitz (Eds.), *Altruism and helping behavior.* New York: Academic Press.

Bandura, A. (1969). *Principles of behavior modification.* New York: Holt.

Bandura, A. (1977). *Social learning theory.* Englewood Cliffs, NJ: Prentice-Hall.

Bar-Tal, D., & Raviv, A. A. (1982). A cognitive learning model of helping behavior development: Possible implications and applications. In N. Eisenberg (Ed.) *The development of prosocial behavior* (pp. 199–219). New York: Academic Press.

Berlyne, D. E. (1967). Arousal and reinforcement. In D. Levine (Ed.), *Nebraska Symposium on Motivation* (pp. 1–110). Lincoln, NE; University of Nebraska Press.

Bettelheim, B. (1958). Individual and mass behavior in extreme situation. In E. E. Maccoby, T. M. Newcomb, & E. L. Hartley (Eds.), *Readings in social psychology,* London: Methuen.

Bozowitch, L. J. (1968). *Licznost i jejo formirowanije w detskom wozrastie.* Moskva: Izd. Prosowieszczenije.

Damon, W. (1977). *The social world of the child.* San Francisco: Jossey-Bass.

Damon, W. (1981). The development of justice and self-interest during childhood. In M. Lerner & S. Lerner (Eds.), *The justice motives in social behavior* (pp. 57–73). New York: Plenum.

Deutsch, M. (1985). *Distributive justice.* New Haven: Yale University Press.

Dollard, J., Doob, L. W., Miller, N. E., Mowrer, H. O., & Sears, R. R., (1947). *Frustration and Aggression.* New Haven: Yale University Press.

Eisenberg, N. (1982). The development of reasoning regarding prosocial behavior. In N. Eisenberg (Ed.), *The development of prosocial behavior* (pp. 249–251). New York: Academic Press.

Festinger, L. (1957). *A theory of cognitive dissonance.* Stanford, CA: Stanford University Press.

Fiske, S. F. (1982). Schema-triggered affect: Application to social perception. In M. S. Clark & S. F. Fiske (Eds.), *Affect and cognition* (pp. 55–78). The 17th Annual Carnegie Symposium on Cognition. Hillsdale, NJ: Erlbaum Lawrence Associates.

Gelfand, D.M. & Hartmann, D.P. (1979). Response consequences and attributions: two contributors to prosocial behavior. In N. Eisenberg (Ed.), *The development of prosocial behavior.* New York: Academic Press.

Grusec, J. (1982). The socialization of altruism. In N. Eisenberg (Ed.), *The development of prosocial behavior* (pp. 139–167). New York: Academic Press.

Hartup, W. W. (1983). Peer relations. In P. H. Mussen (Ed.), *Handbook of child psychology.* New York: J. Wiley.

Hebb, D. O. (1949). *The organization of behavior.* New York: Wiley.

Hoffman, M. L. (1970). Moral development. In P. H. Mussen (Ed.), *Carmichael's manual of child psychology* (Vol. 2, pp. 261–359). New York: Wiley.

Hoffman, M. L. (1976). Empathy, role-taking, guilt and development of altruistic motives. In T. Lickona (Ed.), Moral development and behavior (pp. 124–144). New York: Holt.

Hoffman, M. L. (1984). Parent discipline, moral internalization, and development of prosocial motivation. In E. Staub (Eds.), *Development and maintenance of prosocial behavior* (pp. 117–139). New York: Plenum.

Hoffman, M.L. (1986). *Affect, cognition, and motivation.* In R.M. Sorrentino, E.T. Higgins (Eds.), Handbook of motivation and cognition: foundations of social behavior. NY: Guilford Press.

Hunt, J. McV. (1963). Motivation inherent in information processing and action. In O. J. Harvey (Ed.), *Motivation and social interaction: Cognitive determinants.* New York: Ronald Press.

Jacobson, S. G. (1981). Stanovlenye psihologitcheskih mehanismov etitchescoy regulatsyi poviedenya. In I. N. Antsyferova (Ed.), *Psihologyia formirovanya i razvitya litschnosty* (pp. 320–338). Moskva: Izd. Nauka.

Karyłowski, J. (1984). Focus of attention and altruism: endocentric and exocentric sources of altruistic behavior. In E. Staub et al. (Eds.), *Development and maintenance of prosocial behavior* (pp. 139–155). New York: Plenum.

Kochańska, G. (1980). *Experimental formation of cognitive and helping social motivation in children.* Polish Psycholog. Bulletin, *11,* 75–85.

Kohlberg, L. (1964). Development of moral character and moral ideology. In M. Hoffmann & L. W. Hoffman (Eds.), *Review of child development research.* New York: Russel Sage Fundation.

Kohlberg, L. (1976). Moral stages and moralization: The cognitive-developmental approach. In T. Lickona (Ed.), *Moral development and behavior* (pp. 31–54). New York: Holt.

Kohn, M. L. (1969). *Class and conformity.* Homewood, IL: Dorsey.

Lacey, J., Smith, R. L., & Green, A. (1964). Use of conditioned autonomic responses in the study of anxiety. In C. F. Reed, J. E. Alexander, & S. S. Tomkins (Eds.), *Psychopathology, a source book.* New York: Wiley.

Lickona, T. (1976). Ciritical issues in the study of moral development and behavior. In T. Lickona (Ed.), *Moral development and behavior* (pp. 3–29). New York: Holt.

Mac Arthur, L. Z. (1984). *Judging a book by its cover: Impression of babyfaced adults.* XXIII International Congress of Psychology. Acapulco.

Magnusson, D., & Allen, V. L. (1983). An interactional perspective for human development. In D. Magnusson & V. L. Allen (Eds.), *Human development* (pp. 3–35). New York: Academic Press.

Mandler, G. (1976). *Mind and emotion.* New York: Wiley.

Mowrer, O.H. (1960). Learning theory and behavior. New York: Wiley.

Pavlov, J. P. (1952). *20 lat badań wyższych czynności nerwowych zachowania się zwierząt.* Warszawa: PZWL. (The first edition in Russian 1932).

Piaget J. (1967). *Rozwój ocen moralnych dziecka.* Warszawa: PWN. (The first French edition: 1932).

Piaget J. (1981). *Równoważenie struktur poznawczych (Equilibration of cognitive structures).* Warszawa: PWN (orig. in French).

Reykowski, J. (1979). *Motywacja, postawy prospołeczne a osobowość.* (Prosocial motivation, prosocial attitudes and personality: in Polish). Warszawa: PWN.

Rushton, J. P. (1982). Social learning theory and the development of prosocial behavior. In N. Eisenberg (Ed.), *The development of prosocial behavior* (pp. 77–109). New York: Academic Press.

Schneirla, T. (1959). An evolutionary and developmental theory of biphasic processes underlying approach and withdrawal. In M. Jones (Ed.), *Nebraska Symposium on Motivation* (pp. 1–42). Lincoln, NE: University of Nebraska Press.

Shantz, G. U. (1983). Social cognition. In P. H. Mussen (Ed.), *Handbook of child psychology.* New York: Wiley.

Staub, E. (1979). *Positive social behavior and morality: Socialization and development: vol. 2.* New York: Academic Press.

Staub, E. (1984). Notes towards an interactionist-motivational theory of the determinants and development of (pro) social behavior. In E. Staub, D. Bar-Tal, J. Karylowski, & J. Reykowski (Eds.), *Development and maintenance of prosocial behavior* (pp. 29–51). New York: Plenum.

Strelau, J. (1983). *Temperament-personality-activity.* New York: Academic Press.

Taylor, T. R. (1978). *The construction of an objective method of assessing morality and the testing of Kohlberg's hierarchical theory. Psychologia Africana, 17* (3), 169–201.

Tomkins, S. (1984). In K. Scherer & P. Ekman (Eds.), *Approaches to emotion.* Hillsdale, NJ: Lawrence Erlbaum Associates.

Trzebińska, E. (1978). *Stały i zmienny sposób definiowania relacji z partnerem w toku komunikacji interpersonalnej a niektóre właściwości reprezentacji poznawczych i efektywność komunikowania się.* Unpublished doctoral thesis, University Warsaw.

Ullrich, W. (1976). *Zoopsychologia.* Warszawa: PWN.

Wessells, M. G. (1982). *Cognitive psychology.* New York: Harper & Row.

White, R. W. (1960). *Motivation reconsidered: The concept of competence. Psychological Review, 66,* 297–333.

Volkova, B. D. (1953). O niekatorih osobyennostyah obrasovanya uslovnych reflexov na retchevye rasdrazhitelya u dietiey. *Fizyologitschesky Zhurnal* (No. 5).

Zajonc, R.B. (1968). Cognitive theories in social psychology. In G. Lindzey & E. Aronson (Eds.), *The handbook of social psychology.* New York: Addison-Wesley.

Zuckerman, M. (1980). Sensation seeking and its biological correlates. *Psychological Bulletin, 88,* 187–214.

3 Individual and Societal (Group) Values in a Motivational Perspective and their Role in Benevolence and Harmdoing

Ervin Staub
University of Massachusetts at Amherst

To understand the nature of values and how they affect thought, feeling, and action, we must examine them jointly with other motivational forces. According to Rokeach (1973) "A value is an enduring belief that a specific mode of conduct or end state is personally or socially preferable relative to an opposite or converse mode of conduct or end state of existence" (p. 5). In my view also, values involve preferences. However, I stress more the motivational nature of values. The essential defining element of values is preference or desire for certain outcomes or end states or, more commonly, for classes of outcomes or end states. Associated with these preferences are networks of cognitions or modes of thinking, which include beliefs and reasons that make the desired outcomes preferable. However, this cognitive network may be more or less elaborate, and at times quite limited.

Values are not the only sources of desires or preferences, and when they affect conduct, they do not act alone, separate from other motives. In a series of publications I have evolved a conception, a theory of personal goals, to account for altruism (Staub, 1978a, 1978b, 1980, 1984a, 1984b) and later for aggression as well (Staub, 1986a, 1987), which is now evolving into a more general theory of motivation and action (Staub, in press, 1987). In this chapter I briefly consider the nature and function of values from the standpoint of this general theory. Then I discuss in more detail the nature of both personal and group values, specifically morally relevant values, and of "valuations" of human beings, including the devaluation of outgroup members. I discuss how values and valuations guide the behavior of individuals and groups, especially behaviors that benefit or harm others. I also discuss value change and behavior change, and the relationship between them. I discuss how progressive increases in benevolence or harmdoing (steps along the continuum of destruction) result in changes in individuals and the group and make extreme benevolence or harmdoing (even genocide) possible and probable.

A BRIEF REVIEW OF PERSONAL GOAL THEORY

From the perspective of personal goal theory, to understand behavior that benefits or harms others, or any other behavior, we have to consider the totality of a person's personality and circumstances. Whether people help or harm someone (and whether a society responds to the difficulties of another country in a helpful way or turns against another country) depends on the multiplicity of goals, values, and other motives that the individual (or society) possess and on processes that call forth certain of these motives. How do certain aims arise and become dominant? The focus of the theory has been on motivation, on accounting especially for purposeful behavior guided by goals and values, and more recently on how these and other individual (and group) motivations can be understood in a single, joint framework.

In this conception personal goals and values are similar constructs. Both refer to what is desirable, preferred. In their properties and mode of functioning they are the same. It is worthwhile to distinguish them by their content, by the types of outcomes they refer to. Values are desired outcomes that relate to the welfare of human beings. They guide human relationships in light of considerations of human welfare. At times the awareness of their relationship to human welfare may be lost, the standards derived from values may become reified, as in the case of sexual prohibitions, but on consideration the origins of the standards in values become apparent. Thus, values are always moral or morally relevant, that is, they have clear moral implications. Goals are more self-related, they refer to desired outcomes that have no direct relatonship to others' well-being. Achievement can be such a goal, the desire to do well, to succeed in comparison to standards of excellence. In the following I at times use the generic term motive to refer to goals and values together (and on occasion to other motives as well). I use the term *motivation* to refer to one or more motives in an active state, with the desire to reach relevant outcomes active. (Some readers may object to regarding values as preferences only for morally relevant outcomes. However, if we define values as preferences for any desired outcomes, they will not differ in any way from personal goals, or if we take other conceptual frameworks, from motives in general – see Epstein in this volume).

An important characteristic of goals and values is that they can be arranged in a hierarchy, according to their importance. This is probably true not only of individual, but also of group goals and values. Goals and values function in a unified manner, so that they are best characterized by a single hierarchy. Personal goals and values represent potentials. One goal or value, or a number of "integrated" goals and values that can be satisfied by the same outcome or by different outcomes that can be pursued by the same course of action, will have to become active and dominant if motivated action is to result.

The behavior of individuals and of whole societies depends on the nature of their goals and values and on what goals are in an active state, and on supporting characteristics that determine whether motivation gains expression in action. The role of the environment is very important in activating goals. Certain characteristics of the environment determine the degree to which it has an activating potential for specific goals. The more important a goal or value, the higher in the hierarchy, and the stronger the activating potential of the environment for it, the more likely that it becomes active. Supporting characteristics, such as competencies to pursue outcomes that fulfill the goal or value, affect whether the motive will become active, and whether once active it gains expression in action. The desire to dominate others may not arise in a small and weak person or in a small nation surrounded by powerful neighbors. Even if it does arise, without the capacity to fulfill the goal it will not gain expression in action. However, it is not actual competencies, but how they are perceived by the actor that has primary influence.

Goals and values are activated not only externally, by the environment, but also internally. When no motive is active, and thus there is no preoccupation with motive-related outcomes or with goal-directed action, the internal activation of goals or values becomes more probable. The more important a motive, and the wider and more extensive the network of cognitions associated with it, the more likely that it will be internally activated. When the network of cognitions is extensive, random thoughts, or a wide range of events, can touch on a cognition related to the motive and initiate a sequence of thought that results in its activation. Thus some people may be frequently motivated to fulfill a value, or pursue a goal, even in the absence of direct external instigation.

If a particular aim is "selected" (not necessarily by conscious decision making but by becoming dominant through the processes that I discussed) from the *totality* of motives of different kinds that a person (or society) possesses, then we must also consider motives other than goals and values, and the relative influence of each. All might be regarded for predictive purposes as part of a single hierarchy of motives that vary in their importance to the person (or society). This includes *needs,* which either have a biological basis, or derive from highly important but persistently frustrated goals. They have a pressing, imperative character, and they are likely to frequently override goals and values. The hierarchy includes *unconscious motivation,* which also has a pressing quality. Well-established societal rules and customs that have no clear value implications also are important sources of motivation.

Values exert influence partly as a function of where they are in the hierarchy of motives, partly as a function of their *range of applicability,* which refers to the range of environmental conditions that are regarded as relevant to the value and have activating potential for it. Some values can be of tremendous importance for a person or society. Still, they can be defined as inapplicable to a wide range of people, events, or environmental conditions. Members of out-groups, especially devalued out-groups, are often seen as outside the range of applicability of even basic human values. Their exclusion from the moral realm allows their mistreatment.

Motive Equilibration and Goal Integration. Values, as all other motives, also exert influence as "selectors" or influences that enter into motive equilibration. This refers to a process, itself motivational, that works towards the reduction of conflict among motives. A special case of motive equilibration is *moral* equilibration. Consider, that a goal is activated by circumstances that also potentially activate a value that conflicts with the goal. This is a common occurrence because moral values and rules are the guardians against people acting in their pursuit of self-interest in ways that harm other people. There will be a tendency to "select" a goal and a value in a way that minimizes their conflict. Thus, a person may select a value as relevant that allows the expression of the goal in action. Or if this is impossible a person may choose a goal that is more acceptable in terms of his or her values. This selection probably frequently occurs by a preconscious screening, even before the goal and the value become conscious. Or it can be the result of rationalizations, justifications (when a less high-level value is "chosen") or conscious compromise. Research on moral reasoning has shown that the level of reasoning that people use is affected by circumstances (Staub, 1978a). More specific in their relevance are findings by Eisenberg and her associates (see Eisenberg, 1986) that young children's level of prosocial moral reasoning shifts as a function of the prior arousal of certain goals in them.

Both individuals and societies are likely to function best if they have integrated motivational orientations. Motive equilibration is one process of motive integration. Over time motivational orientations may evolve in which varied motives, including values, are consistent and support each other in selecting outcomes. In contrast, both individuals and societies may find certain motives unacceptable. They exclude them from the self-concept, so that they become unaware of possessing them. The result of this dissociation is lack of integration. To the extent they continue to exist and to exert influence that a person (or society) is unaware of, they represent a constant potential for conflict with conscious motives.

Self-Concept and World View as the Origins of Motives. Specific values and goals may be regarded as independent, relatively separate components of a person's personality. In contrast, they may arise from the self-concept and world views that individuals or groups hold, which together comprise much of a person's assumptive world. For example, a poor self-concept, a sense of weakness, inferiority, or incapacity, results in feelings of vulnerability and threat. This is especially so under conditions of stress, or environmental threat, which activate feelings of weakness or incapacity and are likely to give rise to strong motivation for self-defense. A world view that identifies other people or groups as violent and untrustworthy, and/or violence as a natural, common and perhaps inevitable mode of behavior of persons or groups, also makes the need for self-defense great. With the two combined, a negative self-concept and a view of the world as dangerous, the need for self-defense may arise even without stress or threatening environmental conditions.

The content or nature of the self-concept, in addition to its quality, also affects orientation to others. The basic assumptions one holds about an acceptable or good self, the value placed on certain qualities in the self, will lead to the motivation to create such a self. Toch (1969) noted that many violent criminals are characterized by a value placed on masculine toughness, which leads them to respond to slight and even imagined provocation by violence. They act to maintain the image of toughness and masculinity probably not only in others' eyes, but even in their own, thereby to maintain a positive self-concept.

VALUE ORIENTATIONS OF INDIVIDUALS

Are there certain moral value orientations that tend to characterize individuals? Basically, from their experience and socialization, people can derive one or both of two primary moral value orientations: one that directly focuses on the welfare of human beings, and one that is centered on moral principles and rules. Presumably, the moral principles and rules derive from a valuing of human welfare, and their purpose is to maintain human welfare. However, as this concern is turned into principles and rules, the focus on human welfare can lose its directness, and depending on the way it is shaped by individuals and groups that transmit them, they can become remote from their original purpose.

A number of writers have proposed forms of these two moral value orientations. Durkheim (1961) believed that some people are concerned with promoting the "good" and are inclined to respond to others' needs even if that demand breaks with convention, whereas other people are concerned with the maintenance of the social order. Moreover in his view, in times of stability such as the age of Augustus in ancient Rome, morality will focus on the maintenance of social order. Instability and flux, on the other hand, bring a more direct concern with human welfare, a concern with the good, to the fore.[1] Hoffman

---

[1] Actually, "difficult life conditions," deprivation, and chaos, have the potential as well to activate strong self-protective motives, thus reducing concern for others (Staub, in press).

(1970) identified some children as humanistic, concerned with others' welfare, others as conventional, concerned with conventional rules and with the legal and religious bases of moral judgment. Gilligan (1982) suggested that males' moral thinking has a focus on equality, fairness, the use of logic to derive what is right on the basis of rules, whereas females' moral thinking is more contextual, based on a sense of connectedness to others and of care and responsibility for other people. The former appears to be rule centered; the latter more directly centered on human welfare. Subsequently Gilligan (1984) suggested that these two moral orientations characterize both males and females, but a focus on rules tends to be dominant in males, whereas a focus on care and responsibility in females.

Over time (Staub, 1978a, 1978b, 1980, 1987), I have evolved a distinction between a person-oriented morality that I call *prosocial orientation* and a rule-oriented morality or *rule orientation*. In a number of studies (Staub, Erkut & Jaquette, as described in Staub, 1974; Erqut, Jaquette, & Staub, 1981; Feinberg, 1978: Grodman, 1979; See Staub, 1978a, 1978b, 1987), the factor analysis of a set of value measures provided a factor that I designated as a prosocial orientation factor. Subjects' factor scores were associated with helping a person in physical distress, in a number of different ways, and with helping someone in psychological distress, upset about her boyfriend having unexpectedly left her. The component measures suggested that a prosocial orientation consists of (a) a positive evaluation of human beings, (b) concern about their welfare, and (c) feelings of personal responsibility for people's welfare.

In contrast to person-oriented morality, which probably always has characteristics similar to prosocial orientation, and for which prosocial orientation might be the best index, rule orientation can be quite varied in nature. Its focus may be high-level values or principles, such as justice. However, a belief in justice is insufficient to identify a person's moral orientation, because justice can be seen and perceived in many different ways: as equity, a fair ratio between inputs and outcomes or contributions and rewards; as equality of outcomes; as equality of opportunity to pursue outcomes; or in other ways (Deutsch, 1975; Staub, in press). The sanctity of human life may be another principle. The maintenance of the social order may also be a principle in its own right, a moral one to the extent that it originates in the belief that this is required to maintain or enhance the welfare of the group and its individual members.

The principles mentioned previously, such as justice, which are seemingly and potentially universal, can vary in the extent to which they are concerned with and protect the welfare of all persons, of all humanity, in contrast to the welfare of one's own society and its members, or the welfare of subgroups of society and persons belonging to them. The maintenance of the social order may benefit those who are privileged while harming others. Depending on the kind of justice principle in use, some may benefit, whereas others may be deprived.

Moral value orientations can focus on the individual, or on the group. Although prosocial orientation is usually person oriented, its focus can also be the welfare of the group. Rule orientation can also be either person or group centered, but it tends more to the latter. The maintenance of social order and concern with the social contract are clearly group centered, whereas the norm of social responsibility (see following) person centered. Ideally, moral concerns would focus on both individuals and the group. The danger of group-centered morality is that concern about the welfare of individual members may be lost, so that individuals are sacrificed to the group welfare or in the name of group welfare. As a result, the essence and purpose of morality is lost.

Rule orientation embodies principles and rules that vary along a number of dimensions. One of them is their level of generality. High-level principles are independent and can at times be contradictory, such as the principle of justice and the maintenance of the social order. Rules are usually more specific and are subordinated to principles, the reason for their existence explained by a principle (and at times by person-oriented values such as prosocial orientation). They may be regarded as of lower level than principles. Another variation is in the breadth of the applicability of rules or norms. Although principles are generally broadly applicable, rules, norms, or standards can be more or less specific.

The norm of reciprocity is apparently universal (Gouldner, 1960). This is probably so because it is rooted in the logic of interpersonal relations (Piaget, 1932). It is also broad in applicability. It can in part be derived from principles such as fairness. The "norm of social responsibility" (Bekowitz & Lutterman, 1968; Staub, 1972) makes people responsible for the welfare of other people in need. It is widely held in our society, and it is likely to characterize all societies to some extent. It is derived from values such as a prosocial orientation that is turned into rule orientation. Many low-level rules, norms, and standards exist that guide behavior, different ones in different societies and subgroups.

Lower level rules can become rigid and morally irrelevant or even harmful, unless they specifically aim at promoting human welfare or remain connected to, informed and guided by, higher level rules or principles. Honesty, for example, can be used as a weapon, insisted on regardless of human consequences. Probably the most morally sensitive value orientation, and the most effective one in terms of protecting and promoting human welfare, consists of a combination of prosocial and rule orientations, in which the rules and principles, regardless of their level, remain connected to, are guided by, and tested and evaluated in terms of considerations of human welfare.

Although the domain or breadth of applicability of higher level rules or principles can be delimited, so that practically they are applied only to a limited group of people, potentially they are broadly applicable. Thus, an orientation to the social contract, to a maintenance of the social order, is a very high-level rule. So is an orientation to justice. One is not regarded as higher level than another as they are in Kohlberg's (1969; Kohlberg and Candee, 1984) system. There a level of development refers to the evolution of morality in a person, essentially from lowel level, self-related or egocentric, to higher level, supposedly autonomous morality, universally applicable, as embodied in principles of justice or in valuing the sanctity human life. The moral substance of a social contract orientation or of rule orientation with a focus on justice cannot be judged a priori; it depends on what a person regards as justice, whether the conception of justice is broadly applicable and broadly promotive of human welfare, and on the nature or content of the values and rules embodied in the social contract.

Valuing Connection and Its Role in Empathy. A significant value orientation that ought to be considered in this context is a *valuing of connection* to other people. Connection can be valued for purely functional reason: Through connection, one can gain satisfactions from other people. Cooperation, which is a form of connection, can also be purely functional, valued to the extent it results in personal gain. However, connection and cooperation can also be valued in themselves. Cooperation, helping others, joining others or being joined by them and other activities in which connection is inherent can become valued, desired outcomes, and sources of satisfaction.

Such a valuing of connection goes beyond affiliation as a motive. The value is not only being with other people and/or gaining potential benefits and satisfactions, such as the enjoyment of conversation, of playing basketball, or the lessening of anxiety (Schachter, 1959), but the experiencing of connection to them. As in marriage and other close relationships, through the experience of connectedness the gains of others provide satisfaction to the self. Valuing connection may partly arise from moral values, partly from positive experiences that accompany connection. Intense joy, happiness, fulfillment, and satisfaction can arise from connection to others. As a result of such experiences and of values that orient people to others, the value of connection can come to dominate other values as a source of satisfaction and well-being.

Empathy is an emotional connection to others that is an important source of benefiting them and of inhibiting behavior that harms them. Although empathy is an emotional experience, it is not unrelated to values. Empathy requires the experience of connection to other people. Feeling distant, disconnected, looking at other people and their experience as removed observers (Stotland, 1969), the experience of empathy becomes improbable. Most likely, empathy is "coded" in the value of connectedness, and in valuing human beings (at least those one feels empathy with). It is partly out of these values, which include cognitive *evaluations,* as well as effective preferences and desires (for others' welfare, and so on) that the *experience of connection* arises. This, in turn, is a precondition for empathy. Beyond valuing, the capacity for role taking, for accurately assessing other people's experience or anticipating what they might experience as a result of events in their lives (Hoffman, 1975), is an essential source of empathy. Finally, although an essential aspect of empathy, connection cannot be too intense, if empathy is to result. Being too fused with another person results in too much of a parallel feeling with them, a feeling that is the same as their own. For people to help others in need, to be responsive to others' states a more responsive empathy is required, a sympathetic responsiveness or some other emotion in which the focus remains the other and does not become the self (Staub, 1987).

VALUATIONS OF HUMAN BEINGS

The mistreatment of persons or groups, discrimination, or aggression aimed at them, usually involves devaluation of them. It is difficult to imagine that one person would severely harm another whom he or she sees as a good, worthwhile, deserving person. Although this can happen under special conditions, when there is an overriding motivation for aggression such as hunger or other survival needs, it is not the usual or likely case. Even when there is competition for resources, others are probably usually devalued before they are subject to instrumental aggression. Conversely, helping others usually requires a positive evaluation of them. Again, there can be exceptions, for example, when a religious conception represents all human beings as sinners, while at the same time prescribes helpful conduct.

Individuals and cultures vary in their evaluation of both human beings in general and of specific individuals and groups in particular. An essential aspect of prosocial orientation is a positive evaluation of human beings. Individuals or groups who positively evaluate human beings in general still frequently devalue particular others. People frequently sharply demarcate their ingroup from out-groups and devalue at least some out-groups and their members.

Devaluation and Us-Them Differentiation. Us-them differentiation is a central source of devaluation. Some degree of devaluation as a result of such differentiation alone is usual (Brewer, 1978; Tajfel, Flament, Billig,& Bundy, 1971). In addition, cultures usually evolve conceptions of other groups, stereotypes that are frequently devaluative in nature, that embody negative images of the other group. These stereotypes and negative images are taught to children as part of their socialization, and communicated to them through varied products of the culture, in literature, theater, the arts, and the media. A cultural devaluation of a specific group "preselects" this group for mistreatment. For example, when conditions of life in a society are difficult, motivations arise, such as the need to protect individual and group self-concept, that can be fulfilled by harming others and elevating the self over them. Devaluation of subgroups of society is a cultural characteristic that both makes doing harm more likely and guides the selection of victims (Staub, 1985, in press).

Ingroup out-group differentiation arises from many sources and is affected by many conditions. There seems to be a genetic predisposition for it, embodied in infants' tendency to develop attachment to caretakers and at about the same time anxiety in response to strangers. A related source is the negative emotion generated by a highly unfamiliar stimulus, especially one that deviates from the known and the familiar (e.g., a mismatch between an existing schema, even if nonevaluative, and a stimulus input). Another source is the negative emotion generated by a discrepancy with or deviation from a valued schemata, such as differences between oneself or one's group and others in values, ideals, religion, and so on. Such a discrepancy has implications for the self, raises questions about one's own values, beliefs, and ways of life. The significance and impact of such differences increase given a poor self-concept, circumstances that make a person or group insecure and defensive or the success of members of the other group evident. The latter raises the possibility that their values and ways of life are superior. Active antagonism between groups or individuals, a genuine conflict of interest, can sharpen us-them differentiation and provide an impetus for devaluation.

One function of us-them differentiation and devaluation of them, implied so far, is the defense of self-concept, values, and ways of life. This function is also served by scapegoating. Devaluation makes scapegoating easier and helps to select scapegoats, although inherent in scapegoating is devaluation. One of the several functions of scapegoating is to diminish feeling of one's own responsibility or blame for problems. Another important function of ingroup out-group differentiation is to enhance ingroup cohesion, both a positive evaluation by ingroup members of each other, and a feeling of connectedness among them. Unity and feelings of community can be enhanced by turning against an out-group.

Moral value orientations embody basic assumptions and evaluations. To different extents, they stress an appreciation of and respect for the essential humanity of persons, for their lives and well-being and freedom from suffering. At least implicit in them is the assumption that such respect is required for maintaining the harmony and well-being of the social group. Devaluation makes inapplicable the values and principles embodied in moral value orientations to those devalued, or leads to the application of less stringent values to them. The character and actions of devalued people will be so interpreted that they are perceived as less deserving, or not deserving of well-being and ultimately of life. They are often perceived as morally deficient and even evil, which makes them undeserving of moral concern. As a result they are excluded from the applicability of moral value orientations.

It is unfortunate that the suffering of other people itself results in their devaluation. Just world thinking (Lerner, 1980) leads people to explain others' suffering as due either to their character, or to their actions. At any rate, the suffering is seen as deserved. This is more likely to happen if the others are already devalued. Similarly, empathy is unlikely to arise when people who suffer, who are victimized, have been devalued. The perceptual orientation of persons can be so guided by instructions that they imagine what another person's experience is like, which results in more experience of empathy, or that they distance themselves from the other and assume the stance of an observer (Regan & Totten, 1975; Stotland, 1969). Existing cultural evaluation of groups of people can shape perceptual orientations and affect the likely reaction to their suffering.

There is both experimental and real-life evidence that devaluation makes it easier and more likely, whereas positive evaluation makes it less likely, that people will be harmed (Bandura, Underwood,& Fromson, 1975; Duster, 1971; Staub, 1978a, 1987a, in press; see also research on perceptual sets and on the just world hypothesis noted earlier). When there are essential characteristics of others that make us-them separation and devaluation less likely, and a perception of similarity to the self more likely, helping will increase and harming decrease. In Lebanon, Christians usually massacred Palestinians when they invaded their camps (well before the highly publicized cases of the Sabra and Shatila camps). Kuper (1981) reports, however, instances in which Palestinians were spared because they also were Christians.

To increase caring, connection, and helpfulness by human beings for each other regardless of group membership, and to diminish members of groups mistreating those of other groups, it is essential to shape culture and socialization practices so that they focus on the essential humanity of all persons, on the similarities in basic human needs, strivings, and hopes.

GROUP VALUES AND GOALS: THE ROLE OF CULTURE AND SOCIAL INSTITUTIONS

In groups, as in individuals, values, goals, needs, and dissociated (unconscious) motives can be arranged in a hierarchy, according to their importance. In groups, as in individuals, moral value orientations and other motives can be in conflict or well integrated.

There are important cultural differences in moral value orientations and goals. Mead (1937) noted that cultures differ in how competitive, cooperative, or individualistic they are. Bellah and his associates (1985) recently reported that Americans have continued to be characterized by a strong individualism. This has both positive and negative moral potentials. It makes it less likely, especially in combination with the pluralistic character of America, the range of values that characterize it, and the freedom of their expression, that citizens will unquestioningly follow leaders who might turn subgroups against each other. Under normal conditions, they are likely to question more. (The very diversity, however, also gives rise to a need to overcome differentness and achieve unity, which makes people in societies with diverse subgroups susceptible to leaders who attempt to join them in antagonism against out-groups such as other nations, see Staub, 1986, in press). However, standing relatively alone, without the support of strong connection and community, people are vulnerable to life problems and to intense stress and pressure. Individualistic Americans handled less well, that is, were more susceptible, to the stresses of Chinese "brainwashing" than some others, for example, Turks who provided each other with intense group support (Kinkead, 1959).

Ideologies as Group Values-Goals. Ideologies also emerge or are adopted in a group context. They combine value orientations and goals. "Better world ideologies," which most ideologies are, usually identify a set of desired outcomes, the adoption of ideal values, and an ideal social organization, which is believed to represent an improvement of the group and its ways of life. Frequently ideologies have universal applicability, so that fulfilling the desired outcomes is seen as creating a better world for all humanity. Associated with the desired outcomes is usually an extensive network of cognitions – a body of thoughts, beliefs, conceptualizations, rationalizations, and explanations.

Rationalizations that make any means acceptable for the fulfillment of the ideology are sometimes included in the ideology itself. At other times, as intense commitment to the ideology evolves, so does the belief that all means are justified to fulfill the ideology. For example, the Nazi ideology elevated and celebrated aggression. Because aggression was a component of the ideology, it was hardly necessary to justify its use to fulfill the ideology. Similary, enemies of the ideology may be identified as the ideology is created, in the ideology itself, or at a later time when the ideology proves difficult to fulfill. Usually, however, in case of better world ideologies such enemies are identified, and their destruction sought.

Another type of ideology I designated as "The ideology of antagonism" (Staub, 1986b, in press). A combination of devaluative stereotypes of another country and a past history of antagonism and/or current conflict can lead to the evolution of a conception of both the nature of the existing relationship between one's own and this other country and of the ideal or desired relationship. The existing relationship is one of antagonism that, when an ideology of antagonism evolves, is seen as basic and perhaps inevitable and thus continuing. The ideal or desired relationship is, therefore, one of superiority and dominance, which is not only in the service of one's interests but is required for self – defense, even survival. Superiority and dominance are also necessitated by the devaluation of the other and by seeing one's nation as better. The societal self-concept, values, and ways of life must be protected from and elevated over the other. In extreme cases the ideology requires the destruction of the other. The ideology includes perceptions and representations of what is, what is ideal and desired, and a network or relevant beliefs, explanations, and justifications. Such an ideology is an important source of hostility, especially under certain circumstances: difficult life conditions, difficulties in international relations, and conflict with the "antagonist."

VALUE CHANGES: STEPS ALONG THE CONTINUUM

Values and goals, in combination with the circumstances of either individuals or groups, give rise to motivations. At times, when the competencies and/or other necessary supporting conditions exist, they result in goal-directed action. Extreme harm doing or benefiting others usually result from a progression of increasing helpfulness or harm doing. Genocide and mass killing, for example, are the result of *steps along a continuum of destruction.* They start with lesser mistreatment of a subgroup of society. In Nazi Germany, the first steps leading to the Holocaust were excluding Jews from governement positions and the army and boycotting Jewish stores. One could also argue for historical continuity in "steps," the first steps having been taken long before, in the persecution of the Jews in the Middle Ages and earlier. In Turkey, the steps leading to the genocide of the Armenians began much before those who committed the genocide came to power, and even before they were born (Staub, 1985, in press).

Progressive acts of harming or helping other people result in psychological, cultural and institutional changes. People who help other come to see those they benefited in a more positive light, come to be concerned with their well-being more, and may evolve a feeling of personal responsibility to help them more (Staub, 1975, 1986a, 1987), that is, people will develop a *prosocial orientation towards particular individuals* as a result of their own actions in their behalf. Initial acts of doing harm may result in people devaluing victims, or devaluing them more than before and becoming less concerned with their well-being. The self-perception of individuals will also change, coming to see themselves as more willing to help or to harm (for "justifiable reasons"). In some cases, an intense and even fanatical commitment may develop to helping or saving people, or to destroying people. Such commitment to destruction seems clear in the case of many Nazis, and of Pol Pot and his followers who led the Khmer Rouge in Cambodia to "autogenocide" (Staub, 1987). There are examples of such intense commitment to saving people as well, such as Oscar Schindler, the German who went to Poland in the wake of the German Army to enrich himself and ended up saving the lives of 1200 Jews (Keneally, 1982;

Staub. 1987a, 1987b) and of the inhabitants of the Huegenotte village of La Chambon who saved the lives of thousands of refugees (Hallie, 1979). In addition to real-life events, experimental research also provides evidence of learning and change that result from participation, from people's own prior actions (DeJong, 1979; Freedman & Frazer, 1966; Harris, 1972; Staub, 1975; 1979, Chapter 6; Staub 1987).

As a group progresses along a continuum of destruction or a continuum of benevolence not only individual members change but also group values, group norms, and institutions. Evolving group norms can make aggression and doing harm, or certain types of it, acceptable and even desirable. Lasting changes may result in group values, as expressed in different aspects of the culture: in literature, theatre, the media, or other cultural products, and in how institutions function or what new institutions are created. Discrimination in education and work can become standard operating procedures. The SS or other instituions can administer and enforce new values and norms.

The progressive nature of value changes, and how action that are shaped by values in turn shape values, is evident in many realms. Consider the changes in the family that have taken place in America. The progression is so intertwined and cyclical that it is difficult to pinpoint direct causal relations. Certainly sexual values and values relating to sex roles and work and career for women have changed. The behavior of groups of people changed, resulting in value changes that made further changes in behavior possible. Such continuing and evolving changes were necessary to result in the revolution of cultural mores and practices that has occurred in the last 25 years. Along the way many institutions and government practices have changed, both making further change possible and dictating or creating further change. A detailed study and analysis would probably show that as in the case of genocides and mass killings (Staub, 1985, in press) the nature of the progression, and some of the causal processes along the way, can be identified.

CREATING THE VALUES OF CARING, CONNECTEDNESS, NONAGGRESSION

In place of the aggression among individuals and groups that so characterize human behavior, how can we create cultures and social institutions that would minimize doing harm and maximize connection, caring and cooperation? (see Staub, 1986b, in press) Such cultures would provide the opportunity for the optimal functioning of human beings in their relationship to others, in their ability to pursue and satisfy essential motives, and ultimately in individual satisfaction and happiness.

An essential requirement is the evolution of the values of connectedness, caring, and cooperation. For this to happen, we need to create cross-cutting relations (Deutsch, 1973; Staub, in press) among members of different groups. It is not enough to be near each other, but members of varied groups need to work together and play together. In the case of different nations this may be achieved by joint projects of many different kinds: cultural and academic projects, manufacturing and commercial projects, and scientific work such as developing nuclear fission techniques of energy production. Out of this can develop both a knowing of each other that goes beyond stereotypes and shared interests and superordinate goals that go beyond the separate (and potentially conflicting) goals of each party. Contact between countries can be enhanced by reciprocal peace chores, each country sending its citizens to the other to provide help, instruction – minimally instruction about his or her own culture – or just to work and participate in society as a guest.

Providing people and nations with opportunities to benefit others, and inducing them to use these opportunities, would create or strengthen the values of caring, connection and cooperation, and the valuing of other people. In the case of individuals this would best start early, during the beginning school years, but would ideally continue during the whole life-span. Children will be guided to certain activities and adopt certain values, only if these are part of their culture, that is, part of the behavior and values of adults as well. Nonetheless, childhood experience is crucial. The school instruction ought to stress the shared humanity of all people, similarities in their needs, hopes, and desires. The schools should provide opportunities to act in others' behalf and guide children to use them. The cross-cutting relations, joint projects, reciprocal peace chore activities would be a source of learning by participation of caring and connection between nations.

Ultimately, both the personalities of individuals and the nature of cultures and social institutions may so evolve that cooperation, nonaggressive conflict resolution and mutual help take the place of individual and integroup violence.

REFERENCES

Bandura, A., Underwood, B., & Fromson, M. E. (1975). Disinhibition of aggression through diffusion of responsibility and dehumanization of victims. *Journal of Research in Personality, 9,* 253–269.

Bellah, P. N., Madsen, R., Sullivan, W. M., Swindler, A., & Lipton, S. M. (1985). *Habits of the Heart: Individualism and commitment in Americal life.* New York: Harper & Row.

Berkowitz, L. & Lutterman, K. G. (1968) The traditional socially respondible personality. *Public Opinion Quarterly, 32,* 169–185.

Brewer, M. B. (1978). Ingroup bias in the minimal integroup situation: A cognitive-motivation analysis. *Psychological Bulletin, 86,* 307-324.

DeJong, W. (1979). An examination of self-perception mediation of the foot-in-the-door effect. *Journal of Personality and Social Psychology, 37,* 2221-2239.

Deutsch, M. (1973). *The resolution of conflict: Constructive and destructive processes.* New Haven, CT: Yale University Press.

Deutsch, M. (1975). Equity, equality, and need: What determines which value will be used as the basis of distributive justice? *The Journal of Social Issues, 31,* 137-150.

Durkheim, E. (1961). *Moral education.* New York: The Free Press.

Duster, T. (1971). Conditions for guilt-free massacre. In N. Sanford. & C. Comstock (Eds.), *Sanctions for evil.* San Francisco: Jossey-Bass.

Eisenberg, N. (1986). *Altruistic emotion, cognition and behavior.* Hillsdale, NJ: Lawrence Erlbaum Associates.

Erkut, S., Jaquette, D., & Staub, E. (1981). Moral judgement-situation interaction as a basis for predicting social behavior. *Journal of Personality, 49,* 1-44.

Feinberg, J. K. (1978). *Anatomy of a helping situation: Some personality and situational determinants of helping in a conflict situation involving another's psychological distress.* Unpublished doctoral dissertation, University of Massachusetts, Amherst.

Freedman, J. L., & Fraser, S. C. (1966). Compliance without pressure: The foot-in-the-door technique. *Journal of Personality and Social Psychology, 4,* 195-202.

Gilligan, C. (1982). *In a different voice. Psychological theory and women's development.* Cambridge: Harvard University Press.

Gilligan, C. (1984). *Remapping the moral domain in personality research and assessment.* Paper presented at the 92nd Annual Convention of the American Psychnological Association, Toronto.

Gouldner, A. W. (1960). The norm of reciprocity: A preliminary statement. *Americal Sociological Review, 25,* 161-179.

Grodman, S.M. (1979). *The role of personality and situational variables in responding to and helping an individual in psychological distress.* Unpublished doctoral dissertation, University of Massachusetts, Amherst.

Hallie, P. P. (1979) *Let innocent blood be shed. The story of the village of Le Chambon, and how goodness happened there.* New York: Harper & Row.

Harris, M. B. (1972). The effect of performing one altruistic act on the likelihood of performing another. *Journal of Social Psychology, 88, 65-73.*

Hoffman, M. L. (1970). Conscience, personality, and socialization technique. *Human Development, 13,* 90-126.

Hoffman, M. L. (1975). Developmental synthesis of affect and cognition and its implications for altruistic behavior. *Developmental Psychology, 11,* 607-622.

Keneally, T. (1983). *Schindler's list.* New York: Penguin.

Kinkaid, E. (1959). *In every war but one.* New York: Norton.

Kohlberg, L. (1969). Stage and sequence: The cognitive-developmental approach to socialization. In D. Goslin (Ed.), *Handbook of socialization theory and research.* Chicago: Rand McNally.

Kohlberg, L., & Candee, L. (1984). The relationship of moral judgment to moral action. In W. M. Kurtines & J. L. Gewirtz (Eds.), *Morality moral behavior, and moral development* (pp. 52-73).

Kuper, L. (1981). *Genocide. Its political use in the Twentieth Century.* New Haven, CT: Yale University Press.

Lerner, M. (1980). *The belief in a just world: A fundamental delusion.* New York: Plenum.

Mead, M. (1937). *Cooperation and competition among primitive peoples.* New York: McGraw-Hill.

Piaget, J. (1932). *The moral judgment of the child.* London: Kegan Paul, Trench, Trubner.

Regan, D., & Totten, J. (1975). Empathy and attribution: Turning observers into actors. *Journal of Personality and Social Psychology, 32,* 850-856.

Rokeach, M. (1973). *The nature of human values.* New York: Macmillan.

Schachter, S. (1959). *The psychology of affiliation.* Stanford, CA: Stanford University Press.

Staub, E. (1972). Instigation to goodness: The role of social norms and interpersonal influence. *Journal of Social Issues, 28,* 131-151.

Staub, E. (1974). Helping a distressed person: Social, personality and stimulus determinants. In L. Berkowitz (Ed.), *Advances in experimental social psychology* (Vol. 7). New York: Academic Press.

Staub, E. (1975). To rear a prosocial child: Reasoning, learning by doing and learning by teaching others. In D. DePalma & J. Folley (Eds.), *Moral development: Current theory and research.* Hillsdale, NJ: Lawrence Erlbaum Associates.

Staub, E. (1978a). *Positive social behavior and morality: Social personal influences* (Vol. 1). New York: Academic Press.

Staub, E. (1978b). Predicting prosocial behavior: A model for specifying the nature of personality-situation interaction. In L. Pervin & M. Lewis (Eds.), *Internal and external determinants of behavior* (pp. 87-111). New York: Plenum.

Staub, E. (1980). Social and prosocial behavior: Personal and situational influences and their interactions. In E. Staub (Ed.), *Personality: Basic aspects and current research.* Englewood Cliffs, NJ: Prentice-Hall.

Staub, E. (1981). Promoting positive behavior in schools, in other educational settings, and in the home. In J. P. Rushton & R. M. Sorrentino (Eds.), *Altruism and helping behavior.* Hillsdale, NJ: Lawrence Erlbaum Associates.

Staub, E. (1984a). Steps toward a comprehensive theory of moral conduct: Goal orientation, social behavior, kindness and cruelty. In J. Gewirtz & W. Kurtines, (Eds.), *Morality and moral development.* New York: Wiley-Interscience.

Staub, E. (1984b). Notes toward an interactionist-motivational theory of the determinants and development of prosocial behavior. In E. Staub, D. Bar-Tal, J. Karyłowski, & J. Reykowski (Eds.), *The development and maintenance of prosocial behavior: International perspectives on positive morality.* New York: Plenum.

Staub, E. (1985). The psychology of perpetrators and bystanders. *Political Psychology, 6* 61-86.

Staub, E. (1986a). A conception of the determinants and development of altruism and aggression: Motives. the self, the environment. In C. Zahn-Waxler (Ed.), *Altruism and aggression: Social and biological origins.* Cambridge, MA: Cambridge University Press.

Staub, E. (July, 1986b). *The ideology of antagonism, societal self-concept, and other cultural preconditions of war.* Paper presented at the Symposium, "The social causes and effects of the nuclear arms race," Budapest, Hungary.

Staub, E. (1987). *Social behavior and moral conduct. A personal goal theory account of people benefiting or harming others.* Unpublished manuscript, University of Massachusetts, Amherst.

Staub, E. (in press). *The roots of evil. The psychological and cultural origins of genocide.* New York: Cambridge University Press.

Stotland, E. (1969). Exploratory studies of empathy. In L. Berkowitz (Ed.), *Advances in experimental social psychology,* (Vol. 4). New York: Academic Press.

Tajfel, H., Flamant, C., Billig, M. Y., & Bundy, R. P. (1971). Societal categorization and intergroup behavior. *European Journal of Social Psychology, 1,* 149-177.

Toch, H. (1969). *Violent men.* Chicago, IL: Aldine.

Part 2

DEVELOPMENT OF POSITIVE VALUES

4 Empathy and Prosocial Activism

Martin L. Hoffman
New York University

The question of whether social activism qualifies as moral behavior is difficult to answer, although it seems clear that certain forms of activism are moral. Haan (in press) poses the issue with regard to the 1960s student activism succinctly, as follows:

> (although) the claim of moral purpose seemed too easily made (by the protestors) and in the post-Freudian, older generation's view, might very well mask other phenomena, such as the melancholy outcome of several decades of permissive childrearing, youth's concern with justice for disadvantaged groups, with civil liberties, and with the war against the Vietnamese undeniably involved moral issues.

I agree with Haan, and to reduce any ambiguity about whether activism is moral I deal with a type of activism that is clearly moral, prosocial activism, defined as sustained action in the service of improving another person's or group's life condition either by working with them or by trying to change society on their behalf. This type of activism has an obvious altruistic quality: One is not a victim of society but helps others who are. Prime examples can be found in the pre-1965 white Civil Rights movement. In other types of activism (e.g., free speech, anti-Vietnam War, antinuclear bombs), self-interest, as well as concern for others, may play an important role because one is not only an observer but also a potential victim. These types of activism appear to fit my definition and have a prosocial dimension to the extent that they reflect a concern with victims other than themselves. My aim is to present the case for empathy as a significant motive base for prosocial activism.

There is a large body of research showing a positive relation between empathy and prosocial behavior (Hoffman, 1978). This research has not dealt with sustained action but with discrete momentary acts. I argue, nevertheless, that the general finding that empathy contributes to prosocial behavior applies to sustained prosocial action, hence to activism, as well, though in a more complex manner. In doing this I draw on some of my previous work on empathy including a developmental scheme (Hoffman, 1975a, 1984), a review of empathy's place in Western philosophy (Hoffman 1982c), speculation about its possible roots in human evolution (Hoffman, 1981), and, more recently, an argument for its contribution to caring and justice principles and to moral judgments based on them (Hoffman, 1987).

I begin by describing my developmental scheme for empathy – defined as an affective response more appropriate to someone else's situation than to one's own – and pointing out how empathy may provide a motive base for prosocial activism.[1] Hypothetical examples and anecdotes are used where possible, as there is little relevant research. I then bring in the cognitive dimension in the form of moral principles and ideologies, and how they interact with empathy in fostering prosocial activism. And, finally, I look at the course of prosocial activist involvement from a developmental perspective.

DEVELOPMENT OF EMPATHIC MORAL AFFECT

The scheme for empathic distress, an empathic affective response to another person's distress, starts with a simple innocent-bystander model – one encounters someone in distress – and generates five empathic affects. The affects

TABLE 4.1

Scheme for Development and Transformation of Empathic Distress

I. Modes of Empathic Affect Arousal. Operate singly or in combinations.

(Automatic – non voluntary)

A. Primary circular reaction. Neonate cries to sound of another's cry.
B. Mimicry. Automatic imitation plus afferent feedback.

(continued)

[1] My definition of empathy differs from others, which require a close match between the affective response of the target person and that of the observer. The advantages of my definition have been discussed elsewhere (Hoffman, 1982a).

TABLE 4.1 *(Continued)*

C. Conditioning and direct association.

(Higher level cognitive)

D. Language-mediated association.
E. Putting self in other's place. Other-focused and self-focused.

II. Development of a Cognitive Sense of Others
  A. Self-other fusion.
  B. Object permanence. Other is physical entity distinct from self.
  C. Perspective-taking. Other has independent internal states.
  D. Personal identity. Other has experiences beyond the immediate situation, own history and identity.

III. Developmental Levels of Empathy (Coalescence of I and II).
  A. Global empathy.
  B. "Egocentric" empathy.
  C. Empathy for another's feelings.
  D. Empathy for another's experiences beyond the immediate situation, general condition, future prospects.
    1. Empathy for an entire group.

IV. Partial Transformation of Empathic into Sympathetic Distress
  Begins to occur in transition from IIIA to IIIB. Subsequently, one's affective response to another's distress has a "pure" empathic component and a sympathetic component.

V. Causal Attribution and Shaping of Empathy into Related Moral Affects.
  A. If victim is cause of distress, he may no longer be seen as a victim, removing basis for empathy.
  B. *Sympathetic distress.* Victim has no control over cause of victim's distress.
  C. *Guilt.* Observer is cause of victim's distress.
  Guilt over inaction. Observer, though not cause, does nothing and therefore views self as responsible for continuation of victim's distress.
  Guilt by association. Observer's group is cause of victim's distress. (Observer's group's relative advantage may increase guilt further).
  D. *Empathic anger.* Someone else is cause of victim's distress.
  1. Empathic anger may be reduced and/or turned toward victim depending on context (e.g., if culprit was previously harmed by victim).
  2. If culprit represents society, empathic anger may lead to social criticism and moral-political ideology.
  E. *Empathic injustice.* Contrast between victim's plight and character.

are mediated by social cognitive development and various causal attributions or inferences. The scheme is outlined in Table 4.1.

The scheme includes five hypothesized modes of empathic affect arousal (IA-IE in Table 4.1.), which have been described in detail and documented elsewhere (Hoffman, 1984). I make four points about them here. First, they do not form a strict sequence of stages in the sense of subsequent modes encompassing and replacing preceding modes. The first mode typically drops out after infancy, owing to controls against crying; however, adults may feel sad when they hear a cry and some adults may even feel like crying themselves, although they usually control it. The fifth mode, being deliberate, may be relatively infrequent – for example, it may be used by parents and therapists who believe they can be more effective if they experience some of the child's or patient's feelings. The intermediate three modes enter at various points in development and may continue to operate throughout life.

Second, the existence of live arousal modes suggests that empathy may be overdetermined and hence may be a reliable affective response to another's distress. Thus, if only expressive cues (facial, vocal, postural) from someone in distress are provided, mimicry is available to arouse empathic distress in observers. If only situational cues are provided, conditioning and association are available. Ordinarily, the victim is present and all modes may be brought into play, which mode is dominant depending on which cues are salient. Even if the victim is not present, information about his or her distress communicated by someone else can produce empathy in an observer (through modes ID and IE in Table 4.1.).

Third, empathy may be self-reinforcing. Every time we empathize with someone in distress, the resulting co-occurence of our own distress and distress cues from the other may increase the strength of the connection between cues of another's distress and our own empathic response and thus increase the likelihood that future distress in others will be accompanied by empathic distress in ourselves.

Fourth, most arousal modes require rather "shallow" levels of cognitive processing (e.g., sensory registration, simple pattern matching, conditioning) and are largely involuntary. Thus it should not be surprising that empathy appears to be a universal, largely involuntary response – if one attends to the relevant cues one responds empathically – that may have had survival value in human evolution (Hoffman, 1981).

Although empathy may usually be aroused by these simple involuntary mechanisms, its subjective experience is rather complex. Mature empathizers know the affect aroused in them is due to stimulus events impinging on someone else, and they have an idea of what that person is feeling. Young children who lack the self-other distinction may be empathically aroused without this knowledge. This suggests that the development of empathic distress corresponds to the development of a cognitive sense of others, the four broad stages of which are indicated in IIA-IID in Table 4.1 (See Hoffman, 1975 a for evidence for these stages): (1) fusion, or at least a lack of clear separation between the self and the other; (2) awareness that others are physical entities distinct from the self; (3) awareness that others have feelings and other internal states independent of one's own; and (4) awareness that others have experiences beyond the immediate situation and their own history and identity as individuals. Empathy thus appears to be an affect that is experienced differently as the child progresses through four social-cognitive stages.

The resulting coalescence of empathic affect and social cognitive development yields four levels of empathic distress (IIIA-IIID in Table 4.1), which I now describe briefly (see Hoffman, 1984 for details).

Global Empathy. Infants may experience empathic distress through the simplest arousal modes (IA,B,C, in Table 4.1) long before they acquire a sense of others as physical entities distinct from the self. For most of the first year, then, witnessing someone in distress may produce a global empathic distress response. Distress cues from the dimly perceived "other" are confounded with unpleasant feelings empathically aroused in the self. Consequently, infants may at times act as though what happened to the other happened to themselves. A 11-month-old girl, on seeing a child fall and cry, looked as though she was about to cry herself then put her thumb in her mouth and buried her head in her mother's lap, as she does when she herself is hurt. For other examples, see Hoffman (1975a), Kaplan (1977), and Zahn-Waxler, Radke-Yarrow, & King (1979).

"Egocentric" Empathy. With "object permanence" and the gradual emergence of a sense of the other as physically distinct from the self, the affective portion of the child's global empathic distress may be transferred to the separate image-of-self and image-of-other that emerge. The child may now be aware that another person and not the self is in distress, but the other's internal states remain unknown and may be assumed to be the same as one's own. An 18-month-old boy fetched his own mother to comfort a crying friend although the friend's mother was also present – a behavior that, although confused, is not entirely egocentric (hence the quotation marks) because it indicates the child is responding with appropriate empathic affect.

Empathy for Another's Feelings. With the onset of role taking, at about 2–3 years, one becomes aware that other people's feelings may differ from one's own and are based on their own needs and interpretations of events; consequently one becomes more responsive to cues about what the other is actually feeling. Furthermore, as language is acquired, children become capable of empathizing with a wide range of increasingly complex emotions (e.g., disappointment), and eventually with several conflicting emotions. Empathizing with a victim's distress, children may also eventually become capable of empathizing with the victim's anxiety about the loss of self-esteem, hence with the desire *not* to be helped. Finally, children can be empathically aroused by information about someone's distress even in that person's absence. This leads to the fourth, most advanced level.

Empathy for Another's Life Condition. By late childhood, owing to the emerging conception of oneself and others as continuing people with separate histories and identities, one becomes aware that others feel pleasure and pain not only in the immediate situation but also in their larger life experience. Consequently, though one still responds empathically to another's immediate distress, one's empathic response may be intensified when one realizes the other's distress is not transitory but chronic. Thus, one's empathically aroused affect is combined with a mental representation of another's general level of distress or deprivation. It also seems likely that, as one acquires the ability to form social concepts one's empathic distress may be combined with a mental representation of the plight of an entire group or class of people (e.g., the poor, oppressed, outcast, or retarded).

This stage has great importance for a theory of prosocial activism defined in part as repeated action on behalf of a group, for two reasons. The first is obvious, because this is the stage in which one is capable of being empathic toward groups. The second reason pertains to the chronic nature of the victims' distress. So long as one's empathic response is confined to someone's immediate distress, as in virtually all the altruism and prosocial behavior research, a single act will often suffice to alleviate that distress. If one is empathically motivated to help someone whose plight is chronic, however, the logic of the situation calls for repeated action.

When one has advanced through these four levels and encounters someone in pain, danger, or distress, one is exposed to a network of information about the other's condition. The network may include verbal and nonverbal expressive cues from the victim, situational cues, and one's knowledge about the victim's life beyond the situation. These sources of information should be processed differently: Empathy aroused by nonverbal and situational cues may be mediated by largely involuntary, cognitively shallow processing modes (mimcry; conditioning). Empathy aroused by verbal messages from the victim or by one's knowledge about the victim requires more complex processing, such as language-mediated association or putting oneself in the other's place.

The various cues, arousal modes, and processing levels usually contribute to the same affect, but contradictions may occur, for example, between different expressive cues, such as facial expression and tone of voice, or between expressive and situational cues. If one's knowledge of the other's life condition conflicts with the other's immediate expressive cues, the expressive cues may lose their force for an observer who knows they reflect only a transitory state. Imagine someone who does not know that he or she has a terminal illness laughing and having a good time. A young child might respond with empathic joy, whereas a mature observer might feel empathically sad or a mingling of empathic sadness and empathic joy. Similarly, a mature observer's empathic distress (but not a child's) might decrease if the other person is known to have a generally happy life and his or her immediate distress is just a short-lived exception. Clearly, the most advanced empathic level involves some distancing – responding partly to one's mental image of the other rather than only to the other's immediate stimulus value. This fits my definition of empathy, not as an exact match of another's feelings, but as an affective response more appropriate to another's situation than to one's own.

Partial Transformation of Empathic into Sympathetic Distress (IV in Table 4.1)

The transition from global to "egocentric" empathy may involve an important qualitative shift in feeling: Once children are aware that others are distinct from themselves, their own empathic distress, which is a parallel response – a more or less exact replication of the victim's presumed feeling of distress – may be transformed, at least in part, into reciprocal concern for the victim. That is, they may continue to respond in a purely empathic manner – feeling uncomfortable and highly distressed themselves – but they may also experience a feeling of compassion, or "sympathetic distress" for the victim, along with a conscious desire to help, because they feel sorry for the victim, not just to relieve their own empathic distress.

Evidence for this shift comes from observational research (Murphy, 1937; Zahn-Waxler, Radke-Yarrow, & King, 1979) and from anecdotes such as those cited earlier, which show that: (a) children progress developmentally, first responding to someone's distress by seeking comfort for the self and later trying to help the victim rather than the self; and (b) an inbetween stage, in which children feel sad and comfort both the victim and the self, seems to occur at about the same time that they first become aware that others are distinct from themselves.

What developmental processes account for this shift? I suggested earlier that the unpleasant, vicarious affect that is experienced as a part of the child's initial global, undifferentiated self is transferred to the separate image-of-self and image-of-other that emerge during the self-other differentiation process. It seems likely that the wish, which is not necessarily conscious, to terminate the unpleasant affect is also similarly transferred to the emerging image-of-other and image-of-self. Consequently, the child's empathic response now includes two components: a wish to terminate the other's distress – the sympathetic distress component – and a more purely empathic wish to terminate distress in the self. (See Hoffman, 1984 for a more detailed discussion.) The last three empathy development levels (III B, C, D) may therefore describe the development of an affective response that has both an empathic distress and a sympathetic distress component.

Causal Attribution, Empathy, and Related Moral Affects

People are always making causal attributions and there is evidence that they do this spontaneously (Weiner, 1985). It thus seems reasonable to suppose that, when one encounters someone in distress, one will often make attributions about the cause, and the particular attribution made may determine how empathic affect is experienced. Consider now some causal attributions and the resulting affects (V. A–D in Table 4.1).

Sympathetic Distress. One may respond to another's distress without making a causal attribution when the other's plight is salient, there are no causal situational cues powerful enough to draw one's attention from the other's plight, and one has no prior information about the cause. These conditions often exist when young children witness someone in distress and were therefore assumed in my discussion of early developmental levels of empathy and its transformation into sympathetic distress. One may also feel sympathetic distress when there are cues or when one has information indicating that victims have no control over their plight, as in serious illness or accidental injury.

More germane to the prosocial activism issue are social, political, and economic victims. Consider this example from the book *Uncle Tom's Cabin,* reported by Kaplan in this volume, in which an affluent, politically uninvolved housewife whose empathy for slaves she knew, who "have been abused and oppressed all their lives," leads her to oppose a newly passed law against giving food, clothes, or shelter to escaping slaves. Arguing with her husband, who supports the law on pragmatic and legal grounds, she verbalizes the moral principle of caring – "the Bible says we should feed the hungry, clothe the naked, and comfort the desolate" and "People don't run away when they're happy, but out of suffering." She becomes so intensely opposed to that "shameful, wicked, abominable" law that she vows to break it at the earliest opportunity. This episode suggests that the combination of empathic and sympathetic distress and empathic anger in a particular situation may provide the motive base for (a) affirming the moral principle that one should care and show consideration for the welfare of others, (b) using this principle as a premise for making the moral judgment that a law that violates it is wrong, and (c) on the basis of this moral judgment, engaging in prosocial activism directed against the law.

Sympathetic distress may also be part of a more complex ambivalent response. For example, one may find a man strapped to the electric chair utterly reprehensible for the crimes he committed, and yet also empathize and sympathize with him intensely because of information indicating that his early life experiences, over which he had no control, contributed importantly to the kind of person he became. These feelings might lead to the moral judgment that under these conditions it is wrong to execute the man. If one generalized these feelings and moral judgment to others in the same predicament, one might become an activist against capital punishment.

Empathic Anger. If the cues indicate that someone else caused the victim's plight, one's attention may to some extent be diverted from the victim to the culprit. One may feel anger at the culprit partly because one sympathizes with the victim and partly because one empathizes with the victim and feels oneself vicariously attacked.[2] One's feelings may also alternate between empathic and sympathetic distress, and empathic anger; or empathic anger may crowd out one's empathic and sympathetic distress entirely. A simple example of empathic anger is the 17-month-old boy in the doctor's office who, on seeing another child receive an injection, responds by hitting the doctor.

Empathic anger may also occur in complex contexts in which it is shifted from one target to another, along with the accompanying empathic and sympathetic distress. For example, if one discovers that the victim did harm to the culprit on an earlier occasion, one's empathy for the victim may decrease (he is no longer a victim) and one may begin to feel empathic and sympathetic distress for the culprit because of the hurt that led to the culprit's aggression in the first place; one may even empathize with the culprit's anger. Alternatively one might discover that the victim has a history of being mistreated in his or her relationship with the culprit. In this case, one may assume the victim had a choice (why else would he or she continue the relationship?) and is therefore responsible for his or her own plight and thus is not a victim. One's empathic and sympathetic distress for the victim and empathic anger at the culprit may then decrease sharply. The empathic anger of young children is apt to miss these nuances, and if children's perceptions are confined to the immediate situation they may respond in all these situations with simple empathic anger directed at the visible culprit.

A case of special relevance to prosocial activism is that in which the victim is a very poor or otherwise disadvantaged group and the observer blames the

---

2 Empathic anger should be distinguished from the type of self-righteous indignation that serves to tout one's own moral superiority.

group's plight on someone who represents the larger society or a powerful subgroup within it. For example, one may see the disadvantaged group's basic material needs as not being met because of society's neglect or the lack of an adequate "safety net." One may then feel empathic and sympathetic distress for the group and empathic anger towards the powerful subgroup or towards society as a whole, affects that might provide a motive base for activism on behalf of the group.

Guilt Feeling. The observer thus far in our analysis is an innocent bystander. If one is not innocent but the cause of the other's distress, the condition may be ripe for feeling guilty, that is, for a combination of empathic and sympathetic distress and a self-blame attribution. This type of guilt feeling, which results from the awareness of harming someone in the present, differs from the Freudian guilt, which results from activation of early repressed childhood anxieties about losing parental love, is often unconscious, and may be experienced when no one has been harmed (e.g., masturbation guilt). I have suggested that the combination of empathic affect and self-blame may originate in discipline encounters in which parents point up the harmful consequences of the child's action for others (Hoffman, 1983).

As an illustration of empathy-based guilt, consider this quotation from George Orwell (1958) expressing his feelings over being a British police officer in India as a young adult in the 1920s.

> The wretched prisoners squatting... the gray cowed faces of the long-term convicts, the scarred buttocks of the men who had been flogged, the women and children howling when their menfolk were led away under arrest – things like these are beyond bearing when you are in any way responsible for them. (p. 146) (When I came home on leave) I was haunted by an immense wave of guilt that I had got to expiate... (As a result) I reduced everything to the simple theory that the oppressed are always right and the oppressors are always wrong: a mistaken theory but the natural result of being one of the oppressors yourself... I felt that I had got to escape not merely from imperialism but from every form of man's domination over man. I wanted to submerge myself, to get right down among the oppressed, to be one of them and on their side against the tyrants... failure seemed to me to be the only virtue. Every suspicion of self-advancement, even making a few hundred a year, seemed to me spiritually ugly, a species of bullying. (p. 148).

Especially important for prosocial activism are the many situations in which one may feel guilty even though one is an innocent bystander. If one does not help someone in distress, one may blame oneself and feel guilty not for *causing* the other's plight but for contributing to its continuation by not intervening to help – the guilt is over inaction. In my research on guilt long ago (Hoffman, 1970), I used a story-completion item in which a basically well-meaning protagonist the same age and sex as the subject is hurrying to a movie with a friend and encounters a small boy who seems lost. He suggests they stop and help but his friend talks him out of it. The next day he finds out that the child had been left alone by his baby-sitter, ran into the street, and was killed by a car. In the adult version the victim is an elderly person looking for something lost in the snow. The item was designed to evoke guilt but there were reasons for expecting many subjects to show little or no guilt: The transgression was one of omission – not stopping to help; the protagonist actually *did* nothing wrong and there was no reason for him to anticipate the tragic consequences. And, there were other people to blame – the driver of the car, the friend who talked against stopping, the irresponsible baby-sitter, the parents who hired the sitter. Nevertheless, most subjects (fifth and seventh graders and their parents) gave responses indicating they would feel intensely guilty in such a situation. Furthermore, the protagonists' guilty feelings often led them to engage in prosocial action, such as doing something for the child's family or going out of one's way to help people in similar situations in the future, which suggests that similar guilt feelings in the subjects would dispose them to prosocial action. The most interesting response for present purposes, given mainly by older children and adults, was one in which the protagonist engages in a process of critical self-examination (e.g., "How could I be so selfish"), which results in a reordering of his or her priorities and a resolution to act more thoughtfully of others in the future. It may be through such a process as this that guilt over inaction contributes a motive base for repeated prosocial action on behalf of individuals. And perhaps in certain contexts the same process may contribute to prosocial action on behalf of groups.

The human capacity to experience guilt when one has done nothing wrong is illustrated still more dramatically in the phenomenon of survivor guilt, in which despite one's own plight one may feel guilty and motivated for prosocial action if one feels far better off than others (Hoffman, 1980, Lifton, 1968). More central to our concern is the guilt over affluence reflected in the responses given by the social activists interviewed by Keniston (1968). Keniston notes that these were highly empathic and sympathetic individuals, who experienced a shock when they "really" understood that the benefits they had experienced had not been extended to others and became aware of the vast discrepancy between their own good life and the misery that many others experienced all their lives. Here is a quotation from one of Keniston's interviewees (Keniston, 1968) who was discussing some poor Mexican children he had known years earlier,

> I was the one that lived in a place where there were fans and no flies, and they lived with flies. And I was clearly destined for something, and they were destined for nothing... Well, I sort of made a pact with these people that when I got to be

> powerful I might change some things. And I think I pursued that pact pretty consistently for a long time. (p. 50)

A second quotation (Monroe, 1973), illustrating something between guilt over affluence and over survival, comes not from Keniston's sample but from a black student at Harvard who said that he and others like him,

> ...have had to wrestle with the keen sense of guilt they feel being here while their families still struggle in black ghettoes... The one sure way of easing guilt was (by demanding) "relevance" from Harvard, which means, in effect, instruction that can be directed toward improving the quality of life for blacks as a whole in this country... (and) via building takeovers, strikes, and other kinds of demonstration. (p. 46)

In these quotations the respondent's guilt over his own relative advantage, as well as sympatheic distress and empathic anger, though not always verbalized explicitly, are clear. Both quotations also show a rather direct connection between these affects and prosocial activism. I refer to guilt over relative advantage and survivor guilt as "existential guilt" (Hoffman, 1976) because in both cases one has done nothing wrong but feels culpable because of life circumstances beyond one's control.[3] The possible contribution of existential guilt to prosocial activism is indicated in a recent study of West German college students by Montada, Schmitt, and Dalbert(1986). They found that whereas members of a conservative fraternity obtained very low scores on a questionnaire measure of existential guilt, very high scores were obtained by members of an organizing committee for helping disadvantaged people (Third World, handicapped, and Turkish guest workers). One's existential guilt may be heightened if one is given reason to believe that one's advantage is actually dependent on the victim's distressed condition, as illustrated in this quotation from Orwell (1958):

> (Watching coal-miners working) brings home to you... that... all of us really owe the comparative decency of our lives to poor drudges underground, blackened to the eyes, with their throats full of coal dust, driving their shovels forward. (p. 34-35)

A final point on existential guilt. As a mature observer, one not only categorizes victims into groups but one may also categorize oneself as a member of a group or class. If one's group or class is viewed as causing the

---

[3] Of course one has the power to give up one's advantage, as some do, and it is perhaps because one does not do this that one continues to feel guilty.

victim's distress, or merely benefitting from it, one's empathic distress may then be transformed into a feeling of guilt – guilt by association. Guilt by association with one's class is explicit in this quotation from a 1970 congressional intern who was asked why so many middle-class youth were turned off by the very system that gave them so many advantages and opportunities. The following was stated in The New Republic (November 28, 1970):

> They feel guilty because while they are enjoying this highest standard of living, American Indians are starving and black ghettoes are overrun by rats... This goes on while they eat steak every day. Their sense of moral indignation can't stand this; and they realize that the blame rests on the shoulders of their class. (p.11)

"Empathic Injustice". Other information besides that pertaining to the cause of the victim's distress may shape one's empathic response. I just mentioned that the contrast between the victim's plight and one's own good fortune – one's relative advantage – may produce guilt feeling. Other contrasts are possible, such as that between the victim's plight and *other* people's good fortune. If one observes highly disadvantaged people in a context in which the extravagant life-style of others is salient, one may have a feeling of empathic injustice. Perhaps more important for present purposes is the contrast between the victim's plight and the victim's general conduct or character. Thus if the victim is viewed as bad, immoral, or lazy, one may conclude that his or her fate was deserved, and one's empathic and sympathetic distress might decrease. If the victim is viewed as basically good, however, or at least as not being bad, immoral, or lazy, one might view his or her fate as undeserved or unfair. One's empathic distress (or sympathetic distress, guilt, or empathic anger – whichever is appropriate) might then be expected to increase. Furthermore, the empathic affect may be transformed in part into a feeling that has elements in common with guilt and empathic anger but appears subtly different enough to be called by a new name: empathic injustice. The previous quotations may illustrate empathic injustice as well as guilt over relative advantage.

As a very different example of empathic injustice, consider the 14-year-old Southern male "redneck" described by Coles (1967). After several weeks of joining his friends in harassing black children trying to integrate his school, this boy, a popular athlete,

> ...began to see a kid, not a nigger – a guy who knew how to smile when it was rough going, and who walked straight and tall, and was polite. I told my parents, "It's a real shame that someone like him has to pay for the trouble caused by all those federal judges."
>
> Then it happened. I saw a few people cuss at him. "The dirty nigger," they kept on calling him and soon they were pushing him in a corner, and it looked like trouble, bad trouble. I went over and broke it up... They all looked at me as if I was crazy... Before (everyone) left I spoke to the nigger... I didn't mean to... It just came out of my mouth. I was surprised to hear the words myself: "I'm sorry." (p. 27-28)

After this incident, he began talking to the black youth, championing him personally, while still decrying "integration." Finally, he became the black youth's friend and began advocating "an end to the whole lousy business of segregation." When pressed by Coles to explain his shift, he attributed it to being in school that year and seeing "That kid behave himself, no matter what we called him, and seeing him insulted so bad, so real bad. Something in me just drew the line, and something in me began to change, I think." (p. 28)

The boy clearly seemed to experience sympathetic distress, empathic anger, and guilt. But what really seemed to move him to reverse his attitude toward segregation and in the direction of prosocial activism (though there is no evidence he actually became an activist) was the contrast between the black youth's admirable conduct and the way he was being treated – it was as if the boy felt that this was a fine person who deserves better.

Complex Combinations. Here is an example of the complex combination of empathic affects possible in moral encounters. A shabbily dressed man is observed robbing an obviously affluent person on the street. A young child might feel empathic and sympathetic distress for the victim and anger at the immediate, visible culprit. Mature observers might have these same feelings, but a variety of other empathic affects as well. They might feel guilty over not helping the victim. If they are ideologically liberal, they might empathize and sympathize not only with the victim but also with the culprit because of his poverty. The observers might view the culprit as a victim of society and feel empathic anger toward society. Furthermore, if the observers are affluent as well as liberal, they might feel guilty over being relatively advantaged persons who benefit from the same society. An ideologically conservative observer might not sympathize with the culprit but respond to him with unalloyed empathic anger instead. He might also feel empathic anger towards society, but in this case because he views the victim, not the culprit, as a victim of society (because of inadequate law enforcement and citizen protection).

To summarize, the empathic reaction to someone's distress produces two basic affects: empathic distress and sympathetic distress. In addition – depending on various causal and other attributions – empathic anger, several types of guilt, and a feeling of empathic injustice may be generated. There is considerable research evidence that empathic and sympathetic distress (the research does not separate them) and guilt feelings function as motives for prosocial moral action (Hoffman, 1978, 1982b). Empathic anger has not yet been researched, but it seems reasonable to suppose that such anger includes a disposition to intervene and protect the victim in some way (although egoistic motives like fear may result in inaction). Also, because anger has long been know to "mobilize one's energy and make one capable of defending oneself with great vigor and strength" (Izard, 1977, p. 333), it seems reasonable to expect empathic anger to be an energizer of prosocial action and activism, as suggested in this quote from a letter to the New York Times Editor:

> The pictures of starving children in Ethiopia are heartwrenching but feeling sad isn't enough... we send a check, the pictures disappear from TV screens, and soon we forget that millions are dying... Instead we should feel outraged that in a world of plenty hunger still exists. Outrage produces action... etc. (February, 1985)

Research is needed to see if the letter writer is correct in stating not only that empathic anger leads to prosocial action but also that empathic anger is more likely to do so than is sympathetic distress.

EMPATHY, MORAL COGNITION, AND PROSOCIAL ACTIVISM

Thus far I have tried to show that it is reasonable to expect empathic affects to provide a motive base for prosocial activism. This is only part of the story. Prosocial activism involves not only empathic motivation but it also has a significant moral-cognitive component (principles, values, ideologies). Furthermore, prosocial activism can be a long drawn-out process with its own developmental course, that involves not only empathic affects and moral cognitions but egoistic needs and pressures from the environment as well. I now discuss these issues and then present a rough outline for a developmental model of prosocial activism.

Several theoretical models may be used to explain how empathic affects, which start developing early in life, might contribute to adoption of moral principles and ideologies later in life, say, in adolescence. First, from traditional psychoanalytic theory can be derived a "superego" model, in which one is socialized directly into the parents' ideology from an early age; the ideology is deeply held because of its connections with early emotional ties to one's parents. Psychoanalytic theory has also contributed the "displacement" model, which states that hostility towards parents, largely unconscious, is displaced to other authority figures, providing a powerful motive base for ideologies critical of society and its leaders (e.g.Bettelheim, 1963). The "cafeteria" model (Knutson, 1973) expands on the displacement model and says that people are confronted, mainly in adolescence, with an array of packaged ideologies and are attracted to the one that best fits their needs. A variant of this model says that one does not merely select but more actively tries out or experiments with ideologies until one is found that best fits one's needs. Cognitive developmental theory has an implicit "construction" model in which one does not select from alternatives but constructs an ideology from relevant stored information and direct personal experience, a process that is triggered by being exposed to new realities that contradict one's earlier moral beliefs (Kohlberg & Kramer, 1969). Recent psychoanalytic writers suggest the superego persists through childhood but is disrupted in adolescence due to hormonal changes, social demands, and exposure to new realities that contradict the superego; the disruption motivates a search for more mature moral concepts (e.g., Settlage, 1972).

Each model is limited. The superego and displacement models have been largely discredited by research showing that the ideologies of at least the early 1960s activists were generally consistent with but not mirror images of their parents' ideologies, and their relations with parents were generally warm and close rather than the kind likely to generate intense hostility that is repressed and eventually displaced (Horn & Knott, 1971). The cafeteria model seems to assume a level of passivity that is at variance with available biographical information on prosocial activists (Keniston, 1968). The construction model may be naive in assuming that people mature enough to construct an ideology have not already been exposed to and influenced by packaged ideologies.

Clearly the models are not mutually exclusive and if stated in less extreme form there may be elements of most or all of them in any individual activist. In my own approach, selection (cafeteria model) and construction both play a role. Thus children socialized to be empathic are, later on in life, disposed to select principles and ideologies that support society's disadvantaged members; and when they actually encounter disadvantaged people their causal attributions may not only shape their empathic affect but may also, as indicated in my earlier examples, function as early stages in the construction of an ideology. My primary focus, however, is on the synthesis of empathic affect and moral cognition that both contributes to and results from such construction.

Briefly, people are usually exposed to moral principles and ideologies not in abstract situations such as research interviews but in contexts – moral encounters – involving helpers or people who harm, helpful or harmful actions, and victims or beneficiaries of these actions. Because victims are present, such contexts are likely to arouse empathic affects, especially in people whose socialization has fostered empathic affect development. And, because of the presence of others (e.g., culprits) and other aspects of the context, causal attributions may be triggered in the manner suggested earlier. The sequence in which empathic affects, causal attributions, and moral principles appear may vary. One possibility is that empathic affects and causal attributions occur more or less simultaneously and activate one's relevant moral principles (e.g., the principle that one should consider the welfare of others), in the manner I suggested elsewhere (Hoffman, 1987). Another possibility is that arousal of empathic affects and causal attributions, and activation of moral principles occur independently in response to different aspects of the situation. For example, one may engage in prosocial action in response to others who invoke a principle and indicate their expectation that one will abide by it, but in the course of the action one may encounter victims and have empathic affects aroused. Regardless of which comes first, the important result is that a moral principle may be experienced together with empathic affects.

As a result of this co-occurrence, the principles – as well as the mental representations of the associated victims, culprits, and relevant actions – may become charged with empathic affects, and the principles may be encoded and stored in memory as more or less loosely organized networks of emotionally charged mental representations, or "hot cognitions." It follows that in subsequent moral encounters, a relevant stimulus (victim, culprit, action) may activate one of these emotionally charged representations, releasing the associated empathic feelings; or the entire network may be activated. There may thus be a representation-driven component of the empathic affects aroused in moral encounters. This is in addition to the stimulus-driven component. The representation-driven component may be expected to contribute more of one's total empathic affect in moral encounters as one gets older and has more moral encounter experiences. The total empathic affect (representation-driven plus stimulus-driven) released when the principles and ideologies are activated may have an impact on the moral judgments and decisions one makes, as I have suggested elsewhere (Hoffman, 1987). The cognitive, informational component of activated principles and ideologies may of course also influence one's moral judgments and decisions. For activists, and would-be activists, these decisions may often lead one to seek and engage in further moral encounters, and the entire process may be repeated, in some cases many times. This leads to a consideration of the developmental processes involved in prosocial activism.

A Developmental Perspective on Prosocial Activism

Activism generally begins in adolescence, by which time the development of empathic affects may be assumed to have progressed considerably. We should therefore expect some continuity between empathy development in childhood and the beginnings of prosocial activism in adolescence. And, indeed, it appears from Keniston's interviews that a high level of empathic and sympathetic distress (in keeping with my most advanced empathic level), along with an awareness of oppressed groups, led many of these young adults to engagement in situations involving direct, repeated contact with a disadvantaged group – inner city jobless, for example. I digress here to note that although my empathy-development scheme assumes a bystander model, it is not necessary for victims to be physically present. This is because of the human capacity to represent events, visually or through other sensory modalities, and the power of represented events to evoke affect (See Hoffman, 1987 for documentation). It was therefore possible for budding activists to empathize with a disadvantaged group that they knew about in different ways (e.g., from parents, teachers, newspaper, and television accounts) before having actual contact with the group, although previous contacts were not uncommon.

The activists' direct, repeated contact with a disadvantaged group seemed to have had the effect of intensifying their initial empathic and sympathetic distress. The repeated contact also seemed to diminish their intellectual remoteness and objectivity. In addition, the close personal contact seemed to cut through the stereotypes some of them had about the victims and revealed the victims as basically good, honest people who deserved a better life. This, I suggest, had the effect of transforming the activists' empathic and sympathetic distress in part into empathic feelings of injustice, empathic anger at society, and guilt over their own relatively advantaged position.

Before the repeated contacts with victims, the activists' "ideology" amounted largely to acceptance of society's institutions as compatible with their own loosely held principles of caring, justice and fair play.[4] And their initial judgment of the social system was that it is basically well intentioned, but sometimes does not function properly and when injustice occurs, forces are set in motion to remedy them. The activists' decision was therefore to work within the systems' rules on behalf of its victims (e.g., tenant's rights, voter registration, ghetto tutoring, neighborhood improvement). It was only after repeated broken promises and other formidable obstacles placed in their way by authorities, that their view of society as remedying known injustices began to wane and their moral judgment began to shift in the direction of viewing the system as uncaring and unjust.

This view of society as morally deficient, in turn, seemed to have activated certain cognitive processes among the activists. Some activists began to reflect on how to change the system, and to consider alternative systems including some of the packaged ideologies popular at the time. Whether these ideologies were considered on intellectual grounds only, or actually lived out experimentally (in communes, for example), they often seemed to buttress the activists' view of the current system as being unfair and dominated by various power groups who use it to their own advantage.

The authorities' manner of resisting change seemed not only to intensify the activists' empathic anger and injustice but also introduced a new element: The authorities sometimes attacked or threatened the activists themselves. The result was to arouse direct anger and motivation for aggressive action among some activists. This is not the first egoistic motive generated in the course of

---

[4] I put "ideology" in quotation marks because the acceptance of society's institutions at that point in their lives appears to have been a passive, mindless product of socialization rather than an intellectually arrived at position.

prosocial activism. Other egoistic motives were often recruited and satisfied along the way – peer approval, gratitude from those helped, adventure, excitement, a sense of being part of a growing social movement, a sense of personal continuity and of extending links with one's parents' moral values.

The introduction of the egoistic motivational dimension to prosocial activism has at least two potentially important consequences. On the positive side, it makes prosocial activism less dependent on empathic affects. It may also help neutralize the impact of "empathic overarousal," the tendency, when empathic distress is painfully intense, for people to abandon the empathic mode and focus on their own distress (Hoffman, 1978). On the negative side, one's prosocial activism might become entirely free of its original empathic motivational base ("functionally autonomous"). In that case, the activism's major driving force could become direct anger, a process that may be accelerated because the activist is spending less time helping victims and more time fighting adversaries. Without empathy, the result may ultimately be zealotry and violence, as has been suggested by Berger and Neuhaus (1970). This may in part account for the shift toward violence in the late 1960s and early 1970s.[5]

This developmental account fits the available knowledge about many 1960s prosocial activists, but certainly not all of them. Block, Haan, & Smith (1969), for example, identified a group who appeared to reject parental values, showed little interest in social-service activities and viewed the social order as morally corrupt. They did this from the first, rather than as a result of their experiences with authorities in the course of engaging in prosocial activities. I assume there are other developmental patterns as well.

CONCLUDING REMARKS

I write from the perspective of a psychologist trying to understand the motivational base of prosocial activism. Obviously there is more to activism than its motive base. Why is activism prevalent at certain times and not others? Why in one country rather that others? What accounts for the worldwide, at least Western worldwide activism of the 1960s? Why did it decline in the late 1970s? The answers to these questions may by partly psychological – a decline in empathic socialization perhaps. But, then, why the decline in empathic socialization? The answer must inevitably include economic, political, and probably geo-political forces that create not only the context, or social need, for

[5] It is of course possible that the shift from nonviolence to violence over that period was due to two entirely different cohort groups, rather that a shift that took place within individuals.

activism but also the cultural reinforcement of activism and the conditions that encourage and support empathy-enhancing socialization. My psychological analysis assumes that all these larger forces are operating, as they apparently were during the decade of the 1960s.

REFERENCES

Berger, P. L., & Neuhaus, R. J. (1970). *Movement and revaluation.* New York: Doubleday.

Bettelheim, B. (1963). The problem of generations. In E. H. Erikson (Ed.), *Youth, change, and challenge.* New York: Basic Books.

Block, J., Haan, N., & Smith, M. B. (1969). Socialization correlates of student activism. *Journal of Personality and Social Psychology, 25,* 143-178.

Coles, R. (1967). *Children of crisis: A study of courage and fear.* Boston: Atlantic Monthly Press.

Haan, N. (in press). Activism in moral protest. In L. Kohlberg & E. Turiel (Eds.), *The development of moral judgment and action.* New York: Holt, Rinehart, & Winston.

Hoffman, M. L. (1970). Conscience, personality, and socialization techniques. *Human Development, 13,* 90-126.

Hoffman, M. L. (1975a). Developmental synthesis of affect and cognition and its implications for altruistic motivation. *Developmental Psychology, 11,* 607-622.

Hoffman, M. L. (1975b). Sex differences in moral internalization. *Journal of Personality and Social Psychology, 32,* 720-729.

Hoffman, M. L. (1976). Empathy, role-taking, guilt, and development of altruistic motives. In T. Lickona (Ed.), *Moral development and behavior* (pp. 124-143). New York: Holt, Rinehart, & Winston.

Hoffman, M. L. (1978). Empathy, its development and prosocial implications. In C. B. Keasey (Ed.), *Nebraska Symposium on Motivation, 25,* 169-218.

Hoffman, M. L. (1980). Moral development in adolescence. In J. Adelson (Ed.), *Handbook of adolescent psychology.* New York: Wiley.

Hoffman, M. L. (1981). Is altruism part of human nature? *Journal of Personality and Social Psychology, 40,* 121-137.

Hoffman, M. L. (1982a). Measurement of empathy. In C. Izard (Ed.), *Measurement of emotions in infants and children* (pp. 279-296). New York: Cambridge University Press.

Hoffman, M. L. (1982b). Development of prosocial motivation: Empathy and guilt. In N. Eisenberg, (Ed.), *Development of prosocial behavior,* (pp. 281-313). New York: Academic Press.

Hoffman, M. L. (1982c). Affect and moral development. In D. Cicchetti (Ed.), *New directions in child development* (pp. 83-103). San Francisco: Jossey-Bass.

Hoffman, M. L. (1983). Affective and cognitive processes in moral internalization: An information-processing approach. In E. T. Higgins, D. Ruble, & W. Hartup (Eds.), *Social cognition and social development: A socio-cultural perspective* (pp. 236-274). New York: Cambridge University Press.

Hoffman, M. L. (1984). Interaction of affect and cognition in empathy. In C. Izard, J. Kagan, & R. Zajonc (Eds.), *Emotions, cognition, and behavior* (pp. 103-131). New York: Cambridge University Press.

Hoffman, M. L. (1987). The contribution of empathy to justice and moral judgment. In N. Eisenberg & J. Strayer (Eds.), *Empathy: A developmental perspective.* (pp. 47-80). New York: Cambridge University Press.

Horn, J. L., & Knott, P. D. (1971). Activist youth of the 1960s: Summary and prognosis. *Science, 171,* 977-985.

Izard, C. E. (1977). *Human emotions.* New York: Plenum.

Murphy, L. B. (1937). *Social behavior and child personality.* New York: Columbia University Press.

Keniston, K. (1968). *Young radicals.* New York: Harcourt, Brace, & World.

Knutson, J. (1973). Personality in the study of politics. In J. Knutson (Ed.), *Handbook of political psychology.* San Francisco: Jossey-Bass.

Kohlberg, L., & Kramer, R. (1969). Continuities and discontinuities in childhood and adult moral development. *Human Development, 12,* 93-120.

Lifton, R. (1968). *Death in life: Survivors of Hiroshima.* New York: Random House.

Monroe, S. (1973). Guest in a strange house. *Saturday review of books.* February 1973, pp. 45-48.

Montada, L., Schmitt, M., & Dalbert, C. (1986). Thinking about justice and dealing with one's privileges: A study on existential guilt. In H. W. Bierhoff, R. Cohen, & J. Greenberg (Eds.), *Justice in social relations.* New York: Plenum.

The New Republic, November 28, 1970, p. 11.

Orwell, G. (1958). *The road to Wigan Pier.* New York: Harcourt, Brace, Jovanovitch.

Settlage, C. F. (1972). Cultural values and the superego in late adolescence. *Psychoanalytic Study of the Child, 27;* 57-73.

Weiner, B. (1985). "Spontaneous" causal thinking. *Psychological Bulletin, 97,* 74-84.

Zahn-Waxler, C., Radke-Yarrow, M., & King, R. A. (1979). Childrearing and children's prosocial initiations towards victims of distress. *Child Development, 50,* 319-330.

5 The Development of Prosocial Values

Nancy Eisenberg
Arizona State University

Until relatively recently, the study of moral development was primarily the study of antisocial or immoral behavior. Aggression, dishonesty, inability to resist temptation, and other undesirable behaviors were the topic of concern, whereas positive behaviors were relatively ignored. This focus on negative behavior was reflected in not only the research on moral behavior, but also that related to moral judgment.

In specific, most of the research on moral reasoning until the mid 1970s was based on Kohlberg's (1969, 1976) schema of moral reasoning and his interview materials. The central issues in the hypothetical dilemmas used in this research generally are prohibition-related issues, i.e., they concern laws, rules, punishments, disobeying an authority or his or her dictates, or living up to formal obligations (Eisenberg-Berg, 1979). In none of Kohlberg's standard dilemmas is altruism the primary focus; altruism, if a choice at all, is embedded in a context in which prosocial action constitutes a violation of a prohibition.

In this chapter, cross-sectional, longitudinal, and cross-cultural research concerning moral reasoning about prosocial issues is briefly reviewed. Next, a "model" of moral reasoning is presented. In this model, an individual's level of moral reasoning is viewed as reflecting his or her moral values, as well as other values, needs, and preferences. Moreover, moral reasoning is seen as limited by level of sociocognitive development, and as influenced by situational factors. This model is compared and contrasted with that of Kohlberg.

THE EMPIRICAL RESEARCH

In some of our research on prosocial moral reasoning, we have used an interview technique reminescent of Kohlberg's. The procedure in this research has involved presenting children or adolescents with several (usually four) prosocial dilemmas in an individual interview, and eliciting their reasoning regarding these dilemmas. In each dilemma, the needs or wants of one individual are in direct conflict with those of another individual or group in a context in which the roles of prohibitions, punishments, authorities, and other formal criteria/obligations are irrelevant of minimized. An example of such a dilemma used with younger children (preschool and elementary-school aged) is as follows:

> One day a girl (boy) named Mary (Eric) was going to a friend's birthday party. On her (his) way she (he) saw a girl (boy) who had fallen down and hurt her (his) leg. The girl asked Mary to go to her house and get her parents so the parents could come and take her to the doctor. But if Mary did run and get the child's parents, she would be late for the birthday party and miss the ice cream, cake, and all the games. What should Mary do? Why?

Cross-Sectional Data

In several cross-sectional studies, the prosocial reasoning of children aged 4 to 18 has been examined (e.g., Eisenberg & Shell, 1985; Eisenberg-Berg, 1979; Eisenberg-Berg & Neal, 1981). In these studies, children's responses to four dilemmas were coded into a variety of categories, many of which resemble aspects of Kohlberg's stages (examples of most categories are in Table 5.1). To briefly summarize, across the research we have found that young elementary

TABLE 5.1

Frequently Used Prosocial Moral Reasoning Categories

1. *Obsessive and/or magical view of authority and/or punishments:* Avoidance of punishment and unquestioning deference to power are valued in their own right. The physical consequences of action determine its goodness regardless of human values and needs. Example: "If he didn't help, someone would find out and punish him."

(Continued)

TABLE 5.1 *(Continued)*

2. *Hedonistic reasoning.*

(a) *Pragmatic, hedonistic gain to the self:* Orientation to gain for oneself (besides gain resulting from direct reciprocity). Example: "She wouldn't help because she'd want to go to the party."

(b) *Direct reciprocity:* Orientation to personal gain due to direct reciprocity (or lack of it) from the recipient of an act. Example: "She'd help because they'd give her food the next time she needed it."

(c) *Affectional relationship:* Individuals' identifications with another, their liking for the other, and the other's relation to one's own needs are important considerations in the individual's moral reasoning. Example: "She'd share because she'd probably have friends in the town."

3. *Nonhedonistic pragmatism:* Orientation to practical concerns that are not directly related to either selfish considerations or the other's need. Example: "I'd help because I'm strong."

4. *Concern for other's needs (needs-oriented reasoning).*

(a) *Concern for others' physical and material needs:* Orientation to the physical and material needs of the other person. Examples: "He needs blood," or "She's hurt."

(b) *Stereotyped images of majority behavior:* Orientation to "natural" behavior and and affective states of the other person. Example: "They'd be happy if they had food."

5. *Reference to and concern with humanness:* Orientation to the fact that the other is human, living, a person. Example: He'd help because "they're human," or "they are people, too."

6. *Stereotyped reasoning.*

(a) *Stereotypes of a good or bad person:* Orientation to stereotyped images of a good or bad person. Example: A child would help because "it's nice."

(b) *Stereotyped images of majority behavior:* Orientation to "natural" behavior and what most people would do. Example: "It's only natural to help."

(c) *Stereotyped images of others and their roles:* Orientation to stereotyped images of others and what others do. Example: "I'd help because farmers are nice people."

7. *Approval and interpersonal orientation:* Orientation to others' approval and acceptance in deciding what is the correct behavior. Example: "They'd like her if she helped."

8. *Overt empathic orientations.*

(a) *Sympathetic orientation:* Expression of sympathetic concern and caring for others. Examples: "He would feel sorry for them," "She'd be concerned."

(b) *Role-taking:* The individual takes the perspective of the other and explicitly uses this perspective in his or her reasoning. Examples: "I'm trying to put myself in his or her shoes," or "She'd know how it feels."

(continued)

TABLE 5.1 *(Continued)*

9. *Internalized affect.*

(a) *Simple internalized positive affect and positive affect related to consequences:* The individual simply states that he or she would feel good as a result of a particular course of action without giving a reason or says she or he would feel good because of the consequences of his or her act for the other person. The affect must be used in a context that appears internalized. Example: "She'd help because seeing the villagers fed would make her feel good."

(b) *Internalized positive affect from self-respect and living up to one's values:* Orientation to feeling good as the result of living up to internalized values. Example: "I'd feel good knowing that I had lived up to my principles."

(c) Internalized negative affect over consequences of behavior: Concern with feeling bad or guilty due to the consequences of an act. Example: "She would feel guilty because the girl was hurt."

(d) *Internalized negative affect due to loss of self-respect and/or not living up to one's values:* Orientation to feeling had as the result of not living up to internalized values. Example: "He'd think badly of himself if he didn't do the right thing."

10. *Other abstract and/or internalized types of reasoning.*

(a) *Internalized law, norm, and value orientation:* Orientation to an internalized responsibility, duty, or need to uphold the laws and accepted norms or values. Examples: "She has a duty to help needy others," or "He'd feel he had a responsibility to assist because of his values."

(b) *Concern with the rights of others:* Orientation to protecting individual rights and preventing injustices that violate another's rights. Example: "I'd help because her right to walk down the street was being violated."

c) *Generalized reciprocity:* Orientation to indirect reciprocity in a society (i.e., exchange that is not one-to-one but eventully benefits all). Example: "If everyone helps one another, we'd all be better off."

(d) *Concern with the condition of society:* Orientation to improving the society or community as a whole. Ecample: "If everyone helps, society would be a lot better."

Note: Less frequently use categories such as those related to equality of individuals and social contract are omitted. Adapted from Eisenberg-Berg, 1979. Reprinted from Eisenberg, 1986, with the permission of Lawrence Erlbaum Associates.

school children use little authority- and punishment-oriented reasoning to justify moral decisions; rather, they verbalize much hedonistic and needs-oriented (primitive empathic) reasoning. Moreover, in elementary school, children's judgments begin to reflect approval-oriented considerations, and the desire to behave in stereotypically "good" ways. In contrast, high school students frequently verbalize reasoning reflecting abstract principles, internalized affective reactions (e.g., guilt or positive affect) related to living up to one's principles, and/or self-reflective empathic reasoning, as well as the other less advanced forms of reasoning.

Longitudinal Data

In three longitudinal followups of the preschool children in one of our early studies, we have further delineated developmental changes in children's prosocial moral judgment (Eisenberg, Lennon, & Roth, 1983; Eisenberg, Pasternack, & Lennon, 1984; Eisenberg-Berg & Roth, 1980). Children who initially were aged approximately 4-5 were reinterviewed 1 1/2, 3, and 5 years later. Moreover, a second small cohort of 4-5-year-olds was also reinterviewed at ages 5-6 and 7-8. At all followups, a group of children who had not been previously tested were interviewed to assess the effects of repeated testing.

The results of the three longitudinal followups generally were consistent with the cross-sectional work. Hedonistic reasoning dropped off in use from age 4-5 until mid-elementary school age. Simultaneously, there were significant increases in needs-oriented reasoning which then leveled off by age 9-10. The use of a number of other categories of reasoning increased over the 5-year period: pragmatic reasoning, approval-interpersonal reasoning, stereotypes of good and bad persons, and affectional relationship reasoning. Moreover, two relatively sophisticated categories of reasoning (role taking and positive affect related to consequences of one's behavior for others) were used significantly more than at younger ages.

The results for the younger, smaller cohort were similar to those for the primary cohort. There was a decrement in the use of hedonistic reasoning over the 3-year period, and increments in needs-oriented and stereotypic reasoning. Moreover, children interviewed for the first time at the various followups did not differ in reasoning from that of the primary cohort; thus, there was no evidence of an effect from repeated testing.

Based on both the cross-sectional and longitudinal research described previously, we have delineated an age-related sequence of development of prosocial moral judgment. These levels are presented in Table 5.2; the lowest level (reflecting hedonistic, self-oriented reasoning) has been found to be dominant in the reasoning of only preschool and elementary school children; Levels 4b and 5 (internalized values and related affect) predominate in the reasoning of only a minority of high school students. However, individuals do not reason exclusively at one level, or even at a given level and the adjacent levels. Even adolescents at the highest levels occasionally verbalize Level 1 reasoning when justifying the decision not to assist (Eisenberg-Berg, 1979).

TABLE 5.2

Levels of Prosocial Reasoning

Level 1: Hedonistic, self-focused orientation – the individual is concerned with self-oriented consequences rather than moral considerations. Reasons for assisting or not assisting another include consideration of direct gain to the self, future reciprocity, and concern for others because one needs and/or likes the other (due to the affectional tie) (predominant mode primarily for preschoolers and younger elementary school children).

Level 2: Needs- oriented orientation – the individual expresses concern for the physical, material, and psychological needs of others even though the other's needs conflict with one's own needs. This concern is expressed in the simplest terms, without clear evidence of self-reflective role taking, verbal expressions of sympathy, or reference to internalized affect such as guilt (predominate mode for many preschoolers and many elementary school children).

Level 3: Approval and interpersonal orientation and/or stereotyped orientation – stereotyped images of good and bad persons and behaviors and/or considerations of other's approval and acceptance are used in justifying prosocial or nonhelping behaviors (predominant mode for some elementary and high school students).

Level 4a: Self-reflective empathic orientation – the individual's judgments include evidence of self-reflective sympathetic responding or role taking, concern with the other's humanness, and/or guilt or positive affect related to the consequences of one's actions (predominant mode for a few older elementary school children and many high school students).

Level 4b: Transitional level – the individual's justifications for helping or not helping involve internalized values, norms, duties, or responsibilities, concern for the condition of the larger society, or refer to the necessity of protecting the rights and dignity of other persons; these ideas, however, are not clearly and strongly stated (predominant mode for a minority of people high school age or older).

Level 5: Strongly internalized stage – justifications for helping or not helping are based on internalized values, norm, or responsibilities, the desire to maintain individual and societal contractual obligations or improve the condition of society, the belief in the dignity, rights, and equality of all individuals. Positive or negative affect related to the maintenance of self-respect for living up to one's own values and accepted norms also characterizes this stage (predominant mode for only a small minority of high school students and no elementary school children).

Note: Adapted from Eisenberg et al., 1983.

Cross-Cultural Research

In recent years, the development of prosocial moral judgment has been examined in several different countries. According to Kohlberg (1969), similarities in the developmental pattern of moral judgment are to be expected across cultures. This is due simply to the fact that the capacities for abstract thought and complex perspective taking seem to be necessary for (or at least facilitative of) higher level reasoning (see Kohlberg, 1976). However, individual differences in the level of moral reasoning appear to be related to variations in socialization theory (e.g., Eisenberg et al., 1983; Leahy, 1981; Parikh, 1980); thus, one might expect some cross-cultural variation in level or perhaps even sequencing of children's moral judgment.

German Data. Eisenberg, Boehnke, Schuhler, and Silbereisen (1985) compared the prosocial moral reasoning of American and West German children. Although the German and American cultures are similar in many aspects, there are differences in the two cultures that might lead to differences in the development of moral reasoning. For example, socialization practices in the two countries may differ in important ways. German parents appear to provide more love and support than do American parents (Devereux, Bronfenbrenner, & Suci, 1962), whereas American mothers apparently allow their school-age children more autonomy than do German mothers (Wesley & Karr, 1968).

The participants in this study were 92 Germans and 99 Americans in preschool, second, or fourth grades. Prosocial moral judgment was assessed with the same four moral dilemmas used in the American research with elementary school children, slightly modified for use with the German children.

According to the data for the German children, hedonistic reasoning decreased in use with age whereas needs-oriented, direct reciprocity, approval-interpersonal reasoning, and reference to humanness increased in use with age. As was found in our longitudinal work, needs-oriented reasoning leveled off and decreased nonsignificantly from second to fourth grade. Moreover, the developmental patterns were the same for German and American children. However, German children verbalized more direct reciprocity reasoning than did American children, whereas Americans used considerably more stereotypic reasoning that did Germans.

In summary, developmental changes in the German children's prosocial moral judgment were very similar to those noted in prior cross-sectional and longitudinal research with American children (Eisenberg et al., 1983, 1984; Eisenberg-Berg, 1979). This similarity is probably due to both the role of social cognition in the development of moral reasoning and some basic similarities in the socialization of children in Western cultures.

Israeli Data. In a second study, we (Fuchs, Eisenberg, Hertz-Lazarowitz, & Sharabany, 1986) compared prosocial moral reasoning of Israeli city, kibbutz, and American city children. Based on most of the prior research concerning moral development, it seemed reasonable to expect differences in the reasoning of Israeli city and kibbutz children. In specific, researchers have found that (a) kibbutz children score higher on scales of social responsibility than do city children (Nadler, Romek, & Shapiro-Friedman, 1979); (b) kibbutz children and adults are more prosocial than are city dwellers (Avgar, Bronfenbrenner, & Henderson, 1977; Nadler et al., 1979; Yinon, Sharon, Azgad, & Barshir, 1981); and (c) kibbutz children score higher on Kohlberg's index of moral judgment than doo ity children (Kohlberg, 1976). However, in the one published study of prosocial moral reasoning, Bar-Tal, Raviv, and Shavit (1981) found no difference in the prosocial moral reasoning of kibbutz and city children in Israel.

The prosocial moral reasoning of Israeli children (Kibbutz or city) in comparison to that of American children is also of interest. Israel is a rather diverse society, influenced by both Eastern and Western European (as well as Arabic) cultures. Culturally, it should differ from the the United States at least as much as the difference between German and American children.

Fuchs et al. compared the prosocial moral reasoning of 55 American, 29 kibbutz, and 36 Israeli city children of comparable age. Two sets of analyses were computed, one in which the American data and those of the combined Israeli sample were compared, and one in which all three groups (American, Israeli city, and Israeli kibbutz) were compared.

According to the results, American children used much more physical needs-oriented reasoning. In contrast, Israeli children verbalized more hedonistic, direct reciprocity, affectional relationship, humanness, role taking, and internalized law-norm orientation reasoning. When the reasoning of the children from all three groups were compared, American children scored significantly higher on physical needs-oriented reasoning than did either kibbutz or Israeli city children. In contrast, kibbutz children used more concern with humanness and internalized law-norm orientation reasoning than did either American or Israeli city children, and Israeli city children verbalized more role-taking reasoning than did either of the other two gropus.

To summarize, the American children were especially likely to base their decisions on the relatively immature type of reasoning in which individuals simply orient to others' needs. In contrast, kibbutz children were more likely than other children to justify decisions with an appeal to the notion that the needy other was a "person" (with the implication, direct or implied, that people are special) or by referring to internalized norms, rules, or values. Both of these types of reasoning preferred by the kibbutz children are relatively mature developmentally and seem to reflect the ideological emphasis of the kibbutz.

Moreover, the two immature types of reasoning that were used frequently by the Israeli children (direct reciprocity, affectional relationship) were used considerably (although not significantly) more by kibbutz children and are consistent with the emphasis on relationships and exchange among group members that is characteristic of a communal society. Finally, the fact that Israeli city children expressed somewhat more hedonistic reasoning (the difference between Israelis' and Americans' use of this category was primarily due to the high rate of hedonistic reasoning among Israeli city children) may be due to the emphasis on consumerism in Israeli cities, combined with the fact that many commodities are scarce or expensive.

Papua New Guinea (Maisin) Data. The most informative data concerning prosocial moral reasoning in a nonwestern culture are those collected by Anne Tietjen (1986) from people in two isolated Maisin coastal villages, Uiaku and Ganjiga, Papua New Guinea. In these Maisin villages, the traditional social organization is strong; the people are tightly bound by kinship obligations. Moreover, the Maisin are collectivistic rather than individualistic in orientation (see Tietjen, 1986; Tietjen & Walker, 1985, for more details).

Tietjen interviewed individuals using a slightly modified version of Eisenberg's stories. Sixty-nine children were interviewed in 1982; 34 of these children were reinterviewed in 1983. Eight adolescents and 24 parents also responded to stories.

According to the data, Maisin children as well as adolescents and adults used more physical needs-oriented reasoning than any other type of reasoning. Hedonistic reasoning was next most frequently used. The younger Maisin children's reasoning was similar to that of American children of comparable age in that physical needs-oriented and hedonistic reasoning were the most common modes of judgment, with the former being more prevalent than the latter. However, unlike for Americans, the reasoning of the older Maisin children and adults differed relatively little from that of the children. The most salient developmental changes were significant, moderate increases in affectional relationship, sympathetic and psychological needs-oriented reasoning (especially the latter) with age. Hedonistic reasoning peaked in third grade (perhaps because of the initial effects of exposure to Western values) and dropped off somewhat thereafter. Authority and punishment reasoning was low at all ages, as was the use of higher level reasoning categories. In brief, although the moral judgment of the Maisin clearly fit the coding scheme of Eisenberg (there were no "new" types of reasoning noted by the coders), there are both similarities and clear differences between the reasoning of the Maisin and that of Americans in other research.

The fact that the Maisin adolescents and adults exhibited very little high-level reasoning is consistent with the results of cross-cultural research concerning Kohlbergian moral judgment. Researchers (e.g., Nisan & Kohlberg, 1982; Turiel, Edwards, & Kohlberg, 1978; White, Bushnell, & Regnemer, 1978) have found that people from non-Western, rural and nonindustrial societies exhibit relatively little higher level reasoning. However, in a small, face-to-face, traditional society such as that of the Maisin, it is reasonable that the types of reasoning used by the people reflect attention to others' needs (physical needs-oriented, psychological needs-oriented, and sympathetic reasoning), as well as concern with that which is possible for them to give to others (hedonistic and perhaps pragmatic concerns). A cooperative, other-oriented approach is both necessary for their survival and highly valued.

Summary. Several conclusions can be drawn from the limited cross-cultural research. First, the similarity across cultures in terms of the modes of reasoning that develop first is striking. Needs-oriented and hedonistic reasoning clearly dominate the reasoning of preschool and early elementary children in all cultures studied. Moreover, certain types of reasoning–authority and punishment and the more sophisticated internalized self-reflective categories of reasoning–are seldom verbalized prior to early adolescence.

Despite the similiarites across cultures, cross-cultural differences in moral reasoning are also evident. The moral judgments of children seem to reflect, to some degree, the values and concerns of the culture. Once children are capable of understanding a certain type of reasoning, differential use of that reasoning seems to be linked to the importance of the concerns embedded in the reasoning for persons in the society. Thus, cultural factors seem to affect choice of reasoning within that sphere of moral reasoning accessible to the individual.

MODES OF MORAL JUDGMENT

In this last section of the chapter, a "model" of prosocial moral reasoning, albeit not fully developed, is presented. Because of the familiarity of Kohlberg's model to all researchers and theorists in the area of moral development and the critical role it has played in the study of moral judgment, it is useful to briefly compare our thinking with that of Kohlberg, Colby, and their colleagues.

Kohlberg's Model

According to Kohlberg (Colby, Kohlberg, & Kauffman, 1987), his stages meet the criteria for "hard" structural stage models. In other words, each of his stages is viewed as being qualitatively different in structure from all other stages; the sequence of stages is invariant and universal; each stage is a "structured whole" (i.e., does not represent a specific response determined by knowledge and familiarity with that task or similar tasks but an underlying thought-organization); and each stage displaces or integrates the structures found at lower levels (i.e., stages are hierarchical integrations).

Several aspects of these criteria require further elaboration. The criterion of "structured wholeness" implies that much of an individual's moral reasoning is at a single level. Indeed, Kohlberg and his colleagues have asserted that most of an individual's moral reasoning at a given point in time is at a single stage and the two adjacent stages. Thus, it would appear that people do not use and-or have access to reasoning two or more stages below or above their dominant stage. However, due to the way in which Kohlberg has operationalized moral judgment, this is not really the case.

To some degree, Kohlberg and his colleagues have examined competence, not performance, in the domain of moral reasoning. In other words, the coding system is designed to measure the most advanced or highest level reasoning that an individual uses with any consistency, not the entire range of reasoning verbalized by individuals in their moral reasoning. Indeed, Kohlberg's coding system includes several techniques that systematically exclude, to some degree, reasoning that varies greatly from that of the individual's dominant stage, especially lower level reasoning. For example, stages of reasoning that comprise less than 10% of the individual's reasoning are discarded when computing the person's composite score (Colby, Kohlberg, Gibbs, & Lieberman, 1983). Second, if a lower level idea is expressed in a manner that is not viewed as being prescriptive (i.e., is not used as a moral justification), it is not coded. Third, reasoning at lower levels is eliminated if the same basic idea of concern is also expressed in a more mature version. The rationale for this scoring rule is that the lower level reason is viewed as being conceptually consistent with the higher level reasoning, only expressed incompletely or inadequately (Colby, 1984).

Prosocial Moral Reasoning: Scoring and Conceptual Assumptions

The scoring system that has been used to code prosocial moral judgment differs in a variety of ways from that of Kohlberg. Most important, perhaps, is that with the prosocial scoring system, *all* the individual's reasoning is scored regardless of frequency of use and regardless of whether higher level reasoning concerning the same general idea is used (unless the reasoning is too incomplete to score).

Due, in part, to the fact that Kohlberg and those examining prosocial moral reasoning have coded somewhat different aspects of moral judgment, we do not make all the same assumptions about prosocial moral judgment that Kohlberg has made with regard to Kohlbergian moral judgment. For example, because all of an individual's prosocial moral reasoning is scored (judgments at different levels are not collapsed), we do not find that stages are "structured wholes." Indeed, a single individual often exhibits reasoning at a variety of levels. Moreover, like Rest (1979), we have found that individuals who are capable of higher level reasoning still may express much lower level reasoning. Thus, Kohlberg's criterion of hierarchical integration does not seem to apply to prosocial moral judgment.

We also do not claim that our levels of prosocial reasoning are invariant in sequence. We are still attempting (via longitudinal and cross-cultural research) to further verify the sequence of development. At the present time, it is not altogether clear which categories of reasoning are at equivalent levels; some of those we have combined into a single level may not be entirely equivalent in developmental maturity. For example, direct reciprocity and hedonistic reasoning are combined into a single level although the former seems to develop somewhat later than the latter (e.g., Eisenberg et al., 1983, 1984).

Even if we were more confident that our levels of reasoning were entirely accurate, it would be quite possible that we would discover that the levels were not invariant in sequence. For example, Level 3 including stereotypic and approval/interpersonal oriented reasoning seems to emerge at an earlier age than Level 4 self-reflective empathic reasoning in both our cross-sectional and cross-cultural reasearch. Not all of our longitudinal subjects, however, have exhibited Level 3 reasoning prior to Level 4 reasoning. Thus, based on our data, it would seem that these two levels of reasoning may be neither developmentally equivalent nor invariant in sequence. It should be noted, however, that even if our levels of reasoning were not invariant in sequence, this would not mean that Kohlberg's stages based on level of sociomaral perspective taking are not.

The last of Kohlberg's assumptions with regard to moral stages is that each stage is qualitatively different from other stages of reasoning. Give the dramatic change in the structure of children's reasoning with age, there may be qualitative changes in children's moral reasoning as they develop more sophisticated levels of social-cognitive skills. However, we are uncertain whether or not our levels of prosocial moral reasoning accurately depict qualitatively different stages of reasoning. For example, it is possible that some types of reasoning included in Level 4 are not qualitatively different than some categories of reasoning included in Level 5; rather, some Level 4 and 5 modes of reasoning may represent differences in value orientations (e.g., orientation to other-oriented versus rule-oriented values). Additional research is necessary to determine whether or not there are qualitative changes in prosocial moral judgement, and if so, which modes of reasoning are characteristic of each qualitative stage.

A "Model" of Prosocial Development

Although prosocial moral judgment levels are not asserted to embody all of the criteria of "hard" developmental stages, there are important conceptual similarities between Kohlberg's model of moral judgment and our own model of prosocial moral judgment. The most important of these is the underlying assumption that development is limited, in part, by the individual's level of sociocognitive development, that is, the complexity of the individual's cognition with regard to social phenomena. In Kohlberg's view, individuals who are at a low or moderate level with regard to logical and sociocognitive functioning–often due to their young age and corresponding incomplete development–cannot be expected to understand or use higher level modes of moral judgment (Colby et al., 1987).

The assumption that there is a ceiling set on the individual's level of moral reasoning due to his or her level of logical and/or sociocognitive development seems applicable to the domain of prosocial moral judgment. Young children clearly are incapable of expressing higher level modes of reasoning; level 4 or 5 reasoning is relatively rare even among children in elementary school (e.g., Eisenberg-Berg, 1979; Eisenberg et al., 1983, 1984).

As was discussed previously, within the range of prosocial reasoning accessable to a given individual, a variety of levels may be verbalized. Consequently, an important question concerns the factors that influence an individual's choice of reasoning within his or her range of competence.

In our model (see Fig.5.1), the individual's choice of moral reasoning is influenced by his or her values and goals (which, in turn, are based in part on the indvidual's socialization history). For example, individuals who are concerned about social appearances and others' approval should tend to use approval/interpersonally oriented reasoning whereas empathic persons with other-oriented value systems should tend to use whichever mode of empathic moral reasoning is appropriate for their age (e.g., needs- oriented reasoning for younger children; sympathetic or role-taking reasoning for older children). In contrast, those concerned with material gain should tend to use hedonistic reasoning, whereas the desire to behave in a manner condoned by society would be expected to be associated with stereotypic reasoning. In other words, the type of reasoning preferred by a given individual is expected to be a function of aspects of the person frequently labeled as components of *personality*. These include the individual's value orientation and other characteristics such as degree of positive valuing of people, level of self-esteem, and degree of self-concern, all of which color the individual's needs, goals, and values (see Berkowitz, 1972; Reykowski, 1982; Staub, 1984). Put differently, although the individual's level of competence with regard to moral reasoning is limited by developmental factors, performance within one's sphere of competence is believed to be a function, in part, of individual differences on a variety of personal variables.

Although limited, there is some empirical support for this view. Among fourth graders, we have found that individuals concerned with presenting a socially desirable image tend to use relatively high levels of approval-oriented reasoning (Eisenberg et al., 1984). Similarly, American children who

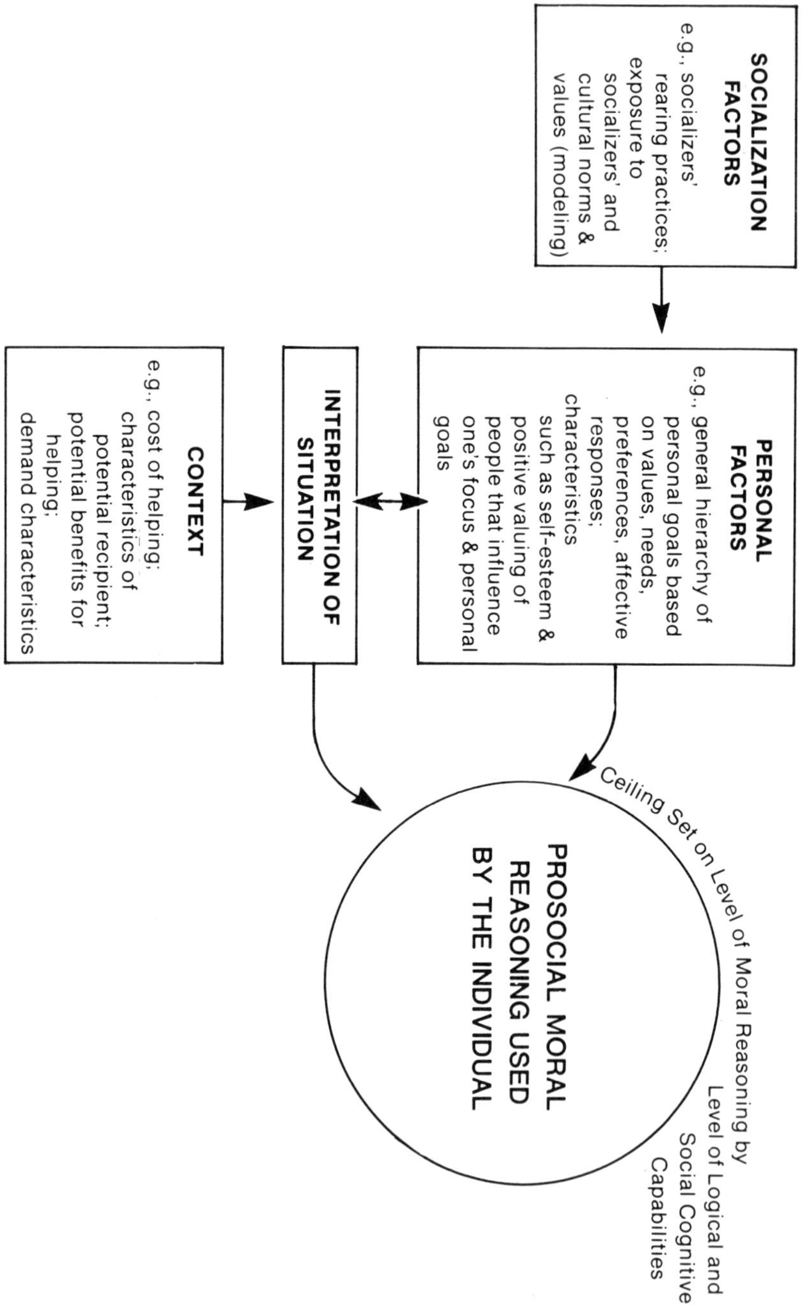

FIGURE 5.1. Factors affecting prosocial moral reasoning.

scored high on Bryant's (1982) empathy scale were found to use relatively high amounts of age-appropriate empathic modes of reasoning (needs-oriented reasoning for second graders; sympathetic reasoning for fourth graders; Eisenberg et al., 1984). A similar relation between needs-oriented reasoning (psychological needs) and empathy scores has been noted amont the Maisin in New Guinea (Tietjen, personal communication, 1984).

Each person has a number of personal goals based on personal values, needs, and preferences (see Staub, 1978, 1984). As was noted by Staub (1978), in a given situation, several of these personal factors may be relevant to moral decision making. Moreover, various personal goals activated in a given context may conflict with one another. For example, in a situation in which a person could publically assist another at a cost to the self, the desire for social approval and/or empathically based concerns may conflict with the desire to preserve one's own resources. In such a circumstance, the relative importance of the various relevant goals in the individual's hierarchy of personal goals should be reflected in his or her choice of moral justifications, as well as in the relative importance of various modes of reasoning (when more than one mode is used).

The context is another important influence on individuals' choices of moral reasoning from those modes available to them. For example, children (Eisenberg & Neal, 1981) and adults (Sobesky, 1983) tend to use more lower level reasoning (e.g., hedonistic rather than needs-oriented) as the cost of assisting another increases. Moreover, there is undoubtedly an interaction between situational and personal factors; which personal goals are salient in a specific situation for a given person will be a function, in part, of characteristics of the context. For example, the goal of obtaining others' approval will be elicited by somewhat different cues (e.g., by different degrees of public visability or the presence or different observers) for different persons. Of course, it is also true that the individual's interpretation of a situation, including which aspects of the situation are apprehended, perceived as salient, and/or are distorted, are a function, in part, of personal characteristics. Indeed, it is unlikely that context alone is ever the sole influence on choice of moral reasoning within the individual's sphere of competence; even in extreme situations in which contextual influences are overwhelming (e.g., if the cost of behaving in a manner consistent with higher level reasoning were death), there would probably still be individual differences in the level of moral judgment expressed (e.g., consider Socrates' behavior and reasoning prior to his death).

The perspective or model of prosocial moral reasoning described earlier is presented in Fig. 5.1. It is not assumed that the factors that influence level of moral reasoning are limited to those in the figure. Nonetheless, it is our view that the model is a useful heuristic when considering the variables that contribute to the individual's level of prosocial moral reasoning concerning moral conflicts in specific contexts.

In summary, our view of the factors influencing the individuals' use of moral reasoning differs somewhat from that of Kohlberg. This is due to both differences in theoretical orientation and in the data on which Kohlberg's and our thinking is based (the data differ with regard to both scoring procedures and in the dilemmas themselves). Personal characteristics, and the socialization influences affecting these characteristics, are much more prominent in our model than in Kohlberg's. Similarly contextual factors, and their interaction with personal factors, are more important in our model. It is hoped that our model and the work on prosocial moral judgment will stimulate greater interest in delineating the factors that affect performance in the domain of moral reasoning.

REFERENCES

Avgar, A., Bronfenbrenner, U., & Henderson, C. R., Socialization practices of parents, teachers, and peers in Israel: Kibbutz, moshav, and city. *Child Development, 48,* 1219-1227.

Bar-Tal, D., Raviv, A., & Shavit, N. (1981). Motives for helping behavior: Kibbutz and city children in kindergarten and school. *Developmental Psychology, 17,* 766-772.

Berkowitz, L. (1972). Social norms, feelings, and other factors affecting helping and altruism. In L. Berkowitz (Ed.), *Advances in experimental social psychology* (Vol. 6, pp. 63-108). New York: Academic Press.

Bryant, B. (1982). An index of empathy for children and adolescents. *Child Development, 53,* 413-425.

Colby, A. (1984). Personal communication.

Colby, A., Kohlberg, L., Gibbs, J., & Lieberman, M. (1983). A longitudinal study of moral judgment. *Monographs of the Society for Research in Child Development, 48* (Serial No. 200), 1-124.

Colby, A., Kohlberg, L., & Kauffman, K. (1987). Theoretical introduction to the measurement of moral judgment. In A. Colby & L. Kohlberg (Eds.), *The measurement of moral judgement* (Vol. 1). New York: Cambridge Press.

Devereux, E. C., Bronfenbrenner, U., & Suci, G. J. (1962). Patterns of parent behavior in the United States of American and in the Federal Republic of Germany: A cross-national comparison. *International Sociological Science Journal, 14,* 488-506.

Eisenberg, N. (1986). Altruistic emotion, cognition, and behavior. Hillsdale, NJ: Lawrence Erlbaum Associates.

Eisenberg, N., Boehnke, K., Schuhler, P., & Silbereisen, R. K. (1985). The development of prosocial behavior and cognitions in German children. *Journal of Cross-Cultural Psychology, 6,* 69-82.

Eisenberg, N., Lennon, R., & Roth, K. (1983). Prosocial development: A longitudinal study. *Developmental Psychology, 19,* 846-855.

Eisenberg, N., Pasternack, J. F., & Lennon, R. (1984, March). *Prosocial development in middle childhood.* Paper presented at the biennial meeting of the Southwestern Society for Research in Human Development, Denver.

Eisenberg, N., & Shell, R. (1985, April). *The relation of prosocial moral judgment and behavior in children: The mediating role of cost.* Paper presented at the biennial meeting of the Society for Research in Child Development, Toronto.

Eisenberg-Berg, N. (1979). Development of children's prosocial moral judgment. *Developmental Psychology, 15,* 128-137.

Eisenberg-Berg, N., & Neal, C. (1981). The effects of person of the protagonist and costs of helping on children's moral judgment. *Personality and Social Psychology Bulletin, 7,* 17-23.

Eisenberg-Berg, N., & Roth, K. ((1980). The development of children's prosocial moral judgment: A longitudinal follow-up. *Developmental Psychology, 16,* 375-376.

Fuchs, I., Eisenberg, N., Hertz-Lazarowitz, R., & Sharabany, R. (1986). Kibbutz, Israeli city, and American children's moral reasoning about prosocial moral conflicts. *Merrill Palmer Quarterly.*

Kohlberg, L. (1969). Stage and sequence: The cognitive-developmental approach to socialization. In D. A. Goslin (Ed.), *Handbook of socialization theory and research* (pp. 325-480). New York: Rand McNally.

Kohlberg, L. (1976). Moral stage and moralization: The cognitive-developmental approach. In T. Lickona (Ed.), *Moral development and behavior: Theory, research, and social issues* (pp. 84-107). New York: Holt, Rinehart, and Winston.

Leahy, R. (1981). Parental practices and the development of moral judgment and self-disparity during adolescence. *Developmental Psychology, 17,* 580-594.

Nadler, A., Romek, E., & Shapiro-Friedman, A. (1979). Living in the kibbutz: Pro-social behavior of city and kibbutz children as affected by social responsibility and social pressure. *Journal of Cross-Cultural Psychology, 10,* 57-72.

Nisan, M., & Kohlberg, L. (1982). Universality and variation in moral judgment: A longitudinal and cross-sectional study in Turkey. *Child Development, 53,* 865-876.

Parikh, B. (1980). Development of moral judgment and its relation to family environment factors in Indian and American families. *Child Development, 51,* 1030-1039.

Rest, J. R. (1979). *Development in judgment moral issues.* Minneapolis: University of Minnesota Press.

Reykowski, J. (1982). Motivation of prosocial behavior. In V. J. Delaga & J. Grzelak (Eds.), *Cooperation and helping behavior: Theories and research* (pp. 355-375). New York: Academic Press.

Sobesky, W. E. (1983). The effects of situational factors on moral judgments. *Child Development, 54,* 575-584.

Staub, E. (1978). *Positive social behavior and morality: Social and personal influences* (Vol. I). New York: Academic Press.

Staub, E. (1984). Steps toward a comprehensive theory of moral conduct: Goal orientation, social behavior, kindness and cruelty. In J. Gerwirtz & W. Kurtines (Eds.), *Morality, moral development, and moral behavior: Basic issues in theory and research* (pp. 241-260). New York: John Wiley & Sons.

Tietjen, A. (1986). Prosocial reasoning among children and adults in a Papua New Guinea society. *Developmental Psychology, 22,* 861–868.

Tietjen, A. M., & Walker, L. J. (1985). Moral reasoning and leadership among men in a Papua New Guinea village. *Developmental Psychology, 21,* 982-992.

Turiel, E., Edwards, C. P., & Kohlberg, L. (1978), Moral development in Turkish children, adolescents, and young adults. *Journal of Cross-Cultural Psychology, 9,* 75-85.

Wesley, F., & Karr, C. (1968). Vergleich der Ansichten und Erziehungshältungen Deutscher und Amerikanischer Müutter. *Psychologische Rundschaú, 19,* 35-46.

White, C. B., Bushnell, N., & Regnemer, J. L. (1978). Moral development in Bahamian school children: A 3-year examination of Kohlberg's stages of moral development. *Developmental Psychology, 14,* 58-65.

Yinon, Y., Sharon, I., Azgad, Z., & Barshir, I. (1981). Helping behavior of urbanites, moshavniks, and kibbutzniks. *Journal of Social Psychology, 113,* 143-144.

6 Contextual Relativism of Moral Judgment in Late Childhood and Early Adolescence

Adam Niemczyński
Agnieszka Maciejowska
Jagiellonian University, Kraków, Poland

We have attempted to probe the possible developmental antecedents of contextual relativism in moral judgment. Contextual relativism is considered as a structural change in early adulthood (e.g., Murphy & Gilligan, 1980). There are several developmental interpretations of relativism as a feature of cognitive functioning after adolescence (Gilligan & Murphy, 1979; Kohlberg, 1984; Labouvie-Vief, 1980, 1982; Perry, 1970; Riegel, 1973). All of them, in one way or another, identify either a structural inadequacy or the functional limitations of formal-operational thought when it is used in contexts of commitment and the responsibility in adulthood. As a result, they stress the connections between postadolescent cognitive development and several ego developments, including the maintenance of identity and autonomy within the context of social interaction and communication. It could be interesting, however, to look at earlier periods of the life – span in order to identify a possible continuity in certain aspects of the basic mechanism from childhood through adolescence into adulthood. If such a basic continuity does exist, then the specificity of adult development could be easier to discern as well as its dependence on earlier development.

AIM AND HYPOTHESES

The notion of relativism is used in two different ways in the study of cognitive and moral development. One of them pertains to epistemological and metaethical issues concerning the nature of rules and principles that underlie knowledge or moral judgment. Here relativism means negation of unconditional and universal rules and principles. The other use of the notion of relativism concerns the nature of criteria against which knowledge and morality claims are to be judged. This time relativism amounts to the negation of logic or moral reasoning as a sufficient condition of adequacy of knowledge or morality.

These issues were recently discussed by Labouvie-Vief (1980, 1982) with reference to postadolescent cognitive development and by Kohlberg (1981, 1984) with regard to the moral domain. It is not our aim to go into this general debate here. We would only like to remark that both Labouvie-Vief and Kohlberg point to a way of approaching the issue of relativism which we also attempt to use. Contextual relativism or intersystemic thought is not to Labouvie-Vief an abandonment of logic or formal operational structures. It is rather a different use of logic, which becomes incorporated and subordinated to a new whole of higher order. In similar vein, what to Gilligan and Murphy (1979) seems to be abandoning of principled morality is no more to Kohlberg (1984, pp. 365-370) than the contextualized search for correct application of principles or struggling to formulate a principle of justice on a higher level. This not only implies that contextual relativism is not a defection from rules and principles but also suggests that postformal or posconventional development takes its route via contextual relativism, which leads to more adequate cognitive organizations. The question arises whether contextualization also is associated with moving to the higher stage of reasoning on both the conventional and preconventional levels.

Edelstein and Noam (1982) have proposed to describe the use of moral principles in the context of real-life situations in terms of struggling for a balance between taking a moral position (principled judgment) and referring to a particular social or interpersonal situation (contextualized judgment) at the same time, without losing sight of either. Edelstein and Noam seem to be interested, first of all, in depicting a way for ego development that would be directed at personal autonomy in the postconventional world. Moral autonomy that "makes use of principled judgments in the context of responsibility beyond early adult legalism" looks like the use of Kohlberg's Stage 6. Adult autonomy might thus be understood as one way of relating the abstract and general ideals of knowledge and morality to concrete and particular demands of the actual situation. It is a rather advanced way of relating the generalities of cognition and judgment to the particularities of context and situation. We attempted to look for other ways of relating generalities with particulars, which are earlier in ontogeny. The simultaneous performance of both functions, i.e., taking the moral position against a situation and meeting the situational requirements for the adequate course of action in the situation, surely is possible during the earlier periods of the life-span.

To summarize, we are interested in answering two related questions: (a) Is contextual relativism linked to the move toward the more advanced stages of moral reasoning at the preconventional and conventional levels as it seems to be at the postconventional level?; (b) Is it possible to find in late childhood and early adolescence the age-related growth in ability to perform the two functions, i.e., taking the moral position against the situation and meeting the situational requirements on the adequate course of action, at the same time and without losing the sight of either?

To explore the phenomena of moral contextualization in later childhood and early adolescence we started with quite a simple model. Taking the moral position against situation is an earlier development that is followed by using the attained moral perspective to plan for morally acceptable action in the situation and to act eventually upon the plan. During ontogeny, the person is confronted again with the task of mastering the moral position taking on each new structural level of moral judgment. One may expect less contextualization of moral judgment at the beginning of each new moral level construction because, at first, moral position taking dominates over meeting the situational requirements. Later on, the domination of moral position taking over meeting the situational requirements is followed by a balance between the two cognitive functions. This way contextualization may lead to a more equilibrated or advanced stage of a given moral level.

We hypothesized alternatively:

1. There is a gradual developmental change in late childhood and early adolescence. At first, the taking of a moral position dominates over meeting the situational requirements. Eventually a balanced relation between the two aspects of cognitive functioning is achieved. Thus, taking a moral position over a situation, i.e., noncontextualized judgment, is an earlier development, that is followed eventually by using the attained moral perspective to plan for morally acceptable action in the situation, i.e., contextualized judgement.

2. The aforementioned pattern of developmental change may be seen in late childhood as well as in early adolescence as two consecutive cycles of domination followed by balance because cognitive and ego changes on entering adolescence again confront a subject with the task of mastering moral-position-taking on the new structural level of moral judgment.

METHOD

Subjects. 192 Ss in four age-groups (48 each), 8, 10, 12 and 14 years old, participated in the study. Half of each age-group, i.e., 24 Ss, 12 girls, and 12 boys, received variant A of the procedure and the other half, again 12 girls and 12 boys, received variant B. Procedure A was designed to foster separation of the two cognitive function, i.e., moral-position-taking and meeting the situational requirements, whereas procedure B was designed to foster integration of the two functions at the same time without losing sight of either. Both of the two variants, with their particular question-order, follow.

Variant A

Question (a). What should you do when it is the name-day of somebody you know?
"Peter liked his teacher very much and on her name-day intended to please her with a gift of flowers, but he had no money and could not buy the flowers."
Question (c). What could Peter do?
"On his way to school that morning, he caught sight of some tulips growing in a flower bed of a city park. He looked around and seeing nobody he stepped in and picked three tulips. He ran off quickly and after arriving at school gave the tulips to his teacher."
Question (b). Was what Peter did good or bad? Why?

Variant B

Question (a). What should you do when it is the name-day of somebody you know?
Subjects then heard the entire story without interruption.
Question (b). Was what Peter did good or bad? Why?
Question (c). What could Peter do instead?

Note that although question (a) was posed first in each variant, the order of questions (b) and (c) was different in each variant. Thus, in variant A, subjects were asked to propose a plan for Peter before hearing what he actually did and before making any moral judgments. This way, pragmatic elaboration of the name-day situation was already completed by the subjects when they judged Peter's violation later on. They simply did not need to make a reference to the situation any more, being encouraged, thus, to focus on Peter's theft independently of the situation in which it was undertaken. In contrast, in variant B, the moral judgment of Peter's behavior was induced before subjects were invited to propose an alternative plan for the name-day situation. This way, variant B encourages subjects to consider simultaneously both situation and violation while making moral judgments. These were the reasons to predict that variant A would elicit more noncontextualized judgments than variant B, which would encourage integration of the two functions, instead of their separate performance as in variant A.

Classification of Responses. Responses to question (b) were classified as norm-centered or noncontextualized judgments (N-category) if a subject concentrated exclusively on the property norm without paying any attention to the name-day issue while judging Peter's action; and contextualized judgments (C-category) when both the property norm and the name-day issue were considered while judging Peter's action. In addition, three subcategories of C-responses were found. These were: (1) instrumental judgments of the type: "What Peter did was good, because his teacher was pleased by the gift of flowers " (CI-subcategory); (2) undecided judgments of the type: "On the one hand, what Peter did was bad because he picked flcwers from the city park, and, on the other hand, it was good what he did, because he gave the flowers to his teacher" (CU-subcategory); and (3) judgments which were underscored by reference to the situation that there was no situational excuse or justification for Peter's violation (CN-subcategory). There were, thus, three types of contextualized judgments: CI – instrumental; CU – undecided; and CN – norm supporting.

All classifications were made by both the authors independently, and only 8 out of 192 cases had to be agreed on afterwards.

Independently of the classifications by contextualization criteria, the responses to question (b) were scored, in addition, as regards Kohlberg's general criteria of preconventional and conventional level of moral judgment. The difference in sociomoral perspective between the two levels, as it is defined in Colby and Kohlberg (1987), was used as a conceptual tool to decide which level was represented by particular Ss in response to question (b). This assessment was done in order to test if there was a difference of moral judgment structural level between the two older groups (12-14 yrs.) and two younger groups (8-10 yrs.), as expected. Two scorers, who were experienced in scoring Kohlbergian interview material, performed this classification independently of each of the other. They achieve 89% of agreement and easily agreed the rest of the cases.

PREDICTIONS

It was assumed that variant A would encourage subjects to focus on Peter's theft independently of the situation in which it was undertaken. In contrast, variant

B would encourage subjects to consider both the name-day situation and violation. Accordingly, prediction (A) was that, at each age level, variant A would elicit more N responses than C responses, whereas variant B would elicit more C responses than N responses.

The next two predictions were concerned with the pattern of age changes in variant B, i.e., the variant that was supposed to encourage the integration of the two functions. Two opposing predictions were tested, the first based on hypothesis (1) was that with increasing age, N responses would decline in frequency and C responses would increase in frequency, prediction (1). The second prediction based on hypothesis (2) was that N responses would predominate at 8 years and again at 12 years, but C responses would predominate at 10 years and 14 years, prediction (2).

RESULTS AND DISCUSSION

In relation to prediction (A), one may observe, as Table 6.1 shows, that the expected domination of C responses (contextualization) in variant B, which was supposed to foster this type of responses, actually occurred only for 10- and 14-year-old groups. In turn, one can find, as Table 6.2 shows, that there is no systematic domination across age levels of N responses (noncontextualized judgment) in variant A, which was supposed to foster the N response type. One may note, however, that there are more N responses than C responses in variant A at each age level, although these differences in frequency are not statistically significant. Thus, we failed to induce with procedure A an increase of noncontextualization, but we succeed with procedure B to induce an increase of contextualization of moral judgment at two age levels, i.e., in 10 and 14 year olds.

TABLE 6.1

N and C Responses by Age. Procedure B Subjects

Response	*Age*	*8*	*10*	*12*	*14*
N category		18	9	18	9
C category		6	15	6	15

Note: Chi-square (3 df) = 13.7143 ($p < 0.0033$)

TABLE 6.2

N and C Responses by Age. Procedure A Subjects

Response	*Age*	*8*	*10*	*12*	*14*
N category		18	14	14	13
C category		6	10	10	11

Note: Chi-square (3 df) = 2.5946 ($p < 0.4585$)

The latter finding allows us to decide between the two alternative predictions, i.e., prediction (1) and prediction (2), regarding age changes (see again Table 6.1) The pattern fits prediction (2). All age-group comparisons except those between 8 and 12 and those between 10 and 14 are significant at 99% level of confidence by the Fisher test for binomial distributions. Thus, the data are contrary to the notion of a monotonic increase in contextualization with age, which was postulated by hypothesis (1). Instead, the data suggest that the pattern of developmental change occurs in late childhood as well as in early adolescence as two consecutive cycles of domination followed by balance. At first, the taking of a moral position dominates over meeting situational requirements (8 year olds). Eventually a balanced relation between the two aspects of cognitive functioning is achieved in late childhood (10 year olds). The cognitive and ego changes on entering adolescence again confront the subject with the task of mastering moral-position-taking on a new structural level of moral judgment, producing thus domination of this function over meeting the situational requirements (12 year olds). And again a balanced relation between the two functions is achieved (14 year olds) on the new structural level of moral judgment.

Table 6.3 shows that the two younger groups taken together scored predominantly at Kohlberg's preconventional level, whereas the two older groups taken together were scored predominantly at the conventional level according to Kolberg's general criteria of differentiation between the two sociomoral perspectives (Colby & Kohlberg, 1984).

We found ex-post facto, as was discussed in the section on the classification of responses, that there were three different types of C responses, i.e., three types of contextualized judgments. The pattern of age changes regarding the frequency of instrumental type (CI), undecided (CU), and norm supporting (CN) judgments, as Tables 6.4 through 6.6 show, makes the global pattern of

TABLE 6.3

Level of Moral Judgment by Age

Level	*Age*	*8–10*	*12–14*
preconventional		34	19
conventional		14	29

Note: Chi-square with cont. corr. (1 df) = 8.2563 ($p < 0.0041$)
Fisher's exact test, $p < 0.0019$

TABLE 6.4

CU Responses by Age

CU	*Age*	*8*	*10*	*12*	*14*
+		3	6	8	7
–		45	42	40	41

Note: Chi-square (3 df) = 2.6667 ($p < 0.4459$)

TABLE 6.5

CI Responses by Age

CI	*Age*	*8*	*10*	*12*	*14*
+		8	14	2	1
–		40	34	46	47

Note: Chi-square (3 df) = 20.0048 ($p < 0.0002$)

TABLE 6.6

CU Responses by Age

CN	*Age*	*8*	*10*	*12*	*14*
+		1	5	6	18
–		47	43	42	30

Note: Chi-square (3 df) = 25.4420 ($p < 0.0000$)

age change in C responses more specific. There was a slight increase of CU responses from 8 to 12 years, and a slight decrease thereafter, but these differences are not statistically significant, and, in general, the undecided judgments were relatively infrequent. In contrast, for both CI responses and CN responses, there is one peak value each. The instrumental contextualization is highest in frequency at 10 years, whereas contextualization supporting the norm is highest at 14 years. Thus, one may identify two qualitatively different contextualizations, each of them representing a balanced judgment on a different structural level. Instrumental contextualization at 10 years fits well the preconventional perspective in Kohlberg's system, whereas contextualization supporting the norm fits well the conventional sociomoral perspective. The pattern of age changes in CI and CN responses strongly suggest, thus, that contextualization is associated with a movement to a higher stage at a given structural level of moral judgment development.

Splitting the total group of subjects into two subgroups according to the procedure variants A and B, one may observe, as Figure 6.1 shows, that there were no age changes in contextualzation by undecided judgment, i.e., CU responses. In contrast, contextualization by instrumental judgment, as well as contextualization by judgment given in support of the norm, i.e., CI responses and CN responses, represents clearly the previously discussed pattern of age changes in the B-procedure group, but not in the group of subjects treated with variant A of the procedure. This reflects again the lack of effects on contextualization of the procedure variant A as well as the efficiency of the procedure variant B in fostering contextualized judgments in the group of 10 year-olds and in the group of 14 year-olds.

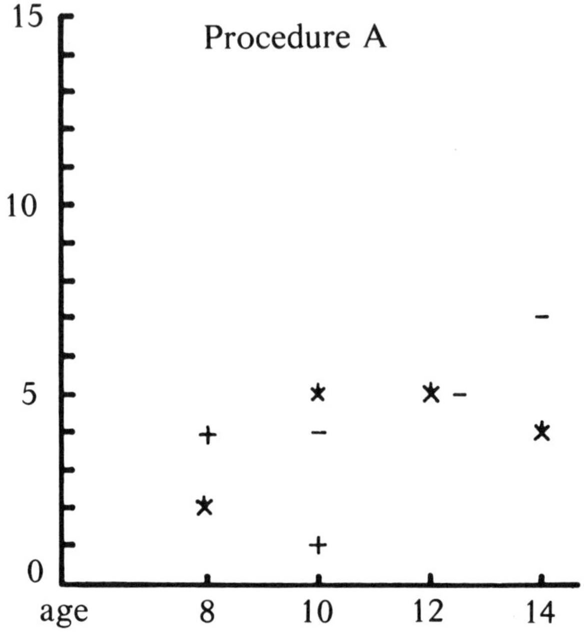

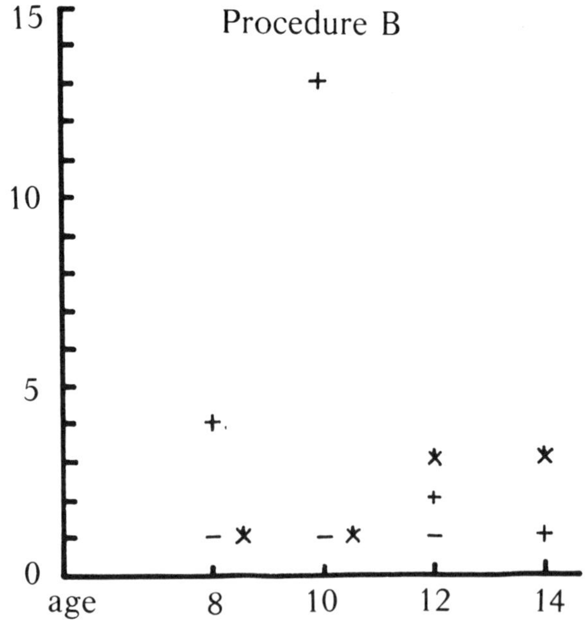

FIGURE 6.1. Frequency of three types of contextualized judgment by age. (+) CI instrumental; (★) CU undecided; (–) CN norm supporting.

CONCLUSION

The data presented can be viewed as strongly suggestive in one general respect, i.e., that it is plausible to expect at each structural level of moral judgment a dynamic developmental pattern in which moral-position-taking predominates over situational or contextual requirements and is eventually replaced by a balance between the two cognitive functions. In other words, the shift from norm or rule-centered judgment toward contextualized judgment without defection from the norm or rule is a move toward a more equilibrated stage at each new structural level of moral judgment. The type of contextualization, however, is qualitatively different at different levels of moral judgment development.

REFERENCES

Colby, A., & Kohlberg, L. (1987). *The measurement of moral judgment.* (Vol. 2). New York: Cambridge University Press.

Edelstein, W., & Noam, G. (1982). Regulatory structures of the self and "postformal" stages in adulthood. *Human Development, 25,* 407-422.

Gilligan, C., & Murphy, J. M. (1979). Development from adolescence to adulthood: The philosopher and the "dilemma of the fact". In D. Kuhn (Ed.), *Intellectual development beyond childhood.* San Francisco: Jossey-Bass.

Kohlberg, L. (1981). *Essays in moral development: Vol. I. The philosophy of moral development.* New York: Harper & Row.

Kohlberg, L. (1984). *Essays in moral development: Vol. II. The psychology of moral development.* New York: Harper & Row.

Labouvie-Vief, G. (1980). Beyond formal operations: Uses and limits of pure logic in life-span development. *Human Development, 23,* 141-161.

Labouvie-Vief, G. (1982). Dynamic development and mature autonomy: A theoretical prologue. *Human Development, 25,* 161-191.

Murphy, J. M., & Gilligan, C. (1980). Moral development in late adolescence and adulthood: A critique and reconstruction of Kohlberg's theory. *Human Development, 23,* 77-104.

Perry, W. B. (1970). *Forms of intellectual and ethical development in the college years.* New York: Holt, Rinehart, & Winston.

Riegel, K. F. (1973). Dialectic operations: The final period of cognitive development. *Human Development, 16,* 346-370.

7 Information Integration in Moral Reasoning: Conceptual and Methodological Implications

Martin F. Kaplan
Northern Illinois University

Moral development is characterized by stage conceptions, in which the individual progresses through a hierarchical series of stages, ordered in a lawful fashion (Kohlberg, 1976; Piaget, 1965; Rest, 1973). People progress at varying rates through a prescribed sequence of stages until some (but not all) reach the theoretically highest stage. Importantly, progression is described as lying in the *reasoning* behind moral behavior and not in the moral *content* or value of the behavior per se (Kohlberg, 1976, Rest, 1973). Much controversy and confusion has arisen over the efficacy of a structural stage analysis and the separation of reasoning and values (see Kohlberg, Levine, & Hewer, 1983, for a review of the controversies). I do not propose to settle questions about structural stages nor to conclude whether development lies in reasoning, values, or both. Instead, I suggest a means of clarifying the reasoning/values distinction by applying a comprehensive model of social judgment to moral judgment. The proposed conceptual and methodological framework enables separation of progressions in reasoning and values and facilitates evaluation of developmental issues. The model also has implications for training moral reasoning, and research on this score is reported.

DEVELOPMENTAL ISSUES

Several paradigms have arisen in the study of moral reasoning, including the judgment of the morality of others' behavior based on their intentions and the consequences of their actions, justice in reward distribution, and reasoning in action choices in moral dilemmas. In the last paradigm, subjects are asked to choose between two actions in a hypothetical scenario, each with positive moral values. This poses a dilemma between the values implied by each choice alternative. Developmental stage or progression is described as lying in the reasoning behind the choice and not in the moral value associated with the chosen alternative (Kohlberg, 1976; Piaget, 1965). A prototypical dilemma, for example, asks whether "Heinz" should steal a drug that may save his wife's life but which is unaffordable. Developmental stage is indexed by the reason given for the choice, and not the choice itself. Kohlberg (1976) described three hierachical reasoning stages. *Preconventional* reasoning emphasizes external rewards and punishments as rationales for choices. *Conventional* reasoning involves acceptance of rules and expectations of significant others, and *Postconventional* reasoning is based on internalized principles of ethical behavior or abstract conceptions of justice. Kohlberg later elaborated the model to include six levels within the original three stage structure.

In addition to movement through the levels of *rationale usage,* a second progression is suggested by Piaget's work in cognition: *Complexity of cognitive processes.* People progress from consideration of choice components as absolutes ("moral realism" or "heteronomous morality") where any component is unchanging in its centrality, to relativistic reasoning ("autonomous reality") where the importance of a particular element (e.g., a conventional rationale) depends on the configuration of other elements. In the former reasoning type, for example, peer approval would have the same influence on choice whether or not the actor is likely to be caught and punished, whereas in the latter type, the impact of peer approval might depend on whether punishment will ensue, whether an ethical principle will be served, and so on. Piaget did not explicitly deal with the question of how people integrate information about preconventional, conventional, and postconventional rationales. Indeed, he thought in terms of isolated variables and the ordering of relations (i.e., importance) among them, and did not address the question of the complexity of these relations (Broughton, 1984). But it can be reasoned that the progression from belief in the immutability of rules (heteronomous morality) to the ability to use different rules at different times (autonomous morality) implies a shift toward determining the influence of each rationale by the context of other information. Recent theorists have considered the question of integrative complexity and suggest that mature reasoning involves higher order reasoning, or the ability to form complex relations among problem terms (Sternberg, 1984). Progression lies in increased sophistication in encoding a wider range of relations (Siegler, 1981). In the realm of moral reasoning, it has been suggested that mature reasoning is contextual, that is, the impact of any single factor depends on the context of other factors (Murphy & Gilligan, 1980). Mature reasoning is not based on universal, invariant principles but involves a stagewise increase in the ability to reflect on more complex social relations (Gibbs

& Widaman, 1982; Roodin, Rybash, & Hoyer, 1984). Thus, there is a trend, beginning with Piaget's suggestion that mature reasoning does not rely on adherance to immutable rules, toward thinking of progression as a matter of increasing complexity in how people relate the variables in a moral problem. There is some evidence for the complexity progression. Wilkening (1979) found that adults are better than children at more complex rules in physical judgments (e.g., multiplying). Anderson and Cuneo (1978) similarly found that multiplying is more chronologically advanced than adding in judgments of area. And Kun, Parsons, and Ruble (1974) report that additive rules give way to multiplying rules in children's predictions of achievement from ability and motivation information. In sum, there is both theory and evidence for a transition from simple, linear modes of reasoning to complex, configural modes in which the contribution of any element is revised in light of the context of other elements. Note that although Kohlberg does not explicitly consider this progression in complexity, his highest stage requires acting solely on the basis of absolute principles of justice, regardless of other factors – an apparent reversal of Piaget's theoretical progression (Murphy & Gilligan, 1980; Rybash, Roodin, & Hoyer, 1983; Sinnott, 1984). Clearly, the issue of integrative complexity requires empirical test.

SOME METHODOLOGICAL AND CONCEPTUAL ISSUES

Reasoning stage has been assessed by interview (Kohlberg, 1976) and paper-pencil (Gibbs & Widaman, 1982; Rest, 1975) techniques. Both techniques are used dually to identify individual reasoning level and to test theory. Subjects are asked to identify (interview) or order (paper-pencil) potential rationales after giving their action choices in dilemma scenarios. Rationales are selected (or scored by the interviewer) from a "shopping list" which reflects the range of pre to postconventional considerations for each choice alternative. For example, in the "Heinz" illustration given earlier, subjects are asked to report the rationales for the action choice of either stealing the drug or not. Several criticisms of stage assessments have emerged (see e.g., Kohlberg et. al., 1983; Kurtines & Greif, 1974) that need not be repeated for our purposes. However, some problems that have received less attention are inherent in these techniques, and these pose methodological and conceptual difficulties for evaluating the central issues in moral reasoning.

One set of problems relates to methodological concerns. First, undue trust is placed on retrospective reports of considerations that putatively influenced the completed choice. Such reports may be inaccurate due to social desirability pressures, rationalization, and so on. Moreover, there is evidence that people do not always know the cues and reasons for their social judgments (Nisbett

& Wilson, 1977). Second, reliance on verbal protocols risks confounding the choice of a particular rationale with verbal fluency (Surber, 1985). Rather than naive reliance on people's reconstruction of their reasoning processes and on uniform verbal fluency, it is preferable (and common practice in the social psychology of judgment) to observe the choices made when different rationales are present or absent in a situation and to infer the relative usage of reasoning elements from the strength and pattern of choice made in the presence of different elements. For a simple example, if we wish to know the relative importance of abstract principles versus reward-punishment rationales, we should covary the likelihood of both elements occurring in the scenario and observe the pattern of choices given different combinations of postconventional and preconventional likelihoods. Will a preconventional rationale be important when a postcoventional element is likely to be present (or absent)? Further illustration of this methodological tact will be given when relevant research is reported.

A third problem with the common questionnaire task is that the dichotomous choice or scoring of rationales loses the subtleties of degrees or mixtures of rationale usage. One cannnot tell whether the respondant used some or all rationale types, and to what degree; nor is there allowance for expression of configural usage (e.g., "A principle of justice is important only when peers will approve of the action"). Uncovering such configuration (or lack therof) is crucial to developmental notions of progressions in complexity but is precluded by present interview and paper-pencil techniques. More on this soon.

The other set of problems strikes at the heart of developmental concepts of progression. First, whereas developmentalists distinguish between moral values ("stealing is bad") and reasoning ("Because you get punished"), the distinction becomes blurred in practice largely because clear conceptualizations and operationalizations are lacking. Evidence shows a link, for example, between particular choices (e.g., "Heinz should steal the drug") and rationales given for the choices (e.g., "Life is more important than property rights"). Some choices are associated with higher level rationales (Martin, Shafto, & Vandeinse, 1977). Second, reasoning levels are explicitly treated as discrete; transition from one level of rationale usage to the next is an all-or-none affair (Kohlberg et. al., 1983). Though the possibility exists that reasoning progresses in degrees (Levine, 1979), assessment and classification are "stacked" to preclude evaluation of continuous developmental changes.

Finally, current conceptions of reasoning progression (and their associated techniques) consider only one aspect of reasoning: usage of rationales. Concern with "reasoning" centers only on the predominant "reason" for a choice and ignores the second aspect of moral cognition that has been identified: the *patterning* or complexity of reasoning. Does one modify reliance on a particular reasoning element when other elements change, that is, is reasoning relative or absolute? Once again, assessment and classification do not permit evaluation of this developmental issue.

The next section introduces a conceptual and methodological means of overcoming these problems in order to evaluate the central issues in moral reasoning development. These issues are (a) whether progressions lie chiefly in values or in reasoning, (b) whether progression is continuous or in discrete stages, (c) whether progression proceeds from greater usage of preconventional, to conventional, then to postconvential rationales, and (d) whether reasoning progresses from simple to more complex forms of rationale usage.

MORAL CHOICE AS INFORMATION INTEGRATION

Information integration theory is a general model of social judgment that has been applied to a wide variety of judgment domains (Anderson, 1981; Kaplan, 1975). In this model, social and other judgments are based on information or beliefs about the judged object. Each piece of information has two subjective properties that can be expressed quantitatively. *Scale value* refers to its value for the dimension of judgment, that is, its evaluative connotation for the judgment in question. For example, the prospect of reward for an action probably has a higher scale value on the dimension "Should (not) steal the drug" than does the prospect of receiving peer disapproval or of being punished; that is, reward has greater value for stealing the drug than does punishment for the act. Each piece of information also has a *weight,* which gives its subjective importance for the judgment. For one person peer (dis-) approval may carry greater weight in determining judgment than the prospect of tangible reward or punishment, whereas for another, the priorities may be reversed. So, scale value refers to the valence of a particular element or rationale of a judgment, and weight refers to *how* that valence is used, that is, the importance of that element to the judgment.

Once information is evaluated and weighed, scale values are integrated into a unitary judgment. For example, knowing that you will be caught and punished (low scale value), that peers will approve your act (high scale value) and that the principle of sancity of life will be served (high scale value), how strongly do you feel that the drug should (should not) be stolen? This shows that moral judgment may be considered as a task (similar to all judgment tasks) of evaluating relevant information, weighing each piece's relative importance, and then "putting it together" to reach the judgment. The integration process is achieved by means on an algebraic cognitive rule, which varies in its complexity. One could, for example, simply add together the values of the information, or one could engage in relative weighting whereby the weighted values are averaged and each weight depends on the value and kind of other information, or even multiply the values so that the effective weight of one piece of information is enhanced by higher values of the other piece of information. The integration process is further illustrated later; for now, note that it involves reasoning about how the pieces "fit together."

Applying an information integration model permits a clear distinction between values and reasoning; indeed, the distinction is at the heart of the model. Moral value refers to the goodness or badness of each piece of information and of the action choice as well, that is, the propitiousness of a particular rationale for an action choice and the overall preference for that choice. In distinction, reasoning resides in the weight assigned to each piece and in the cognitive integration rule used in combining the values. As will be seen, both value and reasoning (weights and integration rule) can be distinctly determined by statistical and graphical analysis.

This distinction permits unambiguous assessment of the locus of developmental progressions. It is possible to see whether progressions lie in values or in reasoning. To illustrate, value progression would be indicated if older children were to choose more strongly to steal the drug, or if they were to feel that peer approval was a better reason for stealing it, compared to younger children. Reasoning progression would be shown if older children were more influenced by peer approval than by potential rewards or punishments, and younger children showed the reverse weighting pattern. And, reasoning progression would also be indexed by shifts to more complex integration rules. There are other advantages to an information integration model. First, the approach looks for patterns of rationale usage (i.e., the integration rule and its complexity), a reasoning function that is overlooked in the Kohlberg approach. Second, the model does not asume a discrete stage structure. It can describe continuous changes in values and reasoning. Weighting is a matter of degree, not an all-or-none usage of a certain rationale type. This results in a more subtle treatment of reasoning. Dichotomous choices of rationales, as made in Kohlbergian interviews or in Rest's paper-pencil test, can mask ambivalence and degrees of rationale usage (Surber, 1985). Kohlberg's theory and method do not lead one to look for degrees of reasoning, nor for changes and interactions in rationale usage as a function of context. The interview task can allow expression of more than one rationale type, and stage mixtures may be scored. However, people are not classed as being in *degrees* of stages but are placed in major and minor or transition stages, retaining a dichotomous flavor. Continuous progression *within* stages is not considered. Subdivision of stages skirts the issue of degree, and classification remains a qualitative, and not a quantitative matter (Gibbs & Widaman, 1982). Specifically, sublevels provided in Kohlberg's theory and scoring do not truly address degrees or mixtures of rationale usage but reflect whether one works within the context of a problem (substage A) or gets to the root of the problem (B) (Gibbs & Widaman, 1982); the distinction is one of depth of insight. The crucial issue remains whether development is in discrete stages (including allowance for transitions) or by continuous accretion (Brainerd, 1978; Levine, 1979; Siegler, 1981). Discovering continous accretions in weighting and integration patterns is integral to the information integration model and permits assessment of the discrete/continous issue.

The model dictates certain methodological practices. Because the focus is on discerning patterns of integration and relative weights of scale values, factorial designs with covariation of information components are desirable. In a typical integration analysis of judgment, the information components are factorially varied, and the subject is asked to judge the object, or make a choice, given the particular configuration of information. Weights and integration rules are then inferred from the patterns of choices and judgments given the systematically varied information components. This permits obtaining continuous estimates of weights of component rationales rather than the dichotomous estimates inherent in the Kohlberg approach. Moreover, this method does not rely on verbal fluency and on retrospective reports of rationale usage, thus avoiding the problems associated with such response requirements.

In summary, the integration conception and methodology is a means of testing implications of Kohlbergian and Piagetian stages while clearly distinguishing between values and reasoning, not assuming discrete stages, and avoiding the problems associated with dichotomous verbal choices and reports. Three expectations are apparent. First, persons located at different reasoning levels will not differ with respect to values assigned to antecedent information components (i.e., rationales) of their choices, or in the choices themselves. Not being punished should be as positive for the decision to steal the drug for people at one level as at another level. Second, persons located at different levels should differ in the weight assigned to given information components. Persons at a higher level should assign more weight to a postconventional rationale, and less to a preconventional rationale, compared to persons at lower reasoning levels. Third, higher level persons should show a more relativistic, complex integration strategy. High-level reasoners might assign little weight to whether they will be punished *if* the likelihood of a principled outcome is high, but greater weight to punishment *if* the principled outcome likelihood is low. Low-level reasoners might assign a constant weight to punishment regardless of the likelihood of postconventional or conventional outcomes.

Brief description of an experiment (Kaplan, 1979) illustrates the model's power to examine these developmental notions. College students, designated as functioning either at a preconventional, conventional, or postconventional level according to the Defining Issues Test (Rest, 1975), indicated on a 20-point scale their strength of belief that an individual should or should not engage in a target act in several different dilemmas. The dilemmas were modifications of those commonly used in assessments of reasoning level (but not those used in the assessment of these subjects). In each dilemma, preconventional, conven-

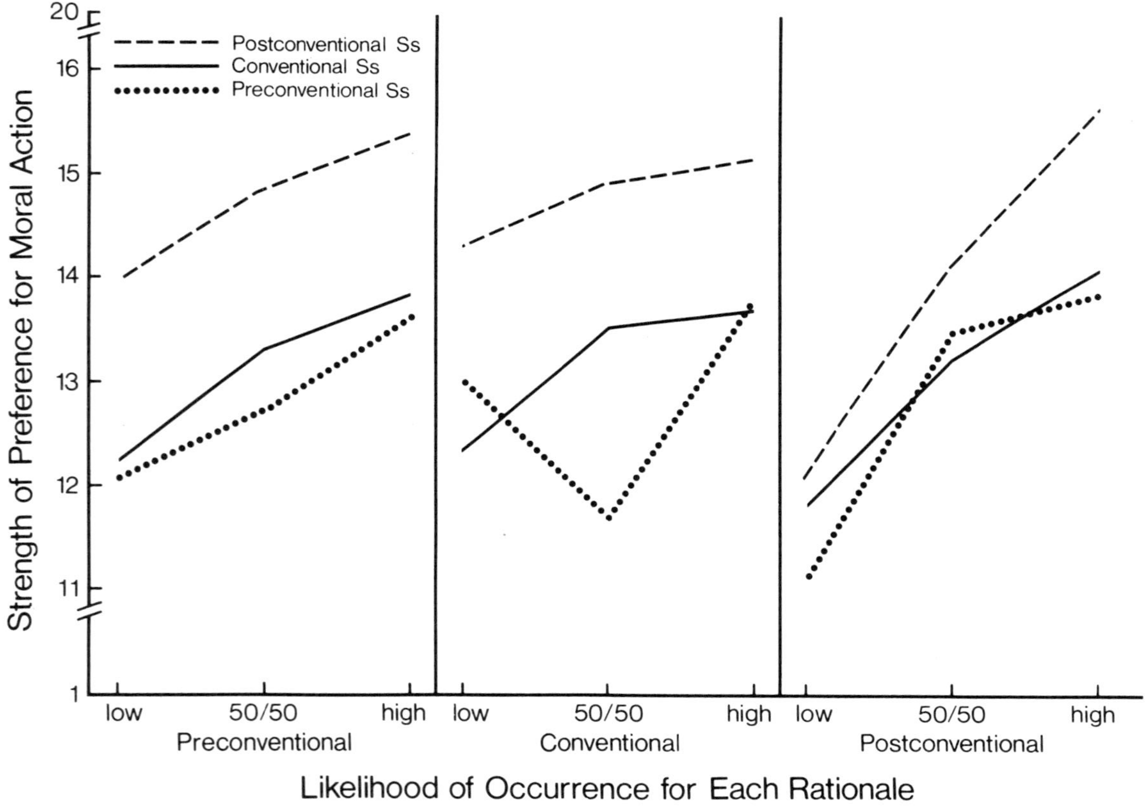

FIGURE 7.1. Choice of moral action as a function of subjects' reasoning level (D.I.T.) and likelihood of preconventional, conventional, and postconventional rationales being present.

tional, and postconventional rationales were given in the form of potential outcomes. Each rationale was also given a likelihood of occurrence, in the form of: "there is a (high/50-50/low) chance that...". For example, "there is a 50-50 chance that family and friends will believe that Heinz was doing his duty as a husband in stealing the drug" gives a medium value, conventional rationale for stealing the drug. There were 27 such dilemmas, constructed from a factorial design with three likelihood levels for each of the three rationale types. Pretesting (see "Training Moral Reasoning," later, for details) disclosed that in each basic scenario, one of the outcomes (e.g., steal the drug) was normatively considered more moral than the other (e.g., don't steal the drug). Responses were scored so that higher ratings reflect a stronger preference for the normatively preferred (more moral) outcome.

A partial account of the results is given in Figure 7.1 which plots the ratings of the subject groups for each pairwise comparison of rationales. Note first that for all subjects, postconventional considerations were weighted most, as shown by the greater slope of the curves in panel C. Second, there was no tendency for any subject group to be more influenced than other groups by rationales "appropriate" to its assessed reasoning level. Conventionals, e.g., do not show a greater slope for variations in conventional rationales than do the other groups (panel B). Statistically, there were no group by likelihood level interactions for any of the rationales. Third, groups did not differ in the complexity of their integration of rationales; the patterns of combination of pairs of rationales were similar for all groups, and the group by rationales by likelihood levels interaction was nonsignificant. This means that groups were similar in how they reacted to different combinations and contexts of rationales and their likelihoods within the factorial design. In short, contrary to developmental notions, the groups did not differ in weight assigned to any given rationale (though they reported such differences in their retrospective accounts on the Defining Issues Test!). Nor did they differ in the complexity of their integration of the rationales. But they did differ in one important way: Students at higher reasoning levels obtained higher overall scores on the experimental dilemmas. Note that the height of the curves in all panels was greatest for postconventional subjects. These subjects simply chose moralistic actions more strongly, a difference between subjects in *value*, not in *reasoning*. Rather than conclude that theory errs in its account of reasoning progression, it is safer to say that the DIT may be measuring *values*, or the preference for moralistic actions, rather that the reasoning process behind choice.

Of course, one may argue that the subject sample was restricted in age and stage difference. But the what is important is that it shows the power of an integration analysis for separating and detecting differences in reasoning and values and testing theoretical assumptions. It also hints that present conceptions and assessments of reasoning levels may confuse values and reasoning. The hint becomes a stronger suspicion in the studies described next.

The reasoning/value confusion becomes particularly troublesome when we consider the widespread use of interventions in schools to advance reasoning levels. These programs generally aim to advance reasoning (the rationales that guide choices) without tampering with underlying values and ultimate choices. Yet, they typically use guided discussion of moral dilemmas and other morally toned materials, with students encouraged to share their opinions. This poses the danger that values will be inculcated during discussion, an outcome that is counter to the developmental principle that reasoning level is independent of values. One should, in principle, be able to advance reasoning level (weighting of rationales and complexity of integration rules) without changing values. But when classes discuss moral dilemmas, individual members may shift their values toward the alternatives that are most normatively preferred and discussed; this is the well-documented "group polarization" effect (Kaplan & Miller, 1983). Polarization, which describes a shift in choices and opinions toward the prevalent or most discussed position, is especially likely in groups that are in extended contact, such as ongoing classes. Consequently, if moral education classes discuss choice dilemmas, and if discussion centers on the "goodness" of choice alternatives and underlying rationales, there is a real possibility of value shifts, in distinction to reasoning progression.

Two studies will now be reported. In one (Kaplan, 1983), information integration methods were used to assess the effects on reasoning and values of an existing training program that was based on Kohlbergian principles. In the other study (Kaplan & Amstutz, 1985), students were given training designed to modify integration rules, and effects on reasoning and values were assessed.

Study 1: Assessing an Ongoing Program

The first task was to construct a set of choice dilemmas that would be close to those typically used in interview and questionnaire assessments, but that would contain the three types of rationales with varying likelihoods of occurrence. Eight moral dilemmas were obtained from the scenarios used in the Defining Issues Test (Rest, 1975) and in standard interviews (Kohlberg, 1976)[1]. In pretesting, it was found that preferences existed for one over the other of the two alternative actions in each scenario; for example, "steal the drug" was preferred over "don't steal the drug." On a scale where "20" represented one

[1] Heinz and the drug, Webster and hiring, The strike, Doctor's dilemma, Student newspaper, Student takeover, Bingo game, Escaped prisoner.

choice and "1" the other, the degree of preference for a given choice ranged from 12.55 to 14.47 (Mean = 13.33); note that an equal preference would incur a mean rating of 10. Preference tendencies were taken into account in the final scenarios and in their presentation (discussed later).

With the help of an educational consultant, scenarios were slightly revised to accomodate a sixth grade reading level. For each scenario, eight modifications were devised varying the likelihood that a preconventional (Pr), conventional (Co), or postconventional (Po) consequence would ensue if one of the actions would be chosen (see following examples). In any scenario there was reported either a high or low chance that each type of consequence would take place. These considerations were worded so that in half the scenarios a high chance of occurence would argue for the less normatively preferred action, and in the remaining half, a high chance would favor the more normatively preferred action. For example, "There is a high chance that the authorities will discover who Thompson really is and Mrs. Jones would be prosecuted for withholding information" gives a high likelihood of a preconventional outcome favoring reporting an escaped prisoner – the less normatively preferred action. "There is a high chance that giving food on credit would teach others that the well-being of people is important for its own sake" illustrates a high likelihood of a postconventional outcome, which favors the normatively preferred action of giving food on credit to strikers. Finally, "There is a low chance that Sam's family and society in general would approve of his giving food" presents a low likelihood of a conventional consequence favoring the normatively preferred action, that is, it illustrates a rationale with a *low* scale value.

In this manner, each scenario was the basis for a 2 x 3 design of high and low likelihood of Pr, Co, and Po considerations. Eight sets of booklets were arranged by cyclical permutation so that each booklet contained a complete design of the eight combinations of Pr, Co, and Po considerations, one combination to each scenario. Across the eight booklets, each basic scenario was ultimately paired with each rationale possibility. In short, combinations of Pr, Co, and Po likelihoods were balanced across the eight scenarios.

Subjects were 128 freshmen in an Illinois high school. Half the subjects were tested immediately after completing a mandatory training course in moral decision making, patterned after the moral education training developed by the Kohlbergians (e.g., Simon, Howe, & Kirschenbaum, 1972), and half were tested prior to taking the course. Sexes were equally distributed within the two groups. The course consisted of a one – week series of daily sessions in which decision making in value-oriented life situations were discussed with the goal of thinking about the components and processes involved in important decisions. None of the experimental dilemmas were used in the course.

Each booklet was evaluated by eight students from the trained and the control groups. Order of scenarios within each booklet was randomized. Students indicated how strongly they felt the character in each dilemma should engage in the alternate acts on a 20-point scale [e.g., "Should not steal the drug

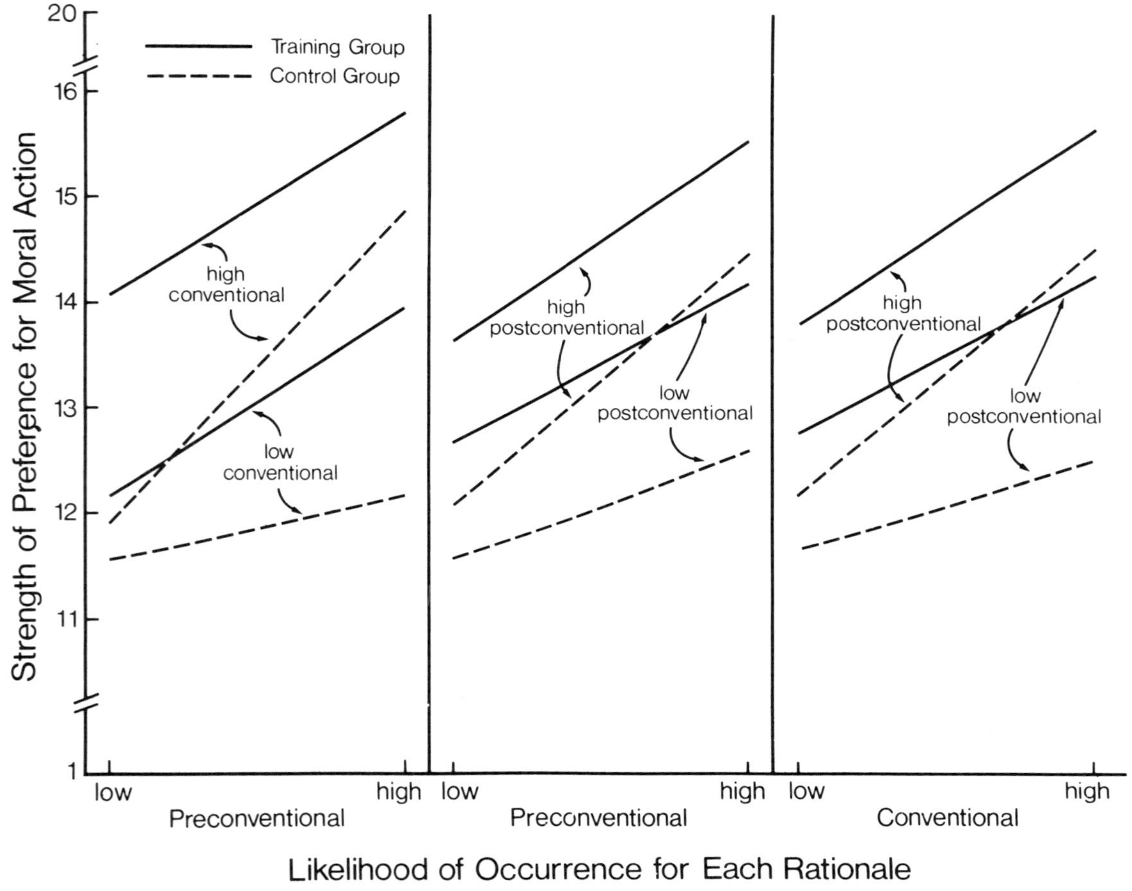

FIGURE 7.2. Choice of moral action by students in a traditional training program and controls as a function of likelihood of preconventional, conventional, and postconventional rationales being present: Plotted by pairs of rationales.

(1)... Should steal the drug (20)"]. Care was taken to balance scale position of the alternative given under (1) or (20) with affirmative or negative wording, and with normative preference (normatively preferred alternative positioned on the left or the right of the scale). By reversing the score of half the responses, higher scores thus reflected more moralistic (i.e., normatively preferred) choices.

Figure 7.2 summarizes the results, plotting pairwise comparisons of rationales. The left panel, for example, plots preferences for the target action given high or low likelihoods of conventional rationales (ordinate) paired with high- or low-preconventional likelihoods (abscissa) collapsing over post-conventional levels. Recall that higher scores reflect a rating more toward the moralistic choice. Trained students differed from controls in two ways: They responded more strongly in the direction of the moralistic choice (higher scores in the Figure), and showed less configuration or relativity in considering rationales. Note the lack of graphical interaction in the curves for trained students, indicating that the effect of a given rationale was independent of the context of other rationales. Trained students' greater moralism is reflected in a statistical effect for training. Considering the groups separately, trained students showed no statistical interactions between pairs of rationales (note the parallel curves in all three panels), whereas controls showed all three possible interactions. Finally, there were no differences between the groups in the effect of any of the rationales, that is, interactions of groups with each of Pr, Co, and Po were not present. In short, trained students were not more influenced by postconventional rationales and were not less influenced by preconventional rationales, compared to controls. *But* they were less contextual in reasoning, and more moralistic in values than the controls.

Proponents of moral education maintain that reasoning, and not values, are being changed (Kohlberg & Mayer, 1972; Simon et al., 1972). Here we see the reverse of these claims. Training resulted in no greater use of postconventional principles, nor lesser reliance on preconventional or conventional. Worse, students who were untouched by training showed the relativism that Piaget attributed to autonomous morality, whereas trained students evidenced more absolutistic reasoning. An example of the former is in the left panel of Figure 7.2: Preconventional rationales were unimportant if a conventional outcome was unlikely but became important (as shown in the relative slopes of the curves) if a conventional outcome was certain. Training imparted a greater sense of moralism, and adding insult to injury, led to retrogression in reasoning complexity. If the goal of moral education is to advance reasoning without directing students toward specific moral choices, something went wrong. What went wrong? First, programs typically make use of morally toned discussion material. This leads students to discuss moral values (it would be hard not to) and produces polarization toward preferred actions. Second, emphasis may be on separating informational elements and considering each singly rather than in relation to one another, leading to a more additive, nonconfigural combination of elements.

It can be argued that the target program was an anomaly, unrepresentative of all such programs. But this would miss the point that all programs can and should be evaluated by these means for their effect on values and reasoning. These results give cause to worry about what they may be accomplishing. Perhaps some programs do meet their goals; this is something we should see.

The next study tried to train reasoning without training moral values. It has two crucial elements: Discussion tasks were unrelated to the moral dilemmas typically used in training and in assessment, and "training" was focused on reasoning about the integration of elements. This strategy goes directly to reasoning, and avoids inculcating moral values.

Study 2: Training Reasoning Without Training Values

Two groups of high schoool freshmen were designated as training and control group, 32 students in each. Students in two sections of a required speech course comprised the training group, and controls were students in other sections of the speech course, but tested in study hall. The former group was given four one-hour sessions of cognitive reasoning training on consecutive days in class. In each session, a different judgmental task was used for illustrating simple and complex integration strategies. Tasks were unrelated to moral dilemmas and involved social issues with moral overtones. All had previously been employed in the author's research and had resulted in nonconfigural averaging of information by college students. In order of daily usage, these were: (a) deciding how likely one would be to help a student by serving in an experiment, given information about experimenter need and subject cost; (b) judging guilt of a student accused of cheating based on his or her actions and the severity of penalties; (c) assigning a sentence to a defendant tried for car theft given his motives and the damage to the car; and (d) attributing suspiciousness to suspects in murder mysteries given their opportunities and motives. The format of each training session was the same. Students made their judgments for the particular task, and an experimenter then described how students often use a simple integration rule to combine the two elements in the task. She went on to describe, with examples, more complex integration, guiding the class to discussion of complex possibilities. For example, she led students to see how, in a mystery, one might give less weight to opportunities if motive is weak, and more if motive is strong. Conversely, one might not be as influenced by motive if opportunity is weak than if it is strong. Each discussion built on the lessons of previous sessions. After the class seemed to understand the principle, it retook the day's task. Responses before and after discussion were on numerical scales of the order: "(1) Would definitely not help the experimenter. Would definitely help the experimenter (20)" and "How suspicious is person X, from 0% to 100% certainty?"

On the 5th day, students completed the eight moral dilemmas previously described without discussion. The control group responded to the four judgment tasks and the moral reasoning instrument on consecutive days, but without guided discussion.

The trained students appeared to have learned their lesson. They showed a progressive increase in use of configural integration rules over the training sessions. For example, after training, students were more affected by a murder suspect's opportunities when he had a strong, compared to weak motive. In contrast, control students used noninteractive combination throughout the sessions with the instruction task.

Did training generalize to choice and reasoning in moral dilemmas? Recall that in the study of a more traditional program, reasoning became *less* complex with training. Here, it became more complex. Note in Figure 7.3 in which all pairwise comparisons between rationales are plotted, all three panels show statistical and graphical divergence (an index of complexity) for trained students. In all instances, a high likelihood of any one outcome increased usage of other outcome rationales. For example, if there is a high likelihood that peers will support the more moral act (right panel), then likelihood of a principled rationale occurring matters more. Note that the distance between postconventional curves (i.e., the difference in action preference as a function of postconventional likelihoods) is greater when conventional likelihood is high. In contrast, significant divergence occurred for controls only in the left panel, which displays the Pr/Co comparisons. In other pairwise comparisons, they seem to have considered rationale components noninteractively.

Unlike the case with the standard program, trained students did not uniformly choose more moral alternatives. The present training did not lead to value change toward greater moralism. This can be credited to the facts that discussion did not employ the target moral dilemmas and that it was guided tackle reasoning about stimulus *use* rather than *values*.

There were no group differences in weight assigned to particular rationales, the other facet of reasoning. This is not surprising because training did not involve moral dilemmas, nor tackle the distinction between principles, social conventions, or personal consequences. It would be useful to next train students in such matters using tasks other than moral dilemmas.

CONCLUDING COMMENTS

This chapter shows the utility of an information integration approach for separating reasoning from values. Because this distinction is fundamental for both information integration and for developmental theorizing, the approach enables the clear investigation of issues central to stage conceptions of moral

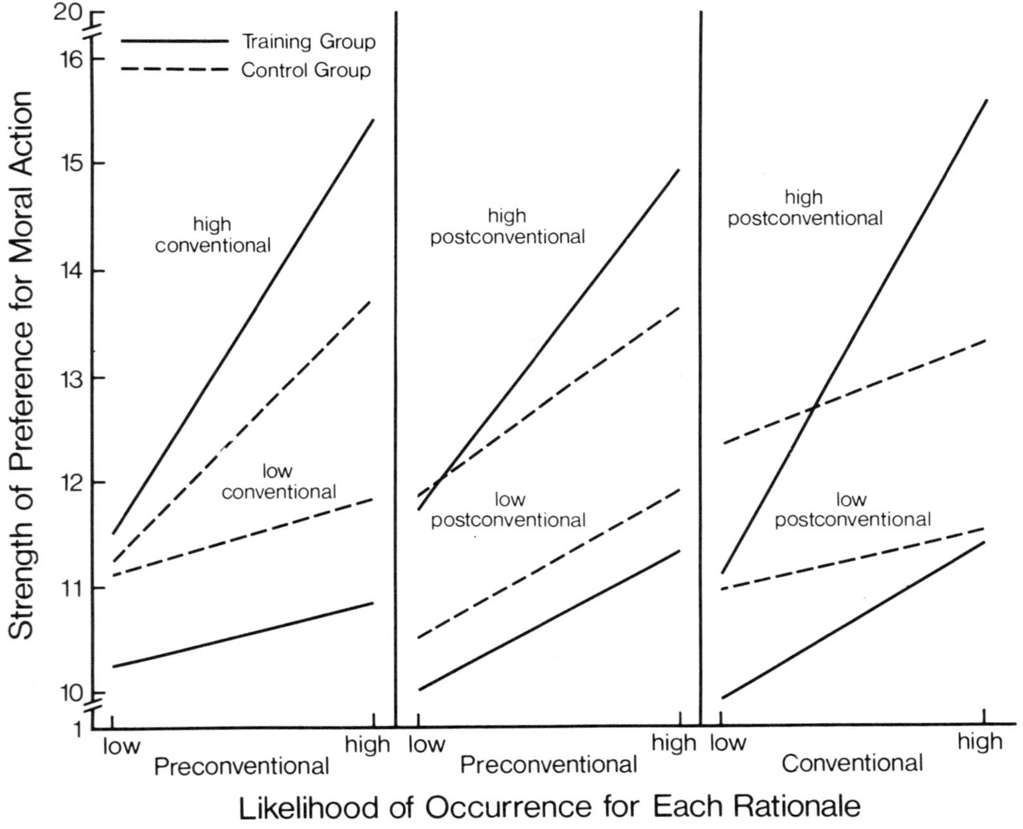

FIGURE 7.3. Choice of moral action by students in an experimental training program and controls as a function of likelihood of preconventional, conventional, and postconventional rationales being present: Plotted by pairs of rationales.

development. Research reported here is illustrative and demonstrates the power of the model to address at least four issues: (a) Whether stage differences lie whether in values or reasoning and to what extent, (b) whether differences between individuals and stages are discrete or continuous, (c) whether reasoning progression proceeds through a sequence of usage of certain rationales for choices, and (d) whether reasoning also progresses from simple to complex or relativistic forms of rationale usage. The last issue has been relatively ignored in moral development work, and the information integration approach ought to refocus attention on this aspect of reasoning.

By use of information integration concepts and methods, we avoid some pitfalls of traditional means of assessing and modifying reasoning stages. We found that questionnaire methods may be tapping value differences rather than reasoning. We also found a harmful and retrogressive effect in a standard training program and showed that reasoning could be modified in a hierarchically advanced direction by training aimed at integration processes.

Findings give comfort to the notion of the unity of cognitive development, or structural parallelism (Piaget, 1965; Tomlinson-Keasey & Keasey, 1974). Students were able to apply rules learned in donor domains of different content (e.g., attributing suspicion in a murder mystery) to the recipient domain of moral choice. On a similar note, cognitive researchers (e.g., Gick & Holyoak, 1983; Reed, Dempster, & Ettinger, 1985) are showing that schemas and rules learned in one sort of word problem can be transferred analogically to other word problems given certain facilitating conditions. It would be fruitful to adopt such transfer techniques for training the integration rule and weighting components of moral reasoning. By using tasks that are unrelated to moral choice in content, discussion would not simultaneously induce certain moral values. The research reported here holds promise for the successful training of moral reasoning by analogy.

There is other work on information integration in moral development. Leon (1980) and Surber (1985) have applied the model to the integration of intentions and consequences in judging the morality of others, and Kaplan and Yehl (1984) report an application to distributive justice in reward allocation. These instances converge to show that central empirical issues in moral values can be approached with methods other than those that have been traditionally used, and with beneficial results.

ACKNOWLEDGMENTS

The author wishes to thank Colleen Surber for her excellent comments on an earlier version of this chapter, and Jane Abramson of Antioch, Illinois High School for her cooperation and help in conducting two studies at the school.

REFERENCES

Anderson, N. H. (1981). *Foundations of information integration theory.* New York: Academic Press.

Anderson, N. H., & Cuneo, D. O. (1978). The height + width rule in children's judgments of quantity. *Journal of Experimental Psychology: General, 107,* 335-378.

Brainerd, C. J. (1978). The stage question in cognitive-developmental theory. *Behavioral and Brain Sciences, 1;* 173-182.

Broughton, J. M. (1984). Not beyond formal operations but beyond Piaget. In M. L. Commons, F. A. Richards, & C. Armon (Eds.), *Beyond formal operations.* New York: Praeger.

Gibbs, J. C., & Widaman, K. FL (1982). *Social intelligence: Measuring the development of sociomoral reflection.* Englewood Cliffs, NJ: Prentice Hall

Gick, M. L., & Holyoak, K. J. (1983). Schema induction and analogical transfer. *Cognitive Psychology, 15,* 1-38.

Kaplan, M. F. (1975). Information integration in social judgment: Interaction of judge and informational components. In M.F. Kaplan & S. Schwartz (Eds.) *Human judgment and decision processes.* New York: Academic Press.

Kaplan, M. F. (1979). *Cognitive processes in morality judgment.* Paper Presented at the annual meeting of the Midwestern Psychological Association, Chicago, IL (May).

Kaplan, M. F. (1983). *Effect of training on reasoning in moral choice.* Paper presented at the annual meeting of the Midwestern Psychological Association, Chicago, IL (May).

Kaplan, M. F., & Amstutz, D. K. (1985) . *Training moral reasoning without training morality.* Paper presented at the annual meeting of the Midwestern Psychological Association, Chicago, IL (May).

Kaplan, M. F., & Miller, C. E. (1983). Group discussion and judgment. In P. Paulus, (Ed.), *Basic group processes.* New York: Springer-Verlag.

Kaplan, M. F., & Yehl, H. M. (1984). *Deservingness and equality in children's reward allocations: Developmental trends.* Paper presented at the annual meeting of the Midwestern Psychological Association. Chicago, IL (May).

Kohlberg, L. (1976). Moral stages and moralization: The cognitive developmental approach. In T. Lickona (Ed), *Moral development and behavior.* New York: Holt, Rinehart, and Winston.

Kohlberg, L., Levine, C., & Hewer, A. (1983). *Moral stages: A current formulation and a response to critics.* New York: Karger.

Kohlberg, L., & Mayer, R. (1972). Development as the aim of education. *Harvard Educational Review, 42,* 449–496.

Kun, A., Parsons, J. E., & Ruble, D. N. (1974). Development of integration processes using ability and effort information to predict outcome. *Developmental Psychology, 10,* 721–732.

Kurtines, W., & Greif, E. G. (1974). The development of moral thought: Review and evaluation of Kohlberg's approach. *Psychological Bulletin, 81,* 453-470.

Leon, M. (1980). Coordination of intent and consequence information in children's moral judgments. In F. Wilkening, J. Becker, & T. Trabasso (Eds.), *Information integration by children. Hillsdale, NJ: Lawrence Erlbaum Associates.*

Levine, C. (1979). Stage acquisition and stage use: An appraisal of stage displacement explanations of variation in moral reasoning. Human Development, 22, 145–164.

Martin, R. M., Shafto, M., & Vandeinse, W. (1977). The reliability, validity, and design of the Defining Issues Test. *Developmental Psychology, 13,* 460-468.

Murphy, J M., & Gilligan, C (1980). Moral development in late adolescence and adulthood: A critique and reconstruction of Kohlberg's theory. *Human Development, 23,* 77-104.

Nisbett, R. E., & Wilson, T. D. (1977). Telling more than we can know: Verbal reports on mental processes. *Psychological Review, 84,* 231–259.

Piaget, J. (1965). *The moral judgment of the child.* New York: The Free Press.

Reed, S. K., Dempster, A., & Ettinger, M. (1985). Usefulness of analogous solutions for solving algebra word problems. *Journal of Experimental Psychology: Learning, Memory, and Cognition, 11,* 106–125.

Rest, J. (1973). The 529 hierarchical nature of moral judgment. *Journal of Personality, 41,* 86–109.

Rest, J. (1975). Longitudinal study of the Defining Issues Test of moral judgment: A strategy for analyzing developmental change. *Developmental Psychology, 11,* 738–748.

Roodin, P. A., Rybash, J. M., & Hoyer, W. J. (1984). Affect in adult congition: A constructivist view of moral thought and action. In C. Z. Malatesta & C. E. Izard (Eds.), *Emotion in adult development.* Beverly Hills, CA: Sage.

Rybash, J. M., Roodin, P. A., & Hoyer, W. J. (1983). Expression of moral thought in late adulthood. *The Gerontologist, 23,* 254-260.

Siegler, R. S. (1981). Developmental sequences within and between concepts. *Monographs of the Society for Child Development, 46,* (2, No. 189).

Simon, S. B., Howe, L. W., & Kirschenbaum, H. (1972). *Values clarification.* New York: Hart.

Sinnott, J. D. (1984). Postformal reasoning: The relativistic stage. In M. L. Commons, F. A. Richards, & C. Armon (Eds.), *Beyond formal operations.* New York: Praeger.

Sternberg, R. J. (1984). Higher order reasoning in postformal operational thought. In M. L. Commons, F. A. Richards, & C. Armon (Eds.), *Beyond formal operations.* New York: Praeger.

Surber, C. F. (1985). Applications of information integration to children's social cognition. In J. B. Pryor & J. D. Day (Eds.), *The development of social cognition.* New York: Springer-Verlag.

Tomlinson-Keasey, C., & Keasey, C. B. (1974). The mediating role of cognitive development in moral judgment. *Child Development, 45,* 291-298.

Wilkening, F. (1979). Combining of stimulus dimensions in children's and adult's judgment of area: An information integration analysis. *Developmental Psychology, 15,* 25-33.

Part 3

MORAL DECISIONS AND FUNCTIONING OF MORAL VALUES

8 Equality and Economic Efficiency: Is There a Trade – off?[1]

Morton Deutsch
Teachers College, Columbia University

Economic inequality tends to undermine equality in other spheres. Economists are aware of this regrettable tendency, but they commonly assume that if the goal of economic equality were to be pursued, economic inefficiency would result. As Okun (1975, p. 48) stated, "Any insistence on carving the pie into equal slices would shrink the pie. That fact poses the trade-off between economic equality and efficiency."

Is there, inevitably, the trade-off between efficiency and equality that is so commonly assumed? This paper summarizes my experimental research, which answers this question. It also reviews scholarly literature relating to work concerning this issue: the diverse research dealing with different forms of work compensation, ownership, participation, and control.

EXPERIMENTAL RESEARCH

Studies of Cooperation-Competition

My early experiment on the effects of cooperation and competition on group process (Deutsch, 1949b) has direct relevance to basic issues relating to the

[1] This paper is based upon material presented more fully in Deutsch, M. (1985). *Distributive justice: A social-psychological perspective*. New Haven: Yale University Press.

consequences of an egalitarian as compared to a meritocratic system of distributing rewards. The experiment studied the effects of two different distributive principles: a competitive – meritocratic principle and a cooperative – egalitarian principle.

The result of the experiment showed striking differences between the cooperative-egalitarian and competitive-meritocratic groups. The students in the groups that operated under the equality principle (i.e., the "cooperative" groups) were not only more productive, they also developed friendlier interpersonal relations, and felt more esteemed and more self-confident as compared to those in the groups that functioned under the competitive – meritocratic principle.[2]

Since my study of cooperation and competition in 1949, hundreds of related studies have been conducted (see Johnson & Johnson, 1983). The results of this extensive research are consistent with my early study. The findings are unequivocal in demonstrating substantial differences in the social psychological effects of the two distributive principles on interpersonal relations, self-attitudes, attitude toward work, and group performance.

Experimental Studies of the Effects of Different System of Distributive Justice

Recently, my students and I (Deutsch, 1985) have conducted a series of studies that was stimulated by the assumption implicit in equity theory that people will be more productive if they are rewarded in proportion to their contribution. The research on cooperation-competition had clearly demonstrated that this assumption is not correct when the individuals are working on tasks where it is helpful for them to cooperate, to share information and resources, or to coordinate their activities. Perhaps the assumption has validity only when the individuals are involved in noninterdependent tasks in work which is not facilitated by effective cooperation. In fact, careful thought about the circumstances under which rewarding members, in proportion to their contribution to a group (or rewarding individuals in proportion to their performance), would most likely induce relatively high productivity suggests that there are a number of basic requisites. These include the following:

---

[2] It should be noted that the meritocratic principle is not always competitive; it is so only when a fixed amount (a constant sum) is being allocated. Hence, the more one person gets, the less is available for another. An individualistic form of this principle occurs whenever the amount of the allocation is variable and dependent on the level of the total contributions; here, the allocations the individuals receive are independent of one another. Thus, the result of this early experiment had no direct relevance to the individualistic form of meritocracy.

1. the task to be accomplished must be clearly defined and specified;
2. the individuals involved must believe that their performance can be measured reliably, validly, and with sufficient precision;
3. achievement must be readily susceptible to continued improvement by increased effort, and this is believed to be so by the individuals involved;
4. the type of reward offered for performance must be desired by the individual, and its value the individual must increase with the amount of reward he or she receives;
5. the dependence of an individual's reward upon his or her accomplishment must be known to the individual and subjectively salient during his or her work; and
6. neither individual nor group task performance should depend upon effective social cooperation.

It is evident that the conditions described above are rarely found in the "real world" of work. However, they can be created in the laboratory. Our first two studies were fashioned to create the conditions likely to maximize the chance of obtaining support for the assumption that performance will be enhanced by the expectation of being rewarded in proportion to one's contributions. In them, the subjects worked in separated cubicles, on identical tasks that were neither interesting nor difficult. Both experiments systematically varied the type of distributive system, using the same task; the second also varied the magnitude of the rewards available to the subjects and used female as well as male subjects. In a third experiment, the subjects worked face to face on several different types of very brief tasks under the different distributive systems. In contrast to the first three, the subjects in the fourth study worked alone under one or another reward system similar in character to the different distributive justice systems. In a fifth study, the subjects worked face to face on a highly interdependent, extended task. In a sixth, the "goods" being distributed within the group were grades rather than money; the grades were distributed either according to the equality or proportionality principle and were based upon either the amount of effort or the level of performance.

Four different principles of allocating the group's earnings to its members were used in a number of the studies. These were described as follows:

> Winner-takes-all: Under this system, whoever best performs the task in the group wins all the money the group is paid.
>
> Proportionality: Under this system, each person is rewarded in proportion to his or her contribution to the group score. In other words, the person who contributes 50% of the group's total output will get 50% of the money to be distributed within the group; a person who contributes 10% of the group's total output would get 10% of the money to be distributed within the group, and so on.

Equality: Under this system, each person in the group will get an equal share of the money to be distributed within the group. In other words, each person will get 1/3 of the group's total earnings.

Need: Under the need distribution system, each group member will be rewarded according to the need expressed on the biographical data sheet. In other words, the person who needs the money most would get proportionately more money; the person who needs the money least would get the least amount of money.

The overall results of the six experiments will be presented in terms of a number of key questions asked of all the data.

Did the different distributive systems have differential effects on performance? There is clear and consistent evidence in all of the relevant experiments that there are no reliable effects of the distribution system on individual or group productivity when neither individual nor group task performance depends on effective social cooperation. This result is obtained when the individual is working in a group context and also when he or she is working alone. That is, there is no evidence to indicate that people work more productively when they are expecting to be rewarded in proportion to their performance than when they are expecting to be rewarded equally or on the basis of need.

Were there initial differences in attitudes toward the different distributive systems? Initially, the subjects strongly preferred proportionality over the other distributive systems. The second most favored was equality; need was disfavored; and they had the most negative reaction to the winner-takes-all system.

Were attitudes toward other group members affected by the different distributive principles? Even when the groups were nominal rather than interacting groups (as in the first two experiments), there were some significant effects of the distributive system on attitudes toward other group members. The subjects in the equality and need conditions reported having cooperative feelings towards one another; those in the winner-takes-all and proportionality conditions reported having "competitive" feelings toward one another.

How were attitudes toward the tasks and work affected by the different distributive systems? Under the equality system, the subjects found the tasks more interesting and more pleasant than in the other systems. They also reported the highest intrinsic motivation to perform well, the highest motivation to perform because of task enjoyment, a high desire to increase the group's performance, and the lowest desire to outperform the other group members. Subjects, in all conditions, indicated very high intrinsic motivation to perform well, and this was rated as the strongest component of their motivation to perform well.

Did the high, medium, and low performers in the various conditions differ in their preferences and attitudes? Even before task performance occurred, those who were to have different performance ranks in their groups had different perferences regarding the distribution principles: the better one's future performance, the more one preferred the winner-takes-all principle and the less one preferred the need and equality principles; the medium performers (those whose performance was neither best nor worst) preferred the proportionality principle more than either the low or high performers. In the nominal group, the relationship between task performance and preferences for distributive principle remained essentially the same from the pre-task to post-task measurement. Parallel results were obtained for the rating of the fairness of the distributive principle.

However, in the face-to-face interacting groups, the relationship between task performance and preferences for the different distributive systems changed during the course of the experiment. After performing the various tasks, the proportionality, equality, and need systems were in each case just as likely to be chosen by high and low performers. Only the choice of the winner-takes-all system appeared to reflect self-interest: being chosen by "winners" only.

What were the pre–experimental correlates of initial attitudes toward the different distributive systems? Preferences for winner-takes-all and, to a lesser extent for proportionality, were associated with a sense of power, toughness, self-confidence, and a more conservative political orientation, a feeling of competitiveness and a tendency to downplay one's groupmates. In contrast, preferences for the equality and need principles were correlated with more favorable attitudes toward one's fellow group members and less favorable views of one's own chances and capabilities. The greater the tendency to be Machiavellian, the higher the subject's preference for the winner-takes-all system and the lower their preference for equality.

Our results provide little support for the common assumption that productivity would be higher when earnings are closely tied to performance. Despite the fact that the tasks were neither particularly interesting nor demanding, and despite participating in the experiment primarily to earn money, the subjects seemed more motivated to perform well by their own needs to do as well as they could rather that by the greater amount of pay they might earn from higher performance in the proportionality and winner-takes-all conditions. Their motivation to perform was determined more by self-standards than by external reward.

These results are not surprising if one takes into account that the subjects were college students who were not alienated from themselves, their colleagues, or the experimenters. They had no reason not to do as well as they could whether or not they would earn money by so doing. If they had felt alienated from themselves and their capabilities and had little pride in their own effectiveness, then their performances might have been more influenced by the external reward. It is possible that the assumption that people will be more productive if they are rewarded in proportion to their contribution is valid only when people are alienated from their work or from those for whom they are working. Given the nature of much work and of many employee-employer relations, it would not be surprising if alienation from work were quite common.

RESEARCH IN THE WORKPLACE

The research that I have summarized in the preceding section clearly indicates that an equal distribution of rewards or earnings within a group does not result in less effective individual or group performance than a meritocratic one; to the contrary, when the task required coordination, sharing, communication, or interdependent activity among group members, the performance of egalitarian groups was superior. However, these were laboratory and classroom groups; the people involved were students, the rewards that were distributed did not affect the individual's standard of living, the groups had short lives, and so on. Perhaps the commonly assumed trade-off between efficiency and equality would appear in research on "real-life" egalitarian work groups, even if it does not necessarily occur in the laboratory or classroom.

Here, I briefly review the scholarly literature dealing with different forms of worker compensation, ownership, participation, and control to see whether equality and efficiency are incompatible. However, before proceeding with this review, the meaning of economic egalitarianism is considered.

The Meaning of Economic Egalitarianism

In the literature on economic democracy, worker cooperatives, and the like, there is a clearly emerging social ideal of economic egalitarianism that has several key components. Central to the ideal of economic egalitarianism is the view that the workplace should be a cooperative rather than an authoritarian or adversarial system (Whyte & Blasi, 1982). A cooperative framework is required to do away with the oppositional, alienating tendencies inherent in the power differences between the bosses and the bossed as well as those implicit in the different economic interests of employers and employees. Worker cooperatives are democratically controlled by those who work in them. In small cooperative enterprises, decisions are usually made by the entire work group in frequent meetings. Larger ones have management positions that are filled by election on the basis of one person, one vote. Such positions are usually subject to rotation and are open to all qualified members. Managers can be recalled by the members; ultimate authority rests in the work force. Full worker participation in decision making exists at all levels of the organization. The opportunity for informed and effective participation is aided by training and full access to relevant information.

How the income and surplus produced by the cooperative should be distributed is decided by the workforce. The tendency is toward equality; differences, when they exist, between the highest and lowest paid worker are much smaller than in privately owned firms. Profit or surplus may be used for reinvestment within the firm to create new jobs, improve working conditions, or improve productivity. It may be invested in education, health clinics, daycare centers, or other social and community purposes; or it may be distributed in the form of bonuses or increased benefits.

Land, buildings, machinery, and other assets and liabilities of the cooperative are owned by the workforce. Unlike the situation in employee-owned corporations, where the shares they own in the corporation can be sold to other individuals (including outsiders), members of a worker cooperative cannot sell their share of ownership except to the cooperative. The value of a cooperative member's share is determined by the value of his or her internal account. The initial balance in this account is determined by the membership fee or the member's initial financial contribution at the start of the cooperative. At the end of each fiscal year, the member's portion of the cooperative's surplus (or loss) is added to (or subtracted from) his or her account balance. When a person terminates membership, the balance in the member's account is paid out to the ex-member over a specified number of years.

Patterns of Compensation

The available research on performance-based pay plans in industry (summarized in Katzell & Yankelovich, 1975, and Lawler, 1971, 1981) does not speak clearly nor reliably to the question of whether there is a trade-off between egalitarian wage structures and work efficiency. Thus, there is some research evidence to suggest that individuals work more efficiently when their pay is clearly linked to their performance. But there are many qualifications that have to be added to this statement. First, the research does not demonstrate that it is the connection between pay and performance rather than the connection with accountability (i.e., with performance appraisal and feedback) or with other confounded factors that is instrumental.

There is also some research evidence suggesting that performance-based pay plans, where the performing unit is the group (department, plant, or firm), can lead to more efficiency than pay plans based on individual performance when cooperative work is required. Such plans tend to be more egalitarian than plans based on individual performance. Group plans, in addition, are less plagued by some of the measurement and other administrative problems of individual merit pay systems.

I could find no research evidence that directly addresses the question of whether individual as compared to group merit pay systems lead to more efficient retention of high performing employess and more efficient elimination of lower performing ones. One reason for assuming that egalitarian pay sysems are relatively inefficient is because high performers presumably could earn more in a nonegalitarian system and, hence, would be likely to leave the egalitarian system; this would not be the case in an individually-based, merit system. There are other reasons to suppose that the closer, personal attachments and the more congenial interpersonal atmosphere associated with the egalitarian as compared to the individualistic - competitive system might lead to a stronger desire to remain in the egalitarian system.

Patterns of Participation and Control

In the doctrine of economic egalitarianism, the ideal of equality of power – the ability to participate equally in making the decisions that control, directly and indirectly, one's work and the organization in which one works – is at least as central as the ideal of an equal standard of living. Worker participation in decision - making within a firm can take place at three levels: the shop floor, the department and plant, and the corporate level. At the department and corporate levels, participation is usually indirect through delegates or representatives. Shop floor participation involves direct personal involvement as an individual or as a member of a small group in such day-to-day operating decisions as: scheduling of work, work methods, workplace layout, quantity of output, quality control, training. Terms such as "Job enrichment," "job redesigning," "job enlargement," "job rotation," "work restructuring," "autonomous work group," and so forth are often used to characterize worker participation and control at the shop level.

At the departmental and plant levels, worker participation is in the administrative decisions, through representatives to "work councils" or "joint labor-management consultative committees," that usually have consequences for weeks to months (at departmental level) or for a year or two (at the plant level). At the departmental level, these include cost and quality control, resource allocations, achievement of targets and quotas, and planning and coordination of activities. At the plant level, the decisions center about product lines: production layouts, plant-wide work arrangements, hiring, firing, and promotion of employees, and the acquisition, organization, and control of resources needed for production. At the corporate level, worker participation is through representatives on corporate boards that are concerned with such long -range strategic policy decisions as setting goals and objectives; choice of products and geographic locations; pricing and marketing policies; major capital expenditures; diversification; mergers, acquisitions, raising of capital; and disposition of profits.

The meager available research evidence about the effects of a more equal sharing of power in the workplace suggests that it increases rather than decreases economic efficiency (see Katzell & Yankelovich, 1975, and Jain, 1980). Although there is a significant push toward more participatory control in the workplace, propelled in part by the increasing education and sophistication of the high tech workforce, neither employers nor unions seem to be eager to extend cooperation to include the corporate board as well as the shop floor.

Employee Ownership

Two forms of employee ownership of firms are emerging in the United States (Woodworth, 1981). Here, we briefly discuss one form, sometimes labeled "worker capitalism," in which employees, as individuals, typically acquire shares in the enterprise through an "employee stock ownership plan" or through direct purchase of a plant that is about to close, be relocated, or be subjected to a takeover by a conglomerate. The employees function as individual shareholders who have a personal economic interest in the profitability of their firm; as shareholders, even when they together own a majority interest (this is often not the case), the employees do not use their shares collectively to determine management decisions. "Worker capitalism" may or may not involve participation and control over their workplace. Rarely does it involve a fundamental change from a capitalist philosophy of ownership and management.

The results of the limited available research (see Conte & Tannenbaum, 1978) indicate that economic egalitarianism, as expressed in the form of employee-ownership of the firm, appears to result in greater productivity and profitability as well as better attitudes. Again, there is little support for the widely - held notion that increased egalitarianism has a trade-off in economic efficiency. Nevertheless, one should recognize that the atmosphere of euphoria that often characterizes a firm after its transformation to employee ownership, after several months is often followed by growing dissatisfaction, sometimes accompanied by sèvere conflict. As Whyte and Blasi (1982, p. 143) point out, "The disillusionment of workers and the resulting conflicts arise out of a failure of management to recognize that an employee-owned firm cannot be managed effectively by following the authoritarian model."

Worker Cooperatives

A second form of worker ownership exists in worker cooperatives. These are usually owned by the workforce of the firm or by the cooperative community in which the enterprise is located (as in the kibbutzim); many such cooperatives do not permit sale or transfer of individual ownership rights. Control of the firm is in the hands of the workforce and is commonly distributed on the egalitarian principles of one person, one vote. However, when the cooperative is part of a cooperative community (as in the kibbutzim) or part of a complex of interrelated cooperatives (as in the Mondragon system), the larger community or cooperative system usually has an important voice in determining policy decisions that would affect the community or system of which it is a component.

There are many examples of successful, well-established, worker-controlled enterprises and of long-lived communes (see Oakeshott, 1978; Lindenfeld & Rothschild-Whitt, 1982; and Simmons & Mares, 1982, for illustrations of worker-cooperatives; and Kanter, 1982, for communes). Below, is a discussion of such enterprises that are structured on the egalitarian principle of one member, one vote including the U.S. Plywood Cooperative, The Mondragon Cooperative System in Spain, and the Kibbutz Cooperative Sector in Israel.

The U.S. Plywood Cooperatives. Various studies have shown that the plywood cooperatives have consistently outperformed private plywood firms substantilally (25–60 %) in productivity and also in the wages received by the workers (about 25 % higher). A large portion of this productivity difference may result from the smaller number of management and supervisory personnel required in the cooperatives. In traditional firms, supervisory personnel are used to police the workforce, checking on goofing off and careless or inefficient work. In the cooperatives, workers police themselves and each another, saving an enormous amount of money that is traditionally spent for supervisors.

The Mondragon Cooperative System The Mondragon Cooperatives in the Basque region in Spain have grown from a single industrial cooperative started by five young men in 1956, to a network of more than 87 cooperatives with 18,000 workers and $1.7 billion in annual sales. Thomas and Logan (1982, pp. 125 – 127) after a careful economic analysis conclude:

> Various indicators have been used to explore the economic efficiency of the Monodragon group of cooperatives. During more than two decydes, a considerable number of cooperative factories have functioned at a level equal or superior in efficiency to that of capitalist enterprises. ... Efficiency in terms of the use made of scarce resources has been higher in the cooperatives; their growth record of sales, exports, and employment, under both favourable and adverse economic conditions, has been superior to that of capitalist enterprises.

The Kibbutz Cooperative Sector in Israel. Menachem Rosner (Rosner et al., 1978), one of the foremost students of the kibbutzim, has written: "The equality of mankind – not merely in its formal connotation but in the true human and social sense as well – is the most fundamental principle upon which kibbutz society is based." Embodied in its basic values are two major conceptions: allowance for the specific and diverse needs of various individuals (and individualized or particularistic equality) and the separation of one's social contribution from the material rewards one receives.

In 1979, there were 254 kibbutz communities with almost 120,000 members, comprising about 3.3 % of the population of Israel (Rosner, 1982). The contribution of the kibbutzim to the Israeli national product greatly outweighs their portion of the population (40% of the agricultural and 6% of the industrial output) and its members have been and are disproportionately represented in the parliament and among the political and military leaders of Israel. At the same time, the various indicators of social pathology – crime, drug addiction, suicide, juvenile delinquency, mental disorder – appear to be disproportionately low in the kibbutzim.

A typical kibbutz is an egalitarian, rural community of several hundred families democratically governed by a General Assembly based on the principle of one member, one vote; the Assembly meets on the average of three times a month. A kibbutz is "owned" by its members but it cannot be sold and its assets cannot be divided by its members. If individual members leave, they have severance pay provisions based on a number of clearly defined factors. Kibbutzim are organized into a "holding company" which is affiliated with the general labor oganization of Israel. Should the majority of a kibbutz decide to dissolve it, the kibbutz's assets would be turned over to the holding company. (For additional descriptions of kibbutz life, see Blasi, 1980; Lieblich, 1982, Rayman, 1982, and Snarey, 1982.)

People who work together in a kibbutz factory, no matter what their positions in the factory, live together in the same community and have equal standards of living as well as equal control over community affairs. The decision making process on issues related to the industrial plant within a kibbutz is partly determined by the nature of the substantive issues. The Kibbutz General Assembly usually makes the decision on the election of a plant manager, the investment plan, the professional training plan, and the hiring of outside workers; the Worker's Assembly, within the plant, commonly makes the decisions with regard to production plans, work arrangements, choice of candidates for training, and election of plan officials other than the manager; and the plant management decides with regard to technical and professional problems. Even when the General Assembly retains final decision power, it will receive suggestions and proposals from the Worker's Assembly and the plant manager with regard to the issue being considered.

For the kibbutz as a whole, as well as for its industrial plants and other branches, all managerial and coordinating positions are rotated in order to prevent the emergence of a managerial elite. Rotation imlies not only a turnover of personnel but also that a factory manager will usually be assigned to other lower levels within the plant after completing his tour of duty as manager.

In addition to job rotation of managers, Leviatan (1980) identifies two other mechanisms that are used in the kibbutzim to counterbalance the ill-effects of hierarchy in organization: direct democracy, which provides rank-and-file workers influence over the selection (via the Worker's Assembly and the General Assembly) of plant officers and influence over many aspects of the plant's functioning; and independence of status dimensions such that the individual's standard of living as well as his or her position in the kibbutz community organization is uncorrelated with his or her position in the factory. That is, a manager has the same standard of living as a worker and is not any more likely to have a high position in the community.

Despite the "handicaps" under which they operate, Levitan (1978, a, b, p. 11) points out that: "Studies and economic analyses of the functioning of kibbutz work organizations have proved that the kibbutzim not only compete with their rival organizations in Israel but that in many instances they function even better than similar organizations outside the kibbutz." He indicates (1978, pp. 23-24) that the following general lessons can be drawn from the kibbutz experience:

> – The kibbutz experience in the spheres of work and economy had proven the feasibility for the successful existence of a nonmarket economics, since the kibbutz had broken down the traditional link between the contribution made by a person and the rewards conferred upon him.
>
> – It serves also as a successful example of functioning of work organizations in a situation where material rewards or their equivalents cannot serve as such because of their nondifferentialilty. So, it highlights the effectiveness of psychological motivations of higher order needs.

– In other word, the kibbutz experience is inconsistent with the assumption of an inevitable trade-off between equality and efficiency.

SUMMARY

I have reviewed an extensive literature (see Deutsch, 1985, for a more extensive review) which indirectly or directly bears upon the issue of whether egalitarian work systems are inherently less efficient than nonegalitarian systems. The existing research is meager and not of high quality, but its findings are concordant with the results of the more carefully controlled laboratory studies described in the first section. There is no reliable or consistent research-based evidence that justifies the conclusion that egalitarian systems are intrinsically less productive than the more traditional, nonegalitarian systems. To the contrary, the available research sugests that when efficient work requires efficient cooperation, almost any movement toward a democratic, egalitarian, cooperative system and away from the more traditional authoritarian, hierachical, adversarial system of work improves productivity and lessens worker alienation. This is so whether the movement is from individual to group performance-based pay, or from nonparticipation to worker participation in decision-making and profit sharing, or from outside ownership to worker ownership, or from authoritarian control to democratic control. This is not to deny the importance of individual performance and accountability, but rather to sugest that when everyone has a stake in your performance, your immediate co-workers as well as yourself, this enhances rather than reduces your accountability and your motivation to work and cooperate effectively. Nor is it to deny that one may work harder if one is paid more when one is alienated from work (because of dissatisfying work) or from one's co-workers (because of competitive relations), or from those for whom one works (because of an adversarial system).

Concluding Comment

After reviewing the literature on worker participation, worker ownership, worker cooperatives, the Kibbutzim, communes, and the like, I am convinced that paradise is not to be found on this earth. I am further persuaded that even the nearest thing to common visions of an earthly utopia–a small, well-functioning, cooperative, egaliatarian community–has to work hard and thoughtfully on a continuing basis to preserve its democracy, cooperativeness, and egalitarianism as well as to survive. The inherent tendency of such communities is to break down; it takes sustained effort to prevent this from happening. If egalitarianism were taken seriously, and the thoughtful effort necessary to establish and maintain such democratic cooperative systems were made, the odds are that we would be more productive and less alienated from ourselves and one another.

REFERENCES

Blasi, J (1980). *The communal future: The kibbutz and the utopian dilemma.* Philadelphia: Norwood Edition.

Conte, M., & Tannenbaum, A. (1978). *Employee ownership: A report.* Presented to the Economic Development Administration, U.S. Department of Commerce. Ann Arbor: University of Michigan Survey Research Center.

Deutsch, M. (1949a). A theory of cooperation and competition. *Human Relations,* 2, 129-51.

Deutsch, M (1949b). *An experimental study of the effects of cooperation and competition upon group processes. Human Relations, 2,* 199-232.

Deutsch, M. (1985). *Distributive justice: A social-psychological perspective.* New Haven: Yale University Press.

Jain, H. C., (Ed.) (1980). *Worker participation: Success and problems.* New York: Praeger.

Johnson, D. W.,& Johnson, R. (1983). The socialization and achievement crisis: Are cooperative learning experiences the solution? In L. Bickman (Ed.), *Applied Social Psychology, Annual 4.* Beverly Hills, CA: Sage Publications.

Kanter, R. M. (1982). *Commitment and community: Communes and utopias in a sociological perspective.* Cambridge, Mass.: Harvard University Press.

Katzell, R. A., & Yankelovich, D. (1975). *Work, productivity and job satisfaction: An evaluation of policy-related research.* New York: Psychological Corporation.

Lawler, E. E. (1971). *Pay and organizational development.* Reading, Mass.: Addison-Wesley.

Lawler, E. E. (1981). *Pay and organizational effectiveness: A psychological view.* New York: McGraw-Hill.

Leviatan, U. (1978). *Some problematic aspects of the work sphere in the kibbutz society.* Haifa, Israel: Institute for Research of the Kibbutz and the Cooperative Idea, University of Haifa.

Leviatan, U. (1980a). *Counterbalancing the ill effects of hierarchy: the case of the kibbutz industrial organization.* Haifa, Israel: Institute for Research of the Kibbutz and the Cooperative Idea, University of Haifa.

Leviatan, U. (1980b). Individual effects of managerial rotation: The case of the "demoted" office holder. Haifa, Israel: Institute for Research of the Kibbutz and the Cooperative Idea, University of Haifa.

Lieblich, A. (1982). *Kibbutz Makon.* New York: Pantheon Books.

Lindenfeld, F., & Rothschild-Whitt, J. (1982). *Workplace democracy and social change.* Boston: Porter-Sargent.

Oakeshott, R (1978). *The case for workers' co-ops.* London: Methuen.

Okun, A. M. (1975). *Equality and efficiency: The big tradeoff.* Washington, D.C.: Brookings Institution.

Rayman, P (1982). *The kibbutz community and nation-building.* Princeton: Princeton University Press.

Rosner, M (1982). *Democracy, equality and change: The kibbutz and social theory.* Darby, Pa.: Norwood.

Rosner, M., Ben-David, Y., Ovant, A., Cohen, N. & Leviatan, U. (1978). *The second generation: Between continuity and change.* Tel-Aviv: Sifriat Poalim. In Hebrew.

Simmons, J., & Mares, W. (1983). *Working together.* New York: Alfred A. Knopf.

Snarey, J. (1982). *The social and moral development of kibbutz sabras and founders.* Cambridge, Mass.: Harvard University Project for Kibbutz Studies.

Thomas, H. & Logan, L. (1982). *Mondragon: An economic analysis.* London: George Allen & Unwin.

Whyte, F. W., & Blasi, J. R. (1982). Worker ownership. participation and control: Toward a theoretical model. *Policy Sciences, 4,* 137–63.

Woodworth, W. (1981). Forms of employee ownership and workers' control. *Sociology of Work and Occupation, 8* (2), 195-200.

9 Evaluative Perspective and Distributive Justice

Krystyna Skarżyńska
Department of Psychology
Polish Academy of Sciences

A considerable body of evidence in general and social psychology strongly supports the argument that the perception and evaluation of an object or phenomenon varies across individuals. Similarly, the evaluation of whether or not something is just seems to depend on certain psychosocial characteristics of the evaluating person. A good deal of attention has been devoted in the literature to the way judgments of justice in interpersonal relations are affected by an evaluator's age, sex, social background, status, occupational role, level of moral development or personality variables, such as the need of social approval or achivement, public versus private self-consciousness, or acceptance of Protestant ethics.

There is also relatively abundant evidence concerning the asymmetry of injustice judgments made by the "victim" (i.e., the wronged person) and by the "victimizer." The most comprehensive explanation of this phenomenon has been proposed by Deutsch (1985).

The aim of this chapter is to analyze the effect of one's evaluative perspective on the evaluation of justice of various allocation decisions. The term *evaluative perspective* denotes the relation of the evaluator to the evaluated event. The relation in question is determined by the consequences of the evaluated fact or event for the subject making the evaluation. In attribution theory the actor is defined as the person or group who is directly affected by the action or events to be evaluated. In contrast, the external observer is defined as the person or group whc makes an evaluation but is not directly affected by the evaluated actions or events.

We sought to answer two main questions: first, what are the differences between justice judgments made from the actor's and observer's perspectives, and second, to what psychological factors are these differences due?

According to the equity theory, external observers witnessing an unjust allocation of goods (or any other unfair interpersonal exchange) also experience distress produced by the injustice–through empathizing with victims of the injustice. Thus, observers' responses to the situation of injustice are similar to these of actors participating in the situation, only they are less intense (Austin, Walster, Utne, 1976).

From the equity theory viewpoint then, evaluation of justice/injustice of a given allocation decision can be similar in actors (i.e., in the decision makers and recipients of the decision) and in observers, with the only difference being that the actors' judgments should be more extreme. Observers and actors share the same justice standards: From both perspectives the decisions are evaluated in terms of the equity formula.

The attribution theory holds that justice evaluations made by the observer should differ from these made by the actor. This is due to differences in the perception of the causes of the actor's "vicitimization" (see Barnes, Ickes, & Kidd, 1977, Utne & Kidd 1980). Both the victim of the injustice (the actor, i.e. the person in a disadvantageous situation) and the external observer ask the same questions: why did it happen, what are the causes of the situation? However, the actor (or the victim) usually gives different answers to these questions than the observer does. As compared to the actor (or "victim"), the observer is more likely to perceive that the underrewarded or wronged person is a "victim" of his or her own behaviors or traits (e.g., the latter may be perceived as unable to organize his or her work properly). The so perceived situation may be tolerated as concordant with the justice rules. On the other hand, the "victim" attributes his or her plight to external circumstances (particularly, to "evil intentions" of other people), which results in his or her evaluation of the situation as unjust and distressing.

The effect of the perceptual perspective (of the victim and observer) on differences in experience of injustice has been studied recently by Mikula and Schlamberger (1985) and by Wosińska (1985). The authors take a phenomenological approach and their essential research technique is the analysis of retrospective reports and daily life events experienced as unjust.

In the study by Mikula and Schlamberger (1984), half of the subjects were asked to report an unjust event in a school situation in which they themselves had played the role of the victim, whereas the other half of the subjects were to describe an unjust event they had witnessed as nonaffected observers. Participants in the study were Austrian secondary school students. Frequencies of occurrence and temporal sequence of various categories included in the reports by victims and observers were compared. Observers, as compared to vicitims, were found more often to use evaluative categories and less frequently to use the so-called attributional elements connected with seeking causes of injustice. This finding seems important for considerations concerning the role of evaluative perspective in the process of justice evaluation. The finding suggests that one difference between the two perspectives is in the evaluative orientation, which is more pronounced in the observers than in actors (or victims).

New data on differences in the perception and evaluation of injustice are provided by Wosińska (1985). Her 237 subjects (nurses and doctors in hospitals) were examined by means of the retrospective report technique. The subjects were first asked to describe an unjust event they had experienced themselves at work; then they were asked to describe an event recognized as unjust, which had not affected them personally, but which they had witnessed in the hospital.

When the reports by "victims" and nonaffected observers of injustice were compared, the following patterns of finding were observed:

Different types of events were perceived as unjust from the observer's perspective than from that of the victim; namely, victims more frequently than observers perceived as unjust the situation of underrating their effort or performance level, whereas observers more frequently evaluated as unjust either certain rules or modes of distribution of goods, or a violation of norms of mutual respect. This result may be interpreted as follows: Victims are more sensitive to the subjective aspect of injustice, whereas observers are oriented to the violation of more salient and better codified norms of interpersonal relations.

Observers more often than victims perceived stable traits of the environment and of the victims themselves as causes of injustice; besides, observers more often attributed to victims the responsibility for their condition. This finding is concordant with predictions of the attribution theory, and it indicates that attributions made by victims have defensive functions.

As compared to victims, observers more often took into consideration many various aspect of the injustice situation they evaluated, whereas victims tended to focus their evaluations on single aspects or elements of the situation (e.g., they evaluated only participants of the situation).

On the grounds of the previously presented findings, the following theoretical hypothesis can be reasonably formulated: The evaluative perspective of persons should affect their evaluative orientation. People evaluating social objects and facts from the perspective of a nonaffected observer refer them to norms appropriate for the evaluation of these objects and facts. On the other hand, "actors," i.e., persons evaluating objects and events in which they participate themselves, are more sensitive to the subjective rather than normative aspects of the evaluated objects and events.

Observers of the allocation situation have certain ideas as to what allocation rules should be employed in a given case. In other words, they have certain schemata of just allocation decisions. Recipients of allocation decisions also have such schemata, but the role of these schemata in the process of evaluation of fairness of allocation decisions is limited by the recipient's sensitivity to the subjective aspect of the allocation situation (as discussed earlier). Consequently, the following hypothesis was posed for study: the type of the allocation decision affects observers' evaluations of fairness of an allocation decision more than those of recipients. On the operational level, the allocation decision type can be said to account for a larger percentage of variance in ratings of justice of this decision when the justice judgments are made from the observer's perspective than when they are made from the perspective of the recipient of an allocation decision.

THE IDEA OF THE EXPERIMENT[1]

The following assumptions were were made in the development of the experimental procedure designed to test the hypothesis about the differing effect of the evaluative perspective on judgments of fairness of allocation decisions:

1. Allocation of goods in a social structure does not have to involve directly all members of the structure. However, those who do not participate directly in the allocation (i.e., are neither the allocation decision recipients nor the decision makers) may be in the role of external evaluating the fairness of the observed decisions. Therefore, it is not artificial to distinguish two evaluative perspectives: one of the recipient and the other of the observer, because this reflects the differentiation of evaluative perspectives in the real-life allocation situations.

2. The following distribution rules are most frequently applied: the equality principle, the contribution principle, and the need principle. Therefore, the allocation decisions made in the experimental situation were exemplifications of the previously listed allocation principles.

3. In the real-life allocation situations, allocation participants (individuals or groups) differ in their need for the distributed goods. Therefore, in our experimental situation the subjects needed either more or less of the allocated goods.

[1] The experiment described in this chapter is a part of a larger research project presented by the author in her book "Psychospołeczne aspekty decyzji alokacyjnych" (Psychosocial aspects of allocation decisions), Wrocław 1985, Ossolineum.

4. In the real-life allocation situations in the social system, the allocation participants (individuals or groups) have various relations with other groups or individuals: The relationship may be positive, neutral, or negative. These relations may be maintained or modified (either in the positive or negative direction) by the allocation decision. The evaluation of fairness of a given allocation decision also may be affected by the type of interpersonal relations in the group. Therefore, in our study the persons playing the role of allocation recipients were represented as having three types of interpersonal relations (i.e., positive, neutral, or negative) with other participants of the allocation situation (or with other recipients of the distributed goods).

5. The psychosocial consequences of allocation decisions vary directly with the value of the distributed goods for the allocation recipients. Mode of allocation of goods that are of little value to the recipients probably has no important psychological consequences. Therefore, the goods to be distributed in the experiment were valuable to the subjects. It was assumed that a premium of 500 zlotys for scoring a specified number of points in a psychological examination taking about 1 hour would be a valuable reward for the population under study (secondary school or university students). The experimenter did not distribute money directly but allotted scores, which were to be the basis for obtaining the promised monetary reward on completion of the whole research.

According to the assumptions of our research project, the following main independent variables were induded in the design of the study. (Greater detail regarding these variables is included in a later section):

type of evaluative perspective: the perspective of the recipient of the allocation and that of the observer of the allocation.

type of allocation decision:

(a) equal allocation to partners who performed equally
(b) unequal allocation based on need to partners whose performance was the same
(c) equal allocation to partners whose performance levels differed
(d) unequal allocation to partners, with the allocation being larger for the needy partner who performed at a lower level
(e) unequal allocation to partners, with the allocation being larger for the partner with the higher level of performance.

type of recipients: recipients who are favored by the allocation decision and recipients disadvantaged by the allocation;

type of interpersonal relations in the group of allocation recipients: mutual liking between the group members, indifference or mutual dislike.

The main dependent variable was evaluation of the justice of allocation decisions, as made by the recipients of allocation and by observers.[2]

THE EXPERIMENTAL METHOD

Subjects

Participants in the study were secondary school or university students from Warsaw, male and female, aged from 19 to 23.

In the preliminary, screening stage of the study 68 groups of subjects were examined. By means of a sociometric technique, 384 dyads were selected. In each dyad the partners were of the same sex and had known each other for at least 2 years. There were 154 dayds of partners who liked each other, 102 dayds of mutually indifferent partners, and 128 dyads of partners who did not like each other.

In the actual experiment, the number of dyads was somewhat smaller: 120 dyads who liked each other, 101 indifferent dyads, and 112 dyads of partners who disliked each other. These dyads were randomly assigned to one of 5 experimental groups (conditions) differing regard the type of the allocation decision.

It was necessary to exclude several additional dyads from the analysis because their responses to a postexperimental questionnaire were either incomplete or illegible. Thus, results for only 300 dyads were analyzed: For each of the 15 experimental conditions (5 types of allocation decisions by 3 types of intermember relations), there were 20 dyads.

The external observers in the study were 330 men and women aged 19 to 23 from the same population as the persons in the experimental groups. They were randomly assigned to 15 control group that differed with regard to type of information given to the observer about the allocation decision made in the group and the nature of the interpersonal relationship between the allocation recipients. Statistical analyses were performed for data obtained from 300 observers (20 subjects in each of the 15 control groups).

---

[2] The other two dependent variables, namely the judged intelligence and friendliness of allocator on the one hand, and perceived goal of allocation on the other hand, were under control in the present experiment. Both were shown to depend on three factors; (a) type of decision, (b) recipient's satisfaction with allocation, and (c) evaluative perspective. In that respect both tend to resemble judgments of justice.

Experimental procedures

The experiment included the following stages:

1. Measurement of the interpersonal relationship between the allocation recipients and assignment to dyads based on this variable;
2. Experimental manipulation of the needs of the allocation recipients;
3. Presentation of the allocation decision by the experimenter.
4. Evaluation of the fairness of the allocation decision.

Measurement of Interpersonal Relations. Interpersonal relationship between participants of the allocation situation were measured by means of the so-called "Friendliness and Dislike Plebiscyte" (Pilkiewicz, 1962). By means of this sociometric technique, we selected three groups of dyads: partners who liked each other, disliked each other, or were mutually indifferent.

Manipulation of Needs of Recipients. Subject participating in the preliminary stage of the experiment were informed that a specified amount of money (up to 500 zlotys) could be earned by those who would take part in psychological experiments, providing that they score a specific number of points. Then an appointment was made for the experiment with the dyads selected by means of the sociometric screening.

Participants in the second stage of the study were given two fragments of the Raven test. This type of experimental task had been chosen because it allowed manipulation of information about subjects' alleged performance level. The subjects themselves were not able to establish if their performance was good or not.

Subjects in each dyad worked individually; they were seated at two separate tables, A and B, placed so that neither could see his or her partner. The experimenter interrupted their work after 20 minutes. They were told that a short break was necessary for the experimenter's collaborator to assess their performance level, and their response sheets were taken to another room. Some minutes later the experimenter returned and the following instruction was given to subjects: "Your performance was analyzed and scored by my colleague. Based on his assessment, each of you still needs some points to obtain the premium. The person sitting at table A needs 20 more points, whereas person at table B needs only 5 points more. There is one more task left, in which 30 points will be allotted."

Actually, subjects performance on the experimental task were not scored, and the same predetermined information about the number of points needed by persons A and B was given to all dyads.

The Allocation Decision. The allocation decision that was to be evaluated later consisted of the distribution of points for the performance in the second experimental task. Subjects were given a list of 30 anagrams with the instruction that various rules could be used in order to transform the anagrams into meaningful words, and that the score would depend both on the number of various transformation rules applied and on originality of the produced solutions.

After 10 minutes the response sheets were taken by the experimenter informing subjects that their performance would be scored by a psychologist. The latter was to propose a distribution of 30 points (thus making a certain allocation decision). Prior to announcing the allocation decision to the subjects, they were informed about their individual performance levels. In the first two groups of dyads, subjects were informed that both partners had performed equally well on the Anagrams Test, scoring 10 points each. The remaining three groups of dyads were informed that the partners' performance had been different; namely partner A (who needed more points to get the premium) always "scored" lower than partner B (who needed less points); partner A had had 10 correct, whereas partner B had 18.

One of the following three principles was applied in the final allocation of the reward (i.e., 30 points): equal allocation to both (A and B received 15 points each); needs-matching allocation (A received 20 and B, 10 points), or contribution-matching allocation (A received 10 points, and B, 20 points).

By combination of the previously described allocation principles with the type of information about subjects' performance level, the following five groups were obtained:

1. The allocation recipients (A and B), perform equally well and were allotted the same number of points. An equality-based decision was made in a situation involving equal contributions but different needs of the allocation recipients. This decision is referred to as D_1.
2. The allocation recipients (A and B) perform equally well but were allotted a different number of points: The more needy partner (A) received more points than partner B who needed fewer points to get the premium. The decision took into account the recipients' needs despite their equal contributions. This decision is referred to as D_2.
3. The allocation recipients (A and B) differed in their performance level (A's performance surpassed that of B), but they were allotted the same number of points. An equality decision was made in the context of differing contributions and different needs of the allocation recipients. This decision is referred to as D_3.
4. The allocation recipients (A and B) differed in their performance level A was inferior to B and are allotted a different number of points, but A receives more points than B. The allocation decision took into account the needs of the inferior performer. This decision is referred to as D_4.

5. The allocation recipients (A and B) differed in their performance level (A was inferior to B) and were allotted a different number of points: A received fewer than B. In the decision, the allocation recipients' contributions are taken into account, while their needs are disregarded. This decision will be referred to as D_5.

Table 9.1 depicts the characteristics of the various allocation decisions.

TABLE 9.1

Comprehensive Characteristics of Allocation Decisions

Type of Decision:	*Performance Level:*	*Needs Level:*	*Allocation of Points:*
D_1	$A = B$	$A > B$	$A = B$
D_2	$A = B$	$A > B$	$A > B$
D_3	$A < B$	$A > B$	$A = B$
D_4	$A < B$	$A > B$	$A > B$
D_5	$A < B$	$A > B$	$A < B$

In each of the five experimental groups distinguished on the grounds of the allocation decision type, there were dyads in which interpersonal relations between the partners were either negative (mutual antipathy), neutral (mutual indifference), or positive (mutual sympathy). Consequently, 15 experimental groups were finally obtained.

The abovementioned manipulations of the recipients' needs and types of the allocation decision presumably produced various types of the recipients: those advantaged by the allocation decision and those recipients disadvantaged by the allocation decision. The allocation decision was presumably satisfactory for the handicapped participant A, provided it discriminated on the basis of differential needs (decisions D_2 and D_4) and, for the better performer B, provided it was based on the equality formula (decisions D_1 and D_3) or on the equity formula decision D_5. On the contrary, decisions disregarding level of needs (i.e., D_1, D_3, D_5) should not satisfy handicapped participants, whereas decisions based on level of needs (D_2, D_4) should not please performers B.

The asumption that variations in participants' needs and in the different types of decisions used result in both satisfied and unsatisfied participants of allocation has been confirmed in previous research.

Evaluation of the Allocation Decision. Justice of allocation decision was rated independently on a 7–point scale by each of the dyad members. The higher the rating, the more fair was the judgment of a given allocation decision. The same rating scale was used by external observers, who were asked to assess the justice of the allocation decisions made in each of the 15 allocation situations described to them.

RESULTS

The aim of the statistical analyses was not only to verify whether judgments of the fairness of various types of allocation decisions were a function of evaluative perspective but also to determine the mode of the fairness evaluations affected by evaluative perspective. Therefore, the first stage of the analysis was devoted to the justice ratings made from the perspective of the allocation recipient, and the second stage – to these made from the perspective of the observer, and the last stage – the comparison of ratings made from both perspectives.

The main method used in the analyses was the linear model of ANOVA. The recipient's perspective case was characterized in terms of a three way ANOVA factorial design with following conditions:

(a) allocation decision condition (5 levels);
(b) recipient condition (2 levels), (for half of the subjects the decision was satisfactory, and for the other half it was not);
(c) and interpersonal relation condition (3 levels: mutually liking, disliking, or indifferent).

The design for the data pertaining to the observers' perspective had two factors: (a) allocation decision condition (5 levels), and (b) interpersonal relation condition (3 levels). Obviously, recipient condition was irrelevant for external observers.

Post hoc comparisons for the dependent variable in the experimental groups within the same evaluative perspective (i.e., within recipients or within observers) were calculated by means of the Scheffe *F* test (Roscoe, 1975, p. 313), whereas the significance of differences between the two evaluative perspectives (i.e., between justice ratings made by observers and by participants) was evaluated by means of Fischer's *t* test (Guilford, 1964).

Evaluation of Justice of Allocation Decisions from the Recipient's Perspective

Theoretically, justice ratings for each decision type could range from 1 to 7, and such a range (1 to 7 points) was obtained. Mean ratings of justice of various decisions are presented in Table 9.2.

TABLE 9.2

Mean Ratings of Justice of Various Decisions

Type of Decision and Interpersonal Relations	*Ratings of Justice* R_1	R_2	*Observers*
D_1			
Sympathy	5.55	4.00	6.20
Antipathy	6.25	3.80	6.88
Indifference	6.60	4.75	6.45
D_2			
Sympathy	6.20	4.70	5.25
Antipathy	6.40	3.25	4.15
Indifference	6.20	3.50	4.25
D_3			
Sympathy	4.85	4.75	6.10
Antipathy	4.35	3.45	5.70
Indifference	5.20	4.60	5.40
D_4			
Sympathy	5.95	3.50	3.55
Antipathy	6.30	2.50	2.40
Indifference	6.10	2.95	2.75
D_5			
Sympathy	6.55	4.45	5.70
Antipathy	6.50	3.55	6.30
Indifference	6.45	3.75	6.50

R_1 – recipients for whom the allocation decision was profitable.
R_2 – recipients for whom the allocation decision was not profitable.

Analysis of the mean ratings of justice of allocation decisions in particular groups showed the following:

1. Mean ratings of the justice of allocation decisions within experimental groups ranged from 2.50 (rating of the D_4 decision by recipients for whom it was unsatisfactory, in the dyads of partners disliking each other) to 6.60 (rating of the D_1 decision in the dyads of mutually indifferent partners, by recipients for whom the decision was satisfactory).
2. Any allocation decision was evaluated as more just by those recipients for whom it was more satisfactory. All the differences were statistically significant, except for the difference in ratings of the equality decision in the situation involving different contributions D_3 and dyads of friends.
3. Type of interpersonal relationship between the allocation recipients affected the size of the difference between the fairness ratings of recipients for whom the allocation was either advantageous or not advantageous (less profitable). The smallest differences in rating of fairness among persons who received unequal distributions were observed when the recipient were friends. In contrast, the largest differences in fairness ratings were obtained for allocation recipients who did not like each other.
4. Type of allocation decision modified the magnitude of the difference between justice ratings made by the recipients advantaged by the allocations and these made by recipients disadvantaged by the allocation. The smallest differences were observed for an equal allocation in the context of unequal contributions and different needs of allocation recipients (D_3), whereas the most pronounced differences were when the stronger needs of the inferior performer had been taken into account (D_4).

TABLE 9.3

Results of the ANOVA for the Recipients' Evaluations of Fairness

Source of Variance	*SS*	*df*	*MS*	*F*	*p*	*Percent of the Variance Explaned*
A type of decision	51.03	4	12.75	22.26	0.010	3.90
B type of recipients	661.50	1	661.50	1154.45	0.001	52.90
C type of interpersonal relations	18.41	2	9.20	16.06	0.010	1.38
A × B	94.49	4	23.62	41.22	0.001	7.37
A × C	42.08	8	5.26	9.18	0.010	3.37
B × C	49.08	2	24.54	42.83	0.001	3.84
A × B × C	5.59	8	0.69	1.22	n.s.	0.08
Error	326.70	570	0.57			

Thus, a preliminary analysis indicated that all the three independent variables, i.e., type of allocation decision, type of recipients (the satisfied and the unsatisfied, and interpersonal relations between the recipients) affected the recipients' evaluations of the justice of alloation decisions. This supposition was confirmed by a three-way analysis of variance. All the main effects were statistically significant; see Table 9.3.

The analysis of variance indicated that recipients' satisfaction with allocation exerted the strongest influence on the evaluation of the fairness of the allocation decision from the actor's perspective. This variable accounted for 52.90% of the variance of rating. The type of allocation decision explained only 3.90% of the variance, whereas the type of interpersonal relationship in the dyads accounted for 1.38% of the variance.

The Evaluation of Justice of the Allocation Decision from the Observers' Perspective

External observers also were asked to rate the abovementioned types of allocation decisions on 7-point scales (the higher the rating score, the more just is a given decision was in the rater's opinion). The observed range of rating scores was from 1 to 7 points.

TABLE 9.4

Results of the ANOVA for the Observers' Evaluations of Fairness

Source of Variance	*SS*	*df*	*MS*	*F*	*p*	*Percent of the Variance Explained*
A type of decision	551.64	4	127.75	211.89	0.001	69.06
B type of interpersonal relations	5.61	2	2.80	4.65	0.010	0.59
A × B	41.31	8	5.16	8.56	0.010	5.03
Error	171.83	285	0.60			

The analysis of mean ratings of fairness showed the following:

1. Decisions D_1 (equal allocation and equal contributions) and D_5 (contribution-related proportional allocations) were considered as most fair.

2. Fairness of the same allocation decision was evaluated differently depending on the type of interpersonal relationship between the allocation recipients.

Specifically, according to the 3 by 5 analysis of variance, all values of *F* were significant. Type of allocation decision explained the largest proportion of variance in justice ratings, namely 69.06%. Type of decision by Type of interpersonal relationship in the dyad accounted for 5.03% of the variance, whereas the main effect for type of interpersonal relationship accounted for only 0.59% of variance.

The Evaluative Perspective and the Evaluation of Decisions

It follows from a comparison of the justice ratings made from the two perspectives (observers and allocation recipients) that the type of allocation decision accounted for a considerably larger portion of variance in observers' ratings than in those made by recipients (69.06 and 3.90%, respectively). Therefore, it can be concluded that our main hypothesis was confirmed.

Apart from the verification of the main hypothesis, another interesting question was how evaluative perspective would affect justice evaluations of various types of allocation for dyads representing various kinds of interpersonal relationships. For this purpose, the observers' mean ratings of justice for each allocation decision made in regard to each type of dyad were compared with respective mean ratings obtained from allocation recipients for whom the allocation decision had been more or less satisfactory, more or less profitable (see Table 9.2). Fisher's *t* tests were used to check the significance of differences between mean ratings. According to these comparisons, evaluative perspective had the following effects on the evaluation of justice of particular types of allocation decisions:

1. The evaluation of fairness of any allocation decision was significantly modified by the evaluative perspective. All differences between the compared means were significant at the $p > 0.01$ level.
2. Decisions D_1, D_3, and D_5 (equal or contribution-proportional allocations) were regarded as more fair by observers than by recipients of the allocation averaged across recipients. Decisions D_2 and D_4 (need-proportional allocations) were evaluated as less fair by observers than by recipients (averaged across recipients).
3. For some types of allocation decisions, fairness ratings made by observers were similar to these made by the allocation recipients for whom the decision was less profitable (that is, in the case of the D_2 decision for the dyads in which partners disliked each other, and for the D_4 decision in regard to all typed of dyads). On the other hand, with regard to the evaluation of justice for decisions D_1 and D_3 with dyads of mutually

indifferent partners, and decision D_5 for all types of dyads, observers' ratings were similar to those of the allocation recipients for whom the decision was profitable.

DISCUSSION

The results obtained indicate that the process of evaluating allocation decisions is complex and determined by many factors. Application of the same allocation principle is variously evaluated, depending on certain parameters of the allocation situation and on the evaluative perspective adopted. An attempt is made here to delineate these modifiers of the allocation evaluation and to outline the mechanisms underlying their effect on the process of evaluating justice.

The largest proportion of variance in the justice ratings for allocation turned out to be explained by consequences of the allocation decision for its recipient performing the act of evaluation. Satisfactory decisions (i.e., profitable), as compared to the less satisfying ones, were evaluated by the recipients as more just. A tendency to maximize gain is rather common; it is not surprising then that it operates also in the experimental situation of allocation of goods. The evalutation of materially (or otherwise) satisfying decisions as just allows the recipients to maximize their gains: Not only are they allotted more than the other participant, but they can feel that their gain is actually deserved and fair.

In our experiment, observers received no material profit from the allocation decisions they evaluated; therefore, their ratings of a decision justice could not operate as a justification for any benefits received as a result of the decision. Most probably, the observers' fairness judgments were determined by the consistency of a given decision with their model of a fair allocation decision. In other words, an analysis of the observers' ratings can be used to determine the nature of observers' models of just allocations.

Recipients of decision also seemed to have certain rules regarding what constituted a fair allocation, but the role of these rules in the process of evaluating the fairness of specific decisions was affected by the previously discussed tendency to justify their own gain.

The type of interpersonal relationship in the group was found to influence fairness ratings made from both perspectives. However, the influence mechanism seemed to differ, depending on the evaluative perspective adopted. This supposition is suggested by the following fact: When degree of personal gain associated with a decision is disregarded, any allocation decision was rated as more just by recipients in dyads of partners who disliked each other. Moreover, the effect of type of interpersonal relationship in the dyad was even more complicated when the evaluation was made from the recipients' perspective. It is our belief that the influence of type of interpersonal relationship on recipients' justice ratings was mediated by emotional processes connected with the fact that recipients of the allocation either liked or disliked their partner, or were indifferent to them, and that this attitude was reciprocated. When the allocation recipients liked their partners and were liked by him or her, then their joint participation in the allocation situation should have been less threatening than in the case of mutual indifference or mutual dislike. In the former case, there is no disagreeable emotional tension, and so the whole experimental situation (or a real-life situation of the allocation of goods) should seem more pleasant to the allocation participants, and all its elements, including allocation decisions, should be evaluated more positively. Another type of halo-effect arises when the allocation participants dislike each other.

The obtained relation in our study between the type of interpersonal relationship in the dyad and the evaluation of justice of allocation decisions has serious implications for the practice of social life. Namely, it may be expected that in large social groups, the evaluation of the fairness of allocation decisions also will be affected by the group climate, or by the type of interpersonal relationships among the group members. In groups in which interpersonal relations are poor and characterized by social conflicts, any decision should be evaluated as less fair than it would be in groups in which intermember relationships are good. Therefore, allocation decisions made by or for conflicted groups (or more generally for groups dissatisfied with their situation) require careful deliberation and care. We believe that clear references to commonly accepted rules of fairness may reduce the likelihood of a negative evaluation of decisions made in such situations.

Observers' evaluations of the justice of allocation decisions apparently were influenced not so much by observers' emotional states connected with the type of intragroup relations, but rather by their knowledge of the specific interpersonal relationships (positive, neutral, or negative) in the observed group. Most probably, rules of just allocation differentiated accordingly to the type of intragroup relationship were used to judge decisions. These rules specify relations between specific types of interpersonal relationships and specific rules regarding the allocation of goods. Our results seem to indicate that these rules are as follows: Need-proportional decisions are rated as more just when they are made in groups of persons who liked each other than when the group members dislike each other. On the other hand, contribution-proportional decisions are evaluated by observers as more fair when they are made in groups of persons who dislike each other than in groups of mutually friendly partners. Such rules of just allocation decisions are most probably based on an assumption that good interpersonal relationships in the group are due to the gratification of the group members' needs, and that group efficiency increased as a consequence of contribution-proportional rewards.

For recipients as a group (i.e., across both types of recipients) evaluations of the fairness of need-proportional decisions varied, and the differences were a function of contributions of the more needy partners. When persons who needed more performed similarly (i.e., made the same contributions) as those who needed less, then need-proportional decisions were evaluated as more fair than they were when the more needy partner's performance was inferior to that of the other group member.

Two explanations of this phenomenon seem possible. According to the first, needy partners who have performed as well as their partners are viewed by their partners as not responsible for their state of need. Because it is generally accepted that is desirable to assist the needy who are unable to help themselves, a decision allotting more goods to the more needy and "helpless" performer is evaluated as fair. In contrast, a motivational deficiency rather than the inability to alleviate one's need is ascribed to a person who needs more, but whose performance is inferior to that of others. This may be why allocation decisions that take into account one individual's needs are evaluated as less fair.

The second interpretation refers to the categorization process and to categories of so-called formal justice. According to the principle of formal justice (which seems to be generally accepted), people belonging to the same category should receive the same treatment. The justice of need-proportional decisions is evaluated differently in the case of equally good performers than in the case on a unequal performance; the differences in fairness ratings may be due to the use of different criteria for categorization of people in the first and in the second situation. In the first situation, the only difference between people is that of degree of their need, and it apparently was their need that served as a salient criterion of categorization. In accordance with the formula for formal justice, those having similar needs should be treated similarly, whereas different treatments should be applied to those having different or stronger needs. In contrast, in the second situation the partners made different contributions and had different needs; thus there was no single salient criterion for their categorization. The obtained results indicate that the choice of the categorization criterion was determined by properties of the situation, or by its task-oriented character. The categorization was based on performance level (i.e., contributions). It seems that the following standard rule began to operate: All equal contributors should be treated similarly. Need was not important in this situation and decisions that were based on contributors' needs were evaluated as unjust.

So far the differences between recipients' and observers' evaluations of the justice of allocation decisions have been explained in terms of two factors that interfere with the functioning of the rules of just allocation for recipients. The first factor is the recipients' seeking a justification for their profitable outcomes, whereas the second is the recipients' emotional responses that vary as a function of the recipients' emotional responses that vary as a function of the type of interpersonal relationship in the group. It can be concluded that the perspective of the evaluator affects his or her evaluative orientation: One's orientation is likely to be individualistic in the case of the recipient, and normative or "social" in the case of the observer. This interpretation is supported by our findings that contribution-proportional decisions were evaluated as more just by observers than by recipients, whereas need-proportional decisions were judged as more fair by recipients than by observers. The individual gain or loss by allocation recipients apparently affected their evaluation of a decision as just. Recall, however, that observers apparently took into account the consequences of the decision, not only for particular individuals, but for the observed group as a whole. They seemed to refer to the common belief that allocations proportional to the group members' contributions are the ones socially most desirable. In other words, it is likely that the observer referred to a standard or rule of just allocation. This interpretation seems to be consistent with the findings of Wosińska (1985) discussed earlier in this chapter.

With regard to their evaluation of justice, observers sometimes resembled the recipients for whom the allocation was not profitable whereas, at other times, they resembled the recipients who benefited the allocation. Observers' evaluations were similar to those made by recipients who received fewer allocated goods when these recipients' contributions were as good (D_2) or even better (D_4) than those of the other group participant. In other words, observers evaluated the allocation decision in a manner similar to recipients who felt they were treated unjustly (because their contribution was disregarded in the allocation decision). This result is consistent with a view expressed in the literature that observers of an unjust allocation also experience distress connected with the injustice, through empathy with the victims. The only difference was that observers' responses were less intense (i.e., their ratings were not so extreme). However, the generality of this thesis is limited by our other results. As was mentioned before, observers' evaluations were sometime similar not to those made by the allocation recipients who felt unjustly treated, but to those made by the recipients for whom the allocation decision was profitable and who evaluated the decision as fair. This is the case when the group members' performance level was taken into account in the allocation decision. It should be noted that observers apparently did not experience distress resulting from other people's feeling of being treated unjustly if the latter were inferior performers. Perhaps in this situation the causes of injustice were perceived by observers as ones that could be controlled by the individual experiencing injustice, i.e., if the individual had wished to work harder, he or she would be allotted more goods, his or her needs would be satisfied, and he or she would not be feeling unjustily treated.

The fact that observers expressed the viewpoint of those satisfied with contribution-proportional decision is indirect evidence that in the observers' opinion, the rule of contribution-proportional rewards was more just than that of need-proportional allocation. The assumption therefore can be made that material profits gained by one's own work are seen as more acceptable than are the profits provided by a form of social welfare that satisfies people's needs irrespective of their activity.

However, it should be noted that our experimental situation was perceived by our subjects as a task situation and the allocation decisions were viewed as a means for rewarding work. Thus, subjects' higher acceptance of "equity" decisions (i.e., the contribution-proportional ones) than of decisions based on individual needs may pertain only to the work situation. When allocations have no character of rewarding for work, other types of decisions may be preferred.

REFERENCES

Austin, W., Walster E., & Utne, M. K. (1976). Equity and the law: The effect of a harmdoers's "suffering in the act" on liking and assigned punishment. In L. Berkowitz, & E. Walster (Eds.), *Advances in experimental social psychology*. New York: Academic Press.

Barnes, R. D., Ickes W., & Kidd F.R. (1977). *Effects of the perceived intentionality and stability of another's dependency on helping behavior. A field experiment.* Unpublished manuscript, University of Wisconsin.

Deutsch, M. (1985). *Distributive justice: A social-psychological perspective.* New Haven: Yale University Press.

Guilford, J. P. (1964). *Podstawowe metdy statystyczne w psychologii i pedagogice.* (Fundamental statistics in psychology and education). Warszawa: PWN.

Mikula, G., & Schlamberger K. (1985). *What people think about an unjust event: Toward a better understanding of the phenomenology of experiences of injustice.* Manuscript. University of Graz.

Pilkiewicz, M. (1962). *Techniki socjometryczne* (Sociometric Techniques). Psychologia Wychowawcza.

Roscoe, J. T. (1975). *Fundamental research statistics for behavioral sciences.* New York: Holt, Rinehart, & Winston.

Skarżyńska, K. (1985). *Psychospołeczne aspekty decyzji alokacyjnych.* (Psychosocial aspects of allocative decisions). Wrocław: Ossolineum.

Utne, M. K., & Kidd R. (1980). Equity and attribution. In G. Mikula (Ed.), *Justice and social interaction.* Bern, Stuttgart, Vienna: Hans Huber Publishers.

Wosińska, W. (1985). *Injustice as experienced and observed by medical staff.* Paper presented at the conference: Justice and Injustice in Interpersonal Relations. Kozubnik.

10 Information and Evaluation Processes in Decision Making

Tadeusz Tyszka
Department of Psychology
Polish Academy of Sciences

DECISION PROBLEMS AND STRATEGIES

Having a choice among various places of employment, among apartments, or among various alternatives for spending a vacation, we find ourselves in a decision situation. If the choice is not determined in advance by someone else or by one's self (e.g. when it is an automatic act), we face a decision problem.

Even such a trivial decision problem as the choice among several kinds of socks in a store, if we focus our attention on it, requires quite numerous information and evaluation processes. We acquire certain information on choice alternatives (on socks), some directly through our senses (e.g., with regard to color), some by making special efforts (e.g., asking the saleslady the price), and still others through making inferences (e.g., about durability). We evaluate the attractiveness of these individual aspects of various alternatives and must arrive at something like a global assessment of a given alternative that determines our choice.

Putting the matter abstractly, a typical decision problem contains some choice alternatives: A_1, A_2, A_3, ... which can be described in various ways (with respect to various attributes): X_1, X_2, X_3... The decision maker generally must acquire information on these characteristics of alternatives. Eventually he or she must also compare this information or process it in some way. The decision maker then must make some evaluation of these characteristics and also arrive at something like a global evaluation of alternatives (not necessarily for all alternatives and not necessarily in the form of one composite index of the attractiveness of alternatives). The manner in which these information and evaluation processes take place is referred to as a decision-making strategy.

One can imagine many possible decision strategies. For example, in searching for information the decision maker can simultaneously investigate all choice alternatives, comparing them with respect to successive attributes (searching for information by attributes), or he or she can investigate a single alternative with respect to its various attributes (searching for information by alternatives). One can investigate all alternatives or only a certain (greater or smaller) part of them. Moreover, one can investigate various alternatives with respect to the same attributes or different ones.

Likewise, as far as evaluation processes are concerned, the decision maker can use evaluations of an absolute type: Alternative A_1 with respect to attribute X_1 is good (satisfying), extremely bad, etc. or one can be use evaluations of a comparative type: Alternative A_1 is better/worse than A_2 with respect to X_1. One can use more or less precise evaluations, e.g., X is better than y, or the preferential "distance" from x to y is greater/lesser than the "distance" from y to z. The decision maker can create from partial evaluations (i.e., evaluation with respect to particular attributes) one global evaluation of an alternative, or can use a nonintegrated index of partial evaluations.

Various combinations of these information and evaluation processes are possible, and so various decision-making strategies can be formulated. Indeed, there are at least a dozen seemingly reasonable strategies described in the literature; that some of them are really used by people has been confirmed empirically (cf. Svenson, 1983).

The two main approaches to understanding decision making that have been developed and expressed in suitably formulated decision strategies are the optimizing model and its opposite, the satisficing model (term introduced by Simon, 1955).

According to the first approach, making a decision is viewed as a search by the decision maker for the best choice, i.e., the best alternative. The concept of "bestness" finds its fullest expression in the decision strategy of maximization of additive utilities. This strategy stipulates the following sequential processes: evaluation of the attractiveness (utilities) of each of the alternatives with respect to a fixed set of attributes; evaluation of the importance of each of the attributes; determining the global attractiveness (utility) of each of the alternatives in the form of a weighted sum of each of the dimensions; comparison of these global evaluations and selection of the alternative with the greatest global attractiveness.

The range of information that the decision maker would need to process in using this strategy is so vast that it is hard to imagine that humans would be able to execute all the steps required here. Consequently various simplified strategies appear to be more consistent with our limited cognitive capacities. For example, instead of precise evaluations of alternatives with respect to individual attributes, decision makers may limit themselves to "rougher" evaluations concerning whether an alternative is positive (plus) or negative (minus) in a certain respect and choose the alternative with the highest weighted combination of pluses and minuses (weighted by the importance of individual attributes). Decision makers can use further simplifications and apply the strategy of choosing the alternative with the highest simple combination of pluses and minuses.

Another group of simple strategies is based on comparing alternatives with respect to individual attributes and counting the advantages of each alternative over others with respect to all attributes. This allows use of the "most pros rule," by which the alternative with the greatest number of advantages is chosen, or the least cons rule, by which the alternative with the least number of "cons" is chosen.

Another mode of simplification consists in resigning from comparison of alternatives with respect to less important attributes if they differ (or differ clearly enough) with respect to more important attributes. The lexicographical rule involves comparison of alternatives beginning with the most important attribute. If with respect to this most important attribute one of the alternatives is better than the others, then it is recognized as the best and is chosen. If with respect to this most important dimension there is no best alternative, then the second most important attribute settles the matter.

A totally different strategy and different model of choice was suggested by Simon (1955, 1957). He criticized the very concept of optimizing as assuming unrealistic human capacities for processing information. In place of the assumption of unlimited information - processing capacities, he introduced the idea of limited rationality of the decision maker. He assumed that the individual is unable to make a comprehensive comparison of various choice alternatives and so is unable to be guided by the principle of optimizing. Persons are guided rather by the satisficing principle – i.e., they choose options that are good enough, and not necessarily optimal.

One of the decision strategies that is based on the satisficing principle consists of checking various alternatives to see whether they meet various requirements (e.g., whether work is sufficiently renumerative, whether it provides a certain level of satisfaction from its performance, whether physical conditions are "tolerable"). The first alternative that is found to meet all of these requirements is choosen, even though some other more attractive alternatives might be discovered if one were to search futher. This is called the conjunctive strategy. Another strategy based on the same satisficing principle is the disjunctive strategy. This involves the choice of an alternative meeting at least one of the criteria for satisfaction.

In the following sections we review the literature concerning information and evaluation processes in decision making. This review is used to evaluate the merit of optimizing and satisficing approaches. Additionally, while reviewing findings on information seeking and even more those on evaluation processes, we will encounter phenomena that are odd and inconsistent with both optimizing and satisficing approaches. This leads to a new conceptualization of the nature of the decision-making process. This new conceptualization seems to leave room for uncertainty and amiguity of human evaluative judgments, which has not been sufficiently recognized neither in the decision making area nor in other fields dealing with human values.

INFORMATION PROCESSES

How does a person who is to make a decision collect information on choice alternatives and their features? How does he or she process this information?

In searching for answers to these questions, several research techniques have been used. One is the eye-movement recording technique. With this technique a special apparatus is used to record visual fixation points, and on this basis the sequence and kind of elements being "investigated" are followed.

A second technique for investigating information collection processes involves following the search for information. Choice alternatives are described according to their various features (attributes) and presented to the subject. Descriptions of individual attributes for various alternatives appear on separate cards, but initially the cards are covered. One follows which cards and in what sequence are "uncovered" by the subject. More convenient than this "manual" procedure is the use of a television screen connected with a microcomputer, which can be used to produce certain information on the screen.

Still another technique for following the process of searching for information was introduced by Engländer and Tyszka (1980). Without identfying any attributes characterizing choice alternatives, they gave subjects the opportunity to obtain any information at all on each of the alternatives. This information was given to the subject by suitably prepared assistants of the experimenter, who were presented as persons very familiar with individual alternatives. In fact, assistants gave information prepared beforehand. This technique most closely approximates real-life decision making situations and allows the recording of aspects of alternatives freely chosen by subjects.

Using techniques of these brands, a number of regularities concerning the search for and processing of information have been observed. In the section that follows, these regularities are discussed with reference to the questions for which they provide at least partial answers.

How Much Information Does the Decision Maker Acquire?

Even when separate attributes of alternatives are identified for them, decision makers do not check all of the information. In particular, it appears that as the complexity of the task increases (number of alternatives and/or number of attributes), decision makers are satisfied with investigating a smaller proportion (but not smaller absolute number!) of aspects; yet, this does not reduce their confidence in the correctness of decisions made (see Jacoby, Chestnut, Weigl, & Fisher, 1976). As van Raaij (1983) has shown, the amount of information acquired is a function of the range of variability for attributes of various alternatives. Namely, it turned out that with greater differentiation of alternatives persons acquire more information before making a decision. This is understandable if one assumes that greater differentiation of alternatives makes the problem more important for the decision maker.

The previously mentioned self-limitation in the amount of information acquired is unquestionably an expression of human's limited information capacity. In the experiment by Engländer and Tyszka (1980), in which the choice of attributes was not imposed by the experimenter, the following additional phenomenon was observed: Some time (approximately 2 weeks) after the subjects had made their choices (concerning place of employement and a book to recommend to a publisher) based on information that each of them requested, the same decision task was given to them once again, this time with expanded information. It turned out that many persons changed their choice when provided with more information. This means, it would seem, that people not only fail to acquire all the available information on choice alternatives, but also that omissions include even information that would have an important influence on their choices.

How is the Information on Choice Alternatives Collected?

When one examines the sequence by which people acquire information concerning various aspect of alternatives, it is possible to distinguish among three types of transitions between successive questions asked by the decision maker. These types are identified by Jacoby et al. (1976) and Payne (1976):

Type 1. The next question concerns the same aspect as the previous one and is addressed to a different alternative; this corresponds to acquiring information by aspects.

Type 2. The next question concerns a different aspect than the previous one and is addressed to the same alternative as the previous one; this corresponds to acquiring information by alternatives.

Type 3. The next question concerns a different aspect than the previous one and is addressed to a different alternative than the previous one; such transitions, if they were numerous, would show a lack of any orderliness in acquiring information.

Figures 10.1 and 10.2 are two empirical schemes for giving questions on alternatives labeled A to E (F is the column designating questions concerning all alternatives at the same time) from Tyszka's experiment (1985a). The numbers on the left side stand for the coded number of the question. Their sequence corresponds to the sequence of the questions asked. Figure 10.1

Aspects	Alternatives					
	A	B	C	D	E	F
0060						x
0020						x
2020						x
3030						x
0030		x				
0070	x		x	x	x	
0130	x		x	x	x	
0132	x		x	x	x	
0132	x		x	x	x	
0040	x			x		
0060			x			
0060				x	x	
1010	x			x		
1020	x			x		
0020	x			x		
3020	x			x		
3020						x
	9	1	5	10	5	5

FIGURE 10.1 Pattern of information searching of subject A-C1.

Aspects	Alternatives					
	A	B	C	D	E	F
1100	x					
3030	x					
0130	x					
0020	x					
0023	x					
0040	x					
1100		x				
3030		x				
1010		x				
0040		x				
0130		x				
0030		x				
3170		x				
1100			x			
3030			x			
0040			x			
0030			x			
3170			x			
0033			x			
0040			x			
3030			x			
0030				x		
3030				x		
0040				x		
3030					x	
0040					x	
0030					x	
0060			x		x	
0040					x	
2020					x	
0050						x
0050	x					
	7	7	9	3	6	1

FIGURE 10.2. Pattern of information searching of subject I-CS.

roughly corresponds to acquiring information by aspects; Figure 10.2 corresponds almost ideally to acquiring information by alternatives. In these studies transitions of these various types were observed, and especially interesting are the proportions of transitions of types 1 and 2. Type 1 corresponds more to optimizing behavior; it suggests comparison of alternatives in various respects. Type 2 suits the search for the satisficing alternative because one alternative is looked at in various respects.

Various circumstances such as the manner of presenting alternatives, their differentiation, and the complexity of the decision problem (number of alternatives) influence the predominance of one transition type or another (see Payne, 1976; van Raaij, 1983). Generally, more transitions of type 1 are observed in the first part of the decision making process (in the first half) and more transitions of type 2 in the final part (Payne, 1976; van Raaij, 1983). This difference would seem to result from a two-stage investigation of alternatives (especially when there are many of them); first the person checks a number of aspects for all alternatives, which presumably serves to reject part of them, after which there is a concentration "in depth" on certain alternatives, that are investigated individually (Payne, 1976; Engländer & Tyszka, 1980).

How Thoroughly are Various Alternatives Investigated?

Note that in accordance with the optimizing approach, all alternatives should be investigated with the same care. In brief, they should be compared with each other to see which of them is the best. The satisficing model, on the other hand, stipulates something quite the opposite. It assumes a mechanism for eliminating alternatives. The alternative, which does not meet some criterion of the decision maker, is immediately rejected and there is no reason to investigate it further; finding a satisficing alternative also makes further investigation superfluous. Therefore, in accordance with the satisficing model, not all alternatives will be investigated with the same thoroughness; some of them will be investigated very thoroughly, others – less so or not at all. The alternative that will be investigated most thoroughly should be the alternative that is finally chosen.

In general, the results of various experiments are completely in agreement with the satisficing model. Indeed, the alternative finally chosen usually attracted the most attention from the decision maker prior to making a choice (Dahlstrand & Montgomery, 1984; Engländer & Tyszka, 1980; Tyszka, 1985a).

Some alternatives are eliminated from the very beginning, sometimes after one or two introductory questions. Engländer and Tyszka (1980) introduced a special measure of the distribution of questions among all choice alternatives – the variability coefficient[1] – and found that for most subjects it was very low, which indicated that subjects concentrated on only a few choice alternatives (the index is 0 when all questions concern only one alternative).

Is Comparable Information Collected Regarding Each Alternative?

In the study by Engländer and Tyszka (1980) it was found that in searching for information on various alternatives, subjects did not always ask about the same aspects of various alternatives. For example, someone choosing between two films might ask whether the first film contained elements of humor and whether the second film contained erotic elements. Making a decision based on such nonparallel information is inconsistent with the principle of optimization that requires complete comparability of alternatives with respect to a fixed set of attributes. Similarly, it is inconsistent with the principle of satisficing choice that also assumes evaluation of alternatives with respect to a fixed set of attributes. Such behavior, however, may make sense when the decision maker already has some picture of the alternatives considered and is searching for additional information to supplement or confirm this picture (Engländer, & Tyszka, 1980).

Is Less Information Collected About a Greater Number of Alternatives or More Information About Only a Few Alternatives?

Another intriguing finding concerning the search for information was obtained by Tyszka (1985). Subjects had a choice among six alternatives (places of work, publications). Initially, they were given only very limited information about these alternatives. More specifically, six attributes were identified with respect to which alternatives differed, but individual alternatives were described with respect to only one, two, or three attributes (see Table 10.1).

---

[1] The variability coefficient of the distribution is defined as:

$$V = \frac{\delta}{\bar{x}} \cdot 100,$$

where: δ is the standard deviation of the distribution, and $\bar{x}$ the mean.
An even better measure is simply the entropy of the distribution, H:
$H = \sum^{n} - p \log p$

TABLE 10.1

Initial Information on Choice Alternatives (T. Tyszka, 1985)

Alternatives	*Attributes* 1	2	3	4	5	6
A_1	not fully satisfactory*		satisfactory°	very good°		
A_2	very good°		nonsatisfactory*	satisfactory°		
A_3		satisfactory°		not fully satisfactory*		
A_4	nonsatisfactory*		very good°			
A_5				very good°		
A_6		not fully satisfactory*			satisfactory°	very good°

Note: Entries marked by * have been revealed in one experimental version. Entries marked by ° – in the other experimental version.

Before making a choice, subjects could obtain a certain amount of further information; that is, they could select a specified number of squares in Table 10.1 about which they would receive answers. One of the independent variables in this experiment was the number of additional squares about which subjects could obtain additional information (6 vs. 12). With less information available, subjects did not simply acquire proportionally less information about each alternative but rather limited the number of alternatives examined, i.e., they concentrated on a smaller number of alternatives that they presumably viewed as most "promising."

In short, during the search for information decision makers hardly treat all choice alternatives the same way. Some are investigated quite thoroughly, others only superficially (or not at all). When decision makers have limited access to information, they concentrate all the more on some of the alternatives only. They do not always investigate various alternatives in the same respects. These features bring to mind the search for information in the postdecisional phase (for the purpose of reducing cognitive dissonance, which was described by Festinger, 1957).

It is interesting that Festinger, describing the information search process in the postdecisional phase, contrasted it with the feature of acquiring information in the predecisional phase. Festinger (1957) wrote: "One may further expect that such a person (in the pre-decisional phase) will search for information in an impartial way. He will not select one type of information in order to accept it and avoid information of another type. Rather he will be motivated to acquire knowledge about all aspects and all alternatives" (p. 127).

The studies cited previously suggest that Festinger's contrast was completely amiss. In both the predecisional and postdecisional phases the search for information is characterized by selectivity and "partiality." The source of selectivity and partiality in the postdecisional phase is, according to Festinger, the desire to reduce the unpleasant state of cognitive dissonance. This reduction takes place as one searches for favorable information about the alternative chosen and unfavorable information about the alternatives rejected.

What can be the source of selectivity and partiality of acquiring information in the predecisional phase? Zajonc (1980) proposed the general hypothesis that people's preferences often precede cognition. He cited experimental data showing that even such simple cognitive judgments as recognition or identification of the features of a perceived object can be preceded by affective reactions, which are probably based on the "rough," partially recognized, global features of the object.

Within the decision-making context, Montgomery (1983) suggested a model in which the decision-making process is viewed as a process of generating and checking hypotheses concerning which of the alternatives is dominant (superior) over the others. This model assumes a preselection of one or more promising alternatives, which are then checked to see whether one is really the best. Then this promising alternative can be regarded as a tentative choice of the decision maker. Checking the correctness of such a choice resembles in certain respects justification of the final choice in the postdecisional phase as described by Festinger.

It is hardly clear, however, how this preselection takes place. According to Zajonc (1980), this process is based on only minimal and very rough, global recognition. In his opinion, this is shown by findings of studies in which persons preferred "old" stimuli (i.e., exhibited earlier) to new ones, even when they were unable to recognize which stimuli were old and which were new. Features used to make discriminations among stimuli (e.g., brightness, hue, and saturation in the discrimination of colors) have not been found to be factors responsible for color preferences. Unfortunately, neither Zajonc nor anyone else has been able to more precisely define which features would be responsible for these preferences.

According to an orthodox view, which Zajonc opposes, recognition procedes preferences. Montgomery, (1983), a proponent of the orthodox view, maintains that the choice of a promising alternative is determined by such factors as its advantage with respect to some attribute, especially if this is an attribute important for the person.

Generally, it appears that little is known at this time about how this preselection takes place, which directs the further course of decision making processes.

EVALUATION PROCESSES

The starting point for every theory of choice is the assumption that decisions are based on the preferences of decision makers, i.e., on their evaluations of the consequences of actions from among which they must chose. As it was stressed previously, these assessments can take various shapes and can be made with varying degrees of accuracy.

According to the two main approaches to the problem of choice that are considered in this chapter, it is important to distinguish comparative and absolute evaluations. The model of optimizing behavior assumes evaluations of the comparative type (e.g., "A is better/worse than B"; "the preferential distance from B to C"). These evaluations are made on at least a pair of alternatives. On the other hand, the satisficing model assumes absolute evaluations (e.g., "A is sufficiently/insuficiently good"). The evaluation is made with respect to some standard that is external to the alternatives considered. Generally speaking, as a process this second type of evaluation is simpler, but the standard that it requires is not always so simple to determine.

A second important difference between these approaches concerns whether or not the integration of partial evaluations is posited. The model of optimizing behavior assumes such integration, i.e., it requires some global evaluation that aggregates evaluations of each alternative (e.g., utility, number of advantages). The satisficing model of behavior assumes the use of unintegrated partial evaluations by decision maker (e.g., their conjunction). The requirements of the satisficing model appear less demanding in this respect.

A recent support for using the type of evaluations consistent with the satisficing model has been provided in my research (Tyszka, 1985a) on the role of familiarity in decision making. As results of this research are referred to in further parts of the chapter, we briefly describe its design.

In this study, persons of two professions participated: architects and engineers involved in automobile design. Two decision tasks were used, the choice of one among five apartments and the choice of one among five automobiles. Half of the 16 architects were faced with one decision task, half with the second. Likewise eight engineers solved the problem of choosing a flat, and eight the problem of choosing an automobile. Thus, two of the four experimental groups made a choice among profesionally familiar alternatives, and two among less familiar alternatives.

The study was carried out by two persons, the experimenter and an assistant – an architect or engineer – whose task was to give each subject information concerning alternatives. The alternatives were especially "designed" for the purposes of this study, i.e., very precisely described and so selected that none of them was superior to others in all respects.

Subjects were simply informed that they had to choose among five alternatives, designated by letters A to E, and that they could obtain unrestricted information on each of the alternatives. They were asked to "think aloud," i.e., to say everything that came into their minds during the course of the investigation. Besides, after answering any question asked by the subject; he or she was asked: "How do you evaluate the information received?" The study concluded for each subject when he or she made a final choice of one of the alternatives.

Analysis of acquiring information by subjects in four experimental groups revealed results consistent with regularities described in Section 2. Different alternatives were investigated with unequal attention. Some of them were eliminated very quickly, others were examined much more thoroughly. Most attention in terms of questions asked and statements addressed to was paid to the alternative finally chosen. Investigation, especially during the second half of question asking, involved in a large measure a series of questions concentrated on a single alternative. These tendencies in information acquisition were accompanied by a tendency to formulate the majority of descriptive and evaluative statements in absolute and not comparative terms. This whole picture is evidently more consistent with satisficing than with optimizing behavior.

The two approaches discussed so far (that of optimizing vs. satisfacing) share the assumption that the process of evaluation is made "impartially," i.e., various alternatives are treated (at least initially) equally. As a result of this evaluation, either the best or the most satisfying alternative is selected.

In contrast to these asumptions, Festinger (1957) has observed that in the postdecisional phase, people's opinions are hardly impartial. He stated that after making a choice, a person not only selectively receives information on choice alternatives but also begins to assess alternatives in a one-sided manner. After making a choice, the discrepancy in attractiveness grows between the chosen and the unchosen alternative. This takes place either through an increase in the attractiveness of the alternative chosen or through a decrease in the attractiveness of the alternative rejected, or through both of these occurring at the same time.

More and more observations show, however, that partiality occurs in the predecisional phase. Having ascertained that a certain alternative is better than others in some respect, the decision maker has a tendency to favor it also with respect to other attributes. Seeing in it a promising alternative decision makers try to show (not only to others but mainly to themselves) that it is at least as good as other options in every respect, that it "dominates" all of the other alternatives. For example, Jarvis (1976) has noted that this is a common practice in making political decisions.

Findings in one of my studies (Tyszka, 1983) may be associated with this tendency. Subjects were asked to choose from among three alternatives concerning various problems (e.g., introducing a new technology, purchase of a license, etc.). The information they were given was the rank ordering of the alternatives relative to each attribute (see Figure 10.3). For example, in the sets

Attributes	
I	II
A	B
C	A
B	C

set 1

Attributes	
I	II
A	B
B	D
D	A

set 2

FIGURE 10.3. Two sets of alternatives T. Tyszka (1983).

1 and 2 shown in the figure, alternatives A,B,C and A,B,D were so arranged that in set 1 the best with respect to feature I is alternative A, then C, then B (i.e., B was the worst here), and with respect to feature II, the order of attractiveness of alternatives was B,A,C. Set 2 contained alternatives A,B,D such that for I the order of their attractiveness was A,B,D and for II, B,D,A. Note that alternatives A and B were ordered, relative one to another, the same way in both sets: A was better than B with respect to feature I and worse that B with respect to feature II. The subjects, however, in set 1 preferred A on the whole, and in set 2, they preferred B. The explanation for this behavior seems to be that in set 1 there is a third alternative C, which in every respect is worse than A (but not B!), and in set 2 there is alternative D, which in every respect is worse than B (but not A). Hence, choosing between two nondominated alternatives, subjects preferred this one that was dominant over the third in the set.

Montgomery (1983) mentioned various processes that on one hand de-emphasize the attractiveness of an alternative and one the other, bolster its attractiveness. For example, the decision maker can de-empasize or bolster the value of a certain attribute with respect to which a promising alternative is worse (or better) than some other one. He or she can reduce or exaggerate the difference between two alternatives in some respect. (Even in the case of such an easily measurable attribute as money, a loss or gain of 1,000 zlotys can be felt differently, depending on what we imagine we can acquire for this 1,000 zlotys). One can use arguments of the probabilistic type, e.g., that it is not certain whether a given negative consequence will occur at all. One can finally "manufacture" additional positive or negative evaluations by making inferences about some features based on information about other features. In any case, according to Montgomery (1983) the process of evaluations is clearly directed and aims at arriving at a dominance structure, i.e., set of opinions such that one of the choice alternatives emerges as definitely better than the others, dominating all of the others. In this way the process of evaluation in the predecisional phase very much resembles the justification of choice in the postdecisional phase.

Dahlstrand and Montgomery (1984) conducted an experiment that to some extent tested Montgomery's idea. The subjects studied by them were to choose one from among five flats. As in studies on search processes, they could acquire information about any aspect (among eight attributes) of any alternative. Information was projected on a television screen connected to a microcomputer, on which the subject pressed a certain key to obtain given information. After acquiring information on a selected aspect of a given alternative, the subject ranked it on an appropriate graphic scale that was shown on the screen. After each series of 10 questions and answers, subjects judged the chances of their eventually selecting each of the alternatives. About half of the subjects during the first half of their questions had already made a tentative choice of the alternative that they finally selected. Just as in other studies on search for information, subjects devoted the most attention to the alternative finally chosen. This alternative also received the highest evaluations, especially in the second half of the decision-making process. These high evaluations resulted in large measure from consideration of attributes that were not looked at in the evaluation of other alternatives.

Also in our research cited earlier (Tyszka, 1985a), we found several hints pointing to subjects' tendency to use dominance structuring. Several protocols ended with the subject emphasizing the advantages and positive aspects of the alternative chosen. The ratio of positive to negative evaluations for that alternative was higher in most instances for the second half of the experiment than for the first one. Explicit de-emphasizing of the negative aspects of the alternative chosen was stated (e.g., "After all, it is not so serious a drawback" or "From another point of view this could be regarded as an advantage").

CHOICES WITH UNCERTAIN PREFERENCES

In the various approaches described earlier regarding the nature of human preferences, it was usually assumed (except, perhaps, for the conception of dominance structure) that these preferences are certain, unambiguous, and consistent. In other words, it is assumed that decision makers know what they want, what they prize more and what less, and that they will be able to compare consistently various likes and dislikes.

It is worth noting that the assumption of clarity regarding opinions (likes and dislikes) is not limited to decision-making theory. It is accepted (usually tacitly) in, for example, theories concerning attitudes and everywhere that human valuations are measured (this volume included).

More and more, observations of human decision making behavior show, however, that our preferences are far from clear in many contexts. This is seen, for example, in the often observed reversal of preferences as a result of a change in the name of the objects compared, or as a result of only a minor change in the formulation of a question (see Fischhoff, Slovic, & Lichtenstein, 1980).

There are data that show that people reverse their preferences depending on whether options are formulated in terms of gains or losses. Tversky (1977) told his subjects that in a certain town a new dangerous variety of influenza had appeared and that it could cause the death of 600 persons. The authorities of the town had two possibilities of counteraction. If they decided on action 1, then it was certain that they could save 200 people. If they decided on action 2, there was a one-third chance (probability) that they could save all 600 people, but there was a two-thirds chance that they would not succeed in saving anyone. The subjects were asked to decide which action they favored. The majority of subjects chose action 1. For another group of similar subjects, the following problem of choice was formulated with the same introduction. There were two possible actions. Action 1 would definitely lead to the death of 400 people. Action 2 gave a one-third chance that no one would die and a two-thirds chance that 600 people would die. Again the subjects were supposed to choose one of these actions. A clear majority favored action 2. However, it is easy to see that the problems concern a identical choice: to save 200 among 600 people it is the same as to allow the other 400 people to die. Similary, to have a one-third probability of saving 600 people and a two-thirds probability of not saving anyone is the same as accepting a one-third chance that no one will die and a two-thirds chance that 600 people will. Thus, depending on whether the problem was described in terms of saving the lives of a certain number of people or in terms of the loss of life of a corresponding number of people, subjects' preferences completely reversed themselves. This seems to suggest that perhaps people do not have very clear and consistent system of values on which they base their preferences.

In my previously cited experiment (Tyszka, 1985a), hints have been found that pointed out to this lack of clarity regarding decision maker's opinions. One of these hints was an increase in the proportion of comparative to absolute judgments among subjects dealing with less familiar alternatives as compared with those dealing with more familiar alternatives. A probable interpretation of this phenomenon is that subjects less familiar with the task lacked clear and precise standards for describing and evaluating choice alternatives. The absence of such standards did not permit the person to make absolute judgements and evaluations, and so he or she was compelled to make greater use of comparing alternatives among themselves. The same absence of standards may underlie another result of our research. We found that persons facing a less familiar decision task were more inclined to limit their evaluative judgements by concentrating on only some alternatives than those more familiar with the task. This tendency may reflect the difficulties of these persons with valuation process.

There are several complex and unfamiliar issues on which people may not have clear, coherent opinions. As March (1978) noted, sometimes we undertake special actions to clarify our preferences to ourselves, to convince ourselves that something really does (or does not) suit us. How do people reach decisions despite uncertainty or incoherence of their preferences? Perhaps most often they do not realize that their preferences are incoherent or ambiguous. According to Montgomery's approach discussed earlier, the decision maker finds a promising alternative and tries to structuralize a situation in such a way to justify a choice of this alternative. Assuming such a nature of the decision making process, uncertainty and ambiguity of preferences need not be an obstacle but may be an advantage in reaching a decision. Manipulating various aspects of evaluation (de-emphasizing, bolstering, etc.) seems to be easier and more natural under ambiguous and uncertain preferences than under precise and exact ones. Perhaps the search for good justification or minimizing doubts may also account for a finding (Tyszka, 1985a) that subjects less familiar with the decision task showed the tendency to make more positive evaluations of the alternative considered than subjects more familiar with the task.

However, human decision makers may be forced or encouraged to consider conflicting values, and hence they may be fully conscious of ambiguity or inconsistency of their preferences. How do they solve this problem? Two options seem to be posible: The decision maker may try to overcome the problem of uncertain preferences by applying a decision strategy, which does not require confrontation of conflicting or uncertain preferences, or he or she may try to order or reconcile his or her preferences. Following the first option, the decision maker may overcome the problem of importance of various attributes by applying a decision strategy that does not require such evaluations (e.g., conjunctive or disjunctive decision strategies). When one is ambiguous about thresholds of satisfaction on attributes, he or she may apply a strategy that is based on comparative and not absolute evaluations. One may adopt a rule or a concept that minimizes his or her doubts, e.g., avoiding alternatives with extreme values (cf. Tyszka, 1983).

Ordering and reconciling ambiguous or incoherent preferences is one of the most painful enterprises, particularly when one has to compare such "incomparable" issues as ethical versus utilitarian or social versus personal values, etc. These confrontations are sensitive to several factors–phrasing questions, labeling options or their consequences, etc.–evoking different considerations (cf. Fischhoff et al., 1980). Formulating our evaluative judgments, we observe others' values and rely to some extent on others' opinions. In my experiment cited earlier (Tyszka, 1985a), some subjects unfamiliar with the choice alternatives manifested need for an opinion or advice rather than descriptive information on choice alternatives. We invoke our own experience or past preferences and try to be consistent with them. In an experiment of Slovic, Fischhoff, Lichtenstein, Corrigan, and Combs (1977), most people preferred a gamble with a 25% chance of losing $ 200 and 75% chance of losing nothing to a sure loss of $ 50. However, they reversed their preferences when the sure loss was called an insurance premium; perhaps because buying insurance had been consistent with their past preferences. Finally, we undertake special actions to clarify or develop or control our preferences.

Discussing the problem of ambiguous human preferences, March (1978) claims that in some conditions they shouldn't be seen as a fault or weakness of the decision maker. He finds sense and intelligence in maintaining ambiguous and inconsistent preferences. One of his arguments is that human beings recognize that they construct or develop their tastes. They may choose to undertake an action that is inconsistent with their preferences and maintain a lack of coherence among their desires, in order to clarify or develop their tastes. Another argument–meaningful in the context of moral values discussed in this volume–is that human beings find sense in treating their preferences strategically. They sense that some of their desires, although powerful, are inappropriate and they engage in activities designed to manage preferences (e.g., they made commitments). Maintaining contradictory and imperfectly reconciled desires allows them "to control the development of tastes or to buffer action from tastes" (March, 1978).

REFERENCES

Dahlstrand, U., & Montgomery, H. (1984). Information search and evaluative processes in decision making: A computer based process tracing study. *Acta Psychologica, 56,* 113-123.

Engländer, T., & Tyszka, T., (1980). Information seeking in open decision situation. *Acta Psychologica, 45,* 169–176.

Festinger, L. (1957). *A theory of cognitive dissonance.* Evanston: Row Peterson.

Fischhoff, B., Slovic, P., & Lichtenstein, S. (1980). Knowing what you want: Measuring labile values. In T. S. Wallsten (Ed.), *Cognitive processes in choice and decision* behavior. Hillsdale, NJ: Lawrence Erlbaum Associates.

Jacoby, J., Chestnut, R. W., Weigl, K. C., & Tisher J. (1976) Pre-purchase information acquistion: Description of a process methodology, research paradigm, and pilot investigation. In B. B. Anderson (Ed.). *Advances in consumer research* (Vol. 3). Cincinnati: Association for Consumer Research.

Jarvis, R. (1976). *Perception and misperception in international politics.* Princeton: University Press.

March, J. G. (1978). Bounded rationality, ambiguity, and the engineering of choice. *Bell Journal of Economics, 9,* 587–608.

Montgomery, H., (1983). Decision rules and the search for a dominance structure: Towards a process model of decision making. In P. Humphreys, O. Svenson, & A. Vari (Eds.), *Analysing and aiding decision processes.* Amsterdam: North-Holland.

Payne, J. N. (1976). Task complexity and contigent processing in decision making: An information search and protocol analysis. *Organizational Behavior and Human Performance, 16,* 366–387.

Simon, H. A. (1955). A behavioral model of rational choice. *Quarterly Journal of Economics, 69,* 99–118.

Simon, H. A. (1957). *Models of man.* New York: Wiley.

Slovic, P., & Fischhoff; B., Lichtenstein, S., Corrigan, B., & Combs, B. (1977). Preferences for insuring against probable small losses: Implications for the theory and practice of insurance. *Journal of Risk and Insurance, 44,* 237–258.

Svenson, O. (1983). Decision rules and information processing In L. Sjöberg, T. Tyszka, & J. Wise (Eds.), *Human decision making.* Lund: Doxa.

Tversky, A. (1977). On the elicitation of preferences: Descripive and prescriptive considerations. In D. E. Bell, R. L. Keeney, & H. Raiffa (Eds.), *Conflicting objectives in decisions.* New York: Wiley.

Tyszka, T. (1983). Contextual multiattribute decision rules. In L. Sjöberg, T. Tyszka, & J. Wise (Eds.), *Human decision making.* Lund: Doxa.

Tyszka, T. (1985). Variability of predecisional information seeking behavior, *Polish Psychological Bulletin, 16,* 275–282.

Tyszka, T. (1985a). Information and evaluative processe in decision making: The role of familiarity. In B. Brehmen, H. Jungermann, P. Lourons, & G. Sevon (Eds.), *New perspectives in decision making.* Amsterdam: North-Holland.

van Raaij, F. W. (1983). Techniques for process tracing in decision making. In L. Sjöberg, T. Tyszka, & J. Wise (Eds.), *Human decision making.* Lund: Doxa.

Zajonc, R. B. (1980). Feeling and thinking: preferences need no inferences. *American Psychologist, 35,* 151–175.

11 Social Values and Multiple Outcome Comparisons

John M. Levine
Richard L. Moreland
University of Pittsburgh

Values have been defined in many different ways by psychologists. One of the most influential definitions was provided by Rokeach (1973, 1979), who suggested that values are enduring beliefs that guide preferences about end states of existence and modes of conduct. More recently, Feather (1982) argued that values can be viewed as a special category of motives, specifically "those motives that involve normative consideratons of 'oughtness' and desirability, linked to an evaluative dimension of goodness and badness" (p. 87).

An important subclass of values, termed *social values*, is applicable to interpersonal situations in which participants can influence both their own and one another's outcomes (see MacCrimmon & Messick, 1976; McClintock, 1972; McClintock & Keil, 1983). When individuals are interdependent in this way, their satisfaction with their own outcomes is influenced by the outcomes that others receive. Social values can thus be defined as "consistent preferences for distributions of outcomes to self and other that may serve a motivational or a strategic purpose" (McClintock & Keil, 1983, p. 124). Reflecting Rokeach's (1973, 1979) distinction between end states of existence and modes of conduct, this definition of social values suggests that an actor may prefer specific levels of self/other outcomes either because these outcomes satisfy a goal that the actor wishes to achieve (motivational purpose) or because they are instrumental to the future attainment of that goal (strategic purpose).

Analyses of social values rely heavily on the process of *outcome comparison*. McClintock and Keil (1983), for example, define social values in terms of preferred relationships between two or more outcomes. These relationships can involve the outcomes of a single person (individualism, altrusim, aggression), the outcomes of two persons (cooperation, competition, equality), or both the inputs and outcomes of two persons (ordinal equity, proportional equity). Although this approach is quite interesting, it ignores several aspects of outcome comparison that may be important in clarifying the operation of social values. Two important aspects of outcome comparison that have been neglected are (a) the group context in which comparison occurs and (b) the occurrence of multiple comparisons.

The goal of the present chapter is to clarify how social values affect multiple outcome comparisons in group contexts. To achieve this goal, we first present and discuss a three-dimensional typology of single outcome comparisons that can occur in group contexts. Then, we consider what happens when individuals make multiple outcome comparisons by combining two or more single comparisons.

OUTCOME COMPARISON IN GROUP CONTEXTS

Previous analyses have considered only a small subset of the outcome comparisons that can occur in group contexts. Comparisons involving one's own and another person's outcomes have received the most theoretical and empirical attention (e.g., Adams, 1965; Austin, 1977; Cook, Crosby, & Hennigan, 1977; Davis, 1959; Goodman, 1974, 1977; Martin, 1981; Walster, Walster, & Berscheid, 1978). In some cases the two people involved in the comparison are identified as members of the same group; in other cases they are identified as members of different groups; in still other cases their group memberships are not specified. These self/other comparisons are usually assumed to occur at one point in time, generally the present. Work has also been done on comparisons involving a single individual's outcomes at two points in time (e.g., Cook et al., 1977; Davies, 1969; Feierabend, Feierabend, & Nesvold, 1969; Goodman, 1974, 1977; Gurr, 1970). In these self/self comparisons, the present is usually compared with the past, but sometimes the present and the future are compared. Finally, some attention has been devoted to comparisons involving the outcomes of two groups (e.g., Crosby, 1982; Guimond & Dube-Simard, 1983; Martin & Murray, 1983, 1984; Runciman, 1966; Williams, 1975). These group/group comparisons, like self/other comparisons, are generally assumed to occur at one point in time, usually the present.

A Typology of Outcome Comparison

In order to provide a general framework for integrating the various approaches mentioned previously we recently developed a three-dimensional typology of outcome comparison in group contexts (Levine & Moreland, 1986, in press). The three dimensions are Type of Comparison, Social Context, and Temporal Context (see Figure 11.1). Type of Comparison refers to the identities of the source and target of comparison. *Self/self* comparisons involve the outcomes of a single individual; *self/other* comparisons involve the outcomes of different individuals; *group/group* comparisons involve the outcomes of one or more groups. Social Context refers to the group identification of the source and target of comparison. *Intragroup* comparisons occur when the source and target are identified with the same group; *intergroup* comparisons occur when the source and target are identified with different groups. Finally, Temporal Context refers to the time period(s) during which the two outcomes under consideration occur. *Intratemporal* comparisons involve outcomes that occur during the same time period (i.e., past-past, present-present, future-future); *intertemporal* comparisons involve outcomes that occur during different time periods (i.e., past-present, past-future, present-future).

Figure 11.1 contains 12 cells reflecting the intersections of the three dimensions described earlier. The top layer of the figure depicts comparisons involving the outcomes of a single individual; the middle layer depicts

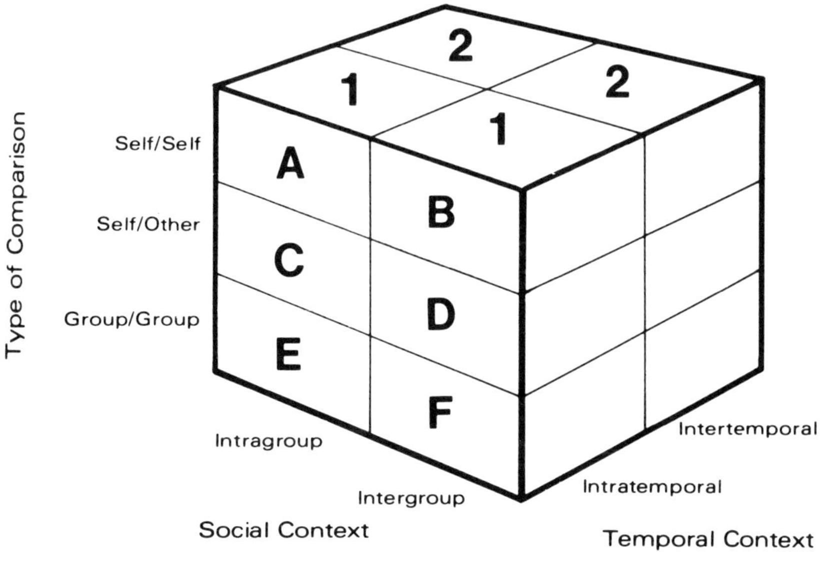

FIGURE 11.1. Varieties of outcome comparison in group contexts (from Levine & Moreland, 1986).

comparisons involving the outcomes of two people; the bottom layer depicts comparisons involving the outcomes of groups. The four cells in each layer differ regarding whether the outcomes involved occur within one group or two groups and at one point in time or two points in time.

Examples of comparisons in the four self/self cells are:

(A1) A faculty member comparing the salary that he currently receives with the salary that he believes he deserves.
(A2) A faculty member comparing her current salary to the salary that she received last year.
(B1) A faculty member comparing his current salary at the university with the income that he currently receives as a member of a consulting firm.
(B2) A faculty member comparing her current salary to the salary that she received last year at another university.

Examples of comparisons in the four self/other cells are:

(C1) A faculty member comparing his current salary to the current salary of a colleague at his own university.
(C2) A faculty member comparing her current salary to the salary received last year by a colleague at her own university.
(D1) A faculty member comparing his current salary to the salary currently received by a colleague at another university.
(D2) A faculty member comparing her current salary to the salary received last year by a colleague at another university.

Examples of comparisons in the four group/group cells are:

(E1) A faculty member comparing the average salary currently received by faculty at his university with the average salary that he believes they deserve.
(E2) A faculty member comparing the average salary currently received by faculty at her university with the average salary that they received last year.
(F1) A faculty member comparing the average salary currently received by faculty at his university with the average salary currently received by faculty at another university.
(F2) A faculty member comparing the average salary currently received by faculty at her university with the average salary received by faculty at another university last year.

Factors That Determine Choice of Comparison Options

Because an individual could select any one of the comparison options depicted in Figure 11.1, it is necessary to consider the factors that determine choices among these options (Levine & Moreland, in press). Two general determinants of comparison choice can be identified; (1) the salience of an individual or a group as a possible target of comparison and (2) the attractiveness of the target as a source of comparison information (cf. Austin, 1977; Goodman, 1977; Singer, 1981). Salience depends on the availability of information concerning the target's outcome (e.g., salary) and any personal characteristics (related attributes) that are presumed to cause that outcome (e.g., seniority). Attractiveness depends on the source's motive for seeking comparison information and the target's assumed instrumentality in satisfying this motive.

Three motives for outcome comparison are particularly important. These motives, which can be viewed as social values, are: (1) the desire for *equity,* or an equal ratio of outcomes to related attributes for oneself and the target of comparison (cf. Adams, 1965; Walster et al., 1978); (2) the desire for *self-enhancement,* or a higher ratio of outcomes to related attributes for oneself than for the target of comparison (cf. Gruder, 1977; Hyman, 1942; Levine, 1983), and (3) the desire for *self-depreciation,* or a lower ratio of outcomes to related attributes for oneself than for the target of comparison (cf. Hyman, 1942; Martin, 1981; Patchen, 1961).

A target's assumed instrumentality in satisfying these three motives depends on the source's perception of his or her own and the target's outcomes and related attributes. A source motivated to achieve equity will prefer a target whose outcomes and related attributes allow an "equal" comparison. A source motivated to achieve self-enhancement will prefer a target whose outcomes and related attributes allow a "downward" comparison (Wills, 1981). A source motivated to achieve self-depreciation will prefer a target whose outcomes and related attributes allow an "upward" comparison.

When many potential targets are available for outcome comparison, the relative salience and attractiveness of these targets will determine which one is selected. Thus, the salience and attractiveness of available targets will influence the probability of (a) self/self versus self/other versus group/group comparisons, (b) intragroup versus intergroup comparisons, and (c) intratemporal versus intertemporal comparisons.

Regarding the Type of Comparison dimension, self/self comparisons are most likely when information about others' outcomes and related attributes is unavailable and when the self is highly salient, perhaps because of objective self-awareness (Carver & Scheier, 1981; Wicklund, 1980). The tendency to focus on oneself can be produced by external cues, such as a mirror (Carver & Scheier, 1978). Also, people who are high in "private self-consciousness" have a dispositional tendency to focus inward (Fenigstein, Scheier, & Buss, 1975). Self/other comparisons are most likely when information about one's own outcomes or related attributes is unavailable, when others are salient comparison objects, when one has a chronic concern about others' evaluations of oneself (Fenigstein, Scheier, & Buss, 1975), or when one desires to see oneself as unique (Lemaine, 1974; Snyder & Fromkin, 1980). Group/group comparisons are most likely when group membership is salient because of group competition, group dissimilarity, or status differentials between groups (Brewer, 1979), when group members seek to enhance their social identity through intergroup comparisons (Tajfel, 1978), or when group members seek to demonstrate their group's inferior outcomes in order to produce social change (Austin, 1977; Patchen, 1961).

Regarding the Social Context dimension, intragroup comparisons are more likely than intergroup comparisons when information about the outcomes or related attributes of targets associated with other groups is unavailable or likely to yield unsatisfying results. Intragroup comparisons are also likely when an individual is strongly identified with one group, because of long membership or high status in the group, or because the group is a "minority group" (Gerard & Hoyt, 1974; McGuire & McGuire, 1981; Mullen, 1983).

Regarding the Temporal Context dimension, intratemporal comparisons are more likely than intertemporal comparisons, because outcomes and related attributes that occur at the same point in time are easier to compare than are those that occur at different points in time. Among intratemporal comparisons, present-present comparisons are more likely than past-past comparisons, which in turn are more likely than future-future comparisons. Among intertemporal comparisons, present-past comparisons are more likely than present-future comparisons, which in turn are more likely than past-future comparisons. These predictions regarding intratemporal and intertemporal comparisons are based on two assumptions: (1) a person's tendency to make a comparison varies directly with his or her confidence in the information underlying the comparison, and (2) confidence is generally highest for information relating to present comparisons, next highest for information relating to past comparisons, and lowest for information relating to future comparisons.

Consequences of Comparison Options

Once an individual has selected a comparison option from those depicted in Figure 11.1,it is necessary to consider the consequences of that choice (Levine & Moreland, 1986). After engaging in social comparison, the source learns that his or her ratio of outcomes to related attributes is higher than, equal to, or lower than the target's ratio. The crucial issue, of course, is not the objective relationship between the source's and the target's ratios, but rather the source's interpretation of this relationship (cf. Adams, 1965; Martin & Murray, 1984; Walster et al., 1978).

Four dimensions of the source's interpetation of his or her superiority, equality, or inferiority seem especially important. One dimension is the *confidence* with which a comparison is made. A source will be confident about a comparison to the extent that he or she has subjectively valid information about (a) his or her own and the target's absolute outcomes and related attributes and (b) the degree of similarity between his or her own and the target's ratio of outcomes to related attributes. A source's confidence regarding absolute outcomes and related attributes will be greater when relevant information is extensive, accurate, quantifiable, and consistent. A source's confidence regarding the degree of similarity between his or her own and the target's ratio of outcomes to related attributes will be greater when both parties' outcomes and related attributes are on the same metrics and are roughly equal in absolute size. A second dimension of interpretation is the *importance* attached to the comparison. Importance is primarily determined by the degree to which the source's outcomes and related attributes are relevant to his or her self-concept (cf. Adams, 1965). The absolute size of the difference between the source's and the target's ratios of outcomes to related attributes can also affect importance. A source's judgment of the *causality* associated with a comparison is a third dimension of interpretation. In seeking to explain his or her superiority, equality, or inferiority, a source considers the locus, stability, and controllability of his or her own and the target's related attributes (cf. Weiner, 1980). The source's causal attribution for an outcome is influenced by the presumed cause of the related attributes that determine the outcome. The final dimension of interpetation is the *acceptability* of the comparison information. Acceptability is based on the source's motive for seeking comparison information (self-enhancement, equity, self-depreciation) and the relationship between the source's and the target's ratios of outcomes to related attributes. It is important to note that, at least under certain circumstances, these four dimensions may not be orthogonal (Levine & Moreland, 1986).

A source's interpretation of a comparison influences his or her affective, behavioral, and cognitive responses to it. We assume, as have others (e.g., Adams, 1965; Homans, 1961; Walster et al., 1978), that affective responses mediate behavioral and cognitive responses. Affective reponses involve the source's positive or negative emotional reactions. Behavioral responses involve efforts by the source to maintain, increase, or decrease his or her actual outcomes or related attributes or those of the target. The source may also change the target of comparison or leave the field. Cognitive responses involve the source's distortions of his or her own outcomes or related attributes or those of the target. These distortions can include changing the perceived levels, relevance, or causes of outcomes or related attributes.

The confidence, importance, causality, and acceptability associated with a comparison can have complex effects on the *latency, strength,* and *duration* of a source's responses and on the specific *type of response* that he or she makes. Responses to a confident and important comparison generally have shorter latency, higher strength, and longer duration than responses to an unconfident and unimportant comparison. The confidence of a comparison can also affect the perceived ease of distorting relevant outcomes and related attributes, which in turn influences the probability that cognitive distortion will be used in response to an unacceptable comparison. Regarding causal attributions, a source who perceives his or her own or the target's outcomes or related attributes as controllable is more likely to try to change these than is a source who perceives them as uncontrollable. Finally, the acceptability of a comparison affects whether a source's affective response is positive or negative and whether behavioral and cognitive responses are designed to maintain, increase, or decrease his or her own or the target's outcomes or related attributes.

These ideas lead to some interesting predictions concerning the consequences of (a) self/self versus self/other versus group/group comparisons, (b) intragroup versus intergroup comparisons, and (c) intratemporal versus intertemporal comparisons (see Figure 11.1). For all three dimensions, it is assumed that efforts to cognitively distort outcomes and related attributes vary inversely with the confidence associated with comparison information, whereas efforts to change actual outcomes and related attributes vary directly with the perceived ease of making these changes.

Regarding the Type of Comparison dimension, we assume that self/self comparisons are made more confidently than self/other comparisons, which in turn are made more confidently than group/group comparisons. In addition, we assume that the perceived ease of changing actual outcomes and related attributes is highest when the self is involved, intermediate when another individual is involved, and lowest when a group is involved. These assumptions lead to the predictions that (a) cognitive distortion efforts will be rank ordered: group/group > self/other > self/self and (b) efforts to produce actual changes will be rank ordered: self/self > self/other > group/group.

Regarding the Social Context dimension, we assume that intragroup comparisons are made more confidently than intergroup comparisons. Moreover, we assume that the perceived ease of changing actual outcomes and related attributes is higher when intragroup rather than intergroup comparisons are involved, as least in the self/other and group/group cases. These assumptions lead to the predictions that (a) cognitive distortion efforts will be rank ordered: intergroup > intragroup and (b) efforts to produce actual changes will be rank ordered: intragroup > intergroup.

Regarding the Temporal Context dimension, we assume that comparisons involving present outcomes and related attributes are made more confidently than those involving past outcomes and related attributes, which in turn are made more confidently than those involving future outcomes and related attributes. In addition, we assume that the perceived ease of changing actual outcomes and related attributes is highest when present information is involved, intermediate when future information is involved, and lowest when past information is involved. These assumptions lead to the predictions that (a) cognitive distortion efforts will be rank ordered: future-future > past-past > present-present (in the intratemporal case) and past-future > present-future > present-past (in the intertemporal case), and (b) efforts to produce actual changes will be rank ordered: present-present > future-future > past-past (in the intratemporal case) and present-future > present-past > past-future (in the intertemporal case).

MULTIPLE OUTCOME COMPARISONS

Our discussion so far has implied that an individual can select only *one* of the twelve comparison options depicted in Figure 11.1. Under some circumstances, however, an individual might consider two or more comparisons when assessing his or her outcomes. When these multiple comparisons occur, issues of sequence and combination arise. Sequence concerns the order in which different comparisons are carried out (Goodman, 1977; Martin, 1981). Combination concerns the way in which the results of different comparisons are integrated to produce an overall assessment of one's outcomes (Austin, 1977; Goodman, 1977; Levine, 1983). In spite of their potential importance, very little is known about either of these aspects of multiple comparison. It seems probable, however, that both the salience and attractiveness of comparison targets will influence the sequence in which multiple comparisons are conducted and the manner in which their results are combined. As mentioned previously, salience depends on the availability of information regarding the target's standing on dimensions relevant to the comparison, and attractiveness depends on the source's motive for seeking comparison information and the target's assumed instrumentality in satisfying that motive. Although we have restricted our attention to the equity, self-enhancement, and self-depreciation motives, additional motives, or social values, may also affect outcome comparison (see MacCrimmon & Messick, 1976; Mc Clintock & Keil, 1983).

Let us first consider the case in which a single motive is operative. When more than one comparison target is available, the most salient and potentially attractive target will be selected first. If comparison with this target yields information that exceeds some threshold of satisfaction, then no further comparison will be made. If comparison with this target does not exceed the threshold, then a comparison will be made with the target that ranks next in salience and potential attractiveness. This process will continue in an iterative fashion until the source's satisfaction threshold is exceeded, the source runs out of comparison targets, or the time and effort required to make these multiple comparisons becomes too great. If two or more comparisons are conducted, then the information obtained from each comparison will be weighted by the degree of satisfaction derived from that comparison (the greater the satisfaction, the greater the weight). These differentially weighted comparisons will then be combined to produce an overall assessment of one's outcomes.

The outcome comparison process is much more complex when two or more motives are operative. In some cases, multiple motives will be operative at the *same* point in time. This might occur, for example, when a person wants to discover that he or she is paid better than some colleagues (in order to feel superior) *and* that he or he is paid worse than others (in order to bargain for a higher salary). In most of these cases, the multiple motives that stimulate comparison will differ in strength. If so, then comparisons designed to satisfy the strongest motive will be made first, followed by comparisons designed to satisfy progressively weaker motives. When more than one comparison is produced by a single motive, the order of comparisons and the weighting of comparison information will occur as described previously for the single-motive case. Moreover, an additional weight will be assigned to each comparison to reflect the relative strength of the motive underlying that comparison. Larger weights will be assigned to comparisons stimulated by stronger motives, and smaller weights will be assigned to comparisons stimulated by weaker motives. Sometimes the multiple motives that stimulate comparison at the same point in time will be equal in strength. If so, then "compromise" comparisons designed to satisfy these motives simultaneously will be made. When more than one compromise comparison is produced by multiple motives, the order of comparisons and the weighting of comparison information will occur as described earlier.

In other cases, multiple motives will be operative at *different* points in time. A single motive at Time 1 might stimulate one or more outcome comparison(s), the results of which produce a new motive at Time 2. This new motive might stimulate additional comparison(s), which in turn produce yet another new motive, and so on. For example, if an individual who is motivated to obtain self-enhancing information learns that his ratio of outcomes to related attributes is lower than that of another person, then he might seek further self-depreciating information in order to justify a demand for higher outcomes. It is also possible, of course, for different *sets* of motives to operate at Time 1, Time 2, Time 3, and so on. In either case, we would expect the weight assigned to any comparison to be affected by the degree of satisfaction derived from the comparison (the more satisfying the comparison, the greater the weight) and the strength of the motive(s) underlying the comparison (the stronger the motive(s), the greater the weight).

In attempting to understand multiple outcome comparisons that are produced either by a single motive or multiple motives, it is useful to consider Figure 11.1 in some detail. Examination of the figure reveals that there are two general kinds of multiple comparisons: "within-cell" comparisons, which involve a single comparison in the figure, and between cell comparisons, which involve two or more cells in the figure. Both kinds of comparisons can be broken down into several categories.

Multiple Within-Cell Comparisons

One category of multiple within-cell comparisons involves the same cell at *different points in time.* For example, an individual might evaluate his salary by conducting a self/self-intragroup-intratemporal comparison on two separate occasions. On two consecutive New Year's Eves, he might compare the salary that he currently receives with the salary that he believes he deserves. Comparisons involving the same cell at two points in time can occur in all 12 cells in Figure 11.1.

A second category of multiple within-cell comparisons involves the same cell with *different temporal constraints.* For example, an individual might evaluate her salary by conducting two self/other-intergroup intertemporal comparisons. She might compare her current salary to the salary that a colleague at another university received last year and to the salary that this colleague is expected to receive next year. Comparisons involving the same cell with different temporal constraints can occur in all 12 cells in Figure 11.1.

A third category of multiple within-cell comparisons involves the same cell with *different types of outcomes.* For example, an individual might evaluate his salary and fringe benefits by conducting two self/self intragroup-intertemporal comparisons. He might compare his current salary and fringe benefits to the salary and fringe benefits that he received last year. Comparisons involving the same cell with different types of outcomes can occur in all 12 cells in Figure 11.1.

A fourth category of multiple within-cell comparisons involves the same cell with *different targets of comparison.* For example, an individual might evaluate her salary by conducting two self/other-intragroup intratemporal comparisons. She might compare her current salary to the current salaries of two colleagues at her own university. Because there is only one "self" that can serve as a comparison target, comparisons involving the same cell with different targets of comparison are restricted to the eight self/other and group/group cells in Figure 11.1.

A fifth category of multiple within-cell comparisons involves the same cell with *different sources of comparison.* For example, an individual might evaluate the average salaries of two groups to which he belongs by conducting two group/group-intergroup-intratemporal comparisons. He might compare the averge salary currently received by faculty at his university and the average salary currently received by members of his own department with the average salary currently received by faculty at another university. Because there is only one "self" that can serve as a comparison source, comparisons involving the same cell with different sources of comparison are restricted to the four group/group cells in Figure 11.1.

All this suggests that multiple within-cell comparisons of outcomes are quite complex. This complexity is even more evident when two additional factors are considered. First, although our example for each category involved only two comparisons, three or more comparisons are possible in each case. Second, within-cell multiple comparisons can involve different categories of comparisons, as well as different examples of a single category. In all 12 cells, it is possible to conduct within cell comparisons that simultaneously involve different points in time, different temporal constraints, and different outcomes. For example, a person might evaluate his current salary and past fringe benefits by conducting self/other-intragroup-intratemporal comparisons on two separate occasions. On the first occasion, he might compare his current salary to the current salary of a colleague at his own university. On the second occasion, he might compare his past fringe benefits to the past fringe benefits of the same colleague. Although within-cell comparisons involving different categories of comparisons can also include different targets and different sources, there are at least some constraints on these comparisons. Because comparisons involving the same cell with different targets are restricted to the eight self/other and group/group cells and because comparisons involving the same cell with different sources are restricted to the four group/group cells, certain combinations involving different targets, sources, points in time, temporal constraints, and outcomes cannot occur. Within-cell multiple comparisons involving all five categories of comparisons can occur only in the four group/group cells.

Multiple Between-Cell Comparisons

One category of multiple between-cell comparisons involves combinations of different within-cell *single* comparisons. Here, we are dealing with the case in which single comparisons are made in at least two of the 12 cells in Figure 11.1. For example, an individual might evaluate his salary by conducting a self/self-intragroup-intratemporal comparison *and* by conducting a self/other-intergroup-intertemporal comparison. He might compare (a) the salary that he currently receives to the salary that he believes he deserves and (b) the salary that he currently receives to the salary that a colleague at another university received last year. Information from such within-cell single comparisons might be combined in several ways. If it is assumed that a comparison occurs in each of the 12 cells, then information might be combined from any set of two cells, any set of three cells, any set of four cells, and so on. The number of possible comparisons for the different set sizes varies from 66 (when set size = 2) to 1 (when set size = 12).

A second category of multiple between-cell comparisons involves combinations of different within-cell *multiple* comparisons. Here, we are dealing with the case in which multiple comparisons are made in at least two of the 12 cells in Figure 11.1. For example, an individual might evaluate her salary by conducting self/self-intragroup-intratemporal comparisons on two separate occasions *and* by conducting two self/other-intergroup intertemporal comparisons. She might compare (a) the salary that she receives on the first occasion to the salary that she believes she deserves at that time and the salary that she receives on the second occasion to the salary that she believes she deserves at that time and (b) the salary that she currently receives to the salary that a colleague at another university received last year and to the salary that this colleague is expected to receive next year. The options for combining information from within-cell multiple comparisons are the same as those for combining information from within-cell single comparisons. A major difference between the two cases may derive from the greater complexity of multiple comparison information. It ssems likely that sources will have more difficulty holding multiple comparison information in memory and will feel less confident about this information. If so, then we might expect sources to have difficulty carrying out between-cell comparisons involving combinations of within-cell multiple comparisons.

A third category of multiple between-cell comparisons involves combinations of different within-cell *single and multiple* comparisons. Here, we are dealing with the case in which a single comparison is made in at least one of the 12 cells in Figure 11.1 and a multiple comparison is made in at least one of the remaining cells. For example, an individual might evaluate his salary by conducting a self/self-intragroup-intratemporal comparison on one occasion *and* by conducting two self/other-intergroup intertemporal comparisons. He might compare (a) the salary that he currently receives to the salary that he believes he deserves and (b) the salary that he currently receives to the salary that a colleague at another university received last year and to the salary that this colleague is expected to receive next year. The options for combining information from within-cell single and multiple comparisons are the same as those discussed earlier. Moreover, depending on the relative amount of multiple and single comparison information that is available, sources might be expected to have more or less difficulty carrying out between-cell comparisons involving combinations of the two types of within-cell information.

SUMMARY

Although analyses of social values rely heavily on the process of outcome comparison, they have neglected both the group context in which such comparison occurs and the occurrence of multiple outcome comparisons. The present chapter sought to clarify how social values influence multiple outcome comparisons in group contexts. To achieve this goal, we presented a three dimensional typology of single outcome comparisons that can occur in group contexts, discussed the factors that determine choice of comparison options, and mentioned the consequences of choosing various options. Next, we dealt with the complexities that arise when individuals make multiple outcome comparisons by combining two or more single comparisons. We discussed the sequence in which multiple comparisons are conducted and the manner in which their results are combined when a single social value is operative and when two or more social values are operative. Finally, we considered various categories of within-cell and between-cell multiple outcome comparisons that are suggested by our three-dimensional typology of single outcome comparisons.

REFERENCES

Adams, J. S (1965). Inequity in social exchange. In L. Berkowitz (Ed.), *Advances in experimental social psychology* (Vol. 2, pp. 267-299). New York: Academic Press.

Austin, W. (1977). Equity theory and social comparison processes. In J. M. Suls & R. L. Miller (Eds.), *Social comparison processes: Theoretical and empirical perspectives* (pp. 279-305). Washington, DC: Hemisphere.

Brewer, M. B. (1979). In-group bias in the minimal intergroup situation: A cognitive-motivational analysis. *Psychological Bulletin, 86,* 307–324.

Carver, C. S., & Scheier, M. F. (1978). Self-focusing effects of dispositional self-consciousness, mirror presence, and audience presence. *Journal of Personality and Social Psychology, 36,* 324–332.

Carver, C. S., & Scheier, M. F. (1981). *Attention and self-regulation: A control-theory approach to human behavior.* New York: Springer-Verlag.

Cook. T.D., Crosby, F., & Hennigan, K. M. (1977). The construct validity of relative deprivation. In J. M. Suls & R. L. Miller (Eds.), *Social comparison processes: In. J. M. Suls & R. L. Miller (Eds.), Social comparison processes: Theoretical and empirical perspectives* (pp. 307-333). Washington, DC: Hemisphere.

Crosby, F. J. (1982). *Relative deprivation and working women.* New York: Oxford.

Davies. J. C (1969). The J-curve of rising and declining satisfactions as a cause of some great revolutions and a contained rebellion. In H. D. Graham & T. R. Gurr (Eds.), *Violence in America: Historical and comparative perspectives* (pp. 671–709). New York: New American LIbrary.

Davis, J. A. (1959). A formal interpretation of the theory of relative deprivation. *Sociometry, 22,* 280-296.

Feather, N. T. (1982). Actions in relation to expected consequences: An overview of a research program. In N. T. Feather (Ed.), *Expectations and actions: Expectancy-value models in psychology* (pp. 53-95). Hillsdale, NJ: Lawrence Erlbaum Associates.

Feierabend, I. K., Feierabend, R. L., & Nesvold, B. A. (1969). Social change and political violence: Cross-national patterns. In H. D. Graham & T. R. Gurr (Eds.), *Violence in America: Historical and comparative perspectives* (pp. 606-668). New York: New American Library.

Fenigstein, A., Scheier, M. F., & Buss, A. H. (1975). Public and private self-consciousness: Assessment and theory. *Journal of Consulting and Clinical Psychology, 43,* 522-527.

Gerard, H. B., & Hoyt, M. F. (1974). Distinctiveness of social categorization and attitude toward ingroup members. *Journal of Personality and Social Psychology, 29,* 836-842.

Goodman, P. S. (1974). An examination of referents used in the evaluation of pay. *Organizational Behavior and Human Performance, 12,* 170-195.

Goodman, P. S. (1977). Social comparison processes in organizations. In B. M. Staw & G.R. Salancik (Eds.), *New directions in organizational behavior* (pp. 97-132). Chicago: St. Clair.

Gruder, C. L. (1977). Choice of comparison persons in evaluating oneself. In J. M. Suls & R. L. Miller (Eds.), *Social comparison processes: Theoretical and empirical perspectives* (pp. 21–41). Washington, DC: Hemisphere.

Guimond, S., & Dube-Simard, L. (1983). Relative deprivation theory and the Quebec Nationalist Movement: The cognition-emotion distinction and the personal-group deprivation issue. *Journal of Personality and Social Psychologdy, 44*,526-535.

Gurr. T. R. (1970). *Why men rebel.* Princeton, NJ: Princeton University Press.

Homans, G. (1961). *Social behavior: Its elementary forms.* New York: Harcourt Brace.

Hyman, H. H. (1942). The psychology of status. *Archives of Psychology, 269,* 5-94.

Lemaine, G. (1974). Social differentiation and social originality. *European Journal of Social Psychology, 4,* 17-52.

Levine, J. M. (1983). Social comparison and education. In J. M. Levine & M. C. Wang (Eds.), *Teacher and student perceptions: Implications for learning* (pp. 29-55). Hillsdale, NJ: Lawrence Erlbaum Associates.

Levine, J. M., & Moreland, R. L. (1986). Outcome comparisons in group contexts: Consequences for the self and others. In R. Schwarzer (Ed.), *Self-related cognitions in anxiety and motivation* (pp. 285-303). Hillsdale, NJ: Lawrence Erlbaum Associates.

Levine, J. M., & Moreland, R. L. (In press). Social comparison and outcome evaluation in group contexts. In J. C. Masters & W. P. Smith (Eds.), *Social comparison and social justice.* Hillsdale, NJ: Lawrence Erlbaum Associates.

MacCrimmon, K. R., & Messick, D. M. (1976). A framework for social motives. *Behavioral Science, 21,* 86-100.

Martin, J. (1981). Relative deprivation: A theory of distributive injustice for an era of shrinking resources. In L. L. Cummings & B. M. Staw (Eds.), *Research in organizational behavior* (Vol. 3, pp. 53-107). Greenwich, CT: JAI Press.

Martin, J., & Murray, A. (1983). Distributive injustice and unfair exchange. In D. M. Messick & K. S. Cook (Eds.), *Equity theory: Psychological and sociological perspectives* (pp. 169-205). New York: Praeger.

Martin, J., & Murray, A. (1984). Catalysts for collective violence: the importance of a psychological approach. In R. Folger (Ed.), *The sense of injustice: Social psychological perspectives* (pp. 95-139). New York: Plenum.

McClintock, C. G. (1972). Social motivation – A set of propositions. *Behavioral Science, 17,* 438–454.

McClintock, C. G., & Keil, L.J. (1983). Social values: Their definition, their development, and their impact on human decision making in settings of outcome interdependence. In H. H. Blumberg, A. P. Hare, V. Kent, & M. Davies (Eds.), *Small groups and social interaction* (Vol. 2, pp. 123-143). Chichester: Wiley.

McGuire, W. J., & McGuire, C. V. (1981). The spontaneous self-concept as affected by personal distinctiveness. In M. D. Lynch, A. A. Norem-Hebeisen, & K. J. Gergen (Eds.), *Self-concept: Advances in theory and research* (pp. 147–172). Cambridge, MA: Ballinger.

Mullen, B. (1983). Operationalizing the effect of the group on the individual: A self-attention perspective. *Journal of Experimental Social Psychology, 19,* 295-322.

Patchen, M. (1961). A conceptual framework and some empirical data regarding comparisons of social rewards. *Sociometry, 24,* 136-156.

Rokeach, M. (1973). *The nature of human values.* New York: Free Press.

Rokeach, M. (Ed.). (1979). *Understanding human values: Indvidual and societal.* New York: Free Press.

Runciman, W. G. (1966). *Relative deprivation and social justice: A study of attitudes to social inequality in twentieth-century England.* London: Routledge & Kegan Paul.

Singer, E. (1981). Reference groups and social evaluations. In M. Rosenberg & R. H. Turner (Eds.), *Social psychology: Sociological perspectives* (pp. 66-93). New York: Basic Books.

Snyder, C. R., & Fromkin, H. L. (1980). *Uniqueness: The human pursuit of difference.* New York: Plenum.

Tajfel, H. (1978). Social categorization, social identity, and social comparison. In H. Tajfel (Ed.), *Differentiation between social groups: Studies in the social psychology of intergroup relations* (pp. 61–76). London: Academic Press.

Walster. E., Walster G. W., & Berscheid, E. (1978). *Equity: Theory and research.* Boston: Allyn & Bacon.

Weiner, B. (1980). *Human motivation.* New York: Holt, Rinehart, & Winston.

Wicklund, R. A. (1980). Group contact and self-focused attention. In P. Paulus (Ed.), *Psychology of group influence* (pp. 189–208). Hillsdale, NJ: Lawrence Erlbaum Associates.

Williams, R. M., Jr. (1975). Relative deprivation. In L. A. Coser (Ed.), *The idea of social structure: Papers in honor of Robert K. Merton* (pp. 355–378). New York: Harcourt, Brace, & Jovanovich.

Wills, T. A. (1981). Downward comparison principles in social psychology. *Psychological Bulletin, 90,* 245-271.

Part 4

VALUES AND THE REGULATION OF BEHAVIOR

12 Personal Values, Moral Principles, and a Three-Path Model of Prosocial Motivation

C. Daniel Batson
University of Kansas

Why do we help others in need, even when we anticipate no payment or praise? It is often assumed that there is a single psychological process, admittedly very complex, that leads to prosocial motivation in the absence of direct material or social rewards. The most popular candidate for this honor is a socialization process: We are taught moral principles (e.g., principles of justice, responsibility, and the like); we internalize these principles as values; and then we act accordingly (Berkowitz, 1972; Schwartz, 1977; Schwartz & Howard, 1982).

By this view, the prosocial motivating force is our sense of moral obligation, duty, or anticipated guilt and shame. One may identify two different sources of a sense of obligation – social expectations and self-expectations. In the words of Schwartz and Howard (1982), some prosocial behavior is "motivated by... group expectations backed by externally defined and imposed rewards and punishments," whereas other prosocial behavior is "motivated by... situation-specific behavioral expectations generated from one's own internalized values, backed by self-administered sanctions and rewards" (p. 329; see also Bar-Tal, 1976; Bar-Tal, Sharabany, & Raviv, 1982; Grusec, 1981; Staub, 1978, 1979). Schwartz and Howard (1982) call the group expectations social norms and the expectations based on internalized values personal norms. But whether socially or self-administered, the prospective helper is assumed to be motivated to gain rewards and avoid punishments. Compliance with social and personal norms is simply a means to this end.

This explanation of prosocial motivation in terms of socialization and internalization of values based on moral principles is not the only explanation that has been proposed. Two others deserve mention. Some psychologists suggest that the central process leading to prosocial motivation is aversive arousal reduction (e.g., Piliavin, Dovidio Gaertner, & Clark, 1981, 1982): Witnessing another's distress causes us to feel empathic distress, and we act in order to reduce this distress (see also Hoffman, 1981a, 1981b, 1982). Other psychologists agree that empathic emotion is a source of prosocial motivation, but they claim that the goal of this motivation is not to reduce our own empathic distress but to reduce the distress of the person in need – i.e., they claim that empathy evokes altruistic rather than egoistic prosocial motivation (Batson, 1987; Batson & Coke, 1981).

Empirical evidence exists to support each of these three views (the evidence is reviewed in the sources cited in the preceding paragraphs). This evidence suggests that we may have to give up the conceptual simplicity of assuming that there is a single psychological process, however complex, that underlies prosocial motivation. Instead, it suggests that there may be at least three distinct prosocial processes: (a) compliance with internalized moral principles, (b) aversive arousal reduction, and (c) desire to have the needy person's distress reduced.

I have recently summarized these three processes in a three-path model of prosocial motivation (Batson, 1987). The model outlines two egoistic paths from perception of another as in need to helping – i.e., two paths on which the goal of benefiting the needy other is only instrumental to reaching the ultimate goal of benefiting oneself – and one altruistic path – i.e., one path on which the ultimate goal is to benefit the needy other, any self-benefits that result are simply unintended consequences. Helping that is egoistically motivated by a desire to comply with socially or self-defined moral principles, as described in the passages from Schwartz and Howard (1982) quoted earlier, is represented on Path 1; helping that is egoistically motivated by a desire to reduce aversive arousal is represented on Path 2; and helping that is altruistically motivated by a desire to have the needy person's distress reduced is represented on Path 3.

My goal here is to employ this three-path model to develop a more differentiated perspective on the relationship between personal values and prosocial motivation – a perspective that takes the discussion of values beyond the customary normative analysis. To start, let me present a brief sketch of the three-path model.

A THREE-PATH MODEL OF PROSOCIAL MOTIVATION

Egoistic Accounts of Prosocial Motivation: Paths 1 and 2

One of two general psychological processes usually underlie egoistic explanations of prosocial motivation. One process involves social learning and a reinforcement model of motivation; the other involves arousal reduction.

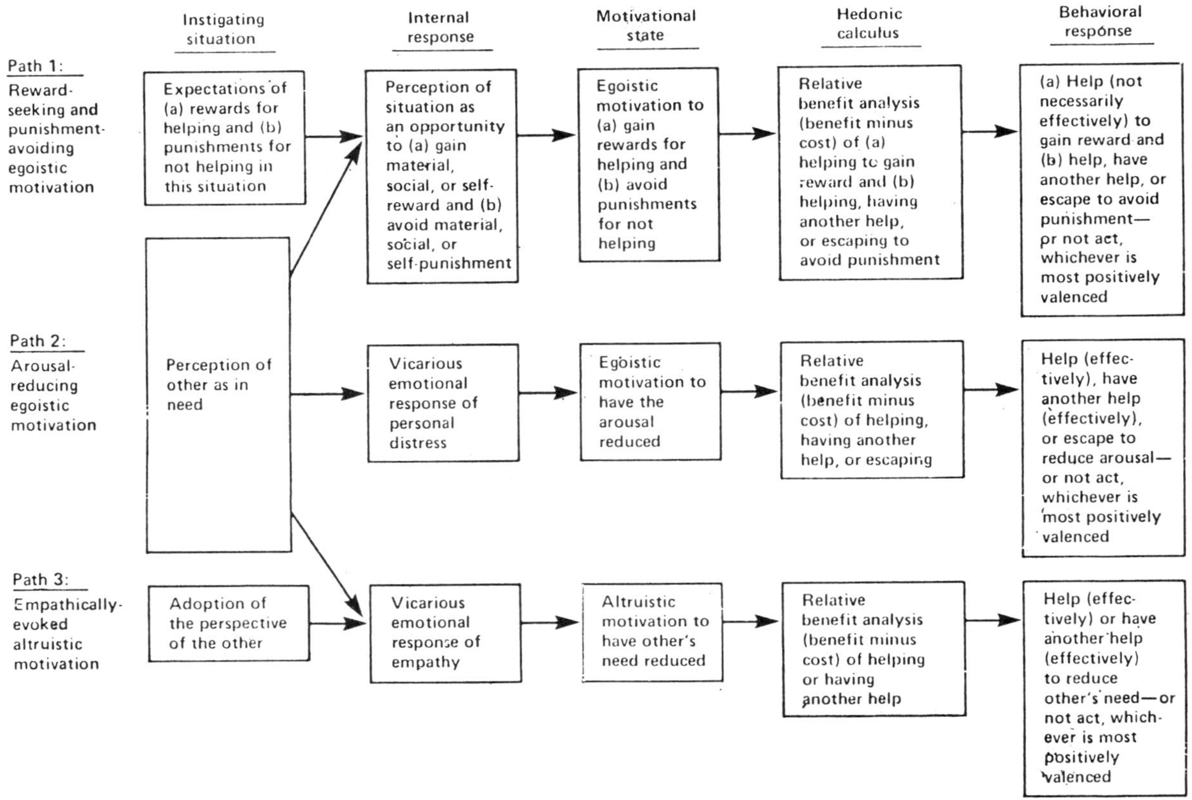

FIGURE 12.1. Flow chart of egoistic and altruistic paths to helping. (Reprinted from Batson, 1987.)

These two egoistic processes are summarized in Paths 1 and 2 of the flow chart in Figure 12.1. The reinforcement model (Path 1) is further subdivided to differentiate (a) reward-seeking and (b) punishment-avoiding motives. Both paths begin with perception of another person in need.

Perception of Another in Need. Perception of another in need involves recognition of a negative discrepancy between the other's current and potential states on one or more dimensions of well-being. Dimensions of well-being include the absence of physical pain, of negative affect, anxiety, stress, and so on, as well as the presence of physical pleasure, of positive affect, security, and so on. The magnitude of the perceived need appears to be a function of three factors: (1) the number of dimensions of well-being on which discrepancies are perceived, (2) the size of each discrepancy, and (3) the potential helper's perception of the importance of each of these dimensions for the person in need (Schaps, 1972).

Expectation of Rewards and Punishments. Perception of another as in need is all that is required to instigate Path 2 motivation, but by itself, this perception is not sufficient to instigate Path 1 motivation. Before motivation to help can be elicited along Path 1, the potential helper must also have the expectation of either receiving rewards for helping or punishments for not helping – or both – in the particular situation. These expectations are the product of the potential helper's learning history, including rewards and punishments he or she has previously received in similiar situations, as well as rewards and punishments he or she has observed others receiving in similar situations. (See Bandura, 1977; Cialdini, Baumann, & Kenrick, 1981; and Eisenberg, 1982, for reviews of research on the social-learning processes by which such expectations are learned.)

Internal Response. Perceiving the other's need, combined with expectations based on one's learning history, can lead to the anticipation of rewards for helping or punishments for not. The anticipated rewards and punishments may be obvious and explicit, such as being paid (Fischer, 1963), gaining social approval (Baumann, Cialdini, & Kenrick, 1981; Gelfand, Hartmann, Cromer, Smith, & Page, 1975; Kenrick, Baumann, & Cialdini, 1979; Moss & Page, 1972), or avoiding censure (Reis & Gruzen, 1976). They may also be more subtle, such as receiving esteem in exchange for helping (Hatfield, Walster, & Piliavin, 1978), complying with social norms (Berkowitz, 1972; Gouldner, 1960; Leeds, 1963; Staub, 1971) complying with internalized personal norms, values, and moral principles (Lerner, 1970; Schwartz, 1977), seeing oneself as a good person (Bandura, 1977; Cialdini, Darby, & Vincent, 1973;

Cialdini & Kenrick, 1976; Weyant, 1978; Wilson, 1976), or avoiding guilt (Hoffman, 1976, 1982; Steele, 1975). This first internal response is represented on Path 1 of Figure 12.1.

Independent of the anticipated rewards and punishments on Path 1, seeing another in need may cause an individual to experience aversive vicarious emotions of personal distress (cf., Hoffman's empathic distress) – to feel upset, anxious, disturbed, and the like (Batson & Coke, 1981; Batson, O'Quin, Fultz, Vanderplas, & Isen, 1983; Hoffman, 1981a, 1981b; Piliavin & Piliavin, 1973; Staub & Baer, 1974). This second internal response is represented on Path 2 of Figure 12.1.

Reward and punishment anticipation (Path 1) and aversive feelings of distress (Path 2) are distinct internal responses to perceiving another in need, but they are not mutually exclusive. In many helping situations, notably emergencies, each of these internal responses will be instigated, and in proportional magnitudes. In other helping situations, such as making a routine annual contribution to a charity, a person may be very aware of the rewards for helping and punishments for not, yet feel little personal distress. In still other situations, such as witnessing a gory accident, much distress may be aroused, and little or no attention paid to the possible reward and punishment opportunities of the situation.

Motivational State. Reward anticipation, punishment avoidance, and feelings of distress each evoke their own form of prosocial motivation. On Path 1, perception of the opportunity to get reward or avoid punishment evokes motivation to gain the reward (Path 1a) or avoid the punishment (Path 1b). The magnitude of the reward-seeking or punishment-avoiding motivation appears to be a function of two factors: (1) the magnitude of the anticipated rewards and punishments, and (2) the potential helper's current need state with regard to the anticipated rewards and punishments. The potential helper's current needs might include, for example, a need for enhanced self-esteem (Steele, 1975), for relief from feeling bad (Cialdini et al., 1973; Weyant, 1978), or for continuance of feeling good (Isen & Levin, 1972).

On Path 2, experiencing personal distress leads to motivation to have this distress reduced. The magnitude of this arousal-reduction motivation appears to be a direct function simply of the magnitude of the distress experienced (Gaertner & Dovidio, 1977; Hoffman, 1981a; Piliavin et al., 1981).

The prosocial motives on Path 1 and Path 2 are distinct but not mutually exclusive; they may be experienced simultaneously. When they are, obtaining their goals may be compatible or incompatible. Sometimes, actions that move one toward gaining reward or avoiding punishment also reduce one's personal distress – as when one saves a person trapped in a burning building by putting out the fire. At other times, acting to gain reward or avoid punishment increases distress – as when one helps by comforting a mangled accident victim. If perception of another in need simultaneously evokes Path 1 and Path 2 prosocial motiviation, then to the extent that the goals of the motives are compatible, their magnitudes should sum.

Hedonic Calculus. If the magnitude of one or more of these motives is above some minimal threshold, then the individual will consider various behavioral means of reaching the goals of these motivational states. Helping may be one means of reaching the goal(s), but often there are other means. Before acting, a "hedonic calculus" is performed; that is, the motivated individual conducts some form of relative-benefit analysis, weighing benefit against cost for each potential response.

The magnitude of the benefit in the hedonic calculus is a function of the magnitude of the motivational state because the benefit is to reach the goal. The magnitude of the cost is the sum of the various costs perceived to be associated with the behavior. Perhaps the simplest way to think about these costs is in terms of conflicting motives. It is likely that the potential helper, in addition to experiencing one or more motives evoked by perception of the other in need, also simultaneously experiences motives to avoid pain or risk of pain, to save time, to keep his or her money, and so on (Piliavin, Piliavin, & Rodin, 1975). As a general principle, if more than one motive exists, and if a given behavior can reach the goal of one of these motives but not others, then failure to obtain the incompatible goals is the cost associated with this behavior. The magnitude of this cost will be a function of the magnitude of the motivational force to reach the unobtained goals.

On Path la, the desired rewards are likely to be associated with being helpful, so the motivation to obtain these rewards specifies the behavioral means: The motivated individual must try to help. The behavioral options are quite different on Path 1b. If another person helps effectively we may escape possible punishments for not helping (including social censure, guilt, shame), because the other's help removes the situation requiring our help. Alternatively, if we can psychologically escape from the need situation – by, for example, becoming involved in a distracting task – then we may successfully escape self-inflicted punishments such as guilt and shame.

The same three behavioral options that can be used to avoid punishment on Path 1b–helping, another person helping, and escaping – can reduce aversive arousal on Path 2. The cause of one's distress can be removed by either helping or another person helping. Alternatively, contact with the cause of one's distress can be removed by escaping. But note that the potential helper is escaping something different on Path 2 than on Path 1b. On Path 1b the escape is from anticipated punishment, especially self-punishment in the form of shame and guilt; on Path 2 the escape is from the stimulus causing one's distress. Given this difference, physical escape may be more effective on Path 2 than Path 1b.

The hedonic calculus is often even more complicated than suggested thus far, because the distressed individual has almost certainly also been socialized to expect rewards for helping and punishments for not. As a result, he or she will likely experience Path 1a and 1b motivation at the same time as Path 2 motivation. The goals of motivation on Paths 1a, 1b, and 2 can all be reached by helping, but escaping will bring no rewards. Thus, the anticipated loss of praise and esteem are part of the cost of escaping in a more comprehensive hedonic calculus that deals with Path 1 and Path 2 motives simultaneously.

Behavioral Response. The motivated individual will help, let someone else help, or escape, whichever available response has the greatest perceived relative benefit to self. If no available response is perceived to have relative benefit, i.e., if the anticipated cost of each exceeds the benefit, then the individual will not respond. He or she will pursue some unrelated goal or will do nothing. If no need-related response occurs, then the force of the Path 1 and Path 2 need-related egoistic motives should slowly dissipate.

Empathically Evoked Altruistic Motivation to Help: Path 3

It has been suggested that these two egoistic paths may not be adequate to provide a full description of why people help. They may need to be supplemented by a third path, one based on the hypothesis that empathic emotion evokes altruistic motivation. This suggestion is reflected in Path 3 of Figure 12.1.

Perception of the Other in Need. Like Paths 1 and 2, Path 3 begins with a perception of need. But on Path 3, perceiving the other's need is claimed to lead to a unique internal response–empathic emotion. Following Hoffman (1975, 1976), Krebs (1975), and Stotland (1969), it is proposed that this unique emotional response is a result of the perceiver adopting the perspective of the other.

Adopting the Perspective of the Other. Taking the other's perspective involves more than simply focusing attention on the other. One may focus attention on another's need but maintain a relatively objective perspective, dispassionately observing that person's plight. In contrast, adopting the other's perspective involves imagining how that person is affected by his or her situation (Stotland, 1969). Recollection of one's own or others' reactions in similar situations–as well as imagining oneself in the other's situation–often provides information that facilitates adopting the other's perspecitve, but there are limits to this facilitation. One may get so wrapped up in reminiscences or in one's own possible reactions to the situation that one fails to consider the specific way the situation is affecting the other (Hygge, 1976; Karniol, 1982). It is this consideration of the effect on the other that is the essence of perspective taking, and it is perspective taking – in combination with a perception of the other as in need – that seems to lead to empathic emotion.

Internal Response of Empathic Emotion. I believe that there are at least two different types of vicarious emotion evoked by perceiving someone in need (Batson, Duncan, Ackerman, Buckley, & Birch, 1981; Batson et al., 1983; Hoffman, 1975, 1976). One, which I am calling *personal distress* (cf., Hoffman's empathic distress), has already been discussed. This vicarious emotion includes feeling anxious, upset, disturbed, distressed, perturbed, and the like, and is assumed to evoke Path 2 egoistic motivation to have the distress reduced. The second vicarious emotion, which I am calling *empathy* (cf., Hoffman's sympathetic distress), includes feeling sympathetic, compassionate, warm, softhearted, tender, and the like.

Empathy, at least as I am using the term, does not mean feeling the same emotions one might imagine the person in need is feeling, nor does it mean feeling the emotions one would if suffering the other's plight. Instead, it is a more other-oriented emotional response elicited by and congruent with the perceived welfare of someone else (see Batson & Coke, 1981). The specific label for this other-directed congruent emotional response is, of course, not crucial. In recent years it has most often been called empathy, but it has also been called sympathy (Heider, 1958; Hoffman, 1975, 1976; Smith, 1759; Wispe, 1968, 1986), compassion (Hume, 1896), and "the tender emotion" (McDougall, 1908).

When perceiving someone in distress, empathy will be an unpleasant, aversive emotion. But it is suggested that empathy–unlike personal distress–does not evoke Path 2 egoistic motivation to have this aversive arousal reduced; instead, it evokes altruistic motivation directed toward the ultimate goal of reducing the other's need.

Altruistic Motivation. The proposal that empathic emotion can evoke motivation directed toward the ultimate goal of reducing the other's need has been called the *empathy-altruism hypothesis* (Batson & Coke, 1981; Batson et al., 1981). According to this hypothesis, the magnitude of the altruistic motivation is assumed to be a direct function of the magnitude of the empathic emotion. Of course, reducing the other's need is likely also to bring social and self-rewards (Path 1a), avoidance of social and self-punishments (Path 1b), and reduction of the helper's own feelings of personal distress (Path 2). But it is proposed that feeling empathy for the person in need evokes a motivation to help in which these benefits to self are not the goal of helping; they are simply consequences of helping.

Even though it is hypothesized that the motivation evoked by empathy is altruistic not egoistic, it is recognized that the instigating conditions that arouse empathic emotion and, as a result, altruistic motivation are also likely to arouse Path 1 and Path 2 egoistic motives. These egoistic and altruistic motives are assumed to be distinct, but to the extent that the goals of these motives are compatible, their magnitudes should sum.

Hedonic Calculus. If the magnitude of the altruistic motivation or the summed egoistic and altruistic motivation is above some minimal threshold, then the individual will proceed to consider behavioral means of reaching the goal of this motivation. As on the egoistic paths, the altruistically motivated individual will perform a relative-benefit analysis before acting. The relative-benefit analysis on Path 3 should be restricted to consideration of helping or having someone alse help; no consideration should be given to the cost of escaping, because escape is not a viable behavioral means of reaching the altruistic goal.

To suggest a relative-benefit analysis for altruistic motivation may seem contradictory, because the goal of this analysis is clearly egoistic–to reach the desired altruistic goal while incurring minimal costs to self. Yet, the existence of this egoistic goal does not mean that the motivation to have the other's need reduced has now become egoistic; it only means that the impulse to act on this altruistic motivation is likely to evoke an egoistic motive as well. The existence of the latter motive need not negate or contaminate the former, although it certainly complicates the relationship betwen the altruistic motive and behavior.

The magnitude of the benefit in the relative-benefit analysis is, as on the egoistic paths, a function of the magnitude of the motivational force because the benefit is to reach the goal or goals. The magnitude of the cost is the sum of the various costs associated with the behavior, including physical harm or risk, discomfort, exertion, mental strain, time, monetary expense, and so on.

Enacting a Behavior to Reach the Altruistic Goal. The altruistically motivated individual will help if: (a) helping is possible, (b) the relative benefit of helping is perceived to be positive, and (c) the relative benefit of helping is perceived to be more positive than the relative benefit of having someone else help (assuming someone else is available to help). If the relative benefit is negative, i.e., the cost of helping exceeds the benefit, then the individual will not help. In this case, the force of the altruistic motivation should slowly dissipate. Alternatively the individual could deny the person's need or change factors leading to adoption of that person's perspective. These responses would not enable the individual to reach the altruistic goal, but they should eliminate the empathic emotion and, hence, the altruistic motivation.

PERSONAL VALUES AND PROSOCIAL MOTIVATION

Now I wish briefly to consider the relationship between personal values and prosocial motivation, employing the three-path model just outlined. I confess that I invoke the concept of value with trepidation. In the past I have shied away from it because it seemed hopelessly vacuous to me; value seemed a term too big and too abstract to be of use in psychological theory. I was a "value phobic." Not that I doubted that people have values; I just did not know how to conceptualize them. So, when someone asserted that people help others because they have prosocial values I could not argue, but I also did not feel that I had learned anything. I simply did not know what a person making such a claim was talking about.

Lest false hopes of imminent enlightenment arise, I hasten to add that I still cannot make sense of most talk about values. Instead, I have begun to take a different tack. Rather than trying to understand what others mean by the term value, I have decided to back off and try to get clear on how I could use the term in a way that makes sense to me. I am at the early stages of thinking about this problem, and my ideas are embarrassingly crude. I have put them down here not because I think they are necessarily right, but because putting them down may help clarify matters—or at least show my confusion for what it is. Perhaps my fumbling will also lead other value phobics to try to render the concept comprehensible.

A Definition of Value. First, I thought about what the word value means. Most generally, it seems to mean relative preference. I value State A over State B if I would choose State A over State B, other things being equal. Some values are very abstract and pervasive (e.g., a preference for personal freedom over oppression); others are very concrete and specific (a preference for chocolate ice cream over vanilla). Moreover, some values are genetically based; they are determined by our structure as organisms (e.g., the preferences we have for certain environmental temperatures, for oxygen to breathe, etc.); other values are learned through classical or operant conditioning, through modeling (see Bandura, 1977), or as a result of the transformation of a means toward some valued end into an end in its own right (cf. Allport's concept of functional autonomy). What is preferred (valued) depends on our current situation; when starved, a steaming bowl of soup is likely to be highly valued; after an elaborate holiday feast, it is not.

The relationship between value and motivation may be summarized as follows: If there is a perceived negative discrepancy between a current or anticipated state and a valued state, then obtaining or maintaining the valued state becomes a goal (wish, desire). Moreover, if the person perceives there to be one or more viable behavioral routes to the goal, and he or she perceives that pursuit of this route is not more costly (i.e., more negatively valued) than the goal is positively valued, then goal-directed activity will ensue. We have motivation.

Although I am not fully satisfied with this conception of value, I was a bit reassured to find that not only was relative preference central to most dictionary definitions of the term but also to the definition proposed by perhaps the best-known current expert on values, Milton Rokeach. Rokeach (1973) says, "A *value* is an enduring belief that a specific mode of conduct or end-state of existence is personally or socially preferable to an opposite or converse mode of conduct or end-state of existence" (p. 5, italics in original).

Of course, I was also chastened by the differences between my conception of value and Rokeach's definition. To qualify as a value for Rokeach, a preference must be relatively enduring; my conception is more situational. Also, to qualify as a value for Rokeach, a preference must be related to some relatively profound aspect of experience; my conception includes rather mundane preferences. Rokeach would not, I think, call a preference for chocolate ice cream over vanilla a value. I use the term value more broadly than Rokeach because I am not yet convinced that qualitatively different psychological processes are involved in more and less enduring or more and less profound preferences; I think these differences may be only quantitative. Moreover, I think it may be useful to demythologize the term value by noting the psychological similarities between, for example, the preference for oxygen to breathe and the preference for freedom of speech.

Three Types of Prosocial Values. Prosocial values are those values that lead to prosocial motivation–i.e., motivation to act in a way that benefits another. But as the three-path model outlined earlier suggests, there are several different types of prosocial motivation. Benefit to the other may be the ultimate goal, as on the altruistic Path 3, or it may only be instrumental for reaching some other ultimate goal, as on the egoistic Paths 1 and 2.

Having proposed (a) a link between prosocial values and prosocial motives and (b) a multiplicity of prosocial motives, I wish also to propose (c) a multiplicity of prosocial values. Specifically, I think one can identify prosocial values associated with each of the three paths in Figure 12.1.

When one hears talk of prosocial values, the speaker most often has in mind some version of Path 1 prosocial motivation: Through socialization, we internalize standards or expectations for appropriate actions and events, and we learn that to deviate from these standards brings unpleasantness in the form of shame, guilt, or moral indignation (Schwartz & Howard, 1982). The prosocial value in this case is, then, that one prefers State A in which oneself and others act in accord with some socialized moral principle (e.g., equity, justice, or concern) to State B, in which self and others do not act morally. Ultimately, it is not the principle of equity, justice, or concern per se that is valued; it is the anticipated social or self rewards for compliance with the principle. The prosocial aspect of such a value is clearly instrumental; it is not ultimate or terminal (to borrow Rokeach's term). This prosocial value might be called *instrumental morality.*

A different instrumental prosocial value underlies Path 2 prosocial motivation; what is valued is *freedom from distress.* Seeing someone else suffer is distressing, and we prefer not to be distressed. In seeking to eliminate our distress, one option is to remove the other's distress, which is the stimulus causing our distress. Once again, the prosocial aspect of this value is instrumental, not ultimate.

Why the distress of others should cause us distress is not entirely clear. In part, we may have learned over the years that when others are suffering there is a greater chance that we will soon suffer too–that such a deviation from our conception of normal portends danger (Reykowski, 1982). There may also be some genetic predisposition to be distressed by the distress of others (Sagi & Hoffman, 1976). Whatever the source, the cry of "change the channel; I can't watch that" in response to television news footage showing the mangled body of a victim of terrorism or the hollow stare of starving refugees suggests that we prefer not to be confronted with the suffering of others. Sometimes this value leads us only to avert our eyes, but at other times it may lead us to act prosocially.

Third, there are at least some other people whose welfare we come to value in its own right. We prefer them to be happy and free of distress, not because it is upsetting to us if they are not–although it quite likely is upsetting to us–but because we value their welfare. This valuing of the *other's welfare* is an ultimate or terminal prosocial value, not simply instrumental. It seems to be an important component of what has been called "attachment" and "care giving" (Ainsworth, Blehar, Waters, & Wall, 1978; Batson, 1987; Bowlby, 1969), and it is a likely precondition for the emergence of empathic emotion and altruistic motivation, as described on Path 3.

Thus, I am suggesting that it is possible to differentiate at least three distinct types of prosocial values, one related to the ultimate goal sought for each of the three different types of prosocial motivation. For the first two, the prosocial aspect of the value is only instrumental; what is valued is actually some positive state for oneself, not for another person. For the third, however, the prosocial aspect is intrinsic to the value; it is the positive state of the other person that is valued.

A Fourth Type of Prosocial Value: Valuing Moral Principles. Having suggested this overly neat typology, let me close by raising the prospect of yet another terminal prosocial value, one that does not fit easily into the three-path model. Can it be that at least some people come to value the internalized moral principles themselves? Analogous to Allport's treatment of the development of functional autonomy, these people may grow beyond instrumental morality and come to value justice–or mercy or thoughtfulness–not because of the rewards or punishments they anticipate for compliance with this prinicple (as on Path 1) but as an abstract principle in its own right. Is so, then it is the *moral principle* itself that is valued.

Kohlberg (1976) has set this intrinsic valuing of moral principles at the pinnacle of his model of moral development. But it is worth noting, first, that although Kohlberg's conception of prosocial values has been quite popular, to the best of my knowledge there is no empirical evidence that clearly demonstrates the existence of moral-principle values independent of the closely-related instrumental moral values described earlier. It is worth noting, second, that if moral-principle values exist and function to evoke a motivational state, the ultimate goal of which is to uphold the moral principle, then this motiviation and the related value lies outside the purview of the three-path model. A fourth path is required. Because the ultimate goal on this path is to uphold or express the moral principle, it would not be appropriate to call the motivation on this path either egoistic or altruistic, at least as I am using those terms. Egoism and altruism are concerned with whether one's ultimate goal is self-benefit or other-benefit, respectively. If one's ultimate goal is to uphold a moral principle such as justice, then neither self nor other benefit is at issue, even though one's actions to uphold the principle may benefit self, other, or both.

The three-path model of prosocial motivation and the three associated prosocial values are person oriented–either self or other–not principle oriented. In this regard, these three prosocial values are far more compatible with Gilligan's (1982) person-oriented view of moral development than with Kohlberg's (1976) principled view. As noted, there is empirical evidence for each of the three forms of prosocial motivation (and values) represented in the three-path model. It remains to be seen whether a fourth path reflecting moral principles as a terminal value needs to be added. What has been called principled morality may be, as Rokeach (1973, p. 8) implies, nothing more than a subtle and sophisticated form of Path 1 instrumental morality. In spite of claims to the contrary, the morally principled individual may comply with abstract moral principles because he or she wishes to avoid shame and guilt.

ACKNOWLEDGMENTS

Preparation of this chapter was supported in part by NSF Grant BSN–8507110, C. Daniel Batson, Principal Investigator.

REFERENCES

Ainsworth, M. D. S., Blehar, M. C., Waters, E., & Wall, S. (1978). *Patterns of attachment: A psychological study of the strange situation.* Hillsdale, NJ: Lawrence Erlbaum Associates.

Bandura, A. (1977). *Social learning theory.* Engelwood Cliffs, NJ: Prentice-Hall.

Bar-Tal, D. (1976). *Prosocial behavior: Theory and research.* Washington, DC: Hemisphere.

Bar-Tal, D., Sharabany, R., & Raviv, A. (1982). Cognitive basis for the development of altruistic behavior. In V.J. Derlega & J. Grzelak (Eds.), *Cooperation and helping behavior: Theories and research* (pp. 377–396). New York: Academic Press.

Batson, C.D. (1987). Prosocial motivation: Is it ever truly altruistic? In L. Berkowitz (Ed.), *Advances in experimental social psychology.* (Vol. 20, pp: 65–122). New York: Academic Press.

Batson, C. D., & Coke, J. S. (1981). Empathy: A source of altruistic motivation for helping? In J. P. Rushton & R.M. Sorrentino (Eds.), *Altruism and helping behavior: Social, personality, and developmental perspectives* (pp. 167–187). Hillsdale, NJ: Lawrence Erlbaum Associates.

Batson, C. D., Duncan, B., Ackerman, P., Buckley, T., & Birch, K. (1981). Is empathic emotion a source of altruistic motivation? *Journal of Personality and Social Psychology, 40,* 290-302.

Batson, C. D., O'Quin, K., Fultz, J., Vanderplas, M., & Isen, A. (1983). Self-reported distress and empathy and egoistic versus altrusitic motivation for helping. *Journal of Personality and Social Psychology, 45,* 706-718.

Baumann, D. J., Cialdini, R. B., & Kenrick, D. T. (1981). Altruism as hedonism: Helping and self-gratification as equivalent responses. *Journal of Personality and Social Psychology, 40,* 1039-1046.

Berkowitz, L. (1972). Social punishments, feelings, and other factors affecting helping and altruism. In L. Berkowitz (Ed.), *Advances in experimental social psychology* (Vol. 6, pp. 63-108). New York: Academic Press.

Bowlby, J. (1969). *Attachment and loss: Vol. 1. Attachment.* New York: Basic Books.

Cialdini, R. B., Baumann, D. J., & Kenrick, D. T. (1981). Insights fron sadness: A three step model of the development of altruism as hedonism. *Developmental Review, 1,* 207-223.

Cialdini, R. B., Darby, B. L., & Vincent, J. E. (1973). Transgression and altruism: A case for hedonism. *Journal of Experimental Social Psychology, 9,* 502-516.

Cialdini, R. B., & Kenrick, D. T. (1976). Altruism as hedonism: A social development perspective on the relationship of negative mood state and helping. *Journal of Personality and Social Psychology, 34,* 907-914.

Eisenberg, N. (Ed.). (1982). *The development of prosocial behavior.* New York: Academic Press.

Fischer, W. F. (1963). Sharing in preschool children as a function of amount and type of reinforcement. *Genetic Psychology Monographs, 68,* 215-245.

Gaertner, S. L., & Dovidio, J. F. (1977). The subtlety of white racism, arousal, and helping behavior. *Journal of Personality and Social Psychology, 35,* 691-708.

Gelfand, D. M., Hartmann, D. P., Cromer, C. C., Smith, C. L., & Page, B. C. (1975). The effects of instructional prompts and praise on children's donation rates. *Child Development, 46,* 980-983.

Gilligan, C. (1982). *In a different voice: Psychological theory and women's development.* Cambridge: Harvard University Press.

Gouldner, A. W. (1960). The punishment of reciprocity: A preliminary statement. *American Sociological Review, 25,* 161-179.

Grusec, J. E. (1981). Socialization processes in the development of altruism. In J. P. Rushton & R. M. Sorrentino (Eds.), *Altruism and helping behavior* (pp. 65-90). Hillsdale, NJ: Lawrence Erlbaum Associates.

Hatfield, E. Walster, G.W., & Piliavin, J. A. (1978). Equity theory and helping relationships. In L. Wispé (Ed.), *Altruism, sympathy, and helping: Psychological and sociological principles* (pp. 115-139). New York: Academic Press.

Heider, F. (1958). *The psychology of interpersonal relations.* New York: Wiley.

Hoffman, M. L. (1975). Developmental synthesis of affect and cognition and its implications for altruistic motivation. *Developmental Psychology, 11,* 607-622.

Hoffman, M. L. (1976). Empathy, role-taking, guilt, and development of altruistic motives. In T. Lickona (Ed.), *Moral development and behavior: Theory, research, and social issues* (pp. 124–143). New York: Holt, Rinehart, & Winston.

Hoffman, M. L. (1981a). Is altruism part of human nature? *Journal of Personality and Social Psychology, 40,* 121-137.

Hoffman, M. L. (1981b). The development of empathy. In J. P. Rushton & R. M. Sorrentino (Eds.), *Altruism and helping behavior: Social, personality, and developmental perspectives* (pp. 41-63). Hillsdale, NJ: Lawrence Erlbaum Associates.

Hoffman, M. L. (1982). Development of prosocial motivation: Empathy and guilt. In N. Eisenberg (Ed.), *The development of prosocial behavior* (pp. 281-313). New York: Academic Press.

Hume, D, (1896). *A treatise of human nature.* (Ed. by L. A. Selby-Bigge). Oxford: Oxford University Press. (first published, 1740)

Hygge, S. (1976). Information about the model's unconditioned stimulus and response in vicarious classical conditioning. *Journal of Personality and Social Psychology, 33,* 764-771.

Isen, A. M., & Levin, P. F. (1971). Effect of feeling good on helping: Cookies and kindness. *Journal of Personality and Social Psychology, 21,* 344-348.

Karniol, R. (1982). Setting, scripts, and self-schemata: A cognitive analysis of the development of prosocial behavior. In N. Eisenberg (Ed.), *The development of prosocial behavior* (pp. 251-278). New York: Academic Press.

Kenrick, D.T., Baumann, D.J., & Cialdini, R.B. (1979). A step in the socialization of altruism as hedonism: Effects of negative mood on children's generosity under public and private conditions. *Journal of Personality and Social Psychology, 37,* 747-755.

Kohlberg, L. (1976). Moral stages and moralization: The cognitive developmental approach. In T. Lickona (Ed.), *Moral development and behavior: Theory, research and social issues.* New York: Holt, Rinehart, & Winston.

Krebs, D.L. (1975). Empathy and altruism. *Journal of Personality and Social Psychology, 32,* 1134-1146.

Leeds, T. (1963). Altruism and the norm of giving. *Merrill-Palmer Quarterly, 9,* 229–240.

Lerner, M. J. (1970). The desire for justice and reactions to victims. In J. Macaulay & L. Berkowitz (Eds.), *Altruism and helping behavior* (pp. 205-229). New York: Academic Press.

McDougall, W. (1908). *Introduction to social psychology.* London: Methuen.

Moss, M. K., & Page, R. A. (1972). Reinforcement and helping behavior. *Journal of Applied Psychology, 2,* 360-371.

Piliavin, I.M., Piliavin, J.A. & Rodin, J. (1975). Costs, diffusion, and the stigmatized victim. *Journal of Personality and Social Psychology, 32,* 429-438.

Piliavin, J. A., Dovid, J. F., Gaertner, S. L., & Clark, R. D., III (1981). *Emergency intervention.* New York: Academic Press.

Piliavin, J. A., Dovidio, J. F., Gaertner, S. L., & Clark, R. D. III (1982). Responsive bystanders: The process of intervention. In V. J. Derlega & J. Grzelak (Eds.), *Cooperation and helping behavior: Theories and research* (pp. 279-304). New York: Academic Press.

Piliavin, J. A., & Piliavin, I. M. (1973). *The Good Samaritan: Why does he help?* Unpublished manuscript, University of Wisconsin.

Reis, H. T., & Gruzen, J. (1976). On mediating equity, equality, and self-interest: The role of self-presentation in social exchange. *Journal of Experimental Social Psychology, 12,* 487-503.

Reykowski, J. (1982). Motivation of prosocial behavior. In V. J. Derlega & J. Grzelak (Eds.), *Cooperation and helping behavior: Theories and research* (pp. 352-375). New York: Academic.

Rokeach, M. (1973). *The nature of human values.* New York: Free Press.

Sagi, A., & Hoffman, M. L. (1976). Empathic distress in newborns. *Developmental psychology, 12,* 175-176.

Schaps, E. (1972). Cost, dependency, and helping. *Journal of Personality and Social Psychology, 21,* 74-78.

Schwartz, S. H. (1977). Normative influences on altruism. In L. Berkowitz (Ed.), *Advances in experimental social psychology* (Vol. 10, pp. 221-279). New York: Academic Press.

Schwartz, S. H., & Howard, J. (1982). Helping and copperation: A self-based motivational model. In V. J. Derlega & J. Grzelak (Eds.), *Cooperation and helping behavior: Theories and research* (pp. 327-353). New York: Academic Press.

Smith, A. (1759). *The theory of moral sentiments.* London: A. Miller.

Staub, E. (1971). Helping a person in distress: The influence of implicit and explicit "rules" of conduct on children and adults. *Journal of Personality and Social Psychology, 17,* 137-145.

Staub E. (1978). *Positive social behavior and morality: Social and personal influences* (Vol. 1). New York: Academic Press.

Staub, E. (1979). *Positive social behavior and morality: Socialization and development* (Vol. 2). New York: Academic Press.

Staub, E., & Baer, R. S., Jr. (1974). Stimulus characteristics of a sufferer and difficulty of escape as determinants of helping. *Journal of Personality and Social Psychology, 30,* 279-285.

Steele, C. M. (1975). Name-calling and compliance. Journal of Personality and Social Psychology, 31, 361-369.

Stotland, E. (1969). Exploratory studies of empathy. In L. Berkowitz (Ed.), *Advances in experimental social psychology* (Vol. 4, pp. 271-313). New York: Academic Press.

Weyant, J.M. (1978). Effects of mood states, costs, and benefits on helping. Journal of Personality and Social Psychology, 36, 1169-1176.

Wilson, J. P. (1976). Motivation, modeling and altruism: A Person X Situation analysis. *Journal of Personaity and Social Psychology, 34,* 1078-1086.

Wispe, L. G. (1968). Sympathy and empathy. In D.L. Sills (Ed.), *International encyclopedia of the social sciences* (Vol. 15, pp. 441-447). New York: Free Press.

Wispe, L. G. (1986). The distinction between sympathy and empathy: To call forth a concept a word is needed. *Journal of Personality and Social Psychology,* 50, 314-321.

13 The System of Personal Values and Behavior

Bogdan Wojciszke
University of Gdańsk, Poland

PERSONAL VALUES AND THE IDEAL SELF

Human values are highly diverse in terms of their contents, expressions, and implications. Most probably different types of values influence human behavior by different routes mediated by various mechanisms. Therefore, only one type of value is addressed in the present chapter – namely personal values.

A personal value is defined here as a cognitive representation of a subjectively desired feature or state of the subject's own self. Positive personality traits – like honesty, intelligence, tenacity, etc. – are the most typical examples of such values. Values of that type are personal in a double sense: they are personally desired by a subject, and they refer to the person of their beholder, i.e., to the subject himself or herself. Obviously personal values defined in such a manner are closely related to another psychological concept of long tradition – the concept of the ideal self.

The ideal self is defined here as a mental structure representing an idealized conception of the subject himself or herself as a person – the desired features, states, and behaviors. *The personal value system* is the most abstract layer of the ideal self-structure, it contains an organized set of personal values defined earlier. Preference is the basic relation organizing a set of distinct values into the system of personal values. In other words, the values are organized hierarchically according to their desirability to the individual. The more a value is subjectively preferable to its opposites, the higher is its position in the hierarchy (Rokeach, 1973). Values of higher hierarchical position are more important as behavioral guides than values of lower positions. According to the control theory of human behavior introduced by Powers (1973) and applied to the psychology of self by Carver and Scheier (1981, 1983), personal values serve as highly abstract reference points in self-regulation of behavior. The subject can compare his or her own current states and behavior with these reference points and adjust successively the former to be consistent with the latter ones. So, personal values serve as a very general guide for behavior, although the specific actions may be sometimes hard to predict based on the values just because of their abstract nature. Even opposite, mutually excluding patterns of behavior may express the same value in extreme cases. For example, in a situation in which there is a discrepancy between the opinions of the subject and his or her peer group, individuals may express and behaviorally fulfil their independence by trying hard to defend their own positions, as well as by an equally strong avoidance of any discussion.

Because the abstract nature of values is difficult to link directly to behavioral consequences, the next layer of ideal self-structure should be postulated – the system of personal norms. Personal values are relatively stable and abstract types of self-related goals, whereas *personal norms* are more transient and specific beliefs of the person about the appropriate behavioral realization of the value in a specific context. Personal norms may be ad hoc in their nature – i.e., people may generate the behavioral implications of their values, implications relevant to the current situation, as Schwartz and Howard (1983) postulate. On the other hand, personal norms may be specific but quite stable rules of behavioral realization of the values in a specified type of situation. Such rules may function as unequivocal implications of the value and they need not be formulated ab initio each time they are concerned. For example, in a temptation situation the rule of behavioral realization of "honesty" value is quite straightforward: "I shouldn't yield to temptation and should not try to obtain an easy profit in a dishonest way."

Whether a personal norm is enduring and well established or transient in nature depends on the situation in which it is applied. It may be hypothesized that enduring, structural norms are established for standard, well-known situations, which have been entered by a person many times in his or her life, whereas transient, newly emerging norms are formulated ad hoc in subjectively new situations. Previous experience with a type of situation results in the development of a personal norm describing the way of realization of personal values concerned in that type of contexts. For example, previous experience with self-other discrepancies of opinions may result in the following rule for fulfilling an individual's need for independence: "Whenever my peers are of different views than me I should try to defend my own position." Such a rule may become so well established that it is automatically accessed in most situations involving a discrepancy of opinions; if this is the case there would be no need for the person to consciously and deliberately construct the value-fulfilling norms in such a situation. On the other hand, in new or unusual circumstances, in which individuals have no ready-made, habitual way of realizing their own values at their disposal, the mode of their behavioral fulfilment must be generated based on value preferences. The process of norm formulation in such a context most probably involves conscious thinking about one's own value preferences and about the implications of several values concerned in the context.

As the previous discussion suggests, the type of situation studied as a context of value fulfilment implies what should be measured as a basis of prediction of behavior: norms or more abstract values. In the case of nonrecurrent behavioral choices the specific, newly formulated norms should be measured as Schwartz and his co-workers did in their studies of such unusual normative behaviors like organ donation or volunteering to tutor blind children (Schwartz & Howard, 1981, 1983). In the case of more frequently faced situations, the behavioral implications of personal values as well as personal norms may be so straightforward for the individual that measurement of personal value preferences may be enough to enable the prediction of behavior.

Because rather commonplace contexts (e.g., temptation situations) were addressed in the present research program, preferences for abstract personal values – not personal norms – were measured as a basis for the prediction of behavior. A Rokeach-type scale of values (cf. Rokeach, 1973) was used in the series of studies described below. In each study subjects were provided with a set of personal values, with each value described by a positive personality trait name, like intelligence, tenacity, modesty, etc. The size of the set varied from 12 to 20 depending on the study. Subjects were asked to rank the provided values according to their subjective preference, i.e., according to the degree to which each personal value is desirable (in comparison with the other values in a set) to the subject with regard to his or her own personality.

VALUES AND BEHAVIOR

The gap between people's dispositions like traits, attitudes, and values on the one side and behavior on the other is usually wide enough to discourage the simple view that to believe in something inevitably (or even frequently) means enacting the belief. This fact has been well documented for years (see Ajzen & Fishbein, 1977; Mischel, 1968; Wicker, 1969), and theories that try to describe and explain the link between hot knowledge and behavior are blooming in social psychology (e.g., Fazio & Zanna, 1981; Fishbein & Ajzen, 1975; Zanna, Higgins, & Herman, 1982). Because personal values and ideal self are defined here as specific instances of mental representations, the problem of the relation between value and behavior may be approached as a specific case of the relation between a cognitive structure and behavior implied by the structure. According to contemporary schemata theory (Taylor & Crocker, 1981; Wojciszke, 1986; Wyer & Srull, 1981), there are at least three preconditions of a structure influence on behavior. First, the structure has to be well established as an enduring entity in a person's cognitive system. Second, it has to be activated or accessed (retrieved) from the long-term memory. Third, the structure must be accepted by a person as a relevant and proper category of conceiving of the current situation. Applying these general rules to the consistency of behavior with personal values results in a following set of predictions concerning the regulatory functions of values.

Personal values constituting the ideal self are able to regulate behavior only for persons who have developed the ideal self or personal values system as a distinct and internally organized structure. For example, the hierarchization of personal values in terms of person's preferences can result in corresponding hierarchization of value-fulfilling behavioral choices only for persons whose verbal declarations of preferences are structurally based. Such declarations are structurally based when the hierarchy of value preferences is characterized by some objective features proving its enduring and organized nature (e.g., the hierarchy is temporally stable and value preferences are transitive – see following). Moreover, even an individual's existing hierarchy of values cannot regulate behavioral choices unless it is activated. Therefore an effect of values on behavior is possible only when a value is both accessed from memory and used to define the meaning of behavioral options which the person is formulating or facing in a specific situation. Any factors that increase the probability of the activation of an individual's personal value system also increase the possibility of its influence on behavior. Some structurally based factors that increase the availability of personal values (like association of values with other highly available cognitive structures) are discussed later.

As the previous discussion implies, interindividual differences in the organization of personal values seem to be a promising point of departure for theorizing and research on value-behavior consistency and psychological mechanisms underlying the consistency. Further elaboration of the idea is presented in the next part of the chapter.

INDIVIDUAL DIFFERENCES IN ORGANIZATION OF PERSONAL VALUES

The Idealism Notion

Most previous research related to the ideal self has been based on the hypothesis that everyone has such a structure in his or her cognitive system (cf. Higgins, Klein & Struman, in press; Markus, 1983; Robinson & Shaver, 1968; Wylie, 1974). The existence of the ideal self-structure has been hypothesized to result in some emotional consequences (especially the experiencing of aversive states because of actual or anticipated behaviors discrepant with the ideal self), and behavioral ones (especially adjusting one's own behavior to the content of the ideal self to avoid such aversive states). Those and similar assumptions underlie most of the research on self-acceptance and real- versus ideal-self discrepancies in which subjecs are asked to describe their ideal selves, usually in terms of some categories provided by the researcher.

However, the study of real- versus ideal-self discrepancies in terms of provided categories precludes the possibility of determining whether subjects actually do have any representation of an ideal concept of their own selves in their cognitive systems. Subjects may simply declare some ideals because they are asked to do so and provided with an easy way to fulfil the demand, even if they actually do not hold any ideals at all. Therefore, it is hypothesized that although every individual is probably able to declare his or her ideal self if required, only for some individuals do such declarations result from the ideal self-structure actually "existing" in their cognitive system. Behavior consistent with verbally declared ideal self may be reasonably expected only in the case of these individuals. Individuals whose ideal selves (especially personal value systems) are established as distinct mental structures and used as a source of information directing their behavioral choices are henceforth labeled as *idealists*. Their counterparts, *nonidealists*, are individuals whose ideal selves are less established and/or not used in the regulation of behavior.

Construction of the Idealism Scale

The Idealism Scale (IS) recently has been devised by the author for the measurement of idealism (Wojciszke, 1987a). The IS is a 31-item, true-false, self-report questionnaire measuring the tendency to report valuing self-related ideals and to report using them as a source of information directing behavioral choices. The IS includes items whose contents express: a) the general approval of ideals – e.g., "I am sure I will never abandon many of my ideals" (true); b) the view that the value of a goal is a more important reason for activity than the probability of goal attainment – e.g., "I do not engage in activity if I see a poor chance of success at the beginning" (false); c) the same view but as related to the self, i.e., in the case of a conflict between behavior implied by the real self and ideal self, the latter tendency overcomes the former – e.g., "I adjust my personal decisions to my capacities rather than my desires" (false).

Persons scoring highly on the IS are individuals who report themselves as being "idealists," i.e., as persons who believe in some ideals, especially those related to themselves, and who try to apply ideals in their own life. The items constituting the final version of IS were selected from an initial 50-item pool of assertions according to criteria of content validity and discriminative power. The content validity of items was based on judgments made by five expert raters (all having a PhD in psychology).

The initial pool of items was also administred to 215 undergraduates and the discriminative power of each item was analyzed by means of biserial correlation computed between individual items and total score. Only items for which discriminative power equaled or exceeded the value of r_{bi}=.45 were selected for the final version of the IS (median r_{bi} of the final version was. 63).

This relatively high discrimination indices resulted in a satisfactory level of internal consistency for the IS. The internal consistency varies from .70 to .95 depending on estimation method and sample. In general, the internal consistency seems satisfactory both for males and females and is higher for high school and university students than for schoolteachers.

The normative data for IS are presented in Wojciszke (1987a) as are data referring to its discriminant validity. Generally speaking, there are low and nonsignificant correlations between the IS and self-monitoring and locus of control indices. For females, the IS shows a low and nonsignificant correlation with social desirability (r=.03) although it is correlated significantly and negatively for males ($r=-.23, p<.05$). The last correlation is too small to threaten the discriminant validity of IS. The results of research demonstrating the construct validity of IS are presented later.

Cognitive-Structural Differences Between Idealists and Nonidealists

Two types of cognitive-structural differences between high- and low IS-scorers are especially important: first, differences in degree of organization of personal value systems, and second, differences in degree of association between value systems and self-structure. Both these differences were studied in empirical research.

Organization of personal value systems. Basically the difference between idealists and nonidealists is that the former actually have developed their ideal selves in their cognitive systems, whereas the latter lack such structures or at least do not use them. The simple description of an object provided by a person cannot be regarded as a proper index of the actual existence of a cognitive structure representing the object in person's mind. The content of such a description may not express any stable internal structure, being only a part of the individual's self-report. But the internal organization of the description can be regarded as such evidence so far as the organization cannot be ascribed only to current situational factors.

The most abstract layer of the ideal-self-structure is viewed here as a hierarchy of personal values, and the preference of values is hypothesized to be the critical factor organizing values into hierarchized system. The assumption of full hierarchization of the personal value system is very strong as it means absolute transitivity of value preferences. According to previously presented theorizing, only idealists are expected to have their value systems organized so well. To verify the hypothesis, the IS and a scale of personal values consisting of 12 items were administered to 70 high school students aged 18-19 (Wojciszke, in press a, Study 1). Subjects were asked to make paired comparisons of the values in terms of subjective desirability, i.e., to choose from each pair of the values the more desired one. The transitivity of value preferences was estimated by means of Kendall's coefficient of consistence K (Ferguson, 1976). The obtained values of K varied from .14 to 1.00 with a median. .84. For only three persons were the Ks nonsignificant. The main hypothesis of the study was that the higher the IS score the better hierarchized is the personal value system (as indicated by the Kendall's K score). As hypothesized, the correlation was relatively high, $r(68) = .734$, $p<.0001$.

The results of this study supported the contention that the content of verbal descriptions of the ideal-self may be to a degree artificially produced by a method of research. When subjects are asked to rank positive personality traits according to their own preferences, they may produce such a ranking even without any structure underlying the ranking, as evidenced by low transitivity of preferences in the case of many subjects of the study. The weak hierarchization of the value system means that different values are equally preferred, whereas strong hierarchization means that the set of values is highly differentiated in terms of their preferences: some values are preferred more than any others. Thus, one may expect that the more hierarchized is the value system, the greater is its influence on the subject's decisions, intentions, and behaviors. In other words, the more hierarchical is the system the better is prediction of value related functioning of the individual. Consistent with this reasoning, Huismans and Kość (1982) showed that the stronger the value hierarchization in their Dutch subjects, the stronger the influence of the single value "equality" on relevant attitudes, intentions, and behaviors.

Whereas the actual hierarchization of the personal value system seems to be a quite convincing measure of the existence of the ideal self, it is not the only possible measure. Other possibilities involve studying the replicability of ranking of personal values and its amenability to current situational influences. If idealist personal value systems are better established than those of nonidealists, they should exhibit relatively greater temporal stability of value preferences as well as lesser amenability to situational influences. This is expected because both high replicability and low amenability to external influences may be conceived as structurally based pehomena. These issues were studied by Wojciszke (in press a, Study 2).

The experiment consisted of two sessions 1 week apart. During the first, the IS and a scale of values (with "honesty" inserted into the set of 16 items) was administered to high school students. The second purportedly unrelated session was run individually by a female experimenter who introduced herself as a psychologist. In one condition the experimenter said that she just started work in a newly opened Young Delinquent Center and asked subjects to formulate as many arguments persuading a youngster to be as honest as possible (on the basis that Center's staff needed such arguments to influence the beliefs of young delinquents). This manipulation was unique for the honesty-activation (experimental) condition. Other steps of procedure were identical for the experimental and control groups. The experimenter also asked subjects to do an incomplete sentence task that measured the intensity of activation of the self-structure. Finally the scale of values was once more administered.

Two hypotheses of the study are relevant to the present discussion. The first of them refers to the control condition only, in which no influences addressed to value systems intervened between the first and second measurement of values. It was hypothesized that they hierarchy of value preferences would be more temporally stable for idealists than for nonidealists. For the idealist subgroup, the correlation (taus) between the first and second value preference indices varied from .28 to .92 with a median of .70, whereas for the nonidealist subgroup it varied from –.03 to .87, with a median of .54. The idealist-nonidealist difference was significant.

The second hypothesis that is relevant pertains to the experimental condition only. Because the second value measurement in that condition followed (by a half of an hour) the procedure designed to activate honesty, it was hypothesized that the value would change its rank position (in comparison with the first value measurement) to a lesser degree in the case of idealists than in the case of nonidealists. The hypothesis was based on the conjecture that idealists' prefrences for honesty (and probably for other values as well) are more structurally based and therefore less susceptible to situational influences. Social psychologists' theorizing and research on the activation of cognitive structures (Higgins & King, 1981; Wyer & Ross, 1980) suggest that an increase in preference of a value should be a natural consequence of its activation, as activated concepts are subjectively more important that nonavailable ones. However, in the context of the present experiment, the activation of honesty involved the experimenter's demand of a verbal defense of the value. For that reason, a decrease in honesty preference resulting from subjects' reactance also could be predicted. Therefore, the instability (in either direction) of the rank position of value "honesty" was analyzed variable.

The data related to this hypothesis are presented in Figure 13.1. As the figure shows, the idealist-nonidealist differences in terms of the instability of honesty preference apparently were strongly influenced by the initial (first measurement) rank position of that value. When the initial preference of honesty was high (median split) there were virtually no differences between idealists and nonidealists, as both groups showed nearly perfect stability of the value preference. Most probably this result is due to the ceiling effect in "honesty" preference. For 65% of the subjects from the "high-honesty" group, honesty was the number one value during the first measurement of value preferences. Therefore, for the majority of that group, any upward change in honesty preference (as a result of the value activation) was impossible for

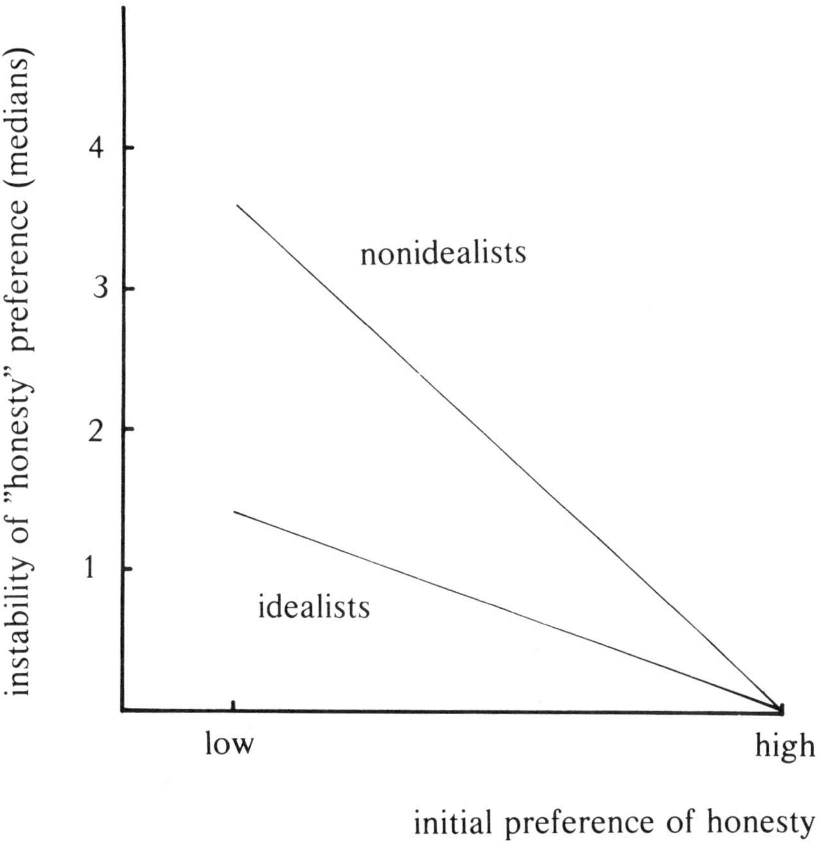

FIGURE 13.1. Instability of rank position of "honesty" value resulting from its recent activation as a function of idealism and initial preference of the value. Source: Wojciszke (1986 b, Study 2)

purely procedural reasons. In such a situation a decisive test of the hypothesis should be made only for those subjects whose initial preference of honesty is relatively low (and upward instability of the value preference is possible). When the initial preference of honesty was low, the nonidealist subgroup exhibited significantly greater instability than did the idealist subgroup (see Figure 13.1).

Taken together the results clearly support the assumption that high-IS-scorers are persons whose self-descriptions of their ideal-selves are more structurally based than are those of low-IS-scores. The idealists' personal value system is more hierarchized and temporally stable, and less amenable to situationally induced influences.

Association between personal values and self. The results discussed so far show important cognitive-structural differences between idealists and nonidealists although they shed little light on the mechanisms mediating the relation between personal values and behavior. It is not clear why the better established personal value systems of idealists are more capable of influencing their behavior. One possibility is that idealists' personal values are more frequently or more easily available as cognitive structures to be used in interpretation of current situations and in forming behavioral choices. The possibility was indirectly addressed in the experiment described previously.

There are many reasons to conjecture that representation of the individual's own self is one of his or her most easily and frequently activated cognitive structures. Situations entered in and persons encountered by an individual vary endlessly and so change the content of cognitive structures activated to deal with the situations and the partners. But one thing varies very little – the individual is always him or herself in those situations. If there is a structure universally activated in a broad variety of contexts, it is individual's self-representation, because many behaviors and activities inevitably require much information about the self to be properly carried out. Also, empirical research demonstrates the high frequency of self-structure activation. Both Polish (Banaśkiewicz & Wojciszke, 1984; Szustrowa, 1976) and American (Carver & Scheier, 1978) researchers have found that when people are asked to complete incomplete sentence tasks, about half of the endings are self-related. The self-structure is also frequently used by people as a cognitive device for the interpretation and understanding of others' behavior (Markus & Smith, 1981) and personalities (Lewicki, 1983). Moreover there are reasons to expect that other cognitive structures associated with the self-structure may be heightened in availability as the activation of any information may result from previous or current activation of strongly related information, according to the theory of spreading activation in the network of semantic memory (Collins & Loftus, 1975; Higgins & King, 1981). So one possible way for the greater influence of idealists' personal values on psychological processes and behavior is a stronger association between values and the self-structure for idealists than nonidealists.

Support for this hypothesis comes from the aforementioned study. Immediately after the honesty activation manipulation, subjects were asked to complete Szustrowa's (1976) Test of Egocentric Associations (TEA). The TEA is a semiprojective, 40-item incomplete sentence task in which the beginning of each sentence is short and vague and does not suggest any specific content of its completion, e.g., "In a situation," "Sometimes" etc. The number of self-referring (mainly containing "I" or "me" pronouns) completions is basic score of the test. Based on the hypothesis that highly preferred personal values of idealists (but not that of nonidealists) are strongly associated with their self-structures and on the widely accepted assumption that the activation of a structure results in the secondary activation of other information associated with the structure, the following hypothesis was formulated. It was predicted that immediately after the activation of "honesty" value, idealists who prefer the value to a high extent would show greater activation of the self-structure than idealists preferring it to a lesser degree. This expectation was held neither for nonidealists in honesty activation condition nor for both groups (idealists as well as nonindealists) in the control condition (for whom no value was activated). In other words, a condition x idealism x honesty preference interaction was predicted for the activation of self-structure as dependent variable.

The results are presented in Figure 13.2. According to an analysis of variance, there was a main effect of idealism, with idealists showing greater activation of the self-structure than nonidealists. The expected interaction was on the border of significance, $p < .10$. However the shape of the interaction depicted in Figure 13.2 (dotted lines) does not support the expectation. The simple effect of value preference for idealists in the honesty activation condition was the essential point of the hypothesis, and the simple effect appeared nonsignificant.

Completion of the TEA consumed on the average 20 minutes and the activation of the self-structure – at least that part that resulted from the experimental manipulation, could dissipate over that time. The activation of a cognitive structure especially when produced by priming or related influences, is rather a short-lived phenomenon; usually it is erased after approximately 10 minutes (Higgins & King, 1981; Wyer & Srull, 1981). For this reason the whole analysis was repeated for the number of self-related completions of the first ten items of TEA, which were completed in the initial about 5-minute period following immediately the experimental manipulation of honesty activation. The results also are presented in Figure 13.2 (solid lines). This time the expected triple interaction was significant, as well as the essential simple effect of the honesty preference for idealists in the honesty activation condition. Thus, the hypothesis was corroborated for the short period of time passing between the priming of a personal walue and the measurement

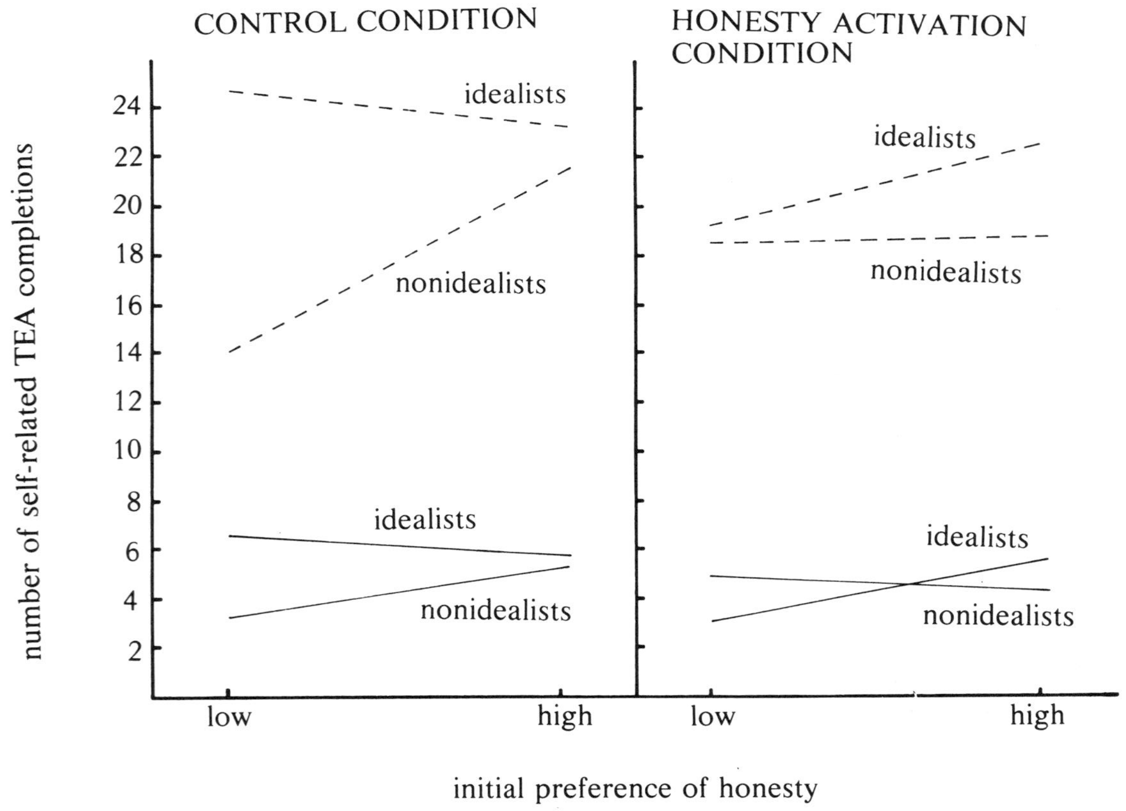

FIGURE 13.2. Intensity of self-structure activation measured by the number of self-related TEA completions as a function of "honesty" activation, the initial preference of the value and idealism for the whole TEA score (dotted lines) and for the first quarter of TEA (solid lines). Source: Wojciszke (1986 b, Study 2).

of the activation of self-structure. Three comments on the results are worth of attention.

First, numerous researchers inspired by the self-awarenes theory (Duval & Wicklund, 1972; Wicklund, 1975) have shown that the consistency of behavior with values (Hormuth, 1982; Karyłowski, 1979) or attitudes (Carver, 1975; Gibbons, 1978) increases in self-focusing conditions. Because self-focusing conditions may be conceived as contexts inducing the activation of the self-structure (Carver & Scheier 1981) and a value-consistent behavior may be treated as a sign of activation of the value, these investigators have shown that the activation of the self-structure results in the activation of the highly preferred values. Interestingly, our study showed that the opposite direction of activation spread is also possible: Activation of a highly regarded value can result in (for idealists) activation of self-structure. Relations between self and values seem to be bidirectional associations.

Second, idealists show generally greater activation of the self-structure than nonidealists. This difference predisposes idealists to greater value-behavior consistency because individuals with the heightened disposition to be self-aware show greater standard-behavior consistency, as a number of studies has shown (see Carver & Scheier, 1981).

Third, the association between personal values and the self-structure apperared detectable only for idealists, which suggests, that the secondary activation of personal values by a previous or concurrent activation of the self-structure may be a mechanism by which values come into play in the regulation of idealists' behavior. Because the self-structure is apparently a frequently activated part of the cognitive system, this mechanism may put values into motion in a variety of situations and actions.

The establishment of a personal value system as a distinct cognitive structure and its activation are necessary although not sufficient preconditions for value-fulfiling behavior. At least one thing more must happen according to the previously presented theorizing. Namely the value has to be accepted by an individual as a proper category for conceptualizing the current situation and the person's own behavioral options. The problem of idealist-nonidealist differences in the tendency to use their personal values as categories of conceiving of social situations was addressed in another experiment (Wojciszke, in press b, Study 3).

Materials used in the experiment consisted of six short stories constructed and selected carefully in a four-stage pilot study. Each story delineated a social situation where the main character behaved in a socially desirable way and the behavior was interpretable as an expression of different positive personality traits (i.e., different personal values). Subjects were asked to describe freely the reason of the character's action in terms of the character's thoughts accompanying each action. Then the experimenter took the story away so that only subject's interpretation was left to her. Next subjects were provided with a ready-made set of the character's thoughts preceeding the action. Finally, the subject estimated how much each of the provided thoughts was present in her own previously written free description of the character's thoughts. The provided thoughts were constructed in such a way that each of them expressed (according to pilot subjects) concern with a specific personal value.

Each story was accompanied by 2-4 value-related thoughts mixed with a few a value-unrelated thoughts serving as buffers. Each of the seven values studied in that way (benevolence, responsibility, tolerance, ambition, independence, self-control, and knowing-what-to-want) appeared in three different stories. The sum of intrasubject acceptance of all three thoughts related to the same value in three different stories constituted the index of the tendency to use the value as interpretation category.

The experiment consisted of two purportedly unrelated sessions. During the first, the IS and a scale of values were administered to 90 female students aged 10-23. During the second session, subjects read the set of stories described earlier. For half of the subjects, the stories were written using "I" and "me" pronouns and subjects were asked to imagine themselves as the main character (activation of self-condition). For the remaining subjects stories were written using "she" and "her" pronouns and the heroine was described as a female student (control conditions). The interindividual correlation between a value preference and its use as an interpretation category was calculated with the expectation that the correlation would be greater for idealists than for nonidealists, especially (or only) in self-activation condition.

The value of the obtained correlations appeared very low (from .03 to .26), probably because of the uninvolving nature of imagined situation and the lack of control of many variables possibly influencing acceptance of an interpretation (e.g., social desirability of interpretation). Only for idealists in the self-activation condition was the average correlation significant. Nevertheless the pattern of data was exactly what was expected. The idealist-nonidealist difference in the correlation was nonsignificant in the control condition and significant in the self-activation condition. The results showed that the more an individual prefers a personal value, the more the concept representing the value functions as an interpretative framework of the individual's own (imagined) behaviors. This is true for idealists only and refers only to the interpretation of subjects' own behavioral choices, but not choices of other persons.

The results of the studies discussed so far support the view that there are essential cognitive differences between idealists and nonidealists. The personal value system of idealists is apparently better established as a mental structure; it is more hierarchized and stable over time, less amenable to current situational influences, and more tuned for use as an interpretative framework for individual's own behavior. All these differences provide rather convincing evidence for the most crucial hypothesis of the program presented here – the hypothesis that idealists show a greater value-behavior consistency than nonidealists. This hypothesis was tested in the next series of studies.

Individual Differences in Value-Behavior Consistency

In a few studies involving diverse methods of data collection we examined the idealist-nonidealist differences in value-behavior consistency. In the first study high school students identified as idealists or nonidealists described themselves and were described by their class-mates (Wojciszke, in press b,

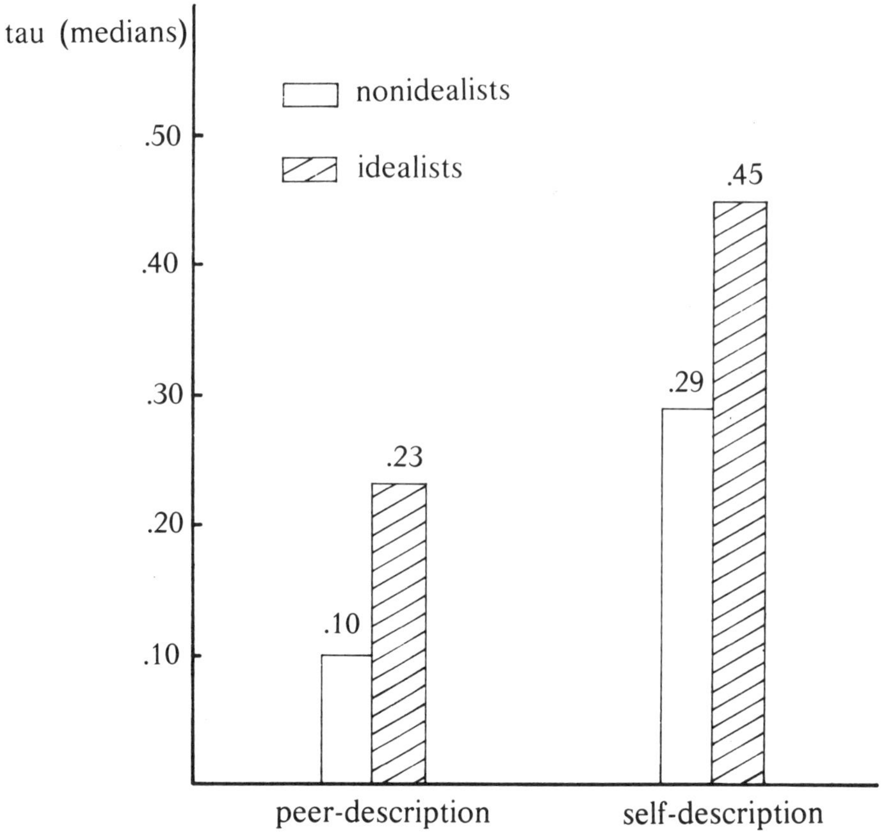

FIGURE 13.3. Median correlations aggregated over 12 values between preference of a value and intensity of behavioral value-fulfillment as rated by observers peer-description and by the subjects themselves self-description for idealists and nonidealists. Source: Wojciszke (1986 c, Study 1).

Study 1). The study involved twelve concepts describing positive personality traits (e.g., helpfulness) that, in the first session, had the status of personal values (and were hierarchized by subjects in terms of their personal desirability). During the second session subjects described themselves on the rating scales, i.e., they estimated how helpful, etc., they actually were, and also described a few of their class-mates using the same rating scales. Each subject was rated by 5 randomly selected peers whose ratings were then averaged. Kendall's tau intersubject correlations between a value preference and rated behavioral fulfilment of the value (calculated for each value separately and then aggregated over values) were the main focus of the analysis.

As can be seen in Figure 13.3, the correlations were generaly higher for idealists than for their counterparts, both for peer- and self-description. When tau correlations for successive values were treated as rank data, the idealist – nonidealist difference was significant both for peer-description and for self-description data. Value-behavior consistency was also substantially higher when behavioral fulfilment of values was estimated by subjects themselves than when it was rated by peers.

It must be noted that idealists' higher self-reported consistency between values and behavior cannot be ascribed to their greater motivation for self-enhancement because the difference was exactly, although on a lower level, replicated for peer-description. Moreover, the idealist – nonidealist difference for self-description was replicated in an independent study involving a larger, 20-item set of personal values (Wojciszke, in press b, Study 2).

The hypothesis of greater value-behavior consistency for idealists was also examined in two additional studies, both of which involved manipulation of self-structure activation. The manipulation was included in the experiments to test the hypothesis that idealism influences value-behavior consistency especially in individuating situations (Abelson, 1982), i.e., in conditions in which the self-structure and values are highly accessible as a source of information directing behavioral decisions. The finding of self-awareness theorists that self-focusing situations increase behavioral consistency (Carver & Scheier, 1981; Wicklund & Frey, 1980) constituted the second reason for inclusion of the self-activation manipulation in the experiments.

One of the experiments (Wojciszke, 1987 b, Study 1) dealt with defensive attribution, i.e, the tendency to ascribe one's own successes to internal rather than external factors, and one's own failures to external rather than internal ones (Nisbett & Ross, 1980; Zuckerman, 1979). It was hypothesized that the defensive attribution pattern represents a specific style of self-presentation as a "man-of-success", whereas the counterdefensive attribution represents a "man-of-modesty" way of self-presentation. It was predicted that the defensive pattern was more characteristic for persons who prefer the value "ambition" to the value "modesty," whereas the counterdefensive attribution was relatively more characteristic for persons who preferred modesty to ambition. In other words, consistency of self presentation with the rank ordering of preferences for the two values was predicted, but only for idealists and especially in a situation in which self and ideal self were readily accessible structures.

The experiment consisted of two sessions with a 3-4-days break inbetween. At the first session the IS and a scale of values (with "ambition" and "modesty" inserted in the set) were administered to a group of high school students aged 18-19 years. The subjects also listened to a short lecture on drug dependency and then they answered several questions related to the material presented during the lecture. The questions constituted the experimental task. The second session was run individually. At the beginning, feedback about subjects' task performance was presented – success for half the participants and failure for the reminder. Then subjects were asked for their attributions. One hundred per cent of responsibility of the task result was divided by each subject and ascribed to the self, the lecturer, and other factors, if any. The defensive attribution index was the percentage of internal responsibility minus percentage of the lecturer's responsibility for the "successful" group, and the percentage of the lecturer's responsibility minus the percentage of internal responsibility for the "failure" group. The self-focus manipulation was fully crossed with previous variables. One third of the subjects ascribed the responsibility for their results in a private self-focus condition (in front of a large mirror), one third in the public self-focus condition (in front of two observers), and the reminder in a low self-focus (control) condition.

The results are depicted in Figure 13.4 (failure-success was deleted from the figure, as the variable did not influence the level of defensive attribution). There was a strong interaction of value preferences with idealism. Idealists provided self-presentation patterns relatively more consistent with their value preferences. Idealists who preferred ambition to modesty were higher on use of defensive attribution than idealists who preferred modesty to ambition (who showed relatively counterdefensive attribution). The nonidealists yielded attributions generally unpredictable from their own value preferences. As a matter of fact, they even tended to give paradoxical attribution patterns, i.e., those who preferred modesty tended to be more defensive than those who preferred ambition.

As can be seen in Figure 13.4, the general shape of the interaction was replicated in all three conditions. Analysis of variance revealed no effect of condition on the basic interaction. This result disconfirms the hypothesis related to the activation of the self-structure; self-focus did not influence idealist versus nonidealist differences in consistency between attribution styles and value preferences. One plausible speculation about the reason of this lack of effect refers to the probably self-focusing nature of the dependent variable measurement. Because this measurement involved self-other comparisons in terms of responsibility for the task result, it may be viewed as a self-focusing procedure. If so, there is the possibility that the self-focus induced by the attribution measurement procedure overcame the effects of

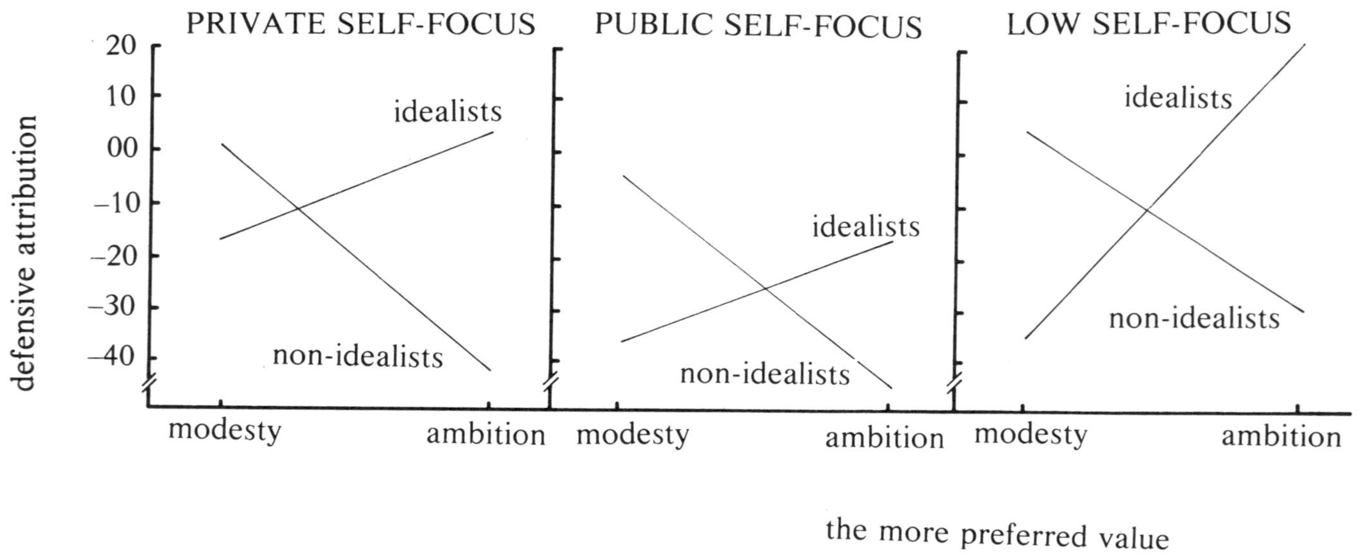

FIGURE 13.4. Defensive attribution level in private versus public low self-focus condition as a function of relative rank position of "modesty" and "ambition" values and the idealism. Source: Wojciszke (in press b, Study 1).

mirrors and observers, and all three conditions were equally highly self-focusing. The idea that self-other comparisons result in a heightened accessibility of self-structure served as one of conceptual bases of the next study.

This experiment (Wojciszke, 1987b, Study 2) was conducted to examine the role of idealism in the context of cheating behavior and to further explore the role of self structure activation in mediating the influence of idealism on value-behavior consistency. For that reason, a new method of self-structure acivation was invented– self-other comparisons. It was hypothesized that any self-other comparison increases activation of the self-structure because such comparison inevitably requires some access to the subject's self-knowledge, especially when the dimension of comparison is subjectively important or ego involving.

The experiment consisted of two, purportedly unrelated, group sessions, which were run by two different researchers. The first session included personality measures (the IS and a scale of value). The second session, which included the self-focus manipulation and the cheating task, was introduced as psychological study on learning ability. Immediately before the task subjects were asked 7 questions referring to learning – the bogus goal of the experiment. In the control (low-self-focus) condition, the questions dealt with learning in animals. In the high-self-focus condition questions referred to the subject and the answers required self-other comparisons on evaluative dimensions. The experimental task involving the possibility of cheating consisted of a series of geometric puzzles identical to those employed by Vallacher and Solodky (1979). The proportion of subjects who cheated in each combination of variables is shown in Table 13.1 as well as the correlations between value "honesty" preference and the intensity of cheating for different combinations of self-focus and idealism.

Chi-square analyses were performed on the relative frequencies of cheaters and noncheaters in each self-focus condition separately, as a function of value preference and idealism. For the high-self-focus condition, four combinations of personality variables produced significantly differing frequencies of cheaters. For the low-self-focus, however, cheating did not differ among the combinations of personality variables. An additional analysis revealed that under high-self-focus, the proportions of cheaters among idealists who valued honesty to a high versus low degree differed significantly. In low-self-focus, however, the analogous proportions did not differ significantly. The same analysis for nonidealists showed an invariable lack of difference between proportions in both conditions. Clearly, the proportion of cheaters was influenced by the rank position of value "honesty" only in the case of idealists who faced the temptation of cheating in high self-focus. This pattern of results was corroborated by the correlational analysis (see Table 13.1).

In conclusion, two studies involving the rating data and two studies involving measurement data provided clear support for the hypothesis that value-behavior consistency is greater for the idealists than for nonidealists. Most probably the difference is pronounced (or observable only) in individuating or self-focusing conditions, i.e., in situations in which the self-structure and personal values associated to the structure are activated and easily accessible as a source of information to be used by the subject in interpreting his or her own current situation and behavioral options.

TABLE 13.1

Proportions of Cheaters and Correlations Between Honesty Preference and Number of Cheatings

	Low-Self–Focus		*High-Self-Focus*	
	Idealists (N = 20)	*Nonidealists (N = 20)*	*Idealists (N = 20)*	*Nonidealists (N = 20)*
Proportion of cheaters				
– highly valuing honesty	.60	.60	.30	.90
– valuing honesty low	.70	.90	.80	.90
Value-behavior correlation	.26[b]	.21	.42[a]	.06

[a] $p < .05$
[b] $p < .10$
Source: Wojciszke (in press b, Study 2).

GENERAL CONCLUSIONS

The results of our research program shed some light on an interesting mechanism mediating between personal value preferences and value-relevant behavior. Differentiated value preferences resulted in corresponding behavior only for persons whose personal value systems were well established (i.e., for whom preferences are more stable over time, less amenable to situational influences and more transitive) and associated with the persons' self-structures. Due to the better organized nature of idealists' value systems, these systems may more efficiently serve as a source of information and thereby influence the process of interpreting the current situation and directing. behavioral choices. Due to the association of idealists' values with their self-structures the activation of self-structure may be – in the case of idealists – an important and frequently operating mechanism for including values in the process of behavioral regulation.

The mechanisms underlying behavioral idealist-nonidealist differences discussed and researched so far are purely cognitive in nature. No attention has been paid to possible emotional or motivational mechanisms (e.g., to the hypothesis that idealists are more likely to base their own self-esteem on the behavioral fulfilment of personally accepted values, whereas nonidealists prefer rather different bases for their own self-regard). Such differences are possible although they were not addressed in the previously presented research. Whereas the whole of social psychology in the last three decades was increasingly cognitive in nature to such a degree, which some theorists found rather fault (e.g., Markus & Zajonc, 1985), the psychology of the self was similarly blamed for being obsessed with purely evaluative factors (McGuire, 1984). The view of the ideal self and personal values presented in this chapter may be accused of being too cognitive, although it is rather free of an evaluative obsession. However, I did not try to show that ideal self and personal values are "nothing more" than cognition. I tried to show that personal values and ideal self are "something more" than internal factors including evaluation, that they are also cognitive structures which may be more or less established, activated, and used as an interpretative framework by a subject. Most probably any evaluative and motivational functions of ideal self are hard to understand and explain without understanding of their nature as mental structures.

ACKNOWLEDGMENTS

The research reported in this chapter was supported by "Problem węzłowy 11.8" Grant to the author. The author wishes to thank Janusz Reykowski for his comments and Nancy Eisenberg and Jerry Tobacyk for language revision of an earlier draft.

REFERENCES

Abelson, R.P. (1982). Three modes of attitude-behavior consistency. In M. P. Zanna, E. T. Higgins, & C. P. Herman (Eds.), *Consistency in social behavior.* The Ontario Symposium (Vol. 2). Hillsdale, NJ: Lawrence Erlabaum Associates.

Ajzen, I., & Fishbein, M. (1977). Attitude-behavior relations: A theoretical analyses and review of empirical research. *Psychological Bulletin, 84,* 888-918.

Banaśkiewicz, R., & Wojciszke, B. (1984). *Comparison of mirror and ego-involving self-other comparisons as a method of self-focus and self-evaluation manipulation.* Unpublished manuscript, University of Gdańsk, Poland.

Carver, C. S. (1975). Physical aggression as a function of objective self-awareness and attitudes toward punishment. *Journal of Experimental Social Psychology, 11,* 510–519.

Carver, C. S., & Scheier, M. F. (1978). Self-focusing effects of dispositional self-consciousness, mirror presence and audience presence, *Journal of Personality and Social Psychology, 36,* 324-332.

Carver, C. S., & Scheier, M. F. (1981). *Attention and self-regulation: A control-theory approach to human behavior.* New York: Springer-Verlag.

Carver, C. S., & Scheier, M. F. (1983). Aspects of self, and the control of behavior. In B.R. Schlenker (Ed.), *The Self and social life.* New York: McGraw-Hill.

Collins, A. M. & Loftus, E. F. (1975). A spreading activation theory of semantic memory. *Psychological Review, 82,* 407–428.

Duval, S., & Wicklund, R. A. (1972). *A theory of objective self-awareness.* New York: Academic.

Fazio, R. H., & Zanna, M.P. (1981). Direct experience and attitude-behavior consistency. In L. Berkowitz (Ed.), *Advances in experimental social psychology* (Vol. 14). New York: Academic.

Ferguson, G. A. (1976). *Statistical analysis in psychology and education* (3rd ed.). New York: McGraw-Hill.

Fishbein, M., & Ajzen, I (1975) *Belief, attitude, intention and behavior: An introduction to theory and research.* Reading, MA: Addison-Wesley.

Gibbons, F. X. (1978). Sexual standards and reactions to pornography: Enhancing behavioral consistency through self-focused attention. *Journal of Personality and Social Psychology, 36,* 976-987.

Higgins, E. T., & King, G. (1981). Accessibility of social constructs: Information-processing consequences of individual and contextual variability. In N. Cantor & J. F. Kihlstrom (Eds.), *Personality, cognition and social interaction.* Hillsdale, NJ: Lawrence Erlbaum Associates.

Higgins, E. T., Klein, R., & Strauman, T. (in press). *Self-concept discrepancy theory: A psychological model for distinguishing among different aspects of depression and anxiety.*

Hormuth, S. E. (1982). Self-awareness and drive theory: Comparing internal standards and dominant responses. *European Journal of Social Psychology, 12,* 31-45.

Huismans, S. E., & Kość, Z. (1982). Wartość "równość" jako predyktor postaw, intencji i zachowania a hierarchizacja systemu wartości. *Studia Psychologiczne, 20,* 49-57.

Karyłowski, J. (1979). Self-focused attention, prosocial norms and prosocial behavior. *Polish Psychological Bulletin, 10,* 57-66.

Lewicki, P. (1983). Self-image bias in person perception. *Journal of Personality and Social Psychology, 45,* 384-393.

Markus, H. (1983). Self-knowledge: An expanded view. *Journal of Personality, 51,* 543-565.

Markus, H., X Smith J. (1981). The influence of self-schema on the perception of others. In N. Cantor and J.F. Kihlstrom (Eds.), *Personality, cognition, and social interaction.* Hillsdale, NJ: Lawrence Erlbaum Associates.

Markus, H., & Zajonc R. B. (1985). The cognitive perspective in social psychology. In G. Lindzey and E. Aronson (Eds.), *The handbook of social psychology* (3rd ed.). New York: Random House.

McGuire, W.J. (1984). Search for the self: Going beyond self-esteem and the reactive self. In R. A. Zucker, J. Aronoff, & A.J. Rubin (Eds.), *Personality and the prediction of behavior,* New York: Academic.

Mischel, W. (1968). *Personality and assessment.* New York: Wiley.

Nisbett, R. E., & Ross, L. (1980). *Human inferences: Stragegies and shortcomings of social judgements.* New York: Prentice-Hall.

Powers, W. T. (1973). *Behavior: The control of perception.* Chicago: Aldine.

Robinson, J. P., & Shaver, P. R. (1968). *Measures of social psychological attitudes.* Ann Arbor: Institute for Social Research.

Rokeach, M. (1973). *The nature of human values.* New York: Free Press.

Schwartz, S. H., & Howard, J. A. (1983). Internalized values as motivators of altruism. In D. Bar-Tal, J. Karyłowski, J. Reykowski, & Staub (Eds.), *The development and maintenance of prosocial behavior,* New York: Academic.

Szustrowa, T. (1976). Test of egocentric associations. *Polish Psychological Bulletin, 7,* 263–267

Taylor, S.E., & Crocker, J. (1981). Schematic bases of social information processing. In E. T.

Higgins, P. Herman, & M. P. Zanna (Eds.), *Social cognition. The Ontario Symposium* (Vol. 2) Hillsdale NJ: Lawrence Erlbaum Associates.

Vallacher, R. R., & Solodky, M. (1979). Objective self-awareness, standards of evaluation and moral behavior. *Journal of Experimental Social Psychology, 15,* 254-262.

Wicker, A. W. (1969). Attitudes vs. actions: The relationship of verbal and overt behavioral response. *Journal of Social Issues, 25,* 41-78.

Wicklund, R.A. (1975). Objective self-awareness. In. L. Berkowitz (Ed.), *Advances in experimental social psychology* (Vol. 8). New York: Academic.

Wicklund, R. A., & Frey, D. (1980. Self-awareness theory: When the self makes a difference. In D. M. Wegner & R. R. Vallacher (Eds.), *The self in social psychology.* New York: Oxford University Press.

Wojciszke, B. (1986). *Teoria schematów społecznych.* Wrocław: Ossolineum.

Wojciszke, B. (in press a). Idealism and cognitive-structural bases of value-behavior consistency. *European Journal of Social Psychology.*

Wojciszke, B. (in press b). Idealism and some cognitive antecedents of value-behavior consistency. *Polish Psychological Bulletin.*

Wojciszke, B. (1987a). Idealism Scale for the measurement of individual differences in regulatory functions of the ideal self. *Polish Psychological Bulletin, 18,* 325–333.

Wojciszke, B. (1987b). Ideal-self, self-focus and value-behavior consistency. *European Journal of Social Psychology, 17,* 187–198.

Wyer, R. S., Srull, T. K. (1981). Category accessibility: Some theoretical and empirical issues concerning the processing of social stimulus information. In E. T. Higgins, C. P. Herman, M. P. Zanna (Eds.), *Social cognition. The Ontario Symposium* (Vol. 1). Hillsdale, NJ: Lawrence Erlbaum Associates.

Wylie, R. (1974). *The self-concept.* (Vol. 1). Lincoln: University of Nebraska Press.

Zanna, M. P., Higgins, E. T., & Herman, C. P. (Eds.). (1982). *Consistency in social behavior. The Ontario Symposium* (Vol. 2). Hillsdale NJ: Lawrence Erlbaum Associates.

Zuckerman, M. (1979). Attribution of success and failure revisited, or: The motivational bias is alive and well in attribution theory. *Journal of Personality, 47,* 245–287.

14 The Development of Motives, Self-Identities, and Values Tied to Blood Donation: A Polish-American Comparison Study

Jane Allyn Piliavin
The University of Wisconsin-Madison

George Herbert Mead (1934) saw two aspects of the self: the "I," which was the source of the impulses to action, and the "me," which represented the person's self-image resulting from the responses of others to those actions. In symbolic interaction theory, no response is truly predictable because the "I" forever remains unknown since it cannot be brought into consciousness. The actions of the self, however, can come to be more and more controlled by the "me," through the development of commitments to certain images of the self. It is the gradual development of commitment to a self-identity of "regular blood donor" and its effect on future behavior that is the focus of this chapter.

The process by which commitments to such new role identities develops should be affected by the structure of the situation and the responses of others to the new "recruit." For example, the development of internalized linkages may well be hindered by the presence of obvious external rewards – such as outright monetary payment – or by attending to other factors in the donation situation, such as social approval or "fringe benefits." On the other hand, the interactions with others in the situation could serve to enhance or accelerate the process, if these others reflect back to the new "recruit" the image of a committed participant.

In order to investigate such propositions, donors in three different blood donation systems were studied. The three systems are as follows: First, there is the United States "community responsibility" system, in which donors receive nothing but thanks, an occasional pin or certificate, and a feeling of having contributed to the collective good. Second, there is the Polish "honorowy" (or voluntary) system, in which donors are *defined* as unpaid, altruistic donors but receive many "fringe benefits," such as a day off work with pay, a free meal, chocolate, and the right to go to the head of queues in pharmacies. Finally, there is the Polish "platny" (paid) system, in which donors receive money for giving blood, as well as some of the fringe benefits, i.e., the free meal and the day off with pay. They do not receive the same kind of respect as the honorowy donors, however, and must defer to them in the queue for giving blood. It is the author's impression that the status of "honorowy donor" in Poland is given a good deal more attention than is the role of voluntary donor in the United States and thus might even come to be a more salient aspect of the self there than in the United States.

Within attribution theory – or even its predecessor, dissonance theory – if there is a clear exernal justification for engaging in an action (for example, a payement of $20 for telling a small lie), there is no need to develop what C. Wright Mills (1940) called "a vocabulary of motives" to justify engaging in it. Similary, there is no pressure to incorporate the meaning of the action into the self – to make a correspondent inference – if there is a clear external reason for having done it. Thus donors in the U.S. system should be most inclined to develop moralistic explanations for their act and to incorporate the behavior into a role identity. Honorowy donors should fall between U.S. donors and platny donors, whereas platny donors should show little tendency to attribute "higher motives" to their act or to incorporate the behavior into their self-concepts.

On the other hand, Deci (1975) argues that it is not merely the presence of external rewards for a behavior that is the important factor in whether the person will attribute the behavior to their effects, but rather whether the person sees the rewards as "controlling" or as merely "informative." Thus, if the honorowy donors see the "fringe benefits" they receive merely as appropriate symbolic indicators of the importance of blood donation rather than as reasons why they are doing it, they should look just like the U.S. voluntary donors, It would be difficult for the platny donors to deny the controlling nature of the payment they receive. Thus, the prediction from Deci would be that Polish honorowy and U.S. voluntary donors should look very much alike, whereas platny donors would be very different.

Reykowski (1982a, b) also sees the individual as pressured to explain his or her actions (to him/herself or others) out of a need for cognitive clarity or consistency. He has presented three categories of motives for prosocial behavior: ipsocentric (external reward), endocentric (self-based morality), and egzocentric (other-oriented morality) and suggests that the role of social situations, in particular the actions of other people, are critical for the process of motive development.

Finally, Kicinski (1978) assumes that the need for self-worth is the most fundamental motivation for action. To the extent that an action can be viewed (by self ond/or others) in a negative light or if "sufficient" social approval is not forthcoming, the individual is motivated to construct justifications for it. In research he did with paid and unpaid Polish donors in the 1960s, he found that the platny donors claimed that the money they received was insufficient to serve as an explanation for their actions and stressed that they felt a moral obligation to give based on perceived need – a highly egzocentric motive in Reykowski's model. (Unpaid donors were more likely to emphasize endocentric – personally altruistic – motives.) Kiciński's model only speaks to the "vocabulary of motives" aspect of development, not to the question of internalization, however. Using his model there is no reason to assume that any of the donors would have to incorporate the role of donor into their self-concept. As long as the donnor is able to believe that the motives are genuine and to convince others, simply expressing the socially acceptable motives should satisfy the postulated needs. Thus, all three groups of donors should look superficially similar but the underlying role-identity structures might well be different.

METHOD

The data used in this chapter were collected in three separate studies. The central data set was collected from November, 1983 to February, 1984 in the "Stacja Krwiodawstwa" in Warsaw, Poland. There were two overlapping samples of donors. First, a brief before-and after-donation questionnaire was given to 915 honorowy and 888 platny donors. This questionnaire included questions concerning reasons for donation, the impetus to donation on that day (e.g., called by the center, just felt like it, etc.), motivation to give, emotional state before and after donation, ratings of the personnel and the donation experience, self-definition as a person who can give blood easily, and measures of commitment to continue. It also included measures of occupation, age, sex, number of prior donations, and amount given that day (which is variable in Poland and under the control of the donor).

A subset of 238 honorowy and 138 platny donors were obtained for a more intensive interview. This schedule included, among other measures, Rokeach's 18 instrumental values, measures of perceived obligation to give blood, bone marrow, or a kindey, and a large number of questions designed to assess the salience, importance, and meaning of the blood donor role identity and its connections to other aspects of the donor's life. The measures will be described as they are used in the data analyses.

The U.S. comparison sample for the first (pre-post) questionnaire consisted of 1800 donors from Red Cross collections in six communities in the South and Midwest of the United States. They filled out the questionnaires at permanent collection stations or mobile drives during the late winter and early spring of 1984. The questionnaires were very similar to, although not identical with, the ones used in Warsaw.

Finally, the U.S. comparsion sample for the more extensive questionnaire consisted of 658 donors from three communities in Wisconsin and one community in Iowa. The data were collected by mailed questionnaire in the fall and early winter of 1982–1983 by Peter Callero, forming the basis for his Ph.D. dissertation The conceptualization of the measurement and analyses of the donor role-identities were his.

RESULTS

Before addressing the various questions that can be put to these data, some descriptive information will be presented (see Table 14.1). A major difference between the platny and honorowy donors in Poland is in the number of donations they have made. The median for the honorowy was just under 10, whereas for the platny it was 30. The U.S. voluntary donors resembled the Polish honorowy donors in this regard. Any direct comparisons between platny donors and the other two groups in motives, values, and attitudes will take this into account. There was also a large sex difference, with almost all Polish donors being male, whereas 43% of U.S. donors were female.

TABLE 14.1

Description of three samples of donors who filled out the pre-post donation questionnaire: Polish honorowy and platny donors and U.S. Red Cross voluntary donors

PRIOR DONATIONS	*Polish Donors* *Honorowy* *(N = 915)*	*Płatny* *(N = 888)*	*U.S. Red Cross* *Voluntary* *(N = 1800)*
0–1	14%	1%	16%
2–5	17%	6%	22%
6–10	18%	9%	15%
11–20	24%	21%	19%
21–50	18%	39%	18%
over 50	5%	24%	5%
MEAN	14.44	36.98	14.66
MEDIAN	9.71	30.07	8.00

(continued)

TABLE 14.1 *(Continued)*

SEX (percent Male)	95%	98%	57%
AGE			
18–25	36%	14%	28%
26–35	48%	42%	33%
over 35	14%	44%	39%
MEAN	29.29	36.98	35.33 (est.)
MEDIAN	27.89	30.07	31.00 (est)
REASONS GIVEN FOR DONATION			
Free day	11%	4%	–
Station Called (1)	9%	58%	27%
Just wanted to (2)	38%	20%	13%
Friend, colleague suggested it	3%	2%	7%
Know there is need (3)	8%	6%	30%
Someone in family needed blood	14%	1%	2%
Organized drive	4%	7%	16%
"Other"	13%	9%	6%
TOTAL INTERNAL	46%	26%	42%
TOTAL EXTERNAL	15%	11%	16%
TOTAL ASKED	26%	61%	35%

(1) Called or received reminder card in U.S. (2) Impulse or heard an ad in U.S. (3) Just knew it was time in U.S.

CAME IN ALONE	72%	97%	62%

Platny and honorowy donors also differ in what they claim was the impetus for their donation. By far the most common answer among the platny donors – over 58% – is that the station called them. Among the honorowy, the most common answer given is "just wanted to" – 38% – followed by someone in the family needing blood, wanting a free day, and the station calling. When these are grouped into "internal," "external," and "asked" categories, the honorowy are heavily represented in the "internal", whereas most platny fall in the "asked" category. The U.S. donors are slightly less "internal" than the honorowy donors and less likely to have been asked than the platny. Nearly all the platny donors came in alone for their donation, whereas this is true of less than 75% of the honorowy, and of only 62% of the U.S. donors. For some unpaid donors, then, blood donation is a social activity, engaged in with friends from outside the donation setting. This is not true among the Polish platny donors.

Differences Between Groups in Expressed Motives for Donation

Our first hypothesis regarding differences between the three groups of donors has to do with expressed motives for donation. Assuming that it is less necessary to develop altruistic motives if an altruistic act is seen as externally controlled, we should find established U.S. donors most likely to agree that their motives for donation are egzocentric or endocentric (using Reykowski's terms) and least likely to agree that they give under social duress, whereas Polish platny donors should be the opposite. Under standard attribution theory, the Polish honorowy should fall between, whereas Deci's model would suggest that should resemble the U.S. donors.

Table 14.2 presents a comparison of selected subsets of established donors from the three groups on motives related to blood donation. Only donors who had given over eight times were compared in order to be able to control for the

TABLE 14.2
Motives and attitudes related to blood donation: established donors (over 8 donations) in 3 samples

	POLISH				*U.S. RED CROSS*
	Honorowy (N = 96)		*Platny (N = 748)*		*Voluntary (N = 723)*
REASONS (% sure it is a reason, unless otherwise indicated)					
1. Like to help	56%	***	41%	***	83%
2. Self-satisfaction	41%	**	31%		34%
3. Not disappoint (% yes)	47%	**	51%	***	28%
4. Obligation to group (% yes)	47%		52%	***	18%
5. Community responsibility	50%		44%	***	74%
6. Blood supply (% yes)	82%		82%		91%
7. Feel I ought to	47%	***	31%	***	72%
8. Moral obligation	42%	***	28%	***	55%

(continued)

TABLE 14.2 *(Continued)*

COMBINATIONS OF REASONS (Mean)					
(1,2) Endocentric	3.68	***	3.98	***	3.31
(3,4) Social pressure	5.27	*	5.08	***	6.36
(5,6) Egzocentric	3.65		3.66	***	2.92
(7,8) Obligation	4.08	**	4.34	***	3.05
MOTIVATION (Mean)	4.07	*	3.84	***	5.86
SELF-CATEGORIZATION (% regular donor)	86%	***	95%	***	86%
THOUGHTS DURING DONATION (% thought very little)					
Goal of giving	43%		43%		–
Image to friends	63%		63%		–
What you will get	77%	***	60%		–
Self-image as donor	57%		50%		–
JUSTIFICATIONS FOR QUITTING (% yes or maybe yes)					
No time	8%		10%		–
Station pleasant	10%		10%		–
Wait is too long	17%	***	22%		–
Blood is wasted	15%	**	22%		–
Bad for health	20%	***	29%		–
Unreasonable demands for giving	36%	.10	40%		–
I've given enough-others' turn now	8%	***	19%		–

Indication of differences between groups: * p=< .05 ** =p< .01 *** p< .001.

differences in the number of be donations between the platny donors and the other two groups. The honorowy and platny donors were significantly different of five of the eight individual items, all in the postulated direction, and on two of the four scales constructed from the items. Honorowy donors were more likely to agree that liking to help, self-satisfaction, and feelings of obligation were reasons for their donation, whereas platny donors agreed more that not wanting to disappoint someone who asked was a reason. U.S. donors were very similar to the honorowy donors in pattern but more extreme in their endorsement of the egzocentric and obligation reasons and in their rejection of social pressure. Although the absolute differences are small, this pattern provides some initial support for the standard attribution theory prediction.

Even within this selected group of experienced donors, a slightly higher proportion of the platny than of the honorowy and U.S. reported that they are "regular donors." In terms of what the donors think about while giving, the only difference is that platny donors are more likely to think about what they will get afterwards. Thus, the platny donors are not afraid to admit to a very external mental content during the course of their donation, supporting the conclusions based on the differences in reported motives for donation discussed earlier. (These questions were not asked of the American donors.)

Finally, in Poland only, a set of questions was asked to try to discover to what extent the donors would find certain conditions, if true, to justify discontinuing donation. The assumption here was that if donation is a behavior that is connected to the self and has meaning in the individual's self-image, it should be more difficult to come up with justifications for abandoning the behavior. Of the seven justifications provided, there were significant differences in the expected direction on four and borderline differences on two more. Platny donors thought that too long a wait, wasting of blood, donation being bad for one's health, and, most strongly, feeling that one has simply done enough could all serve as justifications for quitting, to a greater degree than did the honorowy. To a lesser degree they even thought that unreasonable demands and being short on time would serve as justifications. It is important to note, however, that it is never a majority of the donors in either group who find any of the suggestions to be an acceptable justification.

Differences Between Groups In Measures of Blood Donor Role Identity

Table 14.3 presents some measures of role-identity salience, attitudes towards donation, and the meaning of the donor role identity among the three groups, again using only donors who have given over eight times. These data are taken from the more intensive interview samples. The value measure is simply the mean rank (with "1" equal to the most important value) given by the members of each group to each of the 18 Rokeach instrumental values, followed by the rank of that mean ranking within each group. Note that honorowy and platny donors differed at a borderline level on "helpful," and significantly on ambitious, intellectual, independent, and forgiving. The U.S. donors much more closely resemble the honorowy than the platny. The three groups did not

TABLE 14.3

Values, measures of role-identity salience, connectedness of the blood donor role to other roles, and measures of the meaning of the role of blood donor, established donors (over 8 donations) in three systems

	POLISH						*U.S. RED CROSS*	
	Honorowy			*Platny*			*Voluntary*	
	Mean rank	*Rank*		*Mean rank*	*Rank*		*Mean rank*	*Rank*
Values related to blood donation:								
Loving	6.81	3		7.00	3		7.05	3
Responsible	6.02	2		6.69	2		6.39	2
Helpful	8.03	4	.10	8.94	9		8.63	4
Forgiving	10.58	13	***	12.34	16	***(P)	9.50	6
Ambitious	8.98	9	*	7.60	4	**(P)	9.06	7
Intellectual	10.54	12	**	9.09	10	***(P)	10.96	15
Independent	10.58	13	*	9.74	13	***(H)	8.97	6
Salience rank of three identity categories (Mean)								
Family	1.47			1.40			1.43	
Work	2.59			2.05			2.56	
Religion	3.99			4.20			3.13	
Blood donor	4.30		***	5.23			5.21	
Importance of identities (Mean)								
Family	1.32			1.23			1.29	
Work	2.24			2.05			2.01	
Religion	3.15			3.30		**(H)	2.61	
Blood donor	2.21		***	3.44		***(H)	3.21	
Salience scales (self-based)								
Work	2.97			2.96			2.31 (adj.)	
Religion	3.32			3.55			2.73 (adj.)	
Blood donation	2.79		***	3.73			3.40 (adj.)	
Connectedness								
Blood donation-work	11.45		**	9.04			12.35 (adj.)	
Blood donation-religion	14.41		***	9.94			13.63 (adj.)	
Blood donation-family	17.53		***	12.12			15.25 (adj.)	

(Continued)

TABLE 14.3 *(Continued)*

Meaning of the donor role-identity: (a)			
Honorowy vs. one-time	1.32	*	1.41
Platny vs. one-time	2.12		2.10
Honorowy vs. platny	1.28	***	1.37

Indications of significance between groups: * p=< .05 ** p=< .01 *** p=< .00
(a) The lower the number, the closer is the donor's perceived self-image to the first named of the comparison pair, e.g., 1.32 vs. 1.41 in the first comparison means that honorowy donors see themselves as relatively closer to the honorowy donor (in contrast to the one-time donor) than do the platny donors.

differ on two values found by Callero (1983) to differentiate U.S. donors from the general population norms: "loving," which was ranked third among his U.S. donors, in comparison with the norm of 9, and "responsible," which his donors ranked second, as compared to a norm of 7. Although we do not have norms for the Polish population, these may be seen as specifically "blood donor values."

In the next section of the table, we find that among all three samples, work identities were ranked higher than religious ones, with blood donor identities ranked as less important still. These data come from a part of the questionnaire in which donors were simply asked to place seven categories of roles in a hierarchy of importance. (The other four were family, political, group or organizational, and ethnic or nationality role identities.) The blood donor identity is ranked significantly higher among honorowy than among platny donors, as we would predict if donation becomes part of a self-identity to a greater degree in a unpaid system. No direct comparison is possible to the U.S. sample due to differences in cultures. For example, group identities are much less important in Poland (according to Nowak, a well-regarded Polish sociologist); thus the lists are not comparable across countries. Results on the second measure, which asked donors to rate the importance of the same seven identities on 7-point scales supported the previous analysis. Only the blood donor identity is rated as significantly more important by honorowy donors than by platny. U.S. donors differ from all Polish donors in rating *lower* more highly, but they rate the blood donor identity *lower* in importance than do the honorowy. This again may reflect the fact that more different role identities are available in American society.

Consistent with the findings for the importance ratings are the results for the three self-based salience scales. Each of these consits of seven 7-point scales of response to questions like, "To me, being a blood donor means more than just giving blood," "My job affects the way I do other things" or "My religion is something I rarely ever think about." Honorowy and platny donors differed significantly on blood donor role identity salience. (The scale used in the U.S. employed 9-point scales and thus cannot be directly compared. However, adjusted item averages, as shown in the table, suggest, as did the importance ratings, that on the average the blood identity is if anything *more* salient to the Polish honorowy donor than to the U.S. donor.)

Finally, there are three scales of "connectedness" between blood donation and other role identities. In theory, the more connected to other parts of one's life a given role is, the more committed one should be to it, and, thus, the more likely one should be to perform behavior related to it. On all three measures, honorowy donors rated blood donations as more similar to and more connected to work, family, and religious roles than did platny donors. (Again, a direct comparison with the U.S. data is not possible. However, adjusted scale scores show the U.S. donors much closer to the honorowy than to the platny donors.)

The measure of the meaning of the blood donor identity is much more complex. Devised by Burke and Tully (1977), it uses a two-step procedure. First, ratings of role identities and their counter-identities are obtained on relevant semantic-differential type scales. In the U.S. sample "a regular donor" and "a donor who has given once and dropped out" were used. Then a discriminant function is run to determine the weights for the scales that best differentiate the counter-role identity from the role identity. In the second step, these weights are then multiplied by each donor's ratings, on the same scales, of "As a blood donor I am..." This yields a measure of how close the person's self-image as a donor is to the collective image of the regular donor as compared to the "dropout." The smaller the number, the closer is the self-image to the first of the two role identities being compared.

For the Polish sample, ordinary least squares was employed in place of discriminant analysis, and three role identities were used: honorowy donor, platny donor, and one-time donor. The differentations were done separately for platny and honorowy donors. Thus, for the Polish data there are three possible measures of meaning: the meaning of being an honorowy donor as compared to a dropout, the meaning of being a platny donor, as compared to a dropout, and the meaning of being an honorowy donor as compared to a platny donor.

Means for these three measures are given at the bottom of Table 14.3. Note that honorowy and platny donors do not differ much in the meaning they attach to being a donor in contrast to being a dropout. They differ much more in the meaning of being a donor of their category as contrasted with the other category. (Because the procedure used in the U.S. sample employed discriminant analysis the mean levels are not comparable.) On all of the measures in this table, then, honorowy donors clearly show a stronger commitment to the role identity of blood donor than do platny, and also, it appears, than U.S. donors.

The Development of Donor Motivation

The second major question to be asked of these data has to do with the effects of developing a habit of regular blood donation on expressed motives and values in regard to blood donation and on the structure of role identities. That is, are there changes in the "vocabulary of motives" and in the self-concept as a result of becoming a regular blood donor, and do these effects differ depending on the system in which one is donating?

Of course, it is best not to use cross-sectional data to investigate developmental questions. At present, however, because longitudinal data are not available, all that can be investigated is whether there are differences between the groups in the relationship between the number of prior donations and motives for donation. Please keep in mind that the donors are at different "career stages." Past research has shown that most of the change in motives occurs early in the donor's career. Thus, if the correlations among platny donors are smaller, it may be simply that they are mainly beyond the stage at which they are changing (see Table 14.4).

The first differences that appear in the table cannot be subject to this problem. The perceived impetus to donation clearly becomes more internal among the honorowy and U.S. donors as number of donations increases, whereas motives become slightly more external among the platny donors. It is a significant change among the honorowy and U.S. donors, and the correlations are also significantly different in both cases from the platny. This is an important finding because it shows that the rewards that are offered for the activity do affect the attributions the donors make concerning the impetus to their act. The strength of motivation to give is also greater with more donations among the honorowy and U.S. donors, whereas it is less among the platny. Again, the correlation for the honorowy and U.S. donors is significant, whereas for the platny it is not, but the correlations differ significantly. It is also interesting that negative predonation feelings decrease among the honorowy and U.S. donors, although they do not change significantly for the platny donors. Good feelings before donation as well as after donation increase with donations in all three groups.

TABLE 14.4
Correlation of selected variables with number of prior donations.
(Maturational effects on motives and attitudes)

	Polish				U.S. Red Cross
	Honorowy (N = 914)		*Platny (N = 888)*		*Voluntary N = 1800)*
VARIABLES					
Internal-external (low=int.)	–.155	*	.065	*	–.194
Self-categorization as regular donor	.527	*	.315		.434
Motive	.088	*	–.048	*	.078
Negative feelings before	–.185	*	–.038	*	–.200
Good feelings before	.094		.074		.115
Good feelings after	.122		.127		.074
Reasons for donation					
Like to help	.109		.049		.037
Self-satisfaction	.128		.100		.040
Community responsibility	.062		.095		.080
Blood supply	.115		.062		.120
Feel I ought to	.203		.125		.158
Moral obligation	.178		.146		.120
Obligation to a group	.064		.129	*	.014
Combinations of reasons					
Egzocentric	.108		.085		.118
Endocentric	.147		.088		.048
Social pressure	.046		.109		.020
Obligation	.215		.147		.166
Self-definition as donor	.096		.059		.110
Intention to continue	.311	*	.113		.158

R of .08 is significant at p< .01 in all samples.

R's that differ by .10 or more are significant at p< .05 and are indicated by an asterisk.

Select Samples	(N = 240)	(N = 138)	(N = 658)
Self-based salience	.370 ***	.136 *	.183***
Other-based salience	.375 ***	.210 **	.170***
Attitude towards donation	.225 ***	.257 ***	.145***
Meaning (vs. dropout)	.318 ***	.059	.190***
Meaning (vs. other type donor)	.267 ***	–.149 *	—

Indicators of significance: * =p< .06 ** = p< .01 *** = p< .001

There is a remarkable similarity between the groups in the relationship between participants' agreeing that several suggested potential motives for donation were indeed reasons for their behavior and number of prior donations. Agreement with all of them increases – except for the reasons reflecting social pressure or obligation among the U.S. donors – and these increases usually are significant. The U.S. donors differ significantly from both of the Polish groups in regard to changes in the group obligation question but not in regard to any of the more internal types of motivations. There are again no significant differences between the Polish groups in the relationship between acceptance of the combined reasons and number of prior donations.

Finally, number of prior donations is significantly related to self-categorization as a regular donor (asked before donation) and to intention to continue giving (asked after donation) within all three groups. The relationship is strongest in the honorowy group, next strongest among the U.S. donors, and weakest among the platny.

The process of motive development seems to take place in about the same way in all three groups. The more donations, the more likely are donors to claim that they give blood for a wide variety of altruistic reasons. U.S. donors are somewhat different, in that they clearly reject external "social pressure" reasons as they move through their donation careers, whereas both groups of Polish donors increasingly endorse these reasons as well as internal reasons. This difference may reflect a stronger internalized set of motives among the U.S. donors or merely a cultural difference regarding the evaluation of conforming to social pressure. Blood donation as an activity, then, seems to involve, even for those who are paid for it, the development of a set of moral justifications. Second, all donors come to feel better emotionally, both before and after donation, although the change among the U.S. donors is not significant. This may suggest a difference between the countries in the nature of the donation experience itself or in the amount of dropout among those who do not have a positive experience.

The Development of Role-Identity Commitment, Attitude Towards Donation, and the Meaning of the Blood Donor Role

We can also look at the relations between prior donations and measures of role identity salience, attitude toward donation, and the meaning of the blood donor role, which were measured in the smaller questionnaire/interview sample. Before going on to investigate these relations, however, it is necessary to describe two more measures that were used. The measure of attitude towards donation is made up of two simple scales:positive-negative and favorable-unfavorable, answered in response to the question of what is one's attitude towards donation. Second, there is the variable of other-based salience of the blood donor role identity, which measures perceived expectations of significant others for one's behavior. It is based on seven 7-point scales very like those used for the self-based salience measure. They are questions like "Many people think of me in terms of being a blood donor" or "No one would really be surprised if I just stopped donating blood." Correlations between the number of past donations and the salience, attitude, meaning, and connectedness measures are shown at the bottom of Table 14.4.

Note that for honorowy and U.S. donors, the correlations with attitude, self- and other-based salience, and meaning are positive and significant. In all cases the correlation for Polish honorowy donors is larger than that for U.S. donors, and for both of the salience measures these differences are significant. With more experience in the role, the donor develops more commitment, a more positive attitude, and a view of "self-in role" that is closer to the accepted meaning of the role of regular voluntary donor. The fact that the correlations are larger for the honorowy donors suggests that they are still in an earlier stage of the development of commitment, in spite of the fact that they have on the average the same number of donations as the U.S. donors.

For the platny donor, attitude and other-based salience are postively related to number of past donations and the meaning of the platny role as contrasted with that of honorowy donor is *negatively* related. This last correlation is in the direction one would expect: With more donations, the meaning of self-in-role moves closer to that of platny as contrasted to honorowy donor. However, self-based salience is correlated at only a borderline level, and the meaning of the platny blood donor role as contrasted with that of the dropout is unrelated. Because three of these correlations are indeed significant, one cannot easily suggest that these nonsigificant and borderline findings are due to the fact that most of the platny donors are at a later stage in the donation career; that is, because platny donors are clearly still changing in some ways in response to added donation experiences, their *lack* of change in self-based salience appears to be meaningful. There is somewhat more evidence here for group differences in the development of commitment to the role of blood donor, in contrast to the results regarding development of the "vocabulary of motives."

The Consequences of Commitment to the Donor Role

The last important question to be asked of these data has to do with the consequences of the differential development of motives and self-identities tied to blood donation. Are there behavioral sequelae of increased salience and commitment to the blood donor role? Table 14.5 presents regressions of self- and other-based salience of the blood donor role, controlling for prior donations, on attitude towards donation, a measure of "failure-in-role," ratings

TABLE 14.5
Standardized regression coefficients of regressions of self– and other-based identity salience on attitude to donation, reactions to "failure-inrole," proselytizing, intentions to donate, and meaning of the blood donor role identity

Regressions On:	*Polish Donors* Honorowy (N = 238)	Platny (N = 138)	*U.S. Red Cross* Voluntary (N = 658)
Attitude to donation			
Self-based salience	.394c	.326c	.518c
Other-based salience	-.104	.027	–.105a
Prior donations	.126a	.199a	.064
Reactions to "failure-in-role"*			
Self-based salience	.230a	.063	.143b
Other-based salience	–.152	.110	.030
Prior donations	.015	.110	.056
Proselytizing activity			
Self-based salience	.375c	.366c	.431c
Other-based salience	.105	.207a	.129b
No. of prior donations	.216c	.055	.011
Likelihood of donating in 6 months			
Self-based salience	.281b	.132	.248c
Other-based salience	.033	.109	–.067
No. of prior donations	.198b	.163a	.127b
Meaning of self-as-donor (one-timer as counter-role)			
Self-based salience	.275b	.244a	.327c
Other-based salience	.109	–.171	.010
Prior donations	.176b	.072	.127b
(other group as counter-role)			
Self-based salience	.247b	.057c	–
Other-based salience	.102	.484c	–
No. of prior donations	.366c	–.248b	–
Amount donated			
Self-based salience	.171a	.047	–
Other-based salience	.033	.042	–
No. of prior donations	.366c	.144	–

Indicators of significance: a = $p < .06$; b = $p < .01$; c = $p < .001$
* Six-item scale in U.S., four-item scale in Poland

of likelihood of donation in the next 6 months, proselytizing behavior, and the meaning of the blood donor role (as contrasted with the "dropout") for each of the two groups of Polish donors and for the U.S. sample. For the Polish donors only, regressions on the amount given at the current donation and on the second measure of meaning of the blood donor role (honorowy as compared to platny) are also presented.

Space precludes a variable by variable explication of the findings, presented in Table 14.5. It is evident that for all three groups, personal commitment to donation is important for attitudes towards donation, for proselytizing behavior, and for development of the meaning of self-as-donor as contrasted with a donation dropout. On the other hand, response to failure-in-role is predicted by self-based salience among the U.S. and the honorowy donors, but not among the platny. This is an important finding, and it cannot be attributed solely to the size of the sample because the coefficient itself in the platny analysis is simply very small. What it suggests is that among paid donors, the role is not so internalized as among the U.S. or Polish honorowy donors. To fail at the role thus has no implication for the self, so why would one feel embarrassed or think less of oneself? A similar pattern obtains for the variable of likelihood of donation within the next 6 months.

The findings for the relations with the second measure of meaning are strikingly different between the Polish honorowy and platny donors. Among the honorowy donors, there is a strong relation between self-based salience and the meaning of the honorowy donor role as contrasted with that of platny donor, whereas among the platny there is none. On the other hand, among platny donors, this measure of meaning *is* related significantly to both other-based salience (in a direction such that high other-based salience is associated with a self-in-role perceived as closer to the meaning of the honorowy donor) and to prior donations (in the direction such that more donations are associated with a self-in-role perceived as closer to the meaning of a platny donor). The relation to prior donations is logical: The more one plays a role, the more one should come to see oneself as consistent with one's picture of the typical incumbent of that role. The opposite relation with other-based salience seems to suggest that those whose significant others view them in the donor role are in some conflict regarding their paid donation activity.

The Prediction of Intentions to Donate in the Future

In the preceding analysis, we presented evidence that commitment to the role of blood donor predicted intention to donate in the next 6 months only among U.S. and honorowy donors. Are there other differences between the three groups in the factors predicting future donation? Although we do not have measures of self-identity in our larger samples of donors, with them it *is* possible to investigate the impact of expressed altruistic motives as contrasted with measures of the emotional impact of the donation experience.

We have grouped the available predictor variables into predonation factors (sex of donor, number of prior donations, initial self-description as a regular donor, negative feelings, reasons for giving), donation experience factors (evaluation of staff, unpleasantness of donation experience), and postdonation factors (feelings after donation and self-definition as one who can give easily). We entered them in these three groups into a regression equation in the time order in which they occurred. Table 14.6 presents standardized regression

TABLE 14.6

Standardized regression coefficients for regressions on intentions to give in the next 6 months. Only predictors significant in at least one equation are shown

	Polish Donors				*U.S. Red Cross Voluntary Donors*	
	Honorowy		*Platny*			
Regression on:	*Step 1*	*Step 3*	*Step 1*	*Step 3*	*Step 1*	*Step 3*
INTENTIONS TO GIVE						
Predonation factors:						
Prior donations	.151***	.146***	.058	.048	.027	−.034
Regular donor	.137***	.136***	.137***	.110	.293***	.269***
Motivation	.124***	.120***	−.032	.004	.152***	.146***
Negative feelings	−.114***	−.076*	−.078*	.017	−.152***	−.127***
Like to help	.071*	.073*	.027	.018	.005	.010
Ought to give	.180***	.157***	.064	−.005	.089**	.090**
Donation factors:						
Personal staff	–	.088*	–	.045	–	.085①
Unpleasant exp.	–	.009	–	−.204***	–	.022
Post-donation factors:						
Good feelings	–	.027	–	.065①	–	.013
Self-definition	–	.164***	–	.216***	–	.151***
MULTIPLE R^2	.183	.217	.049	.153	.196	.220

Indicators of significance: ① = $p < .10$ * = $p < .05$ ** = $p < .01$ *** = $p < .001$

coefficients for the prediction of intentions to give in the next 6 months. The first and third steps of the regression are shown. Only predictors significant in at least one equation are presented.

The honorowy donors and the U.S. donors look remarkably alike in this analysis, both in the predictors that are significant and in the amount of variance explained. Self-definition as a regular donor (which may be related to self-identity), motivation, an absence of initial nervousness, and a feeling of moral obligation are all significant predictors in the first block. Of the donation and postdonation factors, self-definition as a person who can give blood easily and ratings of the staff are predictors of continued donation.

Once all of the variables have been entered, platny donors, on the other hand, are significantly affected by only two variables: unpleasantness of the experience and self-definition as a person who can give easily and at a borderline level by good feelings after donation. (On step one, self-definition as a regular donor and negative predonation feelings are significant. But their effects are negated by the later donation and postdonation experiences.) What this appears to imply is that, aside from the obvious monetary payoff, the only factors these donors consider in deciding whether or not to return are matters of emotional comfort and physical ease. In other words, *although they do develop a "vocabulary of motives" consistent with the blood donor role, such motivational factors do not play a causal role in the continuation of their donation behavior.* On the other hand, for the honorowy and U.S. donor, the central factors influencing conscious decisions regarding whether or not to continue are indwelling motivational states brought to the situation. The immediate donation experience has little impact, with the exception of a slight effect of the evaluation of the personnel.

In summary, motivational factors – mainly endocentric motives – appear to be real factors in the continuation decisions of Polish honorowy and U.S. donors, and there appear to be few important differences between them. This begins to suggest that Deci's model is most applicable. The honorowy donors appear to define themselves as voluntary donors and their behavior appears to be under the control of altruistic motives rather than the available fringe benefits. These factors, then, seem to operate as information, not as controlling factors, in the donation decisions of the honorowy donors.

The Role of Salience of the Role Identity in Continuation Decisions

Ajzen and Fishbein (1977) have developed a well-supported model of the attitude-behavior relationship involving the three variables of attitude, norm, and behavioral intention in the prediction of behavior. In this model, attitude and norm combine to predict intention, which alone predicts actual behavior.

However, these authors have not dealt with behaviors linked to roles, nor, in general, have they dealt with repeated, habitual behaviors. It is possible that, if an individual has a well-developed role identity, it is on the basis of that identity, rather than (or in addition to) attitude and perceived norms that the individual constructs his or her behavioral intentions. (This analysis is an extension of an analysis performed by Charng, 1986).

A final analysis was thus performed using the smaller, intensive interview samples, in which this hypothesis could be tested. First, a regression was run for each group testing the basic Ajzen and Fishbein model. Then the variables of self-salience of the blood donor role identity, social relationships tied to blood donation, connectedness to other roles, feelings of moral obligation, and number of prior donations (as an indicator of habit) were added. (The measure of social relations tied to blood donation is the sum of four questions such as "How many people do you know on a first name basis through donating blood?") The measure of intention used was the answer to the question "During the next 6 months, how many times do you intend to donate blood?" These analyses are presented in Table 14.7.

The results are strikingly clear. Other-salience (used as the measure of norms required by the Ajzen & Fishbein model) is most important for honorowy donors and irrelevant for platny. Among all the donors, attitude predicts intentions, as that model requires. When self-salience of the blood donor role identity is brought in, other-salience loses its effect in all groups. Among honorowy donors, attitude is also no longer a predictor after that, whereas among platny donors self-salience has no effect on intentions or on the attitude-intention link. U.S. donors show effects of both the attitude variable and salience. Social relations are a positive factor in the donation decision for all three groups, and the meaning of the donor role is a positive factor for honorowy and U.S. donors. (Among the platny donors, it has a nonsignificant *negative* impact.) These results simply serve to underscore and support the findings of the previous analysis. It is only *feelings,* in this case as represented by the attitude variable, and, in addition, social relationships tied to donation, that are important in the donation decisions of platny donors, whereas for the altruistic donors, both Polish and American both salience of the donor role and meaning of their donor self-image are important additional factors in the decision process. For both samples, social relationships are an additional important factor.

For all three groups, habit, as represented by prior donations, is a highly significant factor in predicting intentions once it is brought in to the equation. In fact, for both Polish samples it becomes the most important predictor in the full equation. Among the honorowy donors, only salience of the role identity continues to predict independently of habit, whereas among U.S. donors, attitude, social relationships, and connectedness to work also retain some effect.

In the U.S. sample a measure of actual donation behavior for the subsequent 6 months is available. (See last panel of Table 14.7.) We present a regression of

TABLE 14.7

Regressions on number of times donor expects to give in the next 6 months and on actual donation (U.S. sample only)

	Polish Honorowy Donors				*Polish Platny Donors*			
	Step 1	*Step 2*	*Step 3*	*Step 4*	*Step 1*	*Step 2*	*Step 3*	*Step 4*
Other salience	.248c	–.011	.006	–.040	.013	–.103	–.112	–.134
Attitude to blood donation	.147a	.048	.044	.001	.237b	.264b	.259b	.211a
Self-salience	–	.249b	.239b	.186a	–	.038	.026	.052
Social Relations	–	.149a	.139a	.025	–	.244a	.237a	.178a
Meaning of blood donor role (1)	–	.142a	.092	.039	–	–.128	–.128	–.124
Connectedness of donor role (2)	–	–	–.147a	–.087	–	–	.052	.042
Obligation to give blood	–	–	.132a	.094	–	–	.008	.008
Prior donations	–	–	–	.476c	–	–	–	.223a
R^2	.100c	.169c	.202c	.357c	.058a	.119b	.121a	.163b
Degrees of freedom	2/219	3/216	7/214	8/213	2/129	5/126	7/124	8/123

	United States Voluntary Donors							
	Regression on intentions				*Regression on actual donation*			
	Step 1	*Step 2*	*Step 3*	*Step 4*	*Step 1*	*Step 2*	*Step 3*	*Step 4*
Other salience	.089a	–.070	–.081	–.093	.137b	.047	.101a	.079
Attitude toward blood donation	.245c	.139b	.107a	.101a	.131b	.074	.003	–.007
Self-salience	–	.223c	.187b	.181b	–	–.024	–.092	–.098
Social relations	–	.101a	.090a	.089a	–	.114b	.077	.089a
Meaning of blood donor role (1)	–	.095a	.089a	.076	–	.098a	.063	.039
Connectedness of donor role (2)	–	–	.078	.084a	–	.030	.004	.013
Obligation to donate blood	–	–	.088	.090	–	.135b	.099a	.105a
Intentions to give – next 6 months	–	–	–	–	–	–	.395c	.375c
Prior donations	–	–	–	.093a	–	–	–	.190c
R^2	.078c	.127c	.138c	.146c	.045c	.083c	.216c	.250c
Degrees of freedom	2/486	5/483	7/481	8/480	2/490	7/485	8/484	9/483

(1) The measure of meaning used is comparing a regular donor to a one time donor. The groups are given their own weights.

(2) The connectedness measure used was to the religious role for honorowy, the family role for platny, and the work role for U.S. donors.

Indicators of significance: a =p< .06 b =p< .01 c =p< .001

all these predictors on donation, mainly in order to show that intentions have a powerful predictive impact on this relatively long-term behavior. This is done to demonstrate the relevance of using intentions as our dependent variable in the foregoing analyses. Habit, feelings of moral obligation, and social relations are significant predictors of actual return in addition to intentions. This further supports the idea that, contrary to the Ajzen and Fishbein model, when established role behavior is involved, intention is not the only important factor in the prediction of behavior.

CONCLUSIONS

There are clear and obvious differences between U.S. donors, honorowy Polish donors, and platny Polish donors. The "vocabularies of motives" developed by platny donors clearly include *less* emphasis on endocentric motives such as moral obligation and liking to help than do those developed by honorowy donors, and U.S. donors are significantly more likely to endorse both endocentric and egzocentric motives than are the honorowy donors. The blood donor role is also clearly more salient, more important, and more tied to other role identities for honorowy and U.S. donors than it is for platny donors, and the meanings that the groups of donors develop in connection with the blood donor role are also different.

Similarly, as platny donors move through their donation career, they appear to become more externally motivated in general, and to develop a meaning of self-in-role that is closer to that of platny than of honorowy donor. The honorowy and U.S. donors, on the other hand, become more internally motivated, more motivated in general, see themselves as closer to the voluntary donor role, and become personally committed to the blood donor role. All groups, however, come to develop the endocentric and egzocentric "vocabularies of motives" to some degree.

The structure of blood donor role identities also differs between the platny group on the one hand and the honorowy and U.S. donors on the other. Self-based salience predicts embarrassment at failure-in-role and the likelihood of donation in the next 6 months for honorowy and U.S. donors, but not for platny donors. The only nonfitting elements in the otherwise rather consistent picture that emerges are that the measure of self-based salience of the blood donor role *does* predict attitudes towards donation, proselytizing behavior, and intentions to continue equally well in all three groups.

The process of commitment to continued role behavior also seems to differ between the platny donors and the other two groups. Past behavior (habit), motivation, and various endocentric reasons for donation do not affect the continuation decisions of platny donors, whereas they do affect those of honorowy and U.S. donors. Only the situational factors of negative feelings before, unpleasant experiences during, and good feelings after donation seem to influence the platny donors' expressed intentions. Consistent with these results, self-salience of the blood donor role identity, meaning of the blood donor role, and feelings of obligation to give blood are related – in addition to social relationship – to intentions to donate in the next 6 months among honorowy and U.S. donors, whereas only attitudes and social relations predict intentions among the platny donors. Thus, although platny donors do develop a "vocabulary of motives" over time that explains their behavior in positive motive language, and although salience of their self-identity is related to some aspects of role-related behavior (e.g., proselytizing) and to attitude towards donation, the salience of their role identity does *not* have an influence on their continuation decisions.

On the whole, the similarities between the U.S. and honorowy donors on the one hand and their differences from the platny donors on the other lend credence to what would be Deci's interpretation as compared with the more general attributional model. The findings can also be seen as consistent with Kicinski's theory, because the "vocabularies of motive" developed by platny donors are much more similar than their underlying role identity structures to those of the honorowy and U.S. voluntary donors.

ACKNOWLEDGMENTS

The data analyzed in this paper were collected under NIH Grant No. HD 24425 to the author, and under a Grant from the Polish Academy of Sciences (11.8). Part of the questionnaire was designed and one set of the U.S. data were collected by Peter Callero, now at the Department of Social Science, Western Oregon State College. Marek Kosewski, with the author, was mainly responsible for translating the questionnaire into Polish and also supervised the Polish data collection, which was ably done by Krystyna Wojciechowska and Małgorzata Binduga. I would like to thank all of them for their help and support.

REFERENCES

Ajzen, I., & Fishbein, M. (1977). Attitude-behavior relations: A theoretical analysis and review of empirical research. *Psychological Bulletin, 84*, 888–918.

Burke, P.J., & Tully, J. (1977). The measurement of role/identity. *Social Forces, 55*, 881–897.

Callero, P. (1983). *Role-identity commitment and regular blood donation*. Unpublished PhD. Dissertation, University of Wisconsin-Madison.

Charng, H. (1986). *Is attitude enough? The influence of role-identity on blood donation.* Unpublished Master's Thesis University of Wisconsin-Madison.

Deci, E.L. (1975). *Intrinsic motivation.* New York: Plenum.

Kicinski, K. (1978). *Egoizm i problem zachowań prospołecznych.* Warszawa: Wydawnictwo UW.

Mead, G.H. (1934). *Mind, self, and society.* Chicago: University of Chicago Press.

Mills, C.W. (1940). Situated actions and vocabularies of motives. *American Journal of Sociology, 5,* 904–913.

Reykowski, J. (1982a). Development of prosocial motivation: A dialectic process. In N. Einsenberg (Ed).), *The development of prosocial behavior.* New York: Academic Press.

Reykowski, J. (1982b). Motivation of prosocial behavior. In V. Derlega & J. Grzelak (Eds.), *Cooperation and helping behavior.* New York: Academic Press.

Schwartz, S.H., & Howard, J. (1982). Helping and cooperation: A self-based motivational model. In V. Derlega & J. Grzelak (Eds), *Cooperation and helping behavior.* New York: Academic Press.

Rokeach, M. (1973). *The Nature of Human Values.* New York: The Free Press. 1973.

Schwartz, S.H. (1977). Normative influences on altruism. In L. Berkowitz (Ed.) *Advances in Experimental Social Psychology,* Vol. 10, New York: Academic Press.

Schwartz, S.H. & Howard, J. (1982). Helping and cooperation: A self-based motivational model. in V. Derlega and J. Grzelczak (Eds.) *Cooperation and helping behavior.* New York: Academic Press.

Stryker, S. (1980). *Symbolic Interactionism: A Social Structural Version.* Menlo Park, Cal: Benjamin/Cummings Publishing Co.

Part 5

SOCIOPOLITICAL, SOCIOECONOMIC, AND HISTORICAL VIEWS ON VALUES

15 Moral Values and Political Attitudes

Aleksandra Jasińska-Kania
Institute of Sociology
University of Warsaw, Poland

The aim of the chapter is to present some results and the theoretical assumptions underlying an ongoing empirical research project dealing with the moral values and political attitudes of the Polish people[1]. Included is a discussion of the main problem addressed in the study, basic hypotheses, and methods of the research and characteristics of the sample, as well as presentation of data collected in September 1984.

PROBLEM

This study was designed to analyze the relation between the structure of moral reasoning, perceptions of justice in society, and tendencies to accept or deny the moral values and political attitudes of the Polish people[1]. Included is was reflected in the moral and political attitudes of the Polish people.

---

[1] In the research directed by the author of this chapter participated the following persons: Grażyna Gęsicka, Grażyna Kacprowicz, Henryk Kliszko, Wojciech Modzelewski, Anna Sawisz. Statistical analysis was carried out by Marek Styczeń. This research was conducted within the Research Program "Cultural Life and Personality Changes Under Conditions of Social Reform" coordinated by Janusz Reykowski.

The concept of political legitimacy refers to a condition in which the political system is positively evaluated in moral terms as being just, proper, and deserving of recognition. Lipset (1960) distinguished evaluation of a political system in terms of its effectiveness and legitimacy. Legitimacy was defined as "the degree to which institutions are valued for themselves and considered right and proper" (p. 46).

Problems of political legitimation recently have been receiving increased attention from scholars of various disciplines. Waves of political protest and the rise of radical social movements in Western democracies, as well as political turbulence in some Eastern European countries in the 1960s and 1970s, have demonstrated the importance of this subject matter and have provoked intense debate about a legitimation crisis (see Jasińska-Kania, 1983).

The fundamental crisis in which the Polish society found itself in the beginning of 1980s can be analyzed according to the conceptual scheme developed by Habermas (1976). The crisis engulfed not only the economic system (unable to produce necessary consumer goods) and the political system (incapable of effectively steering the economy) but also involved an identity crisis constituting a direct threat to social integration. The identity crisis included both a legitimation crisis of the political order and a motivational crisis. A legitimation crisis occurs when the rightness and justice of the system comes to be questioned in public, and when the political order is unable to maintain the necessary level of mass loyalty and compliance. A motivational crisis occurs when the cultural system fails to provide, during the socialization process, individuals with the sense of meaningfulness that would stimulate the kind of activity required by the state and socioeconomic system.

An explanation of the legitimation crisis must take into account both the properties of the system (the performance of the economy and the rationality of administrative decisions) and the evaluation of them by citizens. Although citizens' perceptions and assessments of the political order are largely determined by administrative efficiency and economic prosperity, they are also predicated on the cultural traditions and moral values of the population. Therefore sociological research attempting to identify moral and political attitudes constitutes an essential part of the study of the political legitimation (and delegitimation) process. Such research (Lane, 1979) can provide an empirical answer to the question: "What fraction of the public holds, with what degree of intensity, an opinion treating the economic or political system as illegitimate?" (pp. 55-56). Furthermore, a structural analysis of moral and political consciousness, based on cognitive psychology, can reveal the intellectual capacity of the population to question the legitimacy of the existing system and to assess the possibility of alternatives.

Beyond the immediate interests of diagnosis and explanation of the legitimation crisis in the Polish society, the results of such research can contribute to the development of a general theory of moral and political consciousness formation.

BASIC HYPOTHESES OF THE STUDY

The central hypothesis of the research project was that different structures of moral thinking achieved by people in the process of their cognitive and moral development are related to specific types of meaning of the term *justice* and also are related to distinctive types of arguments for granting or withholding legitimacy to a system. This hypothesis is consistent with prior research in which level of moral judgement has been related to the content of political attitudes, e.g., to the degree to which attitudes are conservative or liberal (see Candee, 1975; Eisenberg-Berg, 1976; Fishkin, Keniston & McKinnon, 1973; Rest, 1979). However, few investigators have examined the relation of moral reasoning to attitudes regarding the legitimacy of political systems.

Kohlberg's theory of moral stage development (1981) was used in this chapter as the basis for constructing my own typology of meanings of the term *justice* and a corresponding typology of arguments brought up in justifying or rejecting the political order's legitimacy. However, Kohlberg's theory includes some controversial and widely disputed assumptions (see Kohlberg, Levine, & Hewer, 1983): that the sequence of stages is invariant and irreversible, that this sequence necessarily reflects higher levels of morality, that each stage forms a "structural whole" of general moral standards applied by a person all the time accross different situations, etc. In order to avoid debate concerning the philosophical and normative assumptions of Kohlberg's theory and to concentrate on a discussion of the empirical data, I use in this chapter the term *moral orientations* instead of *moral stages*. The term *orientations* is more value-neutral and does not presuppose the unilinear direction of moral development. The term *justice* is also understood here in a more empirical sense than in Kohlberg's works, where the notion of justice is discussed as the central and primary domain of moral reasoning. A typology of meanings of justice proposed in this chapter, although guided by Kohlberg's theory, is derived empirically from responses given by our subjects to several forced-choice questions as well as open-ended questions on what the word *justice* meant to them.

Kohlberg distinguishes the following levels and stages of moral reasoning: I. Preconventional level divided into: stage 1 – the punishment avoidance and obedience orientation, and stage 2 – the instrumental purpose and exchange orientation; II. Conventional level divided into: stage 3 – the interpersonal concordance orientation, and stage 4 – the law and order orientation; III. Postconventonal or principled level divided into: stage 5 – the social-contract legalistic orientation, and stage 6 – the universal ethical principle orientation. Kohlberg's labels for the particular types of moral orientations are adopted here, and I hypothesize how they are related to different models of political legitimacy. I also quote Kohlberg's definitions of justice specific for the particular moral orientations, and then I explain the empirical meaning given to them in our study.

According to the basic hypotheses of this study, the following types of meanings of "justice" distinctive for each moral orientation and the corresponding types of arguments used in moral evaluations of the political order can be identified:

I. According to the preconventional or premoral orientations, political authority is evaluated in terms of its power and ability to satisfy material interests. These types of reasoning do not distinguish between evaluations of a political system in terms of its effectiveness and in strictly moral terms.

1. The preconventional morality of "the punishment avoidance and obedience orientation" is related to granting legitimacy only to powerful authorities and withholding it when authority is perceived as weak and unable to use force. Within this orientation justice is understood as "might is right" or, as Kohlberg (1981) has described it: "obedience by weak to the strong and punishment by the strong of those who deviate" (p. 148). Some of our respondents clearly adopt this approach. For them "justice means getting profits and avoiding pains or punishment" and "authority should be strong and able to secure obedience".

2. The person with preconventional "instrumental purpose and exchange orientation" accepts the political order as long as it can provide fulfillment of basic material needs, and rejects its legitimacy when deterioration of the economic situation is perceived. Preconventional thinkers consider only the immediate economic consequences of a crisis. Justice is understood, in Kohlberg's words, as "equal exchanges of favors or blows" (p. 148). In these terms distributive justice means "giving rewards to those who will repay favors", and retributive justice means retaliation or revenge. In our interviews this orientation was expressed in such responses as, for example, "Justice means 'tit-for-tat' or paying back the same" and "authority should improve material standards of the population".

II. The conventional orientations reflect an attitude of conformity to stereotypical images of what is majority behavior and to societal norms that are perceived as objective and unquestionable. We hypothesized this norm-oriented rule-maintaining perspective would be applied in granting legitimacy to a political order.

3. The individual with a conventional "interpersonal concordance orientation" judges authorities by their intentions and ability to avoid conflict. Legitimacy is granted when authorities "mean well" and are able to maintain good interpersonal relations. Perception of the political leadership as dishonest and corrupt is a crucial reason for denying its legitimacy.

Justice is identified with good motives and concern for community approval. According to Kohlberg (1981), "a Stage 3 conception of justice is integrated with a conception of a good (positive and stable) interpersonal relationship" (p. 149). Distributive justice means rewarding those who deserve it for their loyalty and honest motives, whereas retributive justice means evaluating in terms of the intentions rather than the consequences of an act. The following statements were interpreted as examples of this orientation: "justice means having good motives and being concerned about others" and "honesty and truthfulness are the most desirable characteristic of authorities".

4. The conventional "law and order orientation" is related to the maintenance of fixed norms and rules, which demand discipline and unquestioned respect for authority. This type of legitimacy is withdrawn when disorder, chaos, and law-breaking are seen to prevail in society. Kohlberg writes, "For Stage 4, justice and maintenance of the basic rules and structure of society are much the same" (p.151). Distributive justice means that "merit should be rewarded by the system and every individual must contribute to society" (p. 151). Retributive justice is oriented to upholding the law. This orientation was indicated by such responses as "justice means maintaining the law" and "authorities should guarantee law and order in society".

III. Persons with postconventional or principled orientations evaluate a political system in terms of its ability to observe democratic procedures and to put in practice universal ethical principles of justice.

5. The person holding a postconventional "social-contract legalistic orientation" views the legitimacy of authority as dependent on its ability to observe democratic procedures and carry out obligations established in the "social contract". According to Kohlberg (1981) "the typical stage 5 conception of distributive justice is one of equality of opportunity; that is, equality of formal liberty to attain substantive equality" (p. 155). An emphasis also is placed on maintaining legal procedures of due process for those who break the law. These attitudes were expressed by statements such as the following: "justice means to act in accordance with principles and rules that have been democratically agreed on by people", "all members of a group should decide by voting how to distribute rewards," "authorities should be elected in a democratic way".

6. In the postconventional "universal ethical principle orientation" legitimacy is granted to a system seen as functioning in accordance with universal principles of justice, equality of human rights, and respect for the dignity of human beings. Denying legitimacy stems from perceived violation of these principles, inconsistency of the systemic principles, and

a discrepancy between its ideals and reality. According to Kohlberg, "At stage 6, the sense of justice becomes clearly focused on the rights of humanity independent of civil society, and these rights are recognized as having a positive basis in respect for the equal worth of human beings as ends in themselves" (pp. 166–167). Solutions to moral dilemmas concerning breaking a law in order to fulfill a moral duty, as well as solutions to problems of distributive justice, are seen as requiring recourse to the principles of universalizability and reversibility. Such responses as "justice means to act in accord with self-chosen universal ethical principles" and "authority should act in accordance with principles of justice and respect for the human dignity" were interpreted as representing this orientation. However, this does not mean that all respondents who accepted these statements could be classified as persons who had attained the highest stage (or Kohlberg's Stage 6) of moral reasoning.

In the research carried out, we tested the hypothesis that the particular types of reasoning involved in granting or withholding legitimacy to a system are correlated with age, sex, education, socioeconomic status, and occupation of individuals. In this study, we also analyzed the interrelation between these types of reasoning and several other psychological variables, such as satisfaction or frustration, authoritarianism, alienation, perception of conflicts in society, and preferred methods of conflict resolution.

CHARACTERISTICS OF THE SAMPLE AND RESEARCH METHODS

In this chapter empirical data are examined from a survey of some 900 individuals selected for the purpose of studying the influence of age, education, social class background, and family versus school socialization on moral values and political attitudes. The sample included students from various age-groups and levels of education as well as their parents and teachers. Two groups of elementary school pupils (10- year-old fourth graders and 15-year-old eighth graders from the same school) and two groups of secondary school students (17-year-old students from a vocational school for electricians and 17-year-old students from "lyceum" general secondary schoool – both were seniors in the last class before graduation) were selected for interviewing. Parents and teachers were sampled from all these groups. The individuals were interviewed in September 1984 in Toruń.

The interviews lasted 1 1/2 to 2 hours, and were conducted in the respondents' homes by undergraduate students from the Department of Sociology, Warsaw University as a part of their field research studies program. Stress was laid on anonymity. Respondents were given code numbers and were repeatedly assured that no one would know the identity of any subject, that the interview and the tests had nothing to do with evaluation of school work, and that the results would not be seen by the school staff. Sociology students who conducted interviewing (whose own political attitudes were very critical of the government) had the impression that the political nature of many questions had not precluded frankness of responses from a majority of subjects (particularly pupils). Political opinion surveys have become quite popular during the last few years in Poland; the Poles are known for being outspoken and not afraid to express their political views. However, some 20% of parents approached refused to participate in the interview giving the reason that they did not want to discuss political matters. In such cases their children also were not interviewed, even though only one pupil would have been unwilling to answer questions.

The questionnaire included a simple measurement of moral orientations or the types of moral reasoning.[2] This measure was modeled on Rest's Defining Issues Test (1979) and included a list of issues involved in the solution of a moral dilemma reflecting the range of six types of moral orientations discussed previously. Subjects were asked to choose the issue that they thought was the most important. Similar types of questions were used with respect to justice and legitimation (these questions and procedures of measurement are described in the next part of the chapter where some preliminary results of the study are reported). Other questions concerned the concept of justice, perception of the political order's legitimacy, confidence in the leadership of major social institutions, perception of crisis and conflicts in society, measures of acceptance of the system, scales of political alienation and authoritarianism, life goals and parental values, and measures of life satisfaction were also included in the questionnaire. In addition, a shorter version of Rest's Defining Issues Test (3 dilemmas: "Heinz and the drug," "Escaped prisoner," "School newspaper") was administered to 225 students from the oldest group: 17 and 18-year-old seniors in both vocational and general (lyceum) secondary schools. Half of them were included in the sample of those who were interviewed.

---

[2] The questionnaire also contained three Kohlbergian (1983) moral dilemmas ("Heinz and the drug,") "Officer Brown", "John and his father") with open-ended questions designed to uncover the subject's reasons for recommending specific solutions of the dilemmas. Responses were coded and analyzed in accordance with the stage scoring manual elaborated by Colby & Kohlberg (1987). Results of this questionnaire are not reported here because the scoring and analyses have not yet been completed.

RESULTS: THE INFLUENCE OF EDUCATION ON MORAL ORIENTATIONS AND POLITICAL ATTITUDES

Each respondent was asked to choose between alternative solutions for the "Heinz and the drug" moral dilemma (whether the husband should steal the drug to save his wife's life or let his wife die) and then to indicate which rationale from the list of six reasons was the most important one. Accordingly, each subject was placed in one of six categories of moral orientation.[3]

Figures 15.1 (A,B,C) and 15.2 (A,B,C) show the distributions of respondents endorsing particular types of moral orientation among students, their mothers and fathers, with each group classified according to the level of education. As predicted, different moral orientations were systematically related to respondents' level and type of education. Within the group of students, moral orientations also were related to age, because there is a "built in" relation between age and level of education.

The preconventional types of moral reasoning were endorsed relatively more often by the youngest group (10-year-old fourth grades) in primary school, although even among them the modal orientation was the conventional "interpersonal concordance" or Stage 3 moral reasoning. The percentage of those who choose the preconventional orientations steadily diminished in the older groups of students. Among parents the preconventional "punishment avoidance and obedience orientation," or Stage 1 moral reasoning, appeared very rarely and only at lower levels of education. The pattern of distribution of the "instrumental purpose and exchange orientation" or Stage 2 moral reasoning was not so clear; nevertheless, this type of reasoning was seldom found among those with the highest level of education. The conventional types of reasoning (especially "interpersonal concordance" or Stage 3) were the most popular among students, with the exception of the oldest group from general (lyceum) secondary school, and also among parents with only primary and basic vocational education. Preference for these orientations diminished among general secondary school students as well as among parents with secondary and higher levels of education. Again, the pattern of distribution of the "law and order orientation" or Stage 4 moral reasoning was not quite clear. This type was totally absent among adults with general secondary education. It

---

[3] It should be emphasized again that this placement was based on a very crude and preliminary measurement of moral reasoning, and as a result the percentage of those who were included in the postconventional categories is much higher than would be achieved by scoring respondents' own spontaneously expressed reasons, in accordance with the Kohlberg's Manual.

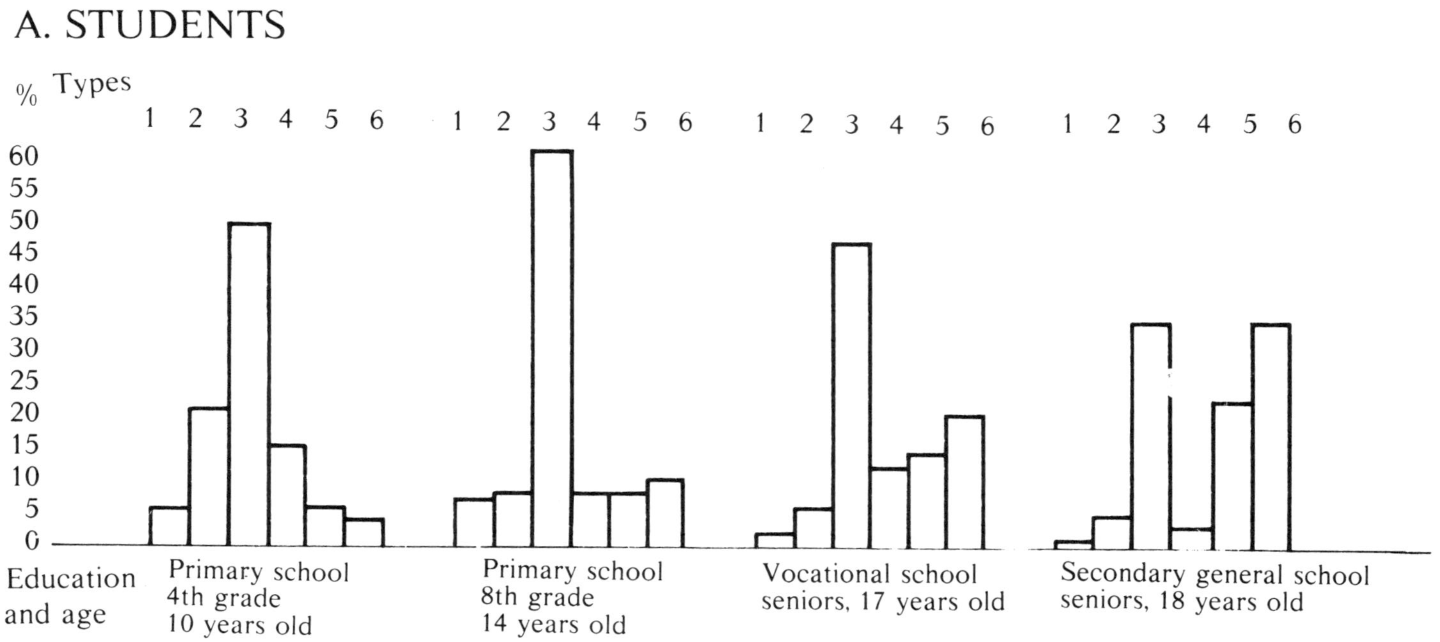

FIGURE 15.1. (A,B,C). Types of moral orientation by education

(continued)

B. MOTHERS

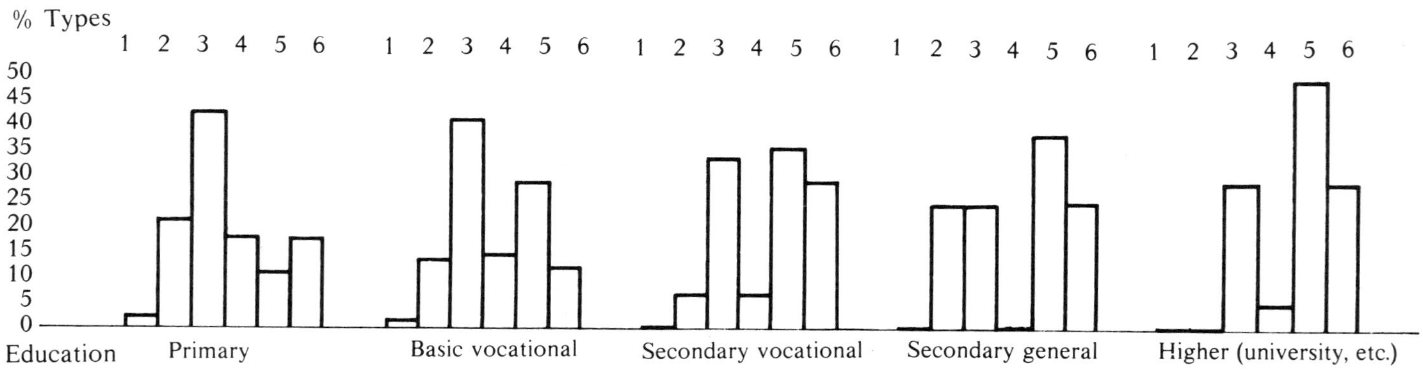

% Types
1 2 3 4 5 6
50
45
40
35
30
25
20
15
10
5
0
Education
Primary
Basic vocational
Secondary vocational
Secondary general
Higher (university, etc.)

C. FATHERS

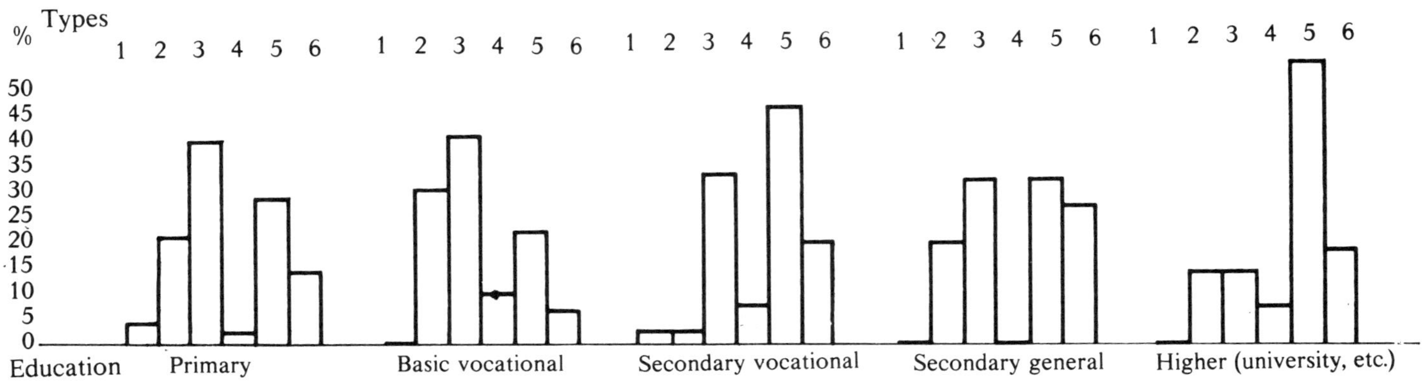

FIGURE 15.1. (A,B,C). Types of moral orientation by education *(Continued)*.

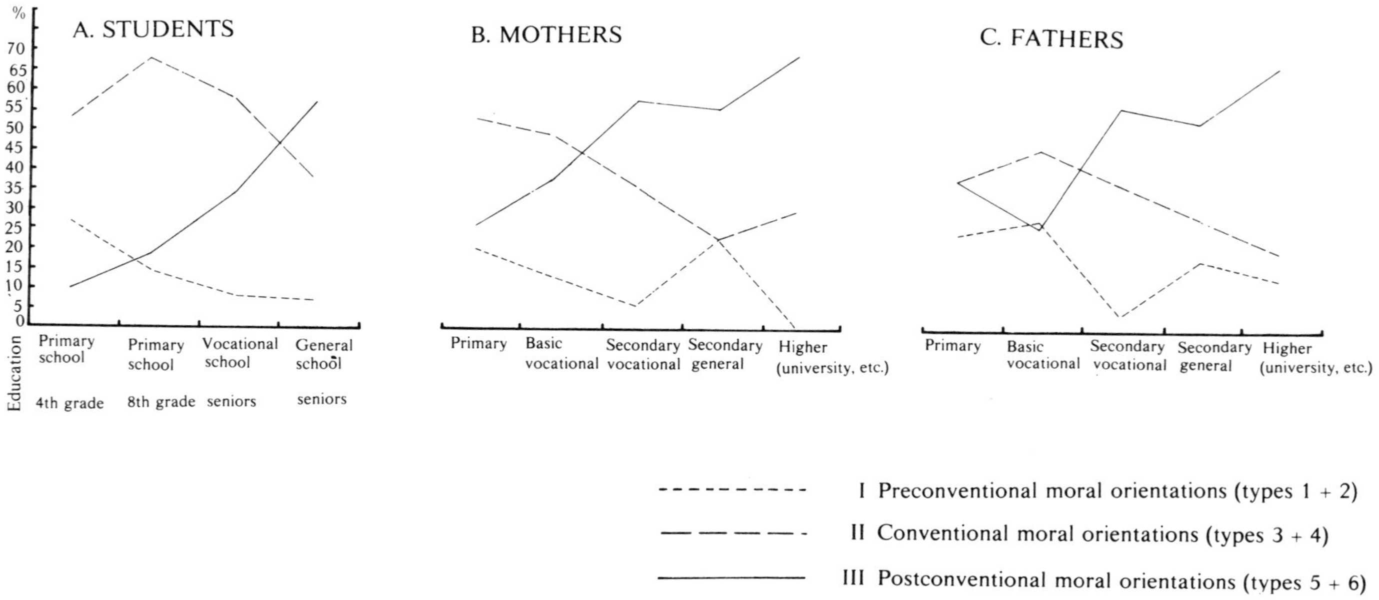

FIGURE 15.2. (A,B,C). Preconventional, conventional and post-conventional moral orientations by education.

should be noted that this type of reasoning (concerned with the issue how to prevent law breaking) was chosen by a strikingly small percentage of the total sample.[4] The frequency of the postconventional moral orientations increased with the age of students and with the level of education among adults. These types of reasoning were used by a majority of respondents with secondary or higher education. However, it should be emphasized that the relatively high percentage of respondents placed in these categories may have resulted from the fact that measurement procedure was a new, adapted version of a standard measure, and thus the results should be interpreted with caution. Nevertheless, this reservation does not undermine our main finding of the relation between type of moral reasoning and levels of education.

Respondents were also given a list of definitions of justice hypothetically related to the previously mentioned six types of moral orientation. They were asked to indicate whether they agreed or disagreed with each of these definitions and then to choose only one that best described their own opinion. On the basis of these choices, subjects were classified in six types. As Figures 15.3 (A,B,C) and 15.4 (A,B,C) illustrate, there was a systematic relation between the types of meaning of justice chosen and levels of education.[5]

The preconventional understanding of justice as "avoiding punishment and getting profits" (type 1) and as "tit-for-tat or paying back the same" (type 2) was very rare; its frequency decreased as the level of education increased (this trend was particularly clear among students and among mothers), and it almost totally disappeared among respondents with the highest level of education. A majority of respondents with primary and basic vocational education (students as well as their parents), and also a majority of mothers with secondary education, chose the conventional definitions of justice. These were "behavior guided by good motives and intentions" (type 3 – the most frequent within these categories of education) and "acting in accord with the law" (type 4). The percentage of responses classified as belonging to these types was much smaller among groups with the highest education, and also among fathers with secondary education. The endorsement of the postconventional meanings of justice increased with the level of education. A majority of adults with the highest education and also a majority of students and their fathers with general secondary education selected such definitions of justice as "acting in accordance with principles and rules which have been agreed on by people in the

---

[4] Kohlberg claims that this particular stage of moral reasoning is the most common among the Americans (1981, pp. 238–239). To answer the question whether the striking difference between the Poles and the Americans in their usage of type 4 "law and order" orientation is related to the specific Polish national character we have to analyze the results of another of our studies based on a national sample and conducted in the fall of 1985.

[5] There are no data for the youngest group of children, because the question was not included in the shorter and simplified version of the questionnaire that was administered to this group.

A. STUDENTS

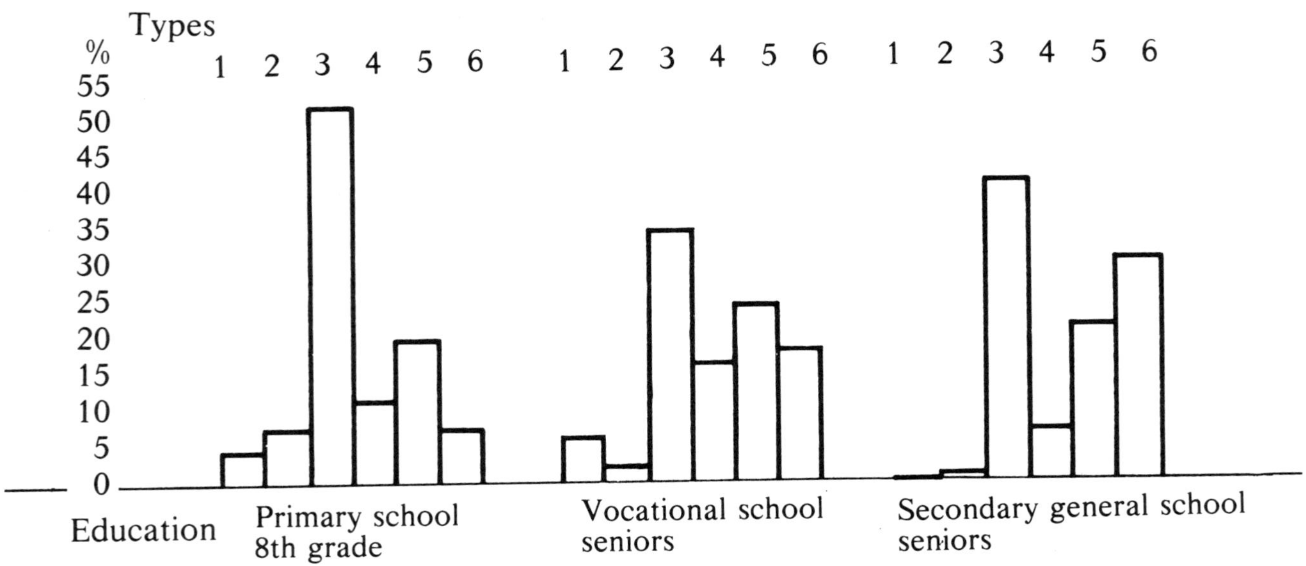
Types
%
1 2 3 4 5 6
55
50
45
40
35
30
25
20
15
10
5
0
Education
Primary school
8th grade
Vocational school
seniors
Secondary general school
seniors

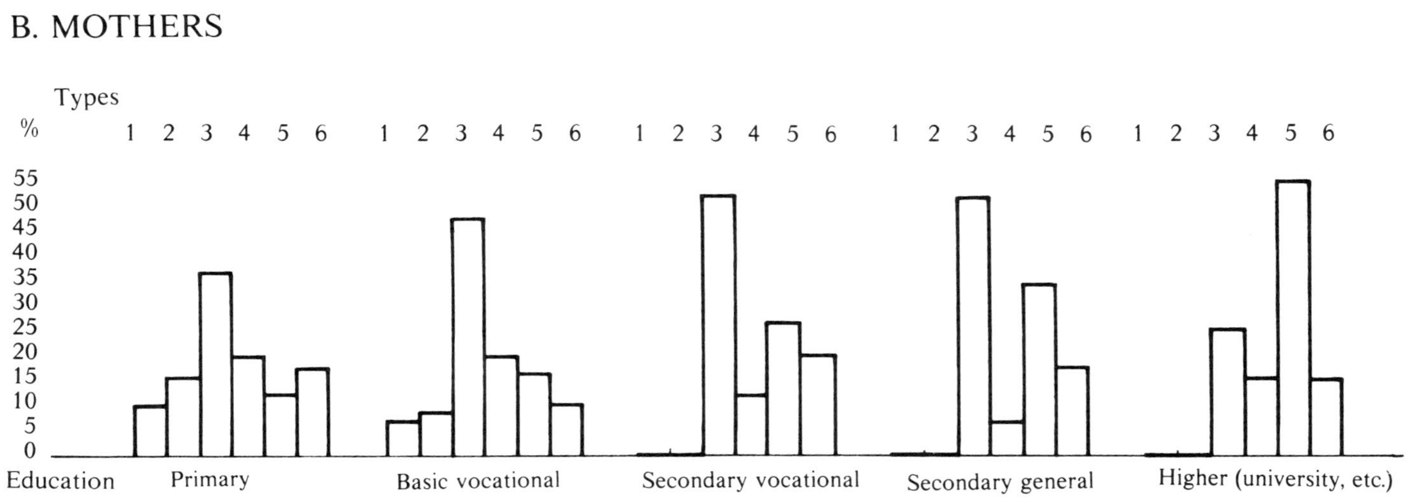

FIGURE 15.3. (A,B,C,). Types of meaning of justice by education.

(continued)

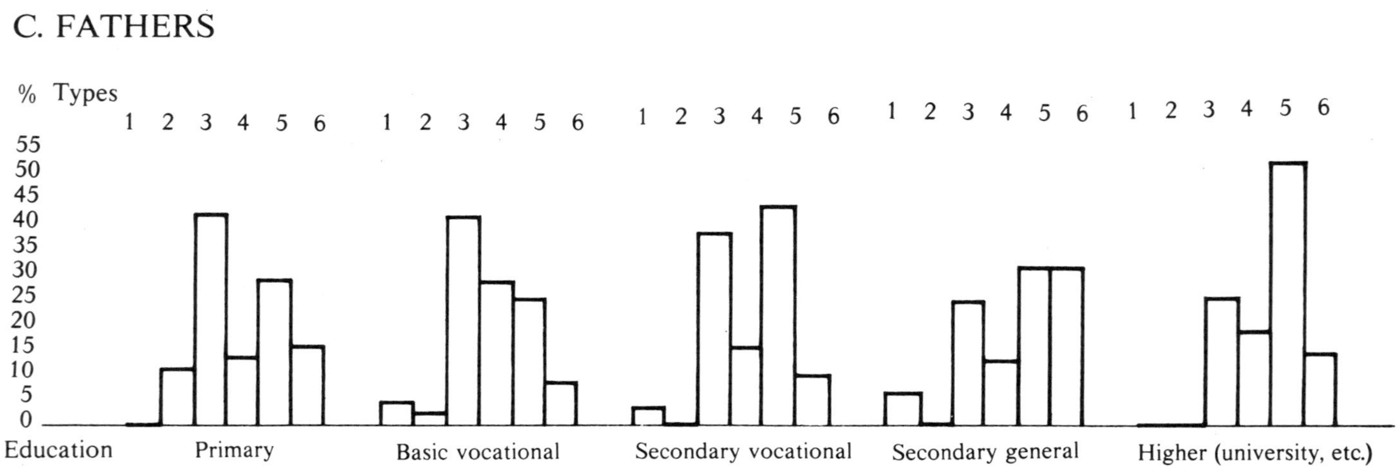

FIGURE 15.3. (A,B,C). Types of meaning of justice by education *(Continued)*.

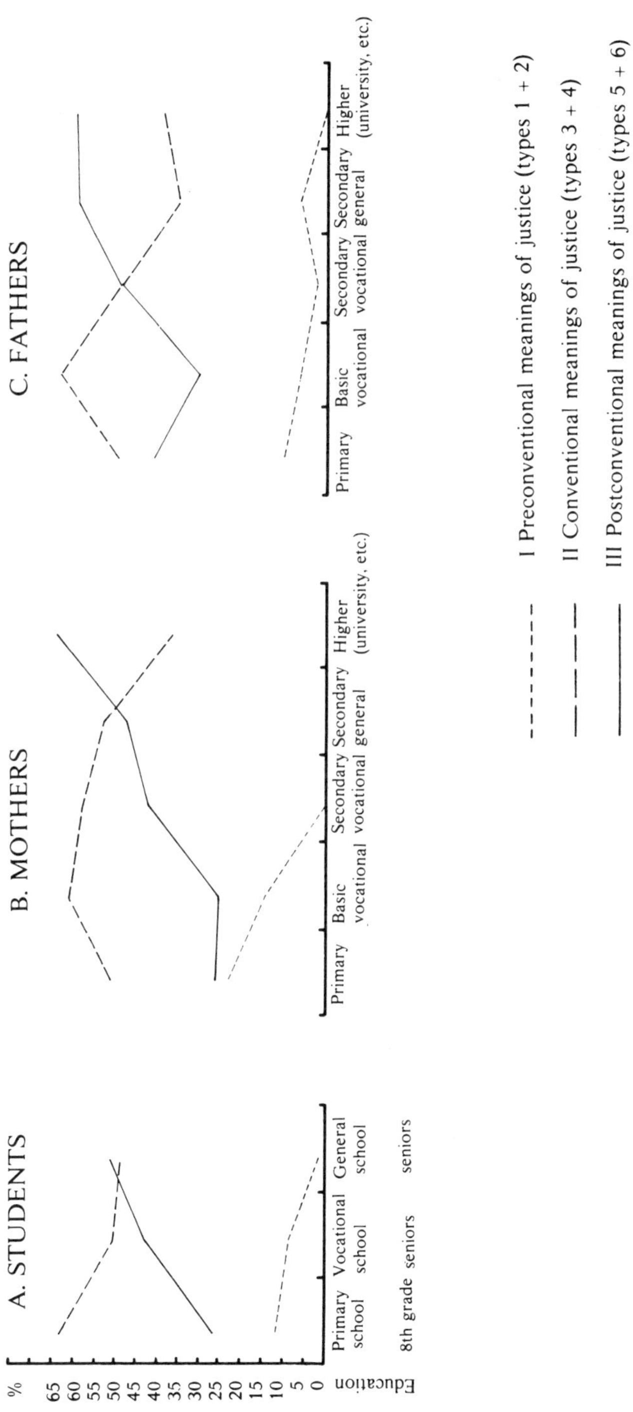

FIGURE 15.4 (A,B,C). Preconventional, conventional and postconventional meanings of justice by education.

social contract'' (type 5) and ''acting in accord with self-chosen universal ethical principles'' (type 6).

The relation between the three general types of moral orientations (i.e., preconventional, conventional, and postconventional) and the corresponding three types of meanings of justice was statistically significant: for students, $x^2 = 36.244$, $p < 0.001$; for mothers, $x^2 = 31.693$, $p < 0.001$. Only for fathers was the level of significance lower, $x^2 = 8.616$, $p < 0.1$.[6] These findings confirm the hypothesis that various meanings of justice are related to particular types of moral orientations.

The typology of standards used to assess legitimacy of the political authority was based on procedures similar to those described previously. Respondents were given a list of attributes considered necessary for a legitimate authority and were asked to choose three desirable characteristics and then to rank them in order of importance. The models of the political legitimacy were classified in six categories corresponding with the Kohlbergian types of moral reasoning. The following statements were interpreted as indicators of particular orientations:

Type 1. Authority should be strong and able to secure obedience.
Type 2. Authority should improve the material standards of the population.
Type 3. Authority should be honest.
Type 4. Authority should guarantee maintenance of law and order in society.
Type 5. Authority should be elected in a democratic way.
Type 6. Authority should act in accordance with principles of justice and respect for human dignity.

The predicted relation between the types of the political legitimacy attributes and levels of education is shown in Figures 15.5 (A, B, C) and 15.6 (A, B, C).

Once again, the percentage of the preconventional types was smaller the higher the level of education. These types selected the following statements: ''Authority should be strong and able to secure the obedience of the people'' (type 1) and ''authority should improve the material standards of the population'' (type 2). The most popular orientation was the conventional ''interpersonal concordance'' orientation (type 3) for which the model of a legitimate authority is that the authority should be honest. This model was selected by a majority of parents. However, another conventional type, expressed in the

[6] An interpretation of this difference, as well as analyses of the relation between attitudes of students and their parents would greatly enlarge this chapter; thus, it will be a subject of a separate publication.

A. STUDENTS

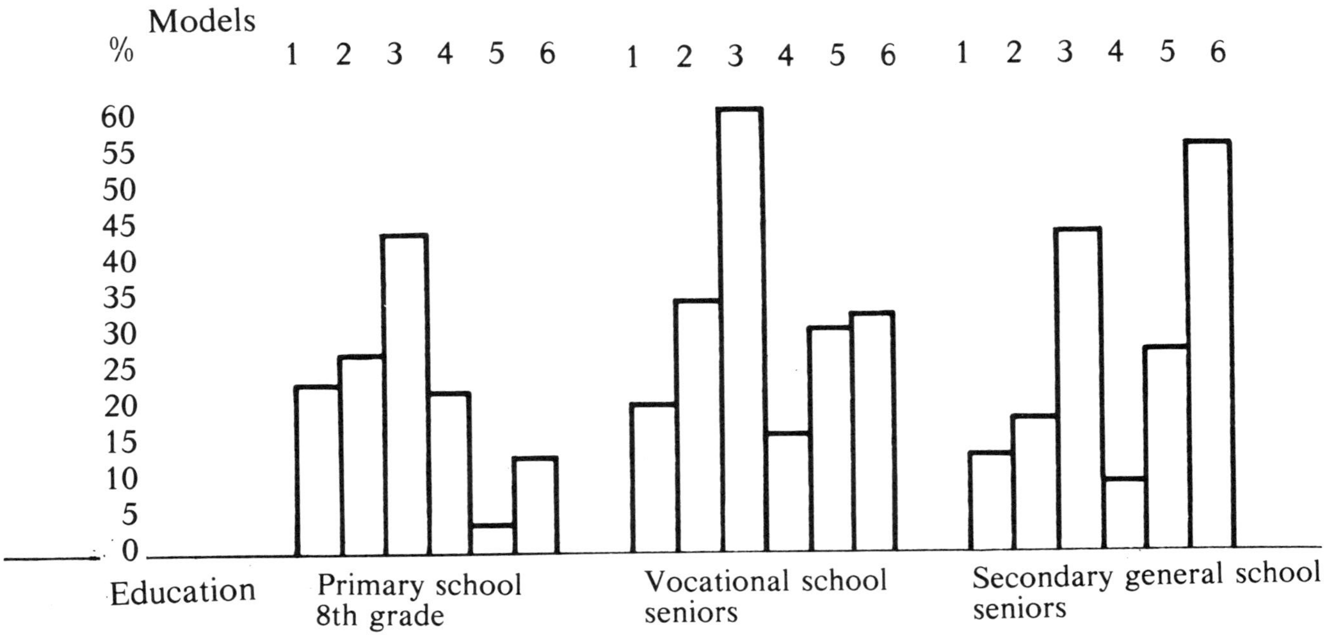

FIGURE 15.5. (A,B,C). Models of the political legitimacy by education.

(continued)

B. MOTHERS

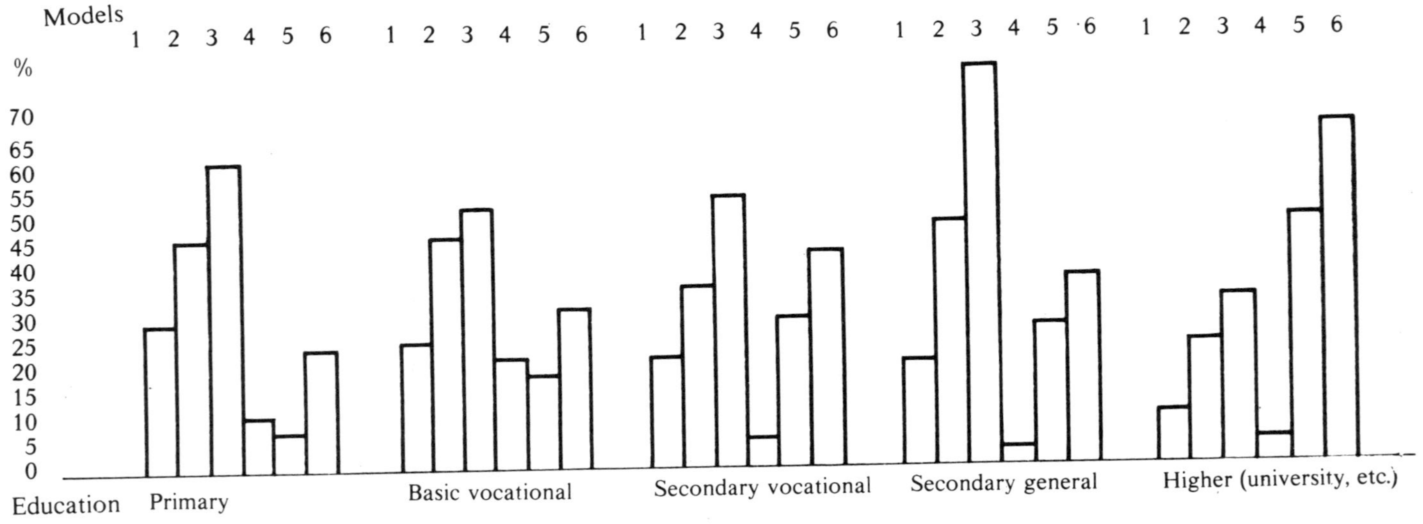

Models
1 2 3 4 5 6 1 2 3 4 5 6 1 2 3 4 5 6 1 2 3 4 5 6 1 2 3 4 5 6
%
70
65
60
55
50
45
40
35
30
25
20
15
10
5
0
Education
Primary
Basic vocational
Secondary vocational
Secondary general
Higher (university, etc.)

C. FATHERS

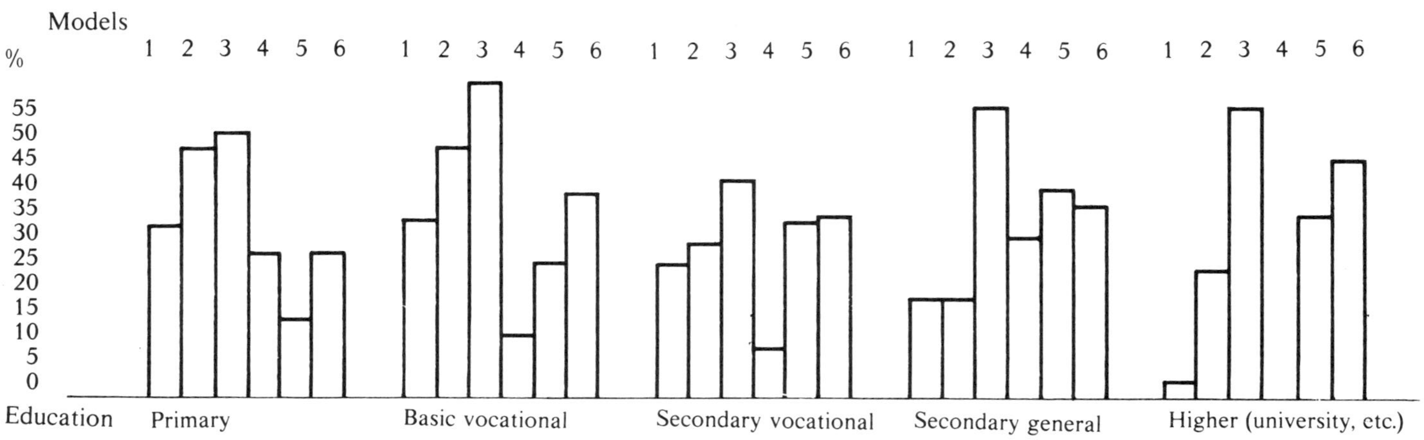

FIGURE 15.5. (A,B,C). Models of the politica. legitimacy by education *(Continued)*.

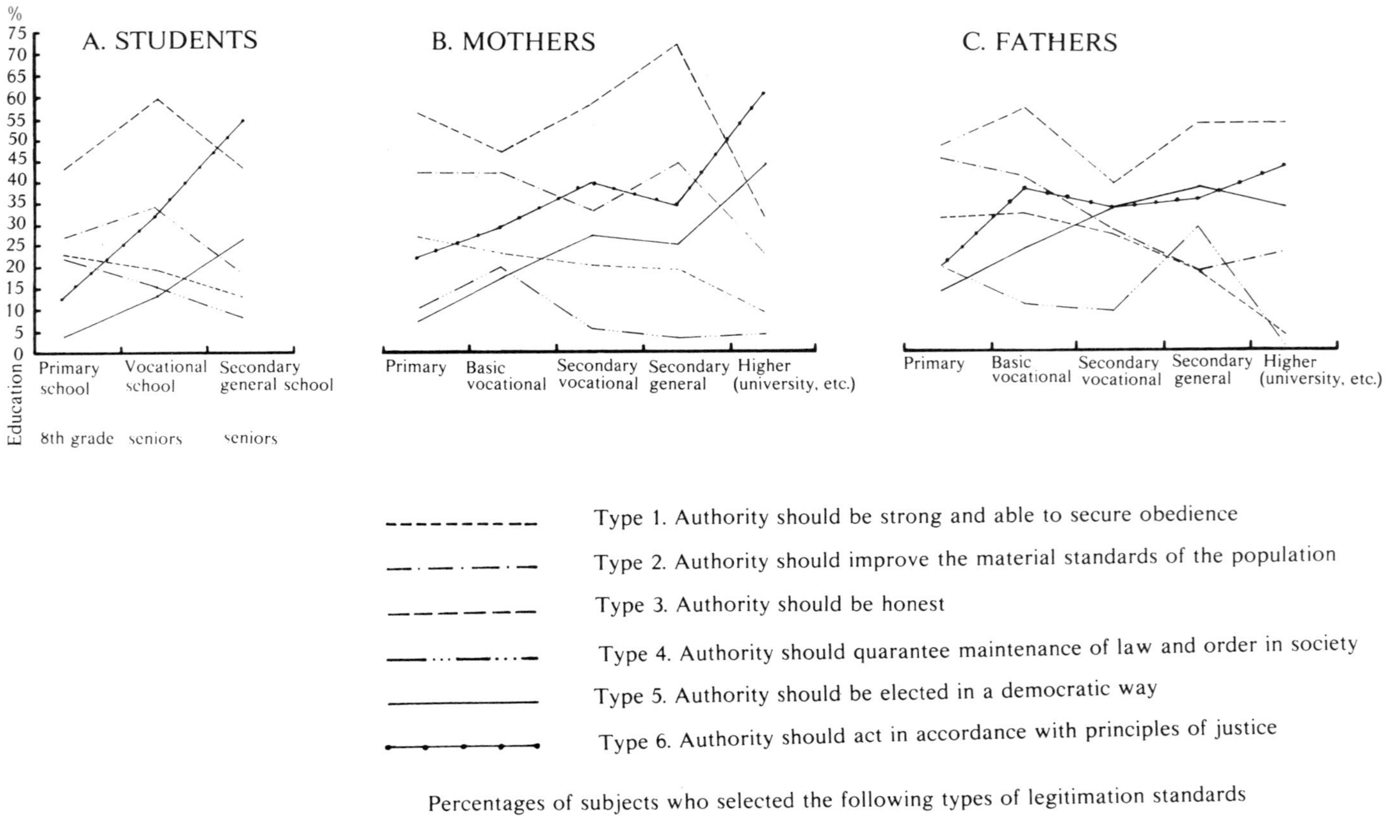

FIGURE 15.6. (A,B,C). Types of legitimation standards by education.

response that "authority should guarantee maintenance of the law and order in society (type 4), was one of the least popular, as was the corresponding type of moral reasoning in general. The frequency of selection of the postconventional models of the political legitimacy, "authority should be elected in a democratic way" (type 5) and "authority should act in accordance with principles of justice and respect for the human dignity" (type 6), increased with the level of education. Here again the findings were consistent with the central hypothesis of the study that distinctive types of arguments for granting or withholding legitimacy to the political system are related to corresponding types of moral reasoning.

Respondents were then asked whether the current political authority in Poland could be described as meeting the required standards of legitimate authority or as not capable of putting these models in practice (the list of attributes considered necessary for a legitimate authority was the same as in the former question). The distribution of responses to this question is shown in Figures 15.7 (A, B, C) and 15.8 (A, B, C).

Here we do not find a uniform relationship between levels of education and tendencies to accept or deny the legitimacy of the present Polish political authorities when they are perceived in terms of particular models of legitimacy or as failing to put them in practice. There is some evidence of a difference in attitudes toward the Polish authority between some categories of education. The majority of the oldest group of the general secondary school students consistently rejected the legitimacy of the authorities in Poland independently of the selected criteria of its evaluation. The majority of adults with the highest education denied the legitimacy of the authorities, describing them as not capable of meeting the postconventional standards that were selected as the most important by this group. Moreover, among almost all groups only a minority agreed that the authorities fulfilled the postconventional standards of legitimacy. With respect to the type 6 model of political legitimacy, only the primary school students took the view that the Polish authorities met the model's requirements, but it should be noted that few members of this group saw this type of model as the most important. Only a minority within all categories of education perceived the authorities as being honest, and for many this was held to be the most important criterion of the political legitimacy. It also should be noted, however, that a relatively large proportion of respondents did not answer the question concerning whether the authorities in Poland were honest.

The majority of respondents recognized that the authorities in Poland were capable of maintaining the law and order in society, but this model of legitimacy was one of the least popular, and it was related to the conventional "law and order" moral orientation that was seldom found in our sample. A relatively large percentage of the sample acknowledged that the authorities in Poland aim to improve the material standards of the population. This type of claim to legitimacy was chosen as an important one by quite a large portion of

A. STUDENTS

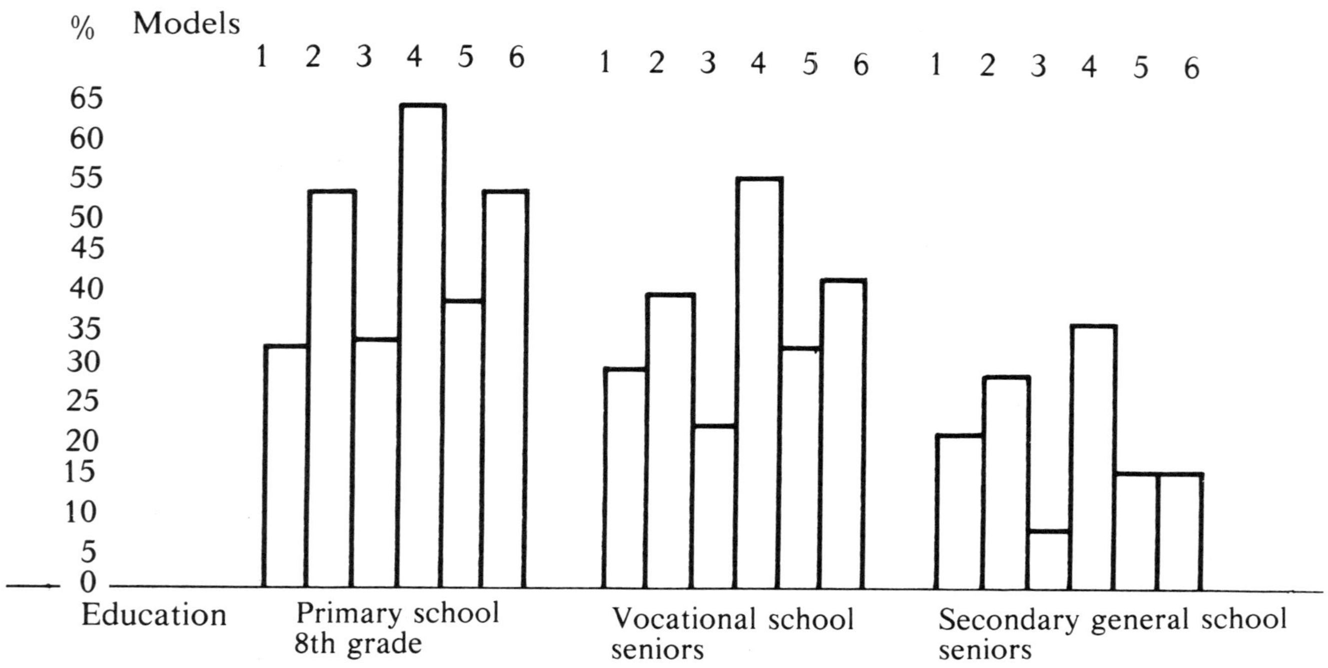
% Models
1 2 3 4 5 6 1 2 3 4 5 6 1 2 3 4 5 6
65
60
55
50
45
40
35
30
25
20
15
10
5
0
Education
Primary school
8th grade
Vocational school
seniors
Secondary general school
seniors

B. MOTHERS

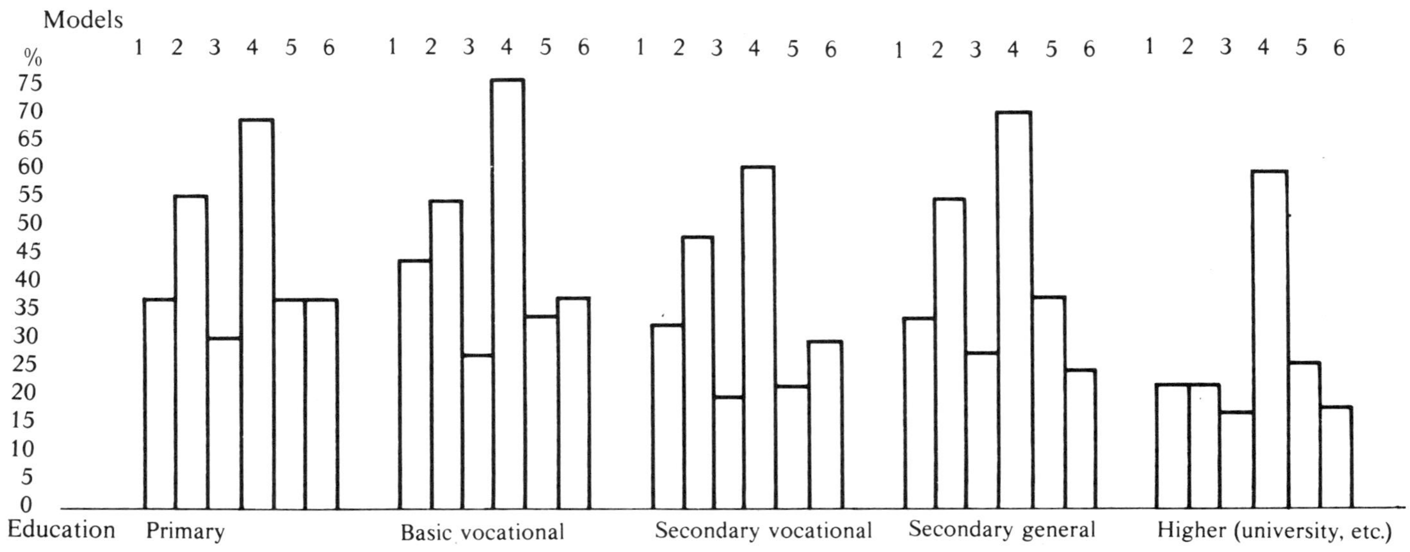

FIGURE 15.7. (A,B,C). Perceived implementation of the political legitimacy models. *(continued)*

C. FATHERS

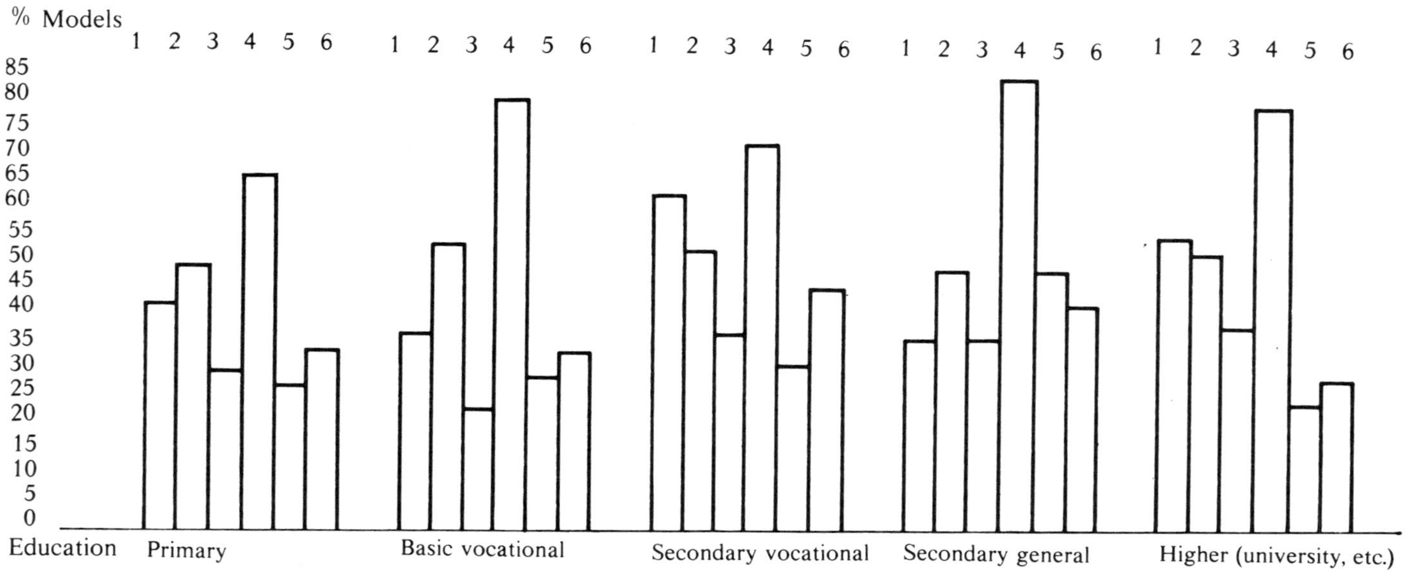

FIGURE 15.7. (A,B,C). Perceived implementation of the political legitimacy models *(Continued)*.

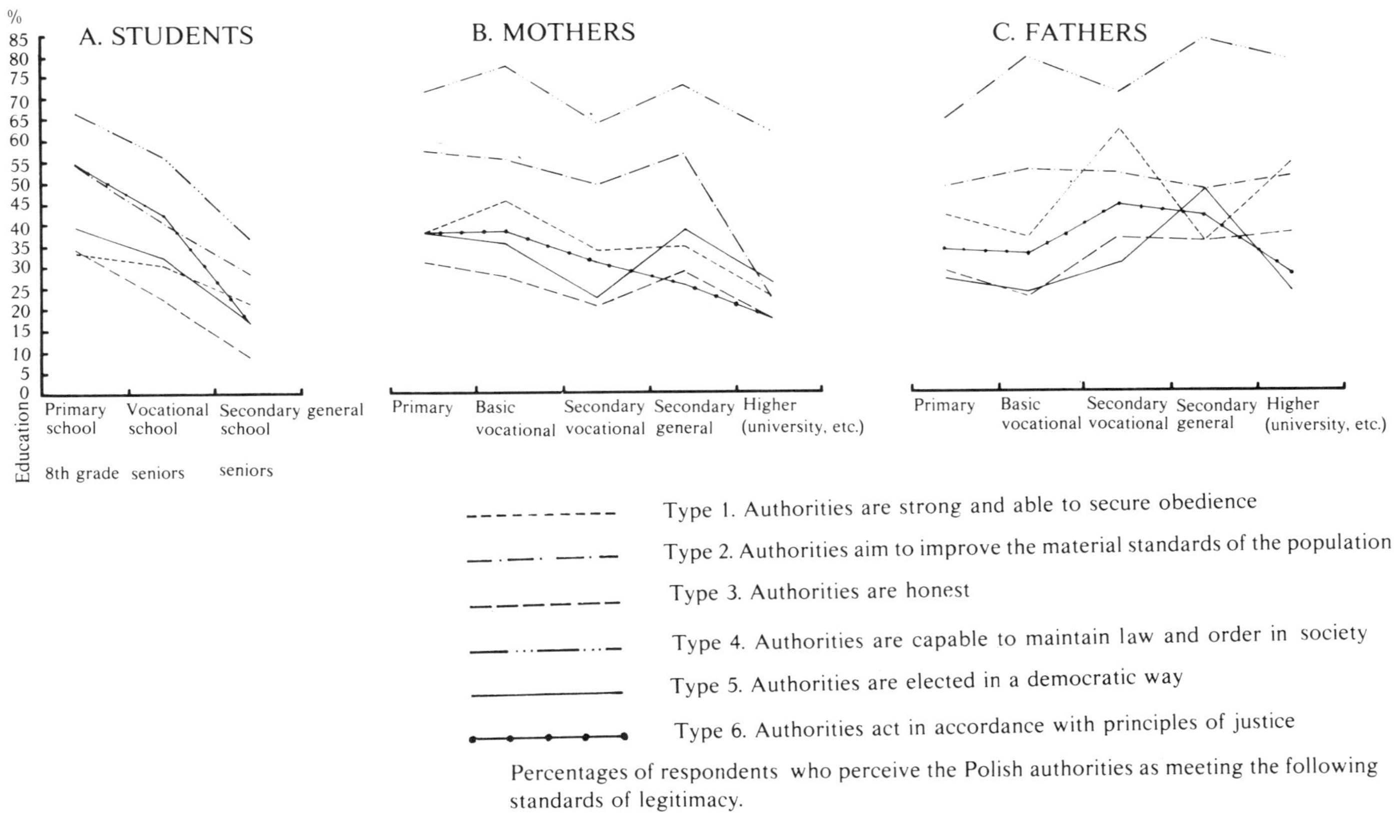

FIGURE 15.8. (A,B,C). Types of legitimacy granted to the Polish authorities (by education).

our respondents (particularly among the less educated), although it is related to the preconventional "instrumental purpose and exchange" moral orientation that was rarely accepted as a general type of moral reasoning by respondents with higher education.

These findings give some evidence of a legitimation crisis in the Polish society in that the authorities were perceived as unable to satisfy post-conventional moral expectations. The authorities' claims to legitimacy were recognized, however, in terms of the types of moral reasoning that were endorsed by a part of population that was relatively less educated and relatively more satisfied with their own living standards. In fact, some of our data indicate a relation between acceptance of the government's legitimacy by respondents and their general level of satisfaction both with their economic or financial situation and with life as a whole. For example, correlations between scores for ratings on Cantril's self-anchoring scale of life satisfaction (see Robinson & Shaver, 1973, p. 13) and acceptance of the government's legitimacy by fathers were from $r = .20$ to $r = .29$, $p < 0.05$. More detailed statistical analysis of the data will be necessary if one is to establish the various factors that influenced respondents' political attitudes.

It seems worthwhile to discuss some additional data derived from testing and interviewing the oldest group of secondary school students. A comparison of students from vocational and general (lyceum) secondary school makes it possible to examine the influence of type of education and social class origin on the moral values and political attitudes of the students, because in this case type of school is strongly related to the social status of parents and to the students' future educational opportunities (both are lower in vocational schools than the general lyceum school).

Many differences in moral values and political attitudes between students from vocational and general secondary schools were found. Vocational school students used the conventional types of moral judgement (3rd and 4th stages) significantly more often than lyceum students, $x^2 = 8.07$, $p < 0.05$. They also showed a higher level of inconsistency than did lyceum students in choosing and ranking items from the Defining Issues Test. In addition, lyceum students obtained higher P scores (interpreted as the relative importance a subject gives to postconventional principled moral considerations in solving moral dilemmas; see Table 15.1).

Vocational school students significantly more often than the others expressed authoritarian attitudes, as indicated by agreement with such statements as "a few strong leaders can do more for this country than all laws and discussions"; "what young people need most of all is strict discipline from their parents"; "one should always show deference to authorities"; "people who don't get ahead just don't have enough will power"; "an insult to one's honor should never be forgotten." Lyceum students more often than the vocational school students expressed feelings of alientation, accepting such statements as "people like myself don't really know what our government is

TABLE 15.1

Means and Standard Deviation on the P index (Principled Postconventional Moral Judgement) and I index (Inconsistency in Selecting and Ranking Moral Reasons) on the Defining Issued Test

	P-Index		*I-Index*		
	X	*S.D.*	*X*	*S.D.*	*N*
Vocational school	5.9	3.1	3.9	4.8	112
General school-lyceum	8.1	4.7	2.6	4.6	125

doing," "those who run the government don't care about ordinary people like myself," "politics is immoral and one should stay away from it."

In their perception of the causes of the Polish crisis vocational school students more often emphasized economic factors, whereas the other group more often mentioned political and moral aspects. Vocational school students also more often declared trust in all political institutions, whereas lyceum students more often showed distrust even in the most trusted institution, the Church (distrusted by 22% in general school and by 6% in vocational school).

In both groups, modal choice of the most adequate definition of "justice" was "an act directed by good intentions" (34% in vocational school, 39% in general school; henceforth labeled v.s. and g.s., respectively). However, lyceum students more often selected a description of justice as acting according to self-chosen moral principles (30% in g.s., 15% in v.s.), whereas vocational school students more often preferred a definition of justice as acting in accordance with the law (17% in v.s., 6% in g.s.). The most acceptable criterion of distributive justice for the vocational school students was an equal distribution, but the lyceum students prefered rewards given for the best and most efficient work.

Although the majority in both groups rejected the form of socialism that exists in Poland, 55% students from vocational school and 42% from general school said that the world should develop toward some form of socialism.

When asked what the most desirable characteristics of legitimate authority are, vocational school students most often linked legitimacy with honesty of leaders (60% in v.s., 43% in g.s.); lyceum students most often said that a legitimate authority would act according to the principles of justice and human dignity. Significantly more vocational school students than others chose the following characteristics of legitimate authority to describe the Polish authorities: safeguarding national security (76% in v.s., 54% in g.s.), achieving national concordance and avoiding conflicts (62% in v.s.; 46% in g.s.), maintaining law and order in the country (56% in v.s., 36% in g.s.).

Vocational school students more often than the other group denied the existence of conflicts in the Polish society, but at the same time they were more inclined to deal with conflicts in a radical way. They were more prepared to justify martial law, as well as to accept radical forms of protest action – strikes, street demonstrations, fighting against the police forces. Lyceum students, on the other hand, more often chose such forms of protest action as writing petitions to the authorities and distributing underground literature.

All subjects were asked to choose one out of the following three basic attitudes toward society: (a) The entire way our society is organized must be radically changed by revolutionary action, (b) our society must be gradually improved by means of reforms, (c) our society must be valiantly defended against all subversive forces. Lyceum students more often preferred reforms (73% in g.s., 53% in v.s.), whereas vocational school students relatively more often chose either revolutionary action (25% in v.s., 17% in g.s.) or defense against subversive forces (21% in v.s., 9% in g.s.).

In summary, the hypothesized relation between the type of education of individuals and their moral values and political attitudes was confirmed by the results. As it had been predicted, vocational school students were more inclined to use conventional types of moral judgements as well as conventional arguments in granting legitimacy to political authorities. This structure of reasoning seems to be related to a higher degree of authoritarianism and political radicalism. Lyceum students more often used postconventional types of moral judgement and postconventional types of arguments denying the legitimacy of authorities. This type of reasoning seems to be related to a greater feeling of political alienation, and to a critical but reform-minded attitude loward society rather than a radical one.

CONCLUDING REMARKS

Our research finding confirmed the central hypothesis of the study that the types of standards used by individuals to assess the legitimacy of the political order are related to specific types of meanings of the term *justice* and also are related to distinctive structures of moral reasoning. The relation was statistically significant and suggested a tendency for persons to apply the same type of reasoning when resolving general moral dilemmas and when evaluating political authorities. However, at the same time our data show that the preconventional "punishment avoidance and obedience" as well as "instrumental purpose and exchange" orientations are applied by adults more often in the political domain than in the sphere of interpersonal relations morality.

Comparing the distribution of the political legitimacy models among various educational groups (see Figure 15.5 A, B, C) with the distribution of responses to the question of whether the present political authorities in Poland were perceived as meeting the required standards of legitimate authority (see Figure 15.7 A, B, C), we are able to differentiate the structures of moral and political judgement from the content of the political attitudes. Whereas the structure of judgement is clearly determined by an individual's level of education (and presumably related cognitive abilities), the content of political attitudes is less influenced by educational level and more by an individual's satisfaction with his or her own living standards. However, there seems to be a linkage between the structure and content of judgements. Consistent with Kohlberg's (1981) statement that "there is a probabilistic tendency for certain stage structures to generate specific moral attitudes" (p.270), we found a tendency for certain moral orientation structures to be associated with specific political attitudes. Those subjects using the postconventional "democratic social-contract" and "universal ethical principle" orientations expressed more critical attitudes toward the political order and more often tended to deny its legitimacy than did persons using the conventional "law and order" orientations (who were more often inclined to grant legitimacy to the Polish authorities).

On the whole, our results, as well as those of others (e.g., Rest, 1979), are consistent with the view that the cognitive developmental perspective can be fruitful means for examining political attitudes. Further, such an approach would seem to represent a promising method for expanding the interface between sociological and psychological perspectives.

REFERENCES

Candee, D. (1975) The moral psychology of Watergate. *Journal of Social Issues. 31*, 183-192.

Colby, A., Kohlberg L. et al. (1987). *The measurement of moral judgment: A manual and its results.* New York: Cambridge University Press.

Eisenberg-Berg (1976). The relation of political attitudes to constrain oriented and prosocial moral reasoning. *Developmental Psychology, 12*, 552-553.

Fishkin, J., Keniston, K., & McKinnon, C. (1973). Moral reasoning and political ideology. *Journal of Personality and Social Psychology, 27*, 109-119.

Habermas, J. (1976). Legitimation crisis. London: Heinemann.

Jasińska-Kania, A. (1983). Rationalization and legitimation crisis: The relevance of Marxian and Weberian works for an explanation of the political order's legitimacy crisis in Poland. Sociology: *The Journal of the British Sociological Association.* Vol. *17*, No. *2*, 157–163.

Kohlberg, L. (1981). Essays in moral development. (Vol. 1). The philosophy of moral development. .San Francisco: Harper & Row.

Kohlberg, L. (1983). *Essays in moral development. (Vol. II). The psychology of moral development.* San Francisco: Harper & Row.

Kohlberg, L., Levine, C., & Hewer, A. (1983). *Contribution to human development.* (Vol. 10). *Moral stages: a current formula and a response to critics.* Basel: Karger.

Lane, R. (1979). The legitimacy bias. In B. Denitch (Ed.), Legitimation of regimes. London: Sage.
Lipset, S. M. (1960). *Political* man. New York: Doubleday.
Rest, J. (1979). *Development in judging moral issues.* Minneapolis: University of Minnesota Press.
Robinson, J.P., & Shaver, P. R. (1973). *Measures of social psychological attitudes.* Ann Arbor, MI: ISR.

16 Perception of the Sociopolitical System and Sense of Political Autonomy-Alienation[1]

Krzysztof Korzeniowski
Department of Psychology
Polish Academy of Sciences

THEORETICAL INTRODUCTION

Sense of Autonomy-Alienation

Robinson and Shaver (1970) have asserted that alienation is one of the most frequently used and misused concepts of our times. The body of knowledge on this subject is characterized by an unusual amount of terminological confusion. For example, Schacht (1971) cited and discussed a few dozen interpretations of this concept. Others, such as Seeman (1959), have made an attempt to introduce some order into this field. Seeman proposed a multidimensional model of alienation, distinguishing five kinds: powerlessness, meaninglessness, normlessness (anomia), social isolation, and self-estrangement (see Korzeniowski, 1983). Because these concepts are defined as categories of subjectively experienced beliefs, feelings, or expectations, a more adequate term seems to be *senses of alienation*.[2]

---

[1] The chapter is based on initial investigations conducted within the fifth thematic group of model problem 11.8, sponsored by the Polish Academy of Sciences.

[2] Maybe the distinction between alienation and sense of alienation requires a few words of explanation. Alienation we understand after Marx to be an objective property of an individual (his or her situation), which consists of his or her objective powerlessness and/or estrangement. Sense of alienation, on the other hand, is a subjectively experienced state of consciousness that may accompany alienation but need not.

During the 28 years that have passed since Seeman's aforementioned article was published, several dozen alienation scales have been constructed (see Ray, 1982), and many new forms and modalities have been proposed. There appear to be no theoretical or metatheoretical perspectives enabling a consistent systematization of sense of alienation modalities. Attempts of this kind have been made by Allard (1972) and Twining (1980), but their proposals have not been followed up by others.

A theory of autonomy (Korzeniowski, Zieliński, & Daniecki, 1983) would seem to provide a foundation for a theoretically coherent integration of at least some of the modalities of a sense of alienation. Autonomy is defined as a conscious activity, initiated and developed by the individual according to his or her own values and standards. It is a specific regulative process, characterized by two properties: awareness of this process (a reflective attitude), and the fact that it is "set in motion" by the individual's personal choice. It may be said that being autonomous depends on being in control, but with awareness; moreover, this control is of a degree and nature that the individual himself or herself has decided.

The question arises concerning domains of autonomy – when can one be autonomous? In the literature, two aspects of activity or relating to reality are distinguished (see, for example, Reykowski, 1975). The first of these is practical behavior, the effect of which may be events or changes in the state of objects. Second, a symbolic aspect of activity may be distinguished. People relate to the world not only in a practical sense; they also think about it and evaluate it. Thus, the individual may be considered as the author of sense or meaning. By this, we mean that individuals give the world their own personal order of meanings. People may discover or create meanings, or else unreflectively take over a whole system of them from their social environment. Individuals may be the authors of values and endow objects or ideas with values, but they also may utilize the system of values society has offered to them. In both cases, consistent with the terminology proposed here, the individual is autonomous in the sphere of meanings. Moreover, as has just been noted, the model distinguishes two aspects of cognitive activities – the descriptive and the evaluative. Thus, the individual may be autonomous with respect to objective events and states of reality, or with regard to his or her own system of descriptive and evaluative meanings.

We mentioned previously that one of the central features of autonomy is an awareness of the regulation of relations with the environment. That is why a particular state of consciousness – a sense of autonomy – accompanies this process. A sense of autonomy is defined as the belief that the extent to which one creates events and states, and/or is the author of meanings, is consistent with one's own values and standards regarding either of these. The opposite conviction, that one is incapable of creating events and states, or of being the author of meanings consistent with one's values or standards, has been termed a sense of alienation.

To conclude our introduction of this concept, it is worth comparing it with another, ostensibly very similar one. A sense of autonomy differs from internal locus of control in that the extent of one's influence on reality is not measured against an "absolute value," but against one's *own standards.* For instance, the belief that one controls a very small area (where all else depends on fate) may be accompanied by a strong sense of autonomy, if the individual's standards of control are not extensive. On the other hand, persons may perceive that they are in control of large areas of reality, but if their "appetites" are greater, they may experience powerlessness.

The modalities of a sense of political autonomy-alienation that are the topic of this chapter have been defined as follows:

1. a sense of efficacy-powerlessness – the individual's belief that he or she affects the course of sociopolitical processes versus that he or she is unable to affect them in the direction expected,

2. a sense of meaningfulness-meaninglessness – the individual's belief that he or she cognitively or conceptually orders versus that he or she is unable to order the sociopolitical reality to an extent that is satisfying,

3. a sense of eunomia-anomia[3] – the individual's belief that he or she evaluates versus that he or she is unable to evaluate the sociopolitical reality in a manner considered accurate and/or coherent.

The model presented here seems to consistently order some of the types of alienation distinguished in the sociological literature, e.g., Seeman's by now classical theory and those of his many followers. Note that the objection most frequently raised with respect to these models is that the forms of alienation distinguished are in a state of logical chaos (Harvey et. al., 1984; Israel, 1971; Schacht, 1971; Schweitzer, 1981). Our approach has one more advantage in comparison with the classical approach (such as Seeman's): the concept of alienation is not confused with that of a sense (or feeling) of alienation (Harvey et al., 1984; Schweitzer, 1981).

Results of research indicate that the kinds of sense of alienation dis-

---

[3] None of the sense of alienation modalities distinguished by Seeman has found so many definitions, or has been comprehended in so many ways, as anomia (see Schacht 1971, pp. 194–197). It has come to denote moral confusion and cynicism. The concept has been used to characterize social systems and single individuals. In this work we refer on the one hand to the ideas of the creator of this category, E. Durkheim, for whom anomia relates to situations where "limits are unknown between the possible and the impossible, what is just and what is unjust, legitimate claims and hopes and those which are immoderate" (Durkheim 1972, p. 22).

tinguished by Seeman are strongly related or constitute one factor of a higher order (Dean, 1961; Neal & Retting, 1967; Zeller, Neal, & Groat, 1980).[4] It is an open question whether the autonomy-alienation modalities distinguished here are intercorrelated in Polish society.

Social Structure and a Sense of Alienation: Review of Research Results

Among attempts to find out where lie the origins and determinants of a sense of alienation, noteworthy are those that focus on the properties of the social structure in which the individual lives or spends most of his or her time. A number of institutions, social groups, and social systems have been investigated. Before reporting these results, however, an important issue should be noted. All the features of social structures spoken of further on are perceived features. Information concerning them was all obtained from subjects (sometimes from others than those tested for alienation) and not based on an objective analysis of the social structure. And so, in principle we will be dealing with relationships between perceived features of the system and a sense of alienation.

Numerous authors have ascertained that strength of alienation is affected by organization centralization, comprehended most frequently as a hierarchy of authority and a lack of participation in decision making (Aiken & Hage, 1966; Beardsley, 1978; Blazovsky, 1978; Cox & Wood, 1980; Wagoner, 1976).

Another of the determinants of a sense of alienation is an extensive system of control and formalization of the social structure (Aiken & Hage, 1966, Beardsley, 1978; Blazowsky, 1978; Cox & Wood, 1980).

Miller (1967) and Barth and Baba (1982) ascertained that when employees' sense of alienation was stronger, the management style they were subjected to was more directive. This result corresponds with Pearlin's data indicating that a sense of alienation appears when authority is communicated in such a way as to prevent or discourage interactions between subordinates, and when the superordinate exercises his or her authority in relative absentia (Pearlin, 1972).

It was also ascertained that employees feel alienated when their organizations do not supply them with professional incentives – do not create possibilities for development or encouragement (Barth & Baba, 1982; Miller, 1967; Mottaz, 1981, 1983) and to not present them with chances for promotion and getting ahead (Pearlin, 1972). A further feature of the social structure, this time inversely related to sense of alienation, is its trustworthiness (Aberbach

---

[4] This result is of special significance for the next part of the exposition. Namely, it allows us to assume that one phenomenon is manifested in the various measures and dimensions of sense of alienation. Hence, the various sense of alienation modalities are comparable.

& Walker, 1972); that is, its perceived legitimacy (Beardsley, 1978). Moreover, Schwartz (1973, after Perkins & Bell, 1980) suggested that people experience alienation when they happen to live in an inefficient sociopolitical system.

Finally, there is the complex of social system features determining a sense of alienation, which we may term the system's axiological orientation. This signifies it is directed toward maintaining and developing such social values as freedom (Long, 1976; Miller, 1967), justice (Schwartz, 1973), and allocentrism of authorities (Perkins & Bell, 1980).

To conclude this section, we may state that human beings do not feel alienated or experience a sense of autonomy, when they perceive the social system in which they find themselves as decentralized, open, permissive, creating chances or activity, trustworthy, effective, and realizing such values as humanism, freedom, equality, law abidingness, and allocentrism.

Mechanisms of Alienation

How then does it happen, one may ask, that if people perceive the social system in a particular way, they experience a sense of alienation from this system?

Pearlin ascertained that an intense feeling of alienation is most likely to occur when authority figures and their subordinates stand in a relation of great positional disparity. This relationship did not occur among "highly obeisant persons." The author's explanation is that an obeisant individual does not feel he or she has the right to share influence with superiors, even when his or her own affairs are involved (Pearlin, 1972).

Miller (quoted earlier) ascertained that various factors determine a sense of alienation, especially among persons who, as one may judge, possess more developed, autonomous standards concerning their place and role in the organization – persons with a PhD and a university education (in comparison with a group of MAs and engineers; Miller, 1967). Barth and Baba (1982) observed that Americans experience a greater sense of alienation than Canadians when they are subjected to a directive management style, and when their freedom of choice of activities is curtailed. For the author this difference is caused by the greater importance of indivdualistic values among Americans.

The results reviewed clearly indicate that a sense of alienation is related not so much to purely descriptive statements concerning properties of the social structure, as to the divergence between the individual's standards or values and these observations. Henceforth, we term the divergence between standards concerning the desired state and the state the sociopolitical system is perceived to be in as one's critical perception of the system.

The question posed at the beginning of this chapter changes slightly but does not lose its significance. In what manner does the individual's perception of the system lead to a sense of alienation?

Long (1976, 1978) proposed an answer to this question for the sense of political alienation. He suggested that one's critical perception may exert an influence in a twofold manner. First, it may bring about feelings of reactance. Then, when individuals feel that both others' and their own liberty and freedom are endangered, they experience alienation. Second, one's critical perception of the sociopolitical system may lead directly to a sense of alienation via simple reasoning and realism. Figure 16.1 presents a model verified using path analysis (from Long, 1978).

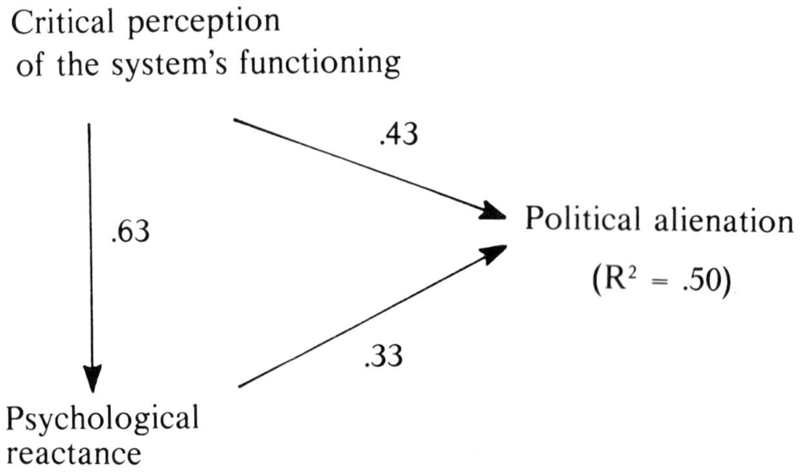

FIGURE 16.1. S. Long's model of political alientation (after Long, 1978).

The unmediated relation between critical perception and a sense of alienation is of special interest as it is in effect uninterpreted in this two-path model. If, as Long maintains, a sense of alienation is a result of a perception of divergence between one's values or standards and the perceived state of the sociopolitical system, one should expect alienation to be stronger among persons whose cognitive representations of the system are considerably developed and complex. This expectation is founded on the rather trivial assumption that to deduce accurately, one have at one's disposal a developed cognitive representation of the objects about which one is deducing. However, this reasoning is not confirmed by Harris and Highlen's (1982) results. Their investigation was not directly related to the issues under consideration here; they studied the effect of conceptual complexity on learned helplessness. However, assuming that the experience of learned helplessness may lead to a feeling of powerlessness, and that divergence between standards concerning the desired state and perception of the existing state may be unpleasant or aversive, the results of their investigation may be of value here. The authors ascertained that complexity mediates the experience of learned helplessness; it appeard that the conceptually complex subjects were less negatively affected than simple subjects as a result of exposure to an aversive situation.

Hence it is neither clear nor evident how structural properties of the representation of the socio-political system may modify the relation postulated to exist between individuals' critical perception of the system and a sense of autonomy-alienation. The purpose of this chapter is to attempt to answer this question.

METHOD

Research Design

This investigation constituted the initial stage of a more extensive research program. It was conducted in the Spring of 1984 in two professional training centers and was a paper and pencil study. Groups of 7 to 15 subjects each were tested. The study consisted of four stages, in the course of which the following constructs or variables were measured: critical perception of the system (suing an opinion questionnaire), the sense of feeling the threatened-secure in the system, socieconomic variables,[5] system representation structure (using a modified grid from of the Rep-test), sense of political autonomy-alienation, and level of anxiety.

Subjects

Subjects were volunteers, participants of professional training courses from the whole of Poland who were in professional training centers at the time. Fifty-four persons aged 22-55 years were tested (7 women and 47 men). The sample was differentiated with respect to education and income. Seventy percent of the subjects described themselves as believers (practicing or sporadically practicing religion).

---

5 As neither subjects' age, education, or income correlate significantly with critical perception of the system, or with structural properties of its representations (treated heıe as explanatory variables), they were not considered in the data analysis.

Measurement and Indices of the Variables Reported in this Study

Critical Perception of the Sociopolitical System. The Opinion Questionnaire, constructed for this study, was used to measure perceptions of the sociopolitical system. It consisted of 64 seven-level graphic scales. Their extremities describe opposing characteristics of the system. The scales so constructed were diagnostic of the following traits of the system: decentralization, opennes, permissiveness, creating possibilities for activity, trustworthiness, effectiveness, humanism, authorities' allocentrism, equality, law-abidingness, freedom. Such a procedure enabled critical perception indices for particula properties, as well as a global index, to be constructed. The "positive" ends of the scales were randomly placed to the left or the right.

The subjects first marked on the questionnaire scales what they considered the current state of the system to be, after which they completed the questionnaire once again, marking the desired state. Critical perception was measured as the divergence between the desired and perceived states.

The mean of diveregence on scales diagnostic of a given feature was the index of critical perception of that particular system feature; the global index was the mean of the index values. The greater the index value, the greater the critical perception.

Measures of reliability (internal consistency) ranged between .70 for freedom perception and .90 for trustworthiness.

To the the relation between individuals' critical perception of particular properties of the system, correlation coefficients were computed between the indices of the particular properties. All correlations were significant in the range of .35 to .81. Thus, critical perception of any of the system's properties was accompanied by a similar perception of all of the remaining properties. Hence, we may suppose that critical perception of the sociopolitical system is a uniform, homogeneous variable. For this reason we used only the global index in the analysis that follows.

Structure of the Sociopolitical System Representation. A modified grid form of the Rep-test was used to measure the representation of sociopolitical system (Bieri et al., 1970; Czapinski, 1978). The subjects assessed 14 officially functioning organizations of a diverse nature. Among them were principal State centers of authority (the Cabinet of the minister, parliament, and the Polish United Workers' Party), as well as religious, economic, propaganda, and other oganizations. Subjects were given a list of organization features (compiled on the basis of pilot study results). It contained 27 different traits that could be ascribed to various institutions. Subjects chose at least seven attributes from this list, and next assessed on a 5-point scale the extent to which each of the organizations possessed each of the attributes.

Indices of two features of system representation structure were calculated: cognitive complexity and schematism of authority perception (Czapinski, 1978). The cognitive complexity index was the mean of squared correlation coefficients that were computed between all attributes chosen by the subject. It was an index of the functional independence level of categories used to describe the system. A greater index value indicated lower cognitive complexity.

The index of schematism in perceiving the three state centers of authority provided information about the extent to which the centers were perceived according to the same cognitive schema as all the constituents of the sociopolitical system.[6] The higher the index value, the greater the schematism.

Sense of Political Autonomy-Alienation. The variable of political autonomy-alienation was measured using a questionnaire especially constructed for use in this study. The questionnaire was patterned on existing scales of alienation, and consisted of 40 statements expressed in the first person singular. They were used to create four subscales that measured the modalities of autonomy-alienation and a sense of estrangement-identification (which is not considered in this chapter). Half of the statements in each subscale expressed a sense of alienation, whereas half pertained to a sense of autonomy.

Subjects assessed on 5-point scales the extent to which each statement was consistent with their beliefs about themselves. The sense of autonomy-alienation modality index was the mean of these assessments, computed in such a manner that a higher index value indicated a greater sense of alienation.

Internal consistency measures were as follows: .853 for the efficacy-powerlessness subscale, .695 for meaningfulness-meaninglessness, and .700 for eunomia-anomia. As the possibility of using a global sense of autonomy-alienation index was considered, correlations between its modalities were computed. As only measures of meaninglessness and anomia correlated significantly, the decision was made not to use the sense of autonomy-alienation index.

---

[6] The reasoning underlying the construction of the schematism index was as follows. We say that two organizations are perceived in an independent manner – using different cognitive schemata – when the correlation coefficient between them is equal to zero. When its value approaches +1 or –1, however, we may speak of the interdependence of their perception, as the individual uses one schema to describe them (in the case of $r = -1$, the organizations are perceived to differ as regards content within the one schema). The squaring of correlation coefficient values allows the extent to which perceptions are interdependent to be assessed regardless of the content similarity of organizations. And so, as should be emphasized, the index used does not inform about the content similarity between centers of authority and the whole system, but about the degree to which they are perceived according to the same cognitive schema as the whole of the sociopolitical system.

RESULTS

A significance level of $p < .10$ was used in the data analysis. This decision was dictated by the following reasons. The investigation was highly explorative in character. A problem was broached that had not to date been the subject of empirical studies. This was done using new, untested (although fairly reliable) research tools. In addition, the sample investigated was, for various reasons, rather small. Considering that significance level has nothing to do with the strength of a relation, and is only the probability of a Type I error, the risk was taken.

Parameters of the Distributions of Sense of Autonomy-Alienation Modality Index Values. Before reporting the results proper, let us examine the distribution parameters of the sense of autonomy-alienation modality indices. The means and standard deviations are to be found in Table 16.1.

TABLE 16.1

Means and standard deviations for the modalities of sense of political autonomy-alienation

	Mean	*Standard Deviation*
powerlessness	3.249	1.132
meaninglessness	2.347	1.824
anomia	1.876	2.266

Index values could range from zero to four; hence it may be concluded that subjects experienced a sense of political alienation rather than autonomy. Only the mean sense of eunomia-anomia index value fell slightly above two; that is, was to be found in the interval that may be interpreted as representing a sense of autonomy. For this reason, and also to simplify our exposition, we speak above all of a sense of political alienation.

Critical Perception of the System, Structure of its Representation, and Sense of Political Alienation. Let us recall that we hypothesized that the sense of alienation would be stronger, the greater the divergence between standards and perception of the sociopolitical system. Moreover, we sought to ascertain whether and how this relation is modified by the extent to which the system representation is developed.

To test our hypothesis, correlation coefficients were calculated between the global critical perception of systems index and indices of the modalities of a sense of alienation. The results are presented in Table 16.2.

TABLE 16.2

Coefficients of correlation between critical perception of the sociopolitical system (CPS) and powerlessness (P), meaninglessness (M), and anomia (A)

	r	df	p
CPS/P	.340	47	.05
CPS/M	.278	47	.07
CPS/A	–.024	47	ns

Note: In this and later tables, correlation coefficient singnificance levels are given for two-tailed tests.

The results reported in Table 16.2 indicate that the greater the divergence between standards concerning the desired state of the system and its currently perceived state, the more strongly political powerlessness and meaninglessness are experienced. A sense of anomia was not related directly to divergence level.

With the aim of verifying whether the extent to which one's cognitive representation of the socio-political system is developed modifies this relation, correlation coefficients were calculated between individuals' critical perception and their sense of alienation modalities. This was done separately for groups of subjects with simple versus complex system representations, and for groups featuring low versus considerable schematism in the perception of centers of authority. The results of this analysis are shown in Table 16.3.

The results indicate that cognitive complexity plays a modifying role only in one case, and that to a very weak extent. It turned out that when an individual's representation of the sociopolitical system was fairly simple, sense of powerlessness was positively related to the degree to which the system was critically perceived. However, this relation seemed to be considerably modified by degree of schematism in individuals' perception of authority. Among persons who perceived centers of authority schematically, the sense of meaninglessness was positively related to degree of critical perception of the sociopolitical system. On the other hand, in the group of persons exhibiting low schematism, critical perception of the system was accompanied by a lowered sense of anomia, or rather, a relatively stronger sense of eunomia.

TABLE 16.3

Correlation coefficients between critical perception of the system (CPS) and powerlessness (P), meaninglessness (M), and anomia (A) in groups featuring simple vs. complex representation of the system, and in groups featuring low vs. high schematism in centers of authority perception

	Simple Representation		*Complex Representation*		Z	p
	r	p	r	p		
CPS/P	.362	.10	.139	ns	.73	ns
CPS/M	.264	ns	.197	ns	.20	ns
CPS/A	–.039	ns	.003	ns	.12	ns

	Low Schematism		*High Schematism*		Z	p
	r	p	r	p		
CPS/P	.266	ns	.198	ns	.23	ns
CPS/M	.060	ns	.434	.05	1.23	ns
CPS/A	–.391	.09	.249	ns	2.06	.05

Let us consider in more detail the concept of schematism in the perception of authority. The index of this variable was the mean of "similarities" between each of the three centers of authority, and all the remaining institutions (ie., in this, the two remaining centers of authority). It assessed the extent to which state centers of authority were perceived according to the same cognitive schema as all the constituents of the sociopolitical system. It seems, however, that the variable termed schematism may have reflected another feature of the organization of the system representation, namely the extent to which centers of authority were perceived as separate from the rest of the system. Thus, an index of this variable was computed. It was the mean of "similarities" between each of the three centers of authority and all organizations not being centers of authority. Next, correlation coefficients were calculated to examine the relation between one's critical perception of the system and one's sense of political alienation. This was done separately for groups of persons scoring high and low with regard to cognitive isolation of centers of authority. The results of this analysis are presented in Table 16.4.

The results found in Table 16.4 indicate that extent of cognitive isolation of authority modified the relation between critical perception and a sense of alienation. For persons who did not view centers of authority as being isolated, powerlessness and meaninglessness scores were higher, the more standards of the desired state diverged from perceptions of the current state of the system. This divergence seemed to be accompanied by a considerable sense of anomia when cognitive isolation of the centers of authority was high.

TABLE 16.4

Correlation coefficients between critical perception of the system (CPS) and powerlessness (P), meaninglessness (M), and anomia (A) in groups featuring cognitive isolation vs. cognitive integration of the centers of authority

	Cognitive Isolation		*Cognitive Integration*		Z	p
	r	p	r	p		
CPS/P	.009	ns	.476	.05	1.58	ns
CPS/M	.080	ns	.538	.01	1.62	ns
CPS/A	–.343	ns	.220	ns	1.78	.09

CONCLUSION

One issue seems worthy of emphasis, namely the theoretical and operational separation of the following two variables: the divergence between the perceived and desired state of the system and the sense of alienation. Certain approaches in research define political alienation in terms of disaffection with the system and distinguish the following of the forms: political discontentment, political cynicism, perceived elitism, and the perception of deficiencies in democracy (Long, 1980). When this is the case, it is difficult to distinguish between feelings of alienation and one's critical perception of the sociopolitical system because both of them are forms of political disaffection. The situation is different for our approach. A sense of alienation is not comprehended in terms of one's evaluation of the system. It is taken to be a feeling of personal ineffectiveness with respect to the practical and/or cognitive control one has over the sociopolitical reality. Hence our belief that negative evaluations of the system and a sense of political alienation are two qualitatively different psychological phenomena.

What new information does this investigation supply? To date, formal properties of the representation of sociopolitical reality have not been considered in research on a sense of alienation. At the most, the content of representations was taken into account. What more, though the effect of a critical perception of the social structure on a sense of alienation was known, no questions were posed concerning the effect of formal features of the system's representation on this relation. This question seems to be of importance.

The data analysis allowed us to ascertain that the divergence between standards concerning the desired state of the sociopolitical system and individuals' perceptions of its current state can be related to a sense of alienation, depending on the formal properties of representations of this system. It must be emphasized, however, that due to the correlational character of the research, these interpretations should be treated with great care.

The part played by cognitive complexity turned out to be incompatible with the predictions of Long's model, and to be nearer to the one proposed by Harris and Highlen (1982). According to Lewicki (1977), the "self" concept is the basic cognitive schema of persons featuring low cognitive complexity; they perceive reality as if through the filter of their own being. Hence we may assume that when the perceived state of the system diverges from standards of the desired state, they egocentrically relate this to their own selves and experience powerlessness. On the other hand, persons with a more complex representation of the system, to a lesser extent related the perceived divergence to the "self", have less of a chance of experiencing alienation. Such an interpretation appears to suggest that sense of powerlessness is a "natural" consequence of divergence between standards and perceived state, as long as this divergence is related to the "self." It seems, however, that a significant part may be played in this relationship by the individual's belief that he or she has at his or her disposal programs of activity enabling him or her to reduce this discrepancy. We may consider that a person who trusts in his abilities will not experience powerlessness when he relates the divergence between standards and the perceived state to the "self".

The conclusion that a critical perception of the system is related to a sense of alienation when one's authority representation is integrated with representations of the remaining constituents of the system is interesting, as it was unforeseen. This result may be interpreted with the aid of the alienation category, or more precisely, the estrangement of authority concept. When centers of authority are cognitively estranged from the whole of the sociopolitical system, they cease, as it were, being political. The individual may then perceive them critically, not experiencing political alienation (and even experiencing eunomia). However, when the authorities are cognitively integrated with the other constituents of the system, indentification takes place between them.

Two other observations are of note. First, it seems that the occurrence of the phenomena discussed may be dependent on the content of characteristics used to describe centers of authority. The second of these observations, which is related to the first, concerns the ecological validity of these results. We may judge that cognitive estrangement plays such a role only in those organizations, societies, or countries in which authority is strong and centralized. Where it is weak or decentralized, we cannot expect such relationships to occur.

REFERENCES

Aberbach, J., & Walker, J. (1972). Political trust and racial ideology. In A. Finifter (Ed.), *Alienation and the social system*. New York: Wiley.

Aiken, M., & Hage, J. (1966). Organization alienation: A comparative analysis. *American Sociological Review, 31*, 497-507.

Allard, E. (1972). Types of protest and alienation. In A.Finifter (Ed.), *Alienation and the social system*, New York: Wiley.

Barth, R. T., & Baba, V. V. (1982). Alienation among professional engineers: A Canadian-American comparison. *Relations Industrielles, 37*, 125-140.

Beardsley, W. (1978). The relationship of bureaucratic climate in public schools to alienation of elementary school students. *Dissertation Abstracts International*, 39(2-A), 554.

Bieri, J., Atkins, A. L., Briar, S., Lobeck, R., Miller, H., & Tripoli, T. (1970). The nature of cognitive structure. In P. B. Warr (Ed.), *Thought and personality*. London: Penguin Books Ltd.

Blazovsky, R. A. (1978). School bureaucracy and teacher alienation. *Dissertation Abstracts International*, 38(7-A), 3820-3821.

Cox, H. & Wood, J. R. (1980). Organization structure and professional alienation: The case of public school teacher. *Peabody Journal of Education*, October, 1–6.

Czapiński, J. (1978). Metodologia Rep Testu – podstawy teoretyczne, przykłady technik, ocena wartości pomiarowych (Methodology of the Rep Test – theoretical foundations, examples of techniques, assessment of measurement value). In E. Paszkiewicz (Ed.), *Materiały do nauczania psychologii* (Materials for the Instruction of Psychology), series III, (Vol. 3). Warszawa: University of Warsaw Press.

Dean, D. (1961). Alienation: Its meaning and measurement. *American Sociological Review, 26*, 753-758.

Durkheim, E. (1972). Anomy. In A. Finifter (Ed.), Alienation and the social system. New York: Wiley.

Harris, R.M., & Highlen, P. S. (1982). Conceptual complexity and susceptibility to learned helplessness. *Social Behaviour and Personality, 10(2)*, 183-188.

Harvey, D. L., Warner, L. G., Smith, L., & Harvey, E. S. (1984). Critical analysis of Seeman's concept of alienation. *Humboldt Journal of Social Relations, 11*, 16-52.

Korzeniowski, K. (1983). Alienacja człowieka (Aliention of man). In X. Gliszczyńska (Ed.), *Człowiek jako podmiot życia społecznego* (Man as the Subject of Social Life). Wrocław: Ossolineum.

Korzeniowski, K., Zieliński, R. & Daniecki, W. (1983). *Podmiotowość jednostki w koncepcjach psychologicznych i organizacyjnych* (Human Autonomy in Psychological and Organizational Theories). Wrocław: Ossolineum.

Lewicki, P. (1977). *Przedmiotowy i podmiotowy mechanizm percepcji społecznej*. Unpublished doctoral dissertation. University of Warsaw.

Long, S. (1976). Political alienation among black and white adolescents: A test of the social deprivation and political reality model. *American Politics Quarterly, 4*, 267-303.

Long, S. (1978). Political alienation: Reality and reactance. *Journal of Social Psychology, 104*, 115-121.

Long, S. (1980). Urban adolescents and the political system: Dimensions of disaffection. *Theory and Research in Social Education, 8*, 31-43.

Miller, G. A. (1967). Professionals in bureaucracy: Alienation among industrial scientists and engineers. *American Sociological Review, 32,* 755-768.

Mottaz, C. J. (1981). Some determinants of work alienation. *Sociological Quarterly, 22,* 519-529.

Mottaz, C. J. (1983). Alienation among police officers. *Journal of Police Science and Administration, 11,* 23-30.

Neal, A. G., & Rettig, S. (1967). On the multidimensionality of alienation. *American Sociological Review, 32,* 45-65.

Pearlin, L. I (1972). Alienation from work: A study of nursing personnel. In A. Finifter (Ed.), *Alienation and the social structure.* New York: Wiley.

Perkins, H. W., & Bell, W. (1980). Alienation and social justice in England and the United States: The policy and economy. *Comparative Social Research, 3,* 71-101.

Ray, J. J. (1982). Toward a definitive alienation scale. *Journal of Psychology, 112,* 67-70.

Reykowski, J. (1975). Osobowość (Personality). In T. Tomaszewski (Ed.), *Psychologia* (Psychology). Warsaw: PWN.

Robinson, J. P., & Shaver, P. R. (1970). *Measures of social psychological attitudes.* Ann Arbor, MI: Institute of Social Research.

Schacht, R. (1971). *Alienation,* New York: Anchor Books.

Schwartz, D. (1973). *Political alienation and political behaviour.* Chicago: Aldine.

Schweitzer, D. (1981). Alienation theory and research: Trends, issues, and priorities. *International Social Science Journal,* XXXIII(*3*), 523-556.

Seeman, M. (1959). On the meaning of alienation. *American Sociological Review, 24,* 783-791.

Twining, J. E. (1980). Alienation as a social process. *Sociological Quarterly, 21,* 417-428.

Wagoner, C. P. (1976). Police alienation: Some sources and implications. *Journal of Police Science and Administration, 4,* 389-403.

Zeller, R. A., Neal, A. G., Groat, H. T. (1980). On the reliability and stability of alienation measures: A longitudinal analysis. *Social Forces, 58,* 1195-1205.

17 Social Stratification, Conditions of Work, and Parental Socialization Values

Duane F. Alwin
Institute for Social Research
University of Michigan

INTRODUCTION

Conceptions of childhood and adult values regarding children have received considerable attention in past decades, particularly by sociologists and social psychologists concerned with the persistence of social inequality over generations. The link between the objective conditions of work, subjective orientations, and modes of behaving toward children is well established in this literature. In recent years the work of Melvin Kohn and his colleagues (see e.g., Kohn, Schooler et al., 1983) has been particularly important in establishing the connection between aspects of social structure, psychological functioning, and values.

Although recent authors have attempted to articulate the links between factors representing social structure and personality (e.g., House, 1981), many such discussions have not been embedded in the current research literature and have lacked a sociohistorical perspective. As early as the 1920s, social scientists studying American communities identified parental values as having some basis in socioeconomic life experiences (e.g. Duvall, 1946; Kohn, 1959a, 1963; Lynd & Lynd, 1929). And one of the time-honored interpretations of the persistence of socioeconomic inequality over generations refers to the transmission of values and orientations from parent to child. Research in the recent status attainment tradition, for example, typically assesses the achievement-related consequences of various parental statuses, or other family characteristics such as number of siblings or family intactness. The interpretation of these effects has rested largely on what Hyman (1953) called the "value systems of different classes." Status attainment research has attempted to implicate parental values in the intergenerational transmission of inequality, although it has focused on somewhat circumscribed behaviors exercised by parents rather late in adolescence (see Sewell & Hauser, 1975).

The most persistent theme in the study of parental socialization values and their relationship to social stratification is the contrast between valuation of *autonomy versus conformity.*[1] This theme appears in Piaget's (1965) distinction between *moral autonomy versus moral heteronomy,* and has appeared repeatedly in several separate works in the late 1950s and early 1960s dealing with parental values (Kohn, 1959a, 1963; Lenski, 1961; Miller & Swanson, 1958). This work has been the basis for sociological theorizing regarding the influence of social class on parental values, an embodiment of the link between social structure and personality. However, in recent years we have witnessed some persistent changes in parental values in some segments of the U.S. population (Alwin, 1984; Duncan, Schuman, & Duncan, 1973- Duncan, Duncan, & McRae, 1978). Although these trends accompany other major changes in the nature of the American family in terms of household composition, living arrangements and family life (e.g., Maccoby, 1978; Masnick & Bane, 1980), these factors do not appear to be related to the changes in values about children (Alwin, 1984). Rather, changes in parental values appear to be most strongly related to changes in socioeconomic factors and particularly so for certain ethnic groups experiencing major shifts in socioeconomic well-being in recent decades.

In this chapter I examine potential changes in the relative importance of two major socioeconomic factors, which are known to influence the professed value orientations of parents regarding children, namely educational and occupational experiences. These concerns grow out of a recent study of trends in parental socialization values in which I traced patterns of change and their sources across a time span of 2 1/2 decades. Using survey data from the Detroit metropolitan area obtained in 1958, 1971, and 1983, this study (Alwin, 1984) reported clear and consistent increases over this time period in the valuation of autonomy for children and a decrease in the valuation of conformity or obedience to authority. These results also suggested that whereas educational experiences appear to contribute strongly to variation in parental values in all three surveys, the influence of occupational position in such values appears to be declining. Because of limitations of the available measures of occupational experience in the data sets examined, this conclusion was considered some-

[1] Parental values are defined as the standards of desirability or criteria of preference that govern choices parents make in evaluating the behavior of their children (Kohn, 1969). See Williams (1968) for a discussion of the theoretical basis for this conception of values.

what tentative and subject to further examination.[2] It is possible, however, to engage in a detailed investigation of the role of both educational and occupational experiences and parental values using the data obtained in the 1983 survey, along with data from a 1982 survey of similar breadth and scope.

SOCIOECONOMIC FACTORS IN PARENTAL VALUES

In the mid-1950s Melvin Kohn and his colleagues initiated some work that has had an important impact on the development of research on socialization and social stratification (Gecas, 1979, 1981). The studies Kohn and his colleagues developed were aimed at assessing the impact of parental socioeconomic class on parental child-rearing values.[3] This research found that "working-class" parents stressed reliance on social control and a general orientation of conformity to external authority (obedience, good manners, cleanliness), whereas the "middle classes" were more likely to place an emphasis on their child's self-direction (self-control, responsibility, good judgment). These findings corroborated a number of other results pointing to a relationship between "social class" and parental orientations to children (see Bronfenbrenner, 1958; Gecas, 1979), and have been persuasive in their documentation of the importance of social stratification for the development of values and subjective orientations of members of modern society.[4]

---

2 The basic problem was that the 1958 dataset used in this analysis had limited information on the variety of occupational experiences of respondents, and the analysis was therefore restricted to a somewhat gross measure of occupation, namely whether the respondent was engaged in "white-collar" versus "blue-collar" work (see Alwin, 1984, p. 366).

3 The complete set of citations to this work is as follows: Kohn (1959a, 1959b, 1963, 1969, 1976, 1977, 1981), Kohn and Carroll (1960), Pearlin and Kohn (1966), Schooler (1972a, 1972b), Kohn and Schooler (1973, 1978, 1982), Słomczyński, Miller, and Kohn (1981) and Kohn, Schooler, and colleagues (1983). For most purposes I refer to the major writings from this bibliography dealing with parental values, which are Kohn (1969, 1976, 1977, 1981), but in cases where it is important to track the history of ideas, I cite earlier references.

4 Given the types of variables measured in these investigations, and given current sociological perspectives on "class," a more sociologically precise term for the phenomenon at hand is "social status". See Bendix (1974) for a clarification of meanings of the terms "social class" and "social status" (see also Wright & Perrone, 1977; Robinson and Kelley, 1979; Wright, 1978, 1980). In my reference to these variables I use the term *socio-economic* to encompass the general nature of the experiences, but I prefer to distinguish between the experiences that arise from the educational system and those which arise from the occupational structure.

In addition, and perhaps most importantly, Kohn offered an interpretation of the relationship of social stratification and parental values, which had not been articulated in the previous literature. Kohn (1963) reasoned that these socioeconomic differences in parental valuation of autonomy (or self-direction, as Kohn refers to it) versus conformity originate, in part, from the job activities and duties performed by members of different classes. Jobs described as "middle class" in American society are generally more complex, less heavily supervised, and less subject to routinized forms of activity than is the case for "working class" jobs, which entail less complex, more routinized organization of work and more closely supervised activities.

The critical feature of Kohn's argument involves the concept of occupational self-direction, or the degree to which a person is free in the context of the work setting to control his or her activity and to escape external sources of control, e.g., machines and supervisory personnel. In order to perform in complex, unstructured work setting, persons must be able to handle uncertainty, rely on their own judgments and be able to initiate independent thought and action. And, according to Kohn's thesis, these are the jobs requiring higher levels of educational experience and those with higher status. By contrast, jobs that involve less occupational self-direction (i.e., those having less education and lower occupational status) involve less task complexity, require greater supervision, and greater acquiescence to external sources of behavioral control.

These "structural imperatives" of the job, Kohn argued, were a primary source of observed socioeconomic differences in parental values. Conditions of work represented experiences that shaped a person's views of both the possible and the desirable, for both themselves and their children. Persons in jobs characterized by Kohn as "working class," being more subject to authority and external control would in theory be more likely to express values of conformity for their children, whereas persons in jobs considered "middle class" would tend to express values encouraging independent decision making and freedom from external controls. These conditions of work, then, were instrumental in socializing parents in terms of the values they bring to their interaction with children, and they influence the nature of parental behavior. Although Kohn (1969) does not explicitly formulate a mechanism by which these values translate into action and ultimately affect the life chances of the child, he does argue that "class differences in values contribute to the perpetuation of inequality" by contributing to the development of capacities that will prepare children for different positions in later life.

In the theoretical formulation of Bronfenbrenner's (1979) ecology of human development, these aspects of the parent's job represent an aspect of "exosystem" influences on the developing child. Although praising the contributions of Kohn and his colleagues, Bronfenbrenner (1979) points out that rarely does research on the socialization influences of parental characteristics advance much beyond showing a correlation between indicators of parental status, e.g., marital status, socioeconomic resources, family configuration, and the like, and indicators of their values or orientations to the "behavior setting" of child rearing. This represents a limitation of the line of research being discussed, including the research I present in this chapter. Nevertheless, in terms of assessing the relative role of sources of influence on parental values, it is worthwhile investigating the overall impact of parental characteristics on parental orientations to their children, even if we do not examine the mechanisms by which they translate into the contexts of child-rearing and outcomes for children.

In his empirical analyses Kohn (1969, see also Kohn & Schooler, 1973, 1978, 1982 and Kohn et al., 1983) investigated the extent to which the conditions of work that circumscribed the nature of "occupational self-direction," namely the substantive complexity of the work, the closeness of supervision, and the routinization of the work flow, actually accounted for the observed relationship between "social class" and parental values. Kohn's major finding in this regard is that by controlling the factors making up this conception of occupational self-direction, the relationship between "social class" and parental self-direction/conformity is reduced by nearly two-thirds (1969), although this reduction was disproportionately shared by education and occupational position. Specifically, controlling on occupational self-direction reduces the relationship of values to education by less than 20%, while reducing the relationship to occupational position by over 80% (1969).

In emphasizing the importance of the structural conditions of work in shaping the child-rearing orientations of parents, Kohn and his colleagues have not ignored the potent influences of educational experiences both in providing access to occupations and in directly influencing the nature of values. In fact, Kohn (1969) presents evidence suggesting that experiences linked to tenure in the formal educational system are more strongly related to parental values than are those tied to conditions of work. Comparing the two sources of influence–education and occupation–Kohn (1969) states the following: "Education is the more potent of the two dimensions, being more strongly related to parental values, to self-values, to judgments about the extrinsic feature of jobs, and–most strongly of all–to authoritarian conservatism" (p. 132). Further, he indicates that "the importance of education for men's values and orientation–at least under the conditions of life in the United States in the mid-1960s–is great, no matter what conditions men subsequently encounter" (p. 191). It should perhaps be emphasized that in this early work Kohn assigns a decidedly more important *direct role* to the experiences reflected in differential school attendance; however, in more recent statements he is less sanguine about the relative influence of the two types of variables (Kohn, 1977).

The principal explanation Kohn gives for the influence of education on value orientations is that educational experiences operate via cognitive factors. Specifically, he suggests that "education... seems to matter for values and orientations chiefly because it can be so very important for intellectual flexibility and breadth of perspective'' (p. 188). Kohn (1977) reports that this hypothesis has received empirical confirmation by the fact that when statistically controlling for intellectual flexibility when examining the relationship between education and values and orientations the relationship is reduced.

Of course, education has both direct and indirect effects, and in this regard Kohn (1969) states that ''job conditions determinative of occupational self-direction are of great importance for explaining the *occupational position* component of the class relationships, but are decidedly less important for explaining the *educational* component of these relationships'' (p. 188). More recently, Kohn (1977) indicates that his ''subsequent analyses suggest that the *indirect effects of education may be even more important than the direct effects''* (emphasis added) (p. 43). Because education serves as a screening device for access to jobs that allow freedom from supervision and opportunities for the exercise of control over the environment, it has a determining influence on the nature of work. According to Kohn (1977, 1981) ''it is precisely because education is crucial for the very occupational conditions that most strongly affect values and orientations that education is so powerful; its indirect effects add greatly to its direct effects.''

This thesis, that variation in educational experiences contributes to value orientations in a fashion that makes occupational success more likely, is further articulated by Bowles and Gintis' ''correspondence theory'' of educational socialization. They have argued that various levels in the schooling process socialize young persons to differing kinds of orientations because of the structure of social relationships in the social organization of the school. Values or personality dispositions, acquired within the various levels of the educational system, correspond to the kinds of personal qualities that are necessary for successful job performance at particular levels within industrial and bureaucratic organizations. The social relations of production are anticipated by the structure of socialization experiences in the school, so that different levels of the educational system–junior and senior high school, 2-year community colleges and technical schools, and the elite 4-year institutions of higher education–channel workers into different levels within the occupational structure. This is carried out, Bowles and Gintis in effect argue, via the socialization of young persons along the dimension of autonomy versus conformity in school settings.

Bowles and Gintis (1976) observe, for example, that just as the lower levels of school (junior and senior high school) ''severely limit and channel the activities of students... the lowest levels in the hierarchy of the enterprise emphasize rule-following'' and conformity to the norms of the enterprise. At the middle levels of schooling (teacher and community colleges) ''more independent activity and less overall supervision'' is allowed, corresponding to the middle levels of the hierarchy of the enterprise, where ''dependability, and the capacity to operate without direct and continuous supervision'' is emphasized.

Finally, at the higher levels of the schooling process (elite 4-year colleges and universtities), social relationships are stressed that correspond to the requirements of jobs that exist at the highest levels of the enterprise–the capacity to initiate independent activity and the internalization of the norms of the organization.

According to this view, then, the social relationships that are organized into the schooling process, and that are roughly represented by the length of exposure to schooling, are duplicated in the social relationships in the hierarchy of production, and value orientations required for successful job performance are instilled (or at least believed to be) at the corresponding level of schooling. Values orientations are reflected in the educational practices that anticipate conditions of work. As Bronfenbrenner (1979) succinctly puts it: "The further one goes in school, the more likely one [is] to experience freedom from close supervision, nonroutinized flow, substantively complex work, and opportunity for self-direction" (p. 248).

These and other observations regarding the nature of the schooling process (e.g., Dreeben, 1967) point toward a theoretical expectation that parental appraisals of what is desirable behavior in their children is governed in part by their past exposure to the educational system. Educated parents, having been exposed to settings that require them to "think for themselves" and to conduct themselves according to internalized norms, desire greater amounts of autonomy in their children; whereas less-educated parents, exposed more to settings that require less independence and greater conformity to external requirements, are less likely to desire autonomy in their children and more likely to prefer obedience. As the work of Kohn and his colleagues demonstrates, although some of these effects operate indirectly via the link between education and occupation, most will operate independently. In either case, the effects of educational experience, indexed in most studies as the number of years of schooling completed, originate in school settings and represent the socializing influences of the educational system quite apart from later occupational experiences. Thus, in considering the relative influences of educational and occupational experiences in affecting parental values we consider education to be causally prior to occupational experience[5].

EDUCATION, OCCUPATION, AND PARENTAL VALUES

In this section I present some results from a study of child rearing in the Detroit, Michigan metropolitan area. The analysis reported here is based on re-

[5] In most cases this represents a reasonable assumption, although in a small number of cases educational experiences will not represent exogenous influences on occupation.

spondents from two successive surveys of parents (defined as adults rearing children between the ages of 2 and 18) in Detroit during 1982 and 1983. The surveys used probability samples of parents from a sampling frame of all occupied housing units in the three Michigan counties of Wayne, Oakland, and Macomb. Both samples were multi-stage samples in which the first stage of selection sampled geographically defined clusters of housing units and the second stage sampled individual housing units within selected clusters. Both samples were drawn under the supervision of the Sampling Section of the Survey Research Center of The University of Michigan. The 1982 sample is a standard cross-sectional area probability sample, stratified on race and geographic location. The design for the 1983 supplemental sample was different, involving a disproportionate oversampling of households in high-density black areas. The interviews in both surveys were conducted by professional interviewers trained and employed by the Survey Research Center, with the exception of one-half of the 1982 interviews, where trained graduate student interviewers were used. The response rate was approximately 80%. In the present analyses the data are weighted in order to take into account these differing sampling fractions and response rates.

The major objective in what I report here is to investigate the relative importance of factors representing educational and occupational experiences for parental values, and the extent to which they are transmitted via the conditions of work. Based on the previous discussion and the perspective adopted from Kohn's writings, I propose the model depicted in Figure 17.1 as a guide to causal analysis. As indicated in the figure, the major dependent variables in this analysis were measures of parental relative preferences for autonomy and conformity in their children. I relied on composite scores based

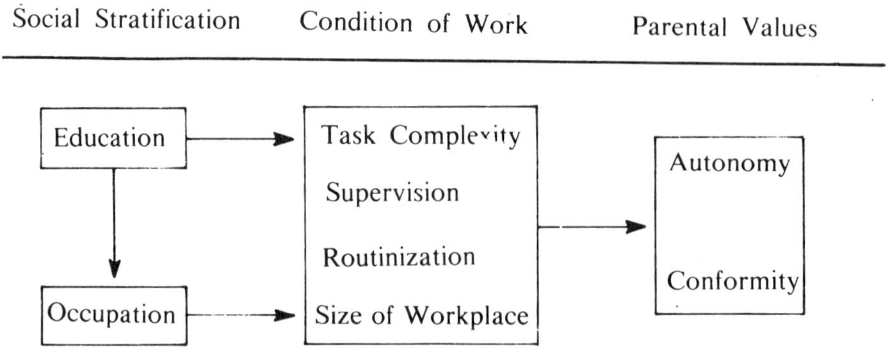

FIGURE 17.1. Causal model for assessing the effects of education and occupation on parental values.

on the measures of parental values from Kohn (1969) and Lenski (1962). In brief, I developed a measure of autonomy and conformity from each of the two measurement approaches, Lenski's simple ranking of five child qualities and Kohn's somewhat more complex reduced-ranking procedure.[6] In both cases the scores were expressd on a 5-point scale, expressing relative preferences among child qualities. I hypothesized, on the basis of prior research literature, that preferences for autonomy would be correlated with high-educational and occupational status and that desires for obedience and conformity in children with lower educational and occupational status. I theorized that this reflects primarily on the experiences persons acquire in educational and occupation settings, and in the case of occupation I was able, following the theoretical developments of Kohn and his colleagues, to examine the extent to which the effects of educational and occupational status were translated into parental values via the structural conditions of work. I was on even more speculative terrain in the case of education, because I had no direct measures of educational experiences (cf. Miller, Kohn, & Schooler, 1985, 1986; Morgan, Alwin, & Griffin, 1979). In this case, I assumed that higher levels of education implicate schooling processes that are distinct from those occurring at lower levels.

The major independent variables in the analysis were measured as follows:

1. Respondent's education: measured in years of formal schooling completed. This involves four basic categories, which accounts for the bulk of the effects: (a) less than 12 years of school attendance, (b) 12 years of school

[6] Lenski's (1961) measure was obtained from respondent ranking of five qualities in terms of their importance "for a child to learn to prepare him for life." The qualities were: (a) to obey, (b) to be well liked or popular, (c) to think for himself (herself), (d) to work hard, and (e) to help others when they need help. Responses to this ranking procedure permit the calculation of a rank-value of each quality for a given respondent, ranging from 1 (low) to 5 (high). Kohn's (1969) procedure is somewhat more complicated. Respondents are asked to review a list of 13 qualities (good manners, tries hard to succeed, honest, neat and clean, good sense and sound judgment, self-control, acts like a boy (acts like a girl) should, gets along well with other children, obeys parents well, responsible, considerate of others, interested in how and why things happen, good student) selecting the three qualities they consider to be the "most desirable." Of these three, respondents are asked to select the one which is "most desirable of all." Then, respondents are asked to review the remaining qualities, selecting the three that they consider "least important," and among these, the one they consider the "least important of all." Responses to these questions are coded as follows: 5 = the most desirable quality, 4 = one of the three valued qualities, but not the most valued, 3 = neither one of the three most or least valued qualities, 2 = one of the three least valued qualities, but not the least valued quality, 1 = the quality least valued of all. Based on prior analyses of responses to these questions (Alwin & Jackson, 1982b; Alwin & Krośnick, 1985; Kohn, 1969, 1976), we use the qualities of "responsible," "good sense and sound judgment," and "interested in how and why things happen" as indications of a preference for autonomy; and the qualities of "obeys," "good manners," and "neat and clean" as indications of a preference for conformity. For the purposes of this analysis, I sum the three qualities in a given domain and divide by three, producing an average rank on a 1 to 5 scale, analogous to the Lenski measure.

attendance, (c) 2-year community college, business, or technical school, (d) 4-year college or university.

2. Respondent's occupational status: measured in the metric of Duncan SEI score (Featherman, Sobel, & Dickens, 1975) based on 1970-detailed Census Bureau occupational categories.

3. Supervisory level of job: measured as a four-category variable assessing the objective position in the job hierarchy, as follows: 1 = self-employed; 2 = employed, but has no director supervisor; 3 = employed, with one supervisory level above; 4 = employed, with two or more supervisory levels above.

4. Closeness of supervision: measured as the unweighted sum of the questions assessing the following: (a) the degree to which the respondent versus his/her supervisor decides what to do (and how to do it) on his/her job; (b) the degree to which the respondent is permitted to discuss what his/her supervisor wants him/her to do; (c) the degree of freedom the respondent has in disagreeing with his/her supervisor; (d) how important it is for doing his/her job well that the respondent do what s/he is told; (e) the degree to which the respondent (versus supervisor and machines) controls the speed of his/her work (see Kohn, 1969). This variable is scored so that a high score reflects greater supervision. Respondents who are self-employed or who have no supervisor are given a score of zero.

5. Substantive complexity of the job: measured on the basis of scores of complexity of work with data, people, and things from the *Dictionary of Occupational Titles* (U.S. Department of Labor, 1977). The present analysis uses the sum of complexity of work with data and complexity of work with people (complexity of work with things is omitted), with greater complexity assigned higher scores (see Kohn, 1969).

6. Complexity of work organization: measured as the unweighted sum of responses to the following questions, (a) how much freedom does your job allow you as to how you do your work? (b) how much does your job allow you to make decisions on your own? (c) how much does it allow you to do a veriety of different things? (d) how much does it allow you to take part in making decisions that affect you? (e) how much does it require you to do things that are very repetitious (do things over and over)? (f) how much is it one where you have a lot of say over what happens on your job? (g) how much does your job allow you to work on a product from beginning to end?

7. Size of workplace: measured as the logarithm of the number of persons who work for the business or company where the respondent works.

8. Family income: measured as the total family income from all sources in the year preceding the survey. The survey questions used to measure family income were open-ended questions, except for a small number of respondents who would report only a range of income. The latter cases were coded to the midpoints of the intervals of the income ranges used. Income values are adjusted to constant 1981 dollars.

Table 17.1 presents the basis for a descriptive bivariate analysis of the major dependent and independent variables.[7] Specifically, using both the Kohn and Lenski measures, the mean rankings of autonomy, conformity, and their contrast (autonomy – conformity) are presented for categories of each independent variable. In the table we also present the number of cases in each category of the independent variables and a measure of the statistical association between the variables involved.[8]

These results show that both educational and occupational experiences are reflected in the kinds of values parents express for children's behavior. Except for the measure of "closeness of supervision," "supervisory level," and "size "size of workplace," all these measures of socioeconomic experiences showed a marked relationship with parental autonomy and conformity values. These results for the most part replicated what would be expected on the basis of past research, that parental values would be predictable from these socioeconomic distinctions, using either the Kohn or Lenski measures. The predictor variables were, of course, correlated, and it proved to be informative to examine their influences within a multivariate framework. Thus, I turned to the use of structural equation models (Duncan, 1975) and multiple regression techniques.

Consistent with the diagram in Figure 17.1, in Table 17.2 I present the regression coefficients (in standard from) from the regression of each of the dependent variables included previously on successive sets of independent variables. Because the "closeness of supervision" and "supervisory level" variables were highly correlated ($r = .86$), they were obviously measuring very closely the same aspect of the phenomenon of interest. Thus, one of the variables was excluded from the analysis. I excluded the "supervisory level" variable primarily because the "closeness of supervision" measure is much closer (virtually an exact replica) to Kohn's measure of the concept.

---

7 Because of the nature of this analysis we exclude persons who have never worked, but this applies to only a small portion. Persons not currently employed who have worked in the past were asked about their last job. Persons who were self-employed or not under direct supervision by others were not asked questions pertaining to supervision – they are scored as zero on all such questions.

8 We use η as an estimate of the square root of the proportion of variance in the dependent variable that lies between categories of the independent variable (see Hays & Winkler, 1971). This is an estimate of amount of nonlinear association between the two variables in the population of interest.

TABLE 17.1

Mean Rankings of Child Qualities by Categories of Education and Occupational Experiences: Detroit Parents, 1982–1983

Predictor Variable	Kohn Measures*				Lenski Measures*			
	n	*(1)*	*(2)*	*(3)*	*n*	*(1)*	*(2)*	*(3)*
Education:								
Less than 12 yr.	201	2.94	3.25	–.32	219	3.82	3.63	.19
12 yr.	362	3.03	3.16	–.14	372	4.32	3.31	1.01
2 yr. college	199	3.08	3.02	.06	204	4.59	2.99	1.60
4 yr. college	248	3.22	2.87	.35	261	4.54	2.73	1.81
Total	1010	3.07	3.07	0.00	1056	4.33	3.16	1.17
η		.188	.273	.258		.243	.238	.280
Occupational Status – SEI:								
High quartile	257	3.25	2.86	.39	234	4.58	2.72	1.85
Second quartile	222	3.01	3.09	–.08	231	4.43	3.13	1.29
Third quartile	284	3.04	3.17	–.13	298	4.25	3.23	1.01
Low quartile	247	2.96	3.21	–.26	262	4.04	3.59	.45
Total	1010	3.07	3.07	0.00	1055	4.33	3.15	1.18
η		.216	.270	.271		.179	.228	.246
Supervisory level:								
Self-employed	78	3.11	2.99	.12	83	4.51	2.73	1.78
Employee/no supr.	57	3.05	2.98	.08	57	4.22	2.89	1.33
Employee/1 level above	573	3.05	3.09	–.04	598	4.33	3.21	1.12
Employee/2+ levels above	96	3.11	3.03	.08	99	4.47	2.71	1.76
Total	804	3.07	3.07	0.00	837	4.37	3.07	1.29
η		.048	.082	.068		.072	.156	.133
Closeness of Supervision:								
High quartile	210	3.08	3.08	0.00	217	4.34	3.19	1.15
Second quartile	218	3.09	3.08	.01	229	4.30	3.15	1.14
Third quartile	295	3.07	3.05	.02	305	4.31	3.15	1.16
Low quartile	193	3.09	3.07	.03	204	4.31	3.17	1.14
Total	916	3.08	3.07	.01	955	4.31	3.17	1.15
η		.018	.025	.011		.015	.010	.003

(continued)

TABLE 17.1 *(Continued)*

Task Complexity:								
High quartile	243	3.21	2.91	.30	251	4.48	2.79	1.69
Second quartile	263	3.12	3.03	.09	269	4.51	3.07	1.45
Third quartile	182	3.05	3.04	.01	191	4.37	3.08	1.29
Low quartile	270	2.94	3.28	–.34	288	4.05	3.54	.51
Total	958	3.09	3.06	.02	999	4.35	3.12	1.24
η		.191	.266	.257		.172	.203	.223
Complexity of Work:								
High quartile	270	3.00	3.11	–.11	286	4.26	3.30	.96
Second quartile	218	3.05	3.15	–.09	224	4.33	3.12	1.21
Third quartile	265	3.06	3.06	0.00	278	4.39	3.11	1.28
Low quartile	227	3.20	2.98	.22	234	4.34	3.06	1.28
Total	980	3.08	3.07	0.01	1022	4.33	3.15	1.18
η		.137	.118	.139		.044	.068	.065
Size of workplace:								
High quartile	109	3.07	3.10	–.03	110	4.42	2.83	1.59
Second quartile	120	3.04	3.02	.02	123	4.51	2.87	1.64
Third quartile	126	3.13	3.00	.13	131	4.35	2.74	1.61
Low quartile	105	3.09	3.01	.08	110	4.35	2.71	1.63
Total	460	3.08	3.03	0.05	474	4.41	2.79	1.62
η		.057	.084	.065		.060	.049	.009
Income:								
High quartile	214	3.20	2.93	.27	217	4.53	2.70	1.83
Second quartile	209	3.13	2.99	.14	218	4.42	2.94	1.48
Third quartile	298	3.05	3.09	–.05	317	4.27	3.33	.94
Low quartile	293	2.92	3.28	–.36	308	4.09	3.61	.49
Total	1014	3.07	3.07	0.00	1060	4.33	3.16	1.17
η		.192	.246	.246		.141	.249	.240

* (1) is Autonomy, (2) is Conformity, (3) is Autonomy – Conformity.

The three equations estimated for each dependent variable shown in Table 17.2 permit the evaluation of the direct and indirect effects of the socioeconomic variables on parental values. This method of successive estimation of reduced-form coefficients in recursive models is described in Alwin and Hauser (1975). In brief, the indirect effects of educational and occupational statuses via the conditions of work variables were obtained by substracting the coefficient in column 3 from the corresponding coefficient in column 2.

TABLE 17.2
Structural Coefficients from the Regression of Parental Values on Relevant Parental Characteristics: Detroit Parents, 1982–83

	Coefficients in standarized form					
	Kohn Measures			*Lenski Measures*		
Predictors	*(1)*	*(2)*	*(3)*	*(1)*	*(2)*	*(3)*
	A. Autonomy					
Educational Level	.184**	.116**	.85*	.231**	.194**	.195**
Occupational Status		.115**	.036		.063	.079
Task Complexity			.103*			–.023
Closeness of Supervision			.040			.000
Complexity of Work			–.020			.058
Size of Workplace			–.088*			–.050
Income			.080*			.048
Multiple Correlation	.184	.206	.249	.231	.237	.250
	B. Conformity					
Educational Level	–.268	–.184**	–.149**	–.233**	–.160**	–.121**
Occupational Status		–.143**	–.059		–.123**	–.072
Task Complexity			–.093*			–.055
Closeness of Supervision			–.023			–.052
Complexity of Work			–.037			–.043
Size of Workplace			.163**			.044
Income			–.164**			–.137**
Multiple Correlation	.268	.292	.364	.233	.253	.290
	C. Autonomy – Conformity					
Educational Level	.254**	.168**	.131**	.278**	.209**	.194**
Occupational Status		.146**	.064		.117**	.092*
Task Complexity			.111*			.025
Closeness of Supervision			.036			.035
Complexity of Work			.010			.060
Size of Workplace			–.141**			–.056
Income			.138**			.115**
Multiple Correlation	.254	.280	.343	.278	.294	.320

* $p < .05$
** $p < .01$

These regression estimates point to several conclusions. First, although both educational level and occupational status, as indicators of socioeconomic experiences, have substantial impact on measures of parental values, education appears uniformly to have the stronger effect. Whether one takes the total effects of education as the measure of relative importance, or the effects of education net of occupational status; in both instances the educational variable consistently shows a somewhat larger role. These findings with regard to the importance of both education and occupation are strongly consistent with those reported by Kohn (1969) and Slomczynski et al. (1981) for the United States and Poland. The contrast in the importance of education over occupational status confirms the findings reported by Kohn (1969); however, in the Polish data the effects of education and occupational status on parental values are roughly the same (see Slomczynski, Miller, & Kohn, 1981). The Slomczynski et al. (1981) paper does not focus on the differences in aspects of these processes across the two countries but emphasizes the similarities and the general support their analysis gives to the interconnections between social structure, psychological functioning, and values. The question of what might account for these differences is an interesting one, but one that is beyond the scope of this presentation.

A second major result of this analysis also confirms the results obtained by Kohn (1969) and Slomczynski et al. (1981) for the United States and Poland, that measures of occupational self-direction transmit considerably more of the effects of occupational position than of education. The results obtained here using Kohn's measures with regard to the indirect effects of education and occupational status are quite similar to those reported by Kohn (1969) and Slomczynski et al. (1981) for the United States, namely that about one-fourth of the effects of education on parental values is transmitted via occupational self-direction, whereas upwards of one-half of the effects of occupational status are so interpreted. The results using Lenski's measures show very little indirect effect of education via occupational self-direction, and considerably smaller indirect effects of occupational position via these mechanisms than is the case using Kohn's measures.

These results are, then, quite consistent with Kohn's (1969) earlier findings that occupational self-direction is much more important for understanding the effects of occupational position than it is for understanding the effects of education. The effects of education operate quite independently of the structural imperatives of the job. The importance of education for parents' values is great no matter what conditions of work they subsequently encounter (Kohn, 1969). Slomczynski et al. (1981) show even a stronger mediating role of occupational self-direction with respect to parental values in the case of Poland. Such measures of occupational self-direction transmit over 80% of the effects of occupational position and 60% of the effect of education. The reason for the stronger role of occupational self-direction in the case of Poland is unclear, but certainly worthy of pursuit.

There is, then, support for the idea that the substantive complexity of work plays a strong mediational role in transmitting the effects of educational level and occupational status. By contrast, the other measures of occupational self-direction (conditions of work), namely the nature of supervision and the routinization of work, did not play a mediational role in these data. Whether this represents an aspect of the changing nature of socioeconomic influences on parental values, or some fundamental differences in the populations studied or methods used, was not at all clear; but it was consistent with the observation made in my earlier analysis of trends in parental values that the importance of occupation for parental values may have been diminishing over time (Alwin, 1984, 1986).

Although there was strong support in these data for conclusions drawn from earlier research regarding the relatively stronger role of education versus occupation in shaping the values parents held for their children, as well as the independent nature of the effects of education, we must take these results as tentative. Specifically, there are a number of issues that need to be addressed in subsequent analyses before generalizing the conclusions drawn from these analyses. Perhaps the most important of these issues has to do with the quality of measurement in the present case. My approach here has been intentionally preliminary and exploratory, and I have not yet completed the analysis required to address the theoretical issues raised here. One of the major difficulties in using ranking measures, as in the present case, stems from their ipsative nature, and this analysis has not incorporated a solution to the ipsative problem. The statistical analysis of rankings requires substantially more complex models for measurement than I have used here (Alwin & Jackson, 1982a, 1982b; Alwin & Krosnick, 1985; see Jackson & Alwin, 1980). By adopting models that allow for patterns of error, both random and systematic, in our measures, it will be possible to improve the level of predictability of our dependent measures, as well as enhance the opportunities for detecting effects of the predictor variables, and this could have implications for the interpretation of our data. Thus, although I do not wish to stress the possible deficiencies of the present analysis, any stronger conclusion than that advanced previously regarding the potentially changing role of occupation as a determinant of parental values must await these further analyses.

CONCLUDING REMARKS

In understanding these results it is important to draw together two perspectives on the role of socioeconomic influences in adult orientations to children. One perspective is that which attests to the important role of social stratification and the nature and organization of work settings in shaping the values and orientations of parents. This perspective rests on a strong empirical base, with confirming evidence spanning many decades and transcending national boundaries. There is little question that socioeconomic experiences play an important role in developing persons' orientations to life and psychological functioning, although there may be some differences in the relative importance of various aspects of socioeconomic experience across time and place.

The second perspective needed to understand the general set of issues connected to the influences of socioeconomic experiences has to do with the changing role of socioeconomic experiences historically. Except for the work of historians of the family (e.g., Schlumbohm, 1980, Stone, 1977), there are few available data on the nature of the connections of socioeconomic experiences to value orientations in past times and places. Some recently assembled data that span the past few decades raise some interesting questions in this regard and demonstrate the importance of considering issues of the role of socioeconomic experiences within a sociohistorical perspective. Even though the problem of disentangling the effects of educational and occupational statuses does not admit to a simple solution, I think it is important to distinguish their influences to the extent possible. The two types of variables quite clearly index different aspects of socioeconomic experience and arise from distinct, though related, areas of socialization. Consequently, as a result of sociohistorical changes these areas of influence may vary in the magnitude of their impact over time and place.

These possibilities not only reinforce the need to distinguish the effects of education and occupation in their impact on parental values, they sensitize us as well to the potential changes in socioeconomic influences that are recorded in our data. Thus, it may be that conditions of work play a less important role in parental values in the contemporary structure of U.S. society than was true in the past, as tentatively suggested in the aformentioned analyses. In any event, it does seem clear that whatever role one were to assign to occupational experiences in shaping the values of parents for the behavior of their children, the role of education is the more powerful. Yet, most of the scholarly work on this topic to date has concentrated exclusively on the conditions of work that explain the nature of occupational influences on parental values. What is needed is a parallel effort aimed at understanding the nature of socialization experiences that are represented by the measure of educational status included in these studies (see e.g., Bowles & Gintis, 1976; Bronfenbrenner, 1979; Miller et al., 1985, 1986; Morgan et al., 1979). Moving in this direction will further clarify the role of social stratification in shaping the lives and orientations of members of society.

ACKNOWLEDGMENTS

An earlier version of the paper was prepared for presentation at a conference on "Social and Moral Values: Development, Organization and Change," sponsored by the Polish Academy of Science and held in Zaborow, Poland, November 23-26, 1984. The research reported here was supported by a grant from the National Institute of Mental Health (MH37289-02). The author wishes to acknowledge the assistance of Lynn Dielman, Mark Glaza, Jon Krosnick, and Marion Wirick in data analysis and manuscript preparation. Requests for copies should be sent to Duane F. Alwin, Institute for Social Research, The University of Michigan, Ann Arbor, Michigan 48106.

REFERENCES

Alwin, D. F. (1984). Trends in parental socialization values: Detroit, 1958-1983. *American Journal of Sociology, 90,* 358382.

Alwin, D. F. (1986). Religion and parental child-rearing orientations: Evidence of Catholic-Protestand convergence. *American Journal of Sociology, 92,* 412-440.

Alwin, D. F., & Hauser, R. M. (1975). The decomposition of effects in path analysis. *American Sociological Review 40,* 37-47.

Alwin, D. F., & Jackson, D. J. (1982a). Adult values for children: An application of factor analysis to ranked preference data. In R. M. Hauser, D. Mechanic, A. O. Haller, & T. S. Hauser (Eds.), *Social Structure and behavior: Essays in honor of William Hamilton Sewell* (pp. 311-329). New York: Academic Press.

Alwin, D. F., & Jackson, D. J. (1982b). The statistical analysis of Kohn's measures of parental values. In K. G. Jöreskog & H. Wold (Eds.), *Systems under indirect observation: Causality, structure and prediction* (pp. 197-223). Amsterdam: North-Holland.

Alwin, D. F., & Krosnick, J. A. (1985). The measurement of values in surveys: A comparison of ratings and rankings. *Public Opinion Quarterly, 49,* 535-552.

Bendix, R. (1974). Inequality and social stucture: A comparison of Marx and Weber. *American Sociological Review, 39,* 149-161.

Bowles, S., & Gintis, H. (1976). *Schooling in capitalist America: Educational reform and the contradictions of economic life.* New York: Basic Books.

Bronfenbrenner, U. (1958). Socialization and social class through time and space. In E. E. Maccoby, T. M. Newcomb & E. L. Hartl (Eds.), *Readings in social psychology* (pp. 400-425). New York: Holt, Rinehart, and Winston.

Bronfenbrenner, U. (1979). *The Ecology of human development: Experiments by nature and design.* Cambridge, MA: Harvard University Press.

Dreeben, R. (1967). The contribution of schooling to the learning of norm. Duncan, B. Duncan, O. D., & McRae, J. A. (1978). *Sex typing and social roles: A research report.* New York: Academic Press.

Duncan, O. D. (1975). *Introduction to structural equation models.* New York: Academic Press.

Duncan, O. D., Schuman, H., & Duncan, B. (1973). *Social change in a metropolitan community.* New York: Russell Sage Foundation.

Duvall, E. M. (1946). Conception of childhood. *American Journal of Sociology,* ux(52), 193-203.

Featherman, D.L., Sobel, M., & Dickens, D. (1975). *A manual for Coding Occupations and*

NORC Prestige Scores. Working paper no. *75-1.* Madison: Center for Demography and Ecology, University of Wisconsin.

Gecas, V. (1979). The influence of social class on socialization. In W. R. Burr, R. Hill, F. I. Nye, & I. L. Reiss (Eds.), *Contemporary theories about the family* (pp. 365-404). New York: Free Press.

Gecas, V. (1981). Contexts of socialization. In M. Rosenberg & R. Turner (Eds.), *Social psychology: Sociological perspectives* (pp. 165-199). New York: Basic Books.

Hays, W. L., & Winkler, H. L. (1971). *Statistics: Probability, inference and decision.* New York: Holt, Rinehart and Winston.

House, J. S. (1981) Social structure and personality. In M. Rosenberg & R. Turner (Eds.), *Social psychology: Sociological perspectives* (pp. 525-561). New York: Basic Books.

Hyman, H. H. (1953). The value systems of different classes: A social psychological contribution to the analysis of stratification. In R. Bendix and S. M. Lipset (Eds.), *Class, status and power: Social stratification in comparative perspective* (pp. 488-499). New York: Free Press.

Jackson, D. J., & Alwin, D. F. (1980). The factor analysis of ipsative measures. *Sociological Methods and Research, 9,* 218-328.

Kohn, M. L. (1959a). Social class and parental values. *American Journal of Sociology, 64,* 337-366.

Kohn, M. L. (1959b). Social class and the excercise of parental authority. *American Sociological Review, 68,* 471-480.

Kohn, M. L. (1963). Social class and parent-child relationships: An interpretation. *American Journal of Sociology, 68,* 471-480.

Kohn, M. L. (1969). *Class and conformity: A study in values.* Homewood, IL: Dorsey Press.

Kohn, M. L. (1976). Social class and parental values: Another confirmation of the relationship. *American Sociological Review, 41,* 538-545.

Kohn, M. L. (1977). Reassessment 1977. In M. L. Kohn (Ed.), *Class and conformity: A study in values* (pp. XXV-1X, 2nd ed.). Chicago: University of Chicago Press.

Kohn, M.L. (1981). Personality, occupation, and social stratification: A frame of reference. In D.J.Trieman & R.V. Robinson (Eds.), *Research in social stratification* (Vol. 1, pp. 267-297). Greenwich, Conn.: JAI Press.

Kohn, M.L., & Carroll, E.E. (1960). Social class and the allocation of parental responsibilities. *Sociometry, 23,* 372-392.

Kohn, M. L., & Schoenbach, C. (1983). Class, stratification, and psychological functioning. In Kohn, et al. *Work and personality: An inquiry into the impact of special stratification* (pp. 154-193). Norwood, NJ: Ablex.

Kohn, M. L., & Schooler, C. (1973). Occupational experience and psychological functioning: An assessment of reciprocal effects. *American Sociological Review, 38,* 97-118.

Kohn, M. L., & Schooler, C. (1978). The reciprocal effects of the substantive complexity ofwork and intellectual flexibility: A longitudinal assessment. *American Journal of Sociology, 84,* 24-52.

Kohn, M. L., & Schooler, C. (1982). Job conditions and personality: A longitudinal assessment of their reciprocal effects. *American Journal of Sociology, 87,* 1257-1286.

Kohn, M. L., Schooler, C., Miller, J., Miller, K. A., Schoenbach, C. & Schoenberg, R. (1983). *Work and personality: An inquiry into the impact of social stratification.* Norwood, NJ: Ablex.

Lenski, G. (1961). *The religious factor.* Garden City, NY: Doubleday.

Lynd, R., & Lynd, H. (1929). *Middletown: A study in contemporary American culture.* New York: Harcourt Brace.

Maccoby, E. E. (1978). Current changes in the family and their impact upon the socialization of children. In J. M. Yinger & S. J. Cutler (Eds.), *Major social issues: A multidisciplinary view.* New York: Free Press.

Masnick, G., & Bane, M. J. (1980). The nation's families: 1900-1990. Boston: Auburn.

Miller, D. R., & Swanson, G. E. (1958). *The changing American parent.* New York: Wiley.

Miller, K. A., Kohn, M. L., & Schooler, C. (1985). Educational self-direction and the cognitive functioning of students. *Social Forces, 63,* 923-944.

Miller, K. A., Kohn, M. L., & Schooler, C. (1986). Educational self-direction and personality. *American Sociological Review, 51,* 372-390.

Morgan, W. R., Alwin, D. F., & Griffin, L. J. (1979). Social origins, parental values, and the transmission of inequality. *American Journal of Sociology, 85,* 156-166.

Pearlin L. I., & Kohn, M. L. (1966). Social class, occupation, and parental values: a cross-national study. *American Sociological Review, 31,* 466-479.

Piaget J. (1965). *The moral development of the child.* New York: Free Press.

Robinson, R. V., & Kelley, J. (1979). Class as conceived by Marx and Dahrendorf. *American Sociological Review, 44,* 38-58.

Schlumbohm, J. (1980). 'Traditional' collectivity and 'modern' individuality: Some questions and suggestions for the historical study of socialization. The examples of the German lower and upper bourgeoisies around 1800. *Social History, 5,* 71-103.

Schooler, C. (1972a). Social antecedents of adult psychological functioning. *American Journal of Sociology, 78,* 299-322.

Schooler, C. (1972b). Childhood family structure and adult psychological functioning. *Sociometry, 35,* 255-269.

Sewell, W. H., & Hauser, R. M. (1975). *Education, occupation and earnings: Achievement in the early career.* New York: Academic Press.

Słomczyński, K. M., Miller, J., & Kohn, M. L. (1981). Stratification work and values: A Polish-United States comparison. *American Sociological Review, 46,*720-744.

Stone, L. (1977). *The family, sex and marriage in England, 1500-1800.* New York: Harper and Row.

U. S. Department of Labor. (1977). *Dictionary of occupatonal titles.* Fourth Edition. Washington DC: U.S. Government Publications Office.

Williams, R. M. (1968). Values. In D. Sills (Ed.), *International encyclopedia of the social sciences.* New York: Macmillan.

Wright, E. O. (1978). *Class, crisis and the state.* London: New Left Books.

Wright, E. O. (1980). Varieties of Marxist conceptions of class structure. *Politics and Society, 9,* 323-370.

Wright, E. O., & Perrone, L. (1977). Marxist class categories and income inequality. *American Sociological Review, 42,* 32-55.

18 Women, Morality, and Social Change from a Discourse Analysis Perspective

E. Ann Kaplan
Rutgers State University
New Brunswick, New Jersey

In recent years, some psychologists and philosophers have shown renewed interest in empathy, caring, and morality (justice ethics).[1] This work may be seen as a series of discourses that stand in an interesting relationship to certain historical discourses that arose before Freud, and therefore before modern psychological views. For my purposes here, a discourse may be defined as a kind of system shared by a socially constituted group of speakers, or as referring to a particular social practice. Gledhill (1978) states that it "provides the terms of what can or cannot be said, and includes all those items, aesthetic, semantic, ideological, social which can be said to speak for or refer to those whose discourse it is" (p. 13).

Looking specifically at statements about women and morality, I argue that current discourses may usefully be linked to an ongoing tradition, dating at least from 1762 and the publication of Rousseau's *Emile*. This tradition may be seen as a kind of gender-based "Master Morality Discourse," to adapt a Nietzschean concept, developed (in its modern form) in the 18th and 19th centuries in response to the rise of industrial capitalism and the bourgeoisie.

My aim in adapting this concept is to demonstrate the continuity of certain culturally constructed (and culturally ingrained) forms of thought; I am interested in the difficulty of eradicating ourselves as thinkers from intellectual traditions that resist change, functioning rather like the needle in the record's groove. Nietzsche, arguably the Father of discourse analysis, was one of the

[1] I am thinking particularly of work by Lawrence Kohlberg, Martin Hoffman, Carol Gilligan, and Nel Noddings. For full citations, see bibliography.

first to perceive and constantly comment on this habit of the human mind. "The masters' right of giving names," he notes in *The Genealogy of Morals,* "goes so far that it is permissible to look on language itself as the expression of the power of the masters: they say, 'this is that, and that,' they seal finally every object and every event with a sound, and thereby at the same time take possession of it." (Nietzsche, 1887, 1954). Nietsche was uninterested in the male domination of the moral traditions he warred against, but this is central to my concerns, influenced as I am by recent feminist discourse. The *Master* Morality Discourse is then aptly named because it was indeed a "discourse of the masters" concerned to position woman in ways that addressed specifically *male bourgeois needs.*

The first half of my chapter briefly summarizes the gender issues in the Master Morality Discourse, after which I turn to recent work by philosophers and psychologists. Psychologists may be distinguished from philosophers in that, as social scientists, their focus is on data collected from living subjects. Such scholars are in a position to explore the relationship between cultural discourses and actual behavior; but usually their object is to test an hypothesis about some particular aspect of behavior rather than to deal with discourses. It is then interesting to find that current data, collected without a particular focus on cultural discourses, betray the legacy of 18th and 19th-century ideas. Men and women are described as thinking of themselves and as adopting moral behavior in accord with what 18th and 19th-century writers and thinkers considered desirable for each gender. In other words, the data that social scientists in the areas of empathy and morality collect are data about contemporary *discourses.*

The fact that the Master Morality Discourse is still the framework within which we think suggests that cultural discourses take root in a way surprisingly resistant to change. Nevertheless, because discourses are partly shaped by social conditions (i.e., stage of technology, economic arrangements, class/race organization), they are subject to change when conditions change. We do thus find interesting alterations in the discourses about women and morality as women have begun to enter the hitherto male-defined public sphere. But the tensions and conflicts that women are now seen as experiencing are nevertheless a result of the 19th-century ideas within whose constraints we still think. It is thus important to be fully aware of the historical roots of contemporary moral discourses that constrain women, if we are to understand what is going on today and see its implications for future social change. It is these historical roots, taking texts as "data," that this chapter addresses.

The positioning of women versus men in moral thinking has a long history, going back at least to the Old and New Testaments; however, as noted, I am concerned here with the development of conceptions in the modern period. Biblical notions, as we see, naturally still invade modern concepts, but the Industrial Revolution may be seen as solidifying modern conceptions in entailing a major shift in the Biblical paradigm.

This shift resulted partly from the economically necessary transition of middle-class women out of their role as producers in the old rural economy into that as consumers in the new bourgeois home (Cott, 1977; Welter, 1966). The change in women's status was simply one of many taking place, and it is also true that many of the ideas forcefully articulated in early 19th-century America had indeed been in practice, to a greater or lesser degree, before that time (Degler, 1980; Leverenz, 1980). The obvious insecurity of great social change is partly compensated for by categorizing and rigidifying gender roles. It is society's way of maintaining a degree of order when all else seems to be slipping out of control.

In addition, at the time of the Industrial Revolution, a new social class, the bourgeoisie, was emerging, entailing a specific need to articulate new and appropriate male-female roles. The text that first synthesizes the new roles, Rousseau's *Emile* (1762), specifically addresses the new middle class in Europe that begins to legislate the moral norms for the society as a whole as it replaces the old aristocracy.

It is significant that from Rousseau on, the conception of women in relation to morality is intricately lined to the new foregrounding of her role as Mother, although this is somewhat underplayed in Rousseau in favor of woman as man's plaything and servant.

Rousseau's conception of women and morality is heavily inflected by remnants of Christian ideology, which dominates the semiotic field in the West up until Marx and Freud, and could always be utilized when female issues were at stake. Rousseau is very much of his century in having abandoned Descartes' notion of innate ideas in favor of Lockean sensationalism, but he still values reason. But when dealing with women, Rousseau reverts to the Christian view of woman's essentially "fallen" nature, which originates with the Biblical Eve. Incipiently lustful and morally weak, woman can be tempted and thus must be carefully schooled in unquestioned precepts, because this alone will secure right behavior.

This underlying, unexplicit Christian ideology accounts for Rousseau's belief that women lack the capacity for abstract reasoning.

Rousseau (1762/1974) states:

> A woman's reason is practical and therefore she soon arrives at a given conclusion but she fails to discover it for herself. The social relation of the sexes... produces a moral person of which the woman is the eye and the man the hand; man teaches woman what to see, she teaches him what to do. (p. 340)

Men, that is, discover the abstract moral principles, whereas women apply them to the practical sphere.

Rousseau had an incipient notion of moral development (anticipating here later thinkers like Piaget and Kohlberg), but woman never gets beyond the first stage, namely that "when what is wrong for young people is what those about them have decided to be wrong; what they are told to do is good, what they are forbidden to do is bad." Rousseau noted that it is especially important for girls to have the right people around them at this stage, because what they learn here is basically all that they will ever learn.

At about age 12, the boy, however, moves on to the next stage, which is "the time when they begin to judge things for themselves," and when "reason becomes enlightenment" as "growing emotion gives a voice to conscience." (p. 340). (Note here that for Rousseau, as not for some later thinkers, emotion prompts moral reasoning.) At this point, significantly, education passes out of woman's hand into those of the Father, or his (male) tutor substitute.

It is only because the early education of man is in woman's hands ("his morals, his passion, his woes, his pleasure, his happiness, depend on her", p. 344) that her education is important. The girl's biological processes shape her to be a mother and require special attention in a way that has no parallel for the boy. The very survival of the human race depends on the woman's function in cementing the family through her skills in emotions and relationships, and in her fidelity.

But man is necessary to her in providing the principles for "right thinking" or justice morality, which women learn by rote because reasons would confuse them. Rousseau thus inscribed in cultural discourse a division of labor exacerbated later on by the Industrial Revolution, re-theorizing the male/public, female/private split that dominated prior discourses and that still shapes contemporary ones.

Rousseau was able to sustain his essentially platonic and utopian view of human nature, and his belief in the beneficence of male reason because he was writing prior to the full impact of both the Industrial and the French Revolutions. These events were to challenge the concept of man's "natural" humanity to his fellow man. (The use of "man" and the male pronoun is deliberate: It embodies Rousseau's philosophy in which woman was part of nature and not part of the moral world. Cf. Wollstonecroft's rebuttal follows). For Rousseau, man in his natural state was good, and all that was needed was to remove the corrupting influences of social organization and habits.

Mary Wollstonecraft's *A Vindication of the Rights of Woman* (1792), written explicitly as an angry rebuttal of Rousseau's treatment of woman in *Emile,* catches Rousseau in the trap of his own social theory, arguing that it is *society* and not nature that has made women vain, weak, and superficial. Believing like Rousseau in the perfection of human reason, Wollstonecraft, however, wanted to bring women into the sphere of the rational denied her by Rousseau. She made three main points, attacking first Rousseau's notion that women are incapable of abstract reasoning. In her view, their apparent "immorality" is merely the effect of man's deliberate enslavement of women.

Wollstonecraft found Sophie "grossly unnatural," believing she merely exemplifies Rousseau's selfish wish to keep women for his playthings and servants. Debunking the Biblical myth of Eve having been made out of Adam's rib, Wollstonecraft appealed to woman's position as a human being, alongside men, differentiated, as is man, from animals by virtue of having Reason. In 17th-century style, Wollstonecraft saw Reason as the supreme human quality, always in combat with the passions that indicate man's brutish remnant: The capacity to reason equals the capacity to be moral and shows man's link to God. If woman be human, her reason must be developed; if her reason is developed, she will stand alongside, and is not different from man.

Second, and following from this, Wollstonecraft argued that morality is also inherently linked to *independence*. As long as women are made slavishly subservient to men, they cannot be truly moral. Wollstonecraft deplores the few opportunities that women are given to exercise their minds on anything other than household duties and suggests, what was at the time revolutionary, that women need representatives in government, might be physicians as well as nurses, or undertake business of various kinds. This might save many women from prostitution, or from wasted, empty lives, devoted to "sensibility."

Finally, realizing that in fact most women will continue to be Mothers, Wollstonecraft (1792/1974) argued that to fulfill this role adequately women need both reason and independence. "Unless," she says, "the understanding of woman be enlarged, and her character rendered more form by being allowed to govern her own conduct, she will never have sufficient sense or command of her temper to manage her childern properly" (p. 227).

Not able to move beyond the constraints of thinking in her historical period and seriously confront the public/male, private/female split, Wollstonecraft nevertheless argued that women must acquire proper cognitive functioning (as we would now phrase it) to carry out their task. Assuming that morality is a purely cognitive function (she does not allow for the empathic base Rousseau had described for the boy), Wollstonecraft anticipates Kohlberg's notion that the highest stage of morality is justice thinking. Wollstonecraft aimed to bring woman into a sphere from which Rousseau excluded her.

But powerful as was Wollstonecraft's argument for women's intellectual/rational capabilities, it was bought at a cost: Mary Wollstonecraft does not confront Rousseau's distrust of femele sexuality, and in fact goes even further that he does in deploring sexual passion and romance (C. Kaplan, 1983). It was as if, given traditional discourses, women of this period had no intellectual constructs through which to argue at once for woman's access to reason *and* for her sexual pleasure. The argument for reason had to rest on its freeing women from their "natural" lasciviousness encouraged by too much idleness and leisure.

Linked by their 17th-century intellectual milieu, although separated in relation to male and female morality, both Rousseau and Wollstonecraft were widely read in Europe and America and together helped shape the American

17th-century discourse of women and morality, which reflects adjustments in the basic model (Cot, 1977; Fliegelman, 1982). Interestingly enough, in America, Rousseau's model of the Father as teacher is replaced by that of the Mother as teacher. As will be clear in the American discourses discussed later, Industrial man is conceived of as requiring woman to act as a "corrective" to the new values of competition and instrumentalism. In this discourse, then, we find a change in the respect and authority accorded woman, correspondingly, in her moral stature. Although Rousseau had inscribed the division of *labor*, the male and female worlds remained united under the moral guidance of the Father's Law. Men and women were seen to have different capacities in relation to an agreed on set of principles (men reason; women enact what men lay down.).

By the 19th-century, discourses show a clear split between the male and the female worlds, with a "higher" morality being implicitly accorded women, at least in women's own discourses. Linda Kerber sees this change as already prepared for in America though the "Revolutionary Rhetoric" of the 1776 rebellion against Colonial oppressors; for, as always, revolutionary idealism filters down to women (and sometimes minorities), forcing attention to their rights. According to Kerber (1980), "the public ideology of individual responsibility and virtue" brought about a change in conception of the mother's role (p. 231). What in Rousseau had been a mere murmer about patriotism only being able to survive "in the soil of that miniature Fatherland, the home," is developed into a whole new discourse about *woman's* service to the nation in the private sphere paralleling men's in the public sphere. "Motherhood," Kerber (1980) notes, "was discussed almost as if it were a fourth branch of gevernment, a device that ensured social control in the gentlest possible way" (p. 200).

Women like Mrs. Sigourney, in the early 19th-century, were perpetuating the idea that the Mother's mission in the home is equal to that of Governors of the State (Sigourney, 1938). Woman was no longer conceived (as Rousseau had conceived Sophie) as a mere male appendagewhose social role was monitored by the Father; instead the Mother is viewed as newly important – as having the responsibility of upholding, continuing, and embodying the old values in danger of being swept away in the tide of changes that were represented as beyond control (Marx, 1963). Although women writers like Sigourney still subscribed to the four qualities of the "Cult of True Womanhood" – namely piety, purity, domesticity, and submissiveness (all qualities already present in Rousseau's Sophie), their discourses now included an image of power over the domestic world undreamt of by Sophie.

The new split between the male and female worlds was obviously complex and contradictory and could be manipulated in various ways. On the one hand, the very relegating of the domestic sphere to the Mother ensured its denigration as "inferior" (women were lesser beings and the central pursuits were obviously the male ones);[2] but on the other hand, that sphere had importance as the training ground for future (male) citizens, and arguably as upholding traditional (Christian) morality.

I want briefly to focus on some arguments by 19th-century American women because they provide important background to those recently advanced by Hoffman, Gilligan, and Noddings. It is significant that 19th-century women did not generally complain about their relegation to the domestic as contemporary women have done. On the whole, women accepted that the domestic was their appropriate (perhaps inevitable) sphere but developed two main lines of argument designed to give them more freedom and to enhance their status, both of which centered on the issue of female morality.

Much indebted to Wollstonecraft, Margaret Fuller insists in her *Woman in the Nineteenth Century* (1845) that women are not only capable of reason and self-reliance but must be encouraged in both. Writing 50 years or so after Wollstonecraft, Fuller was keenly aware, as Wollstonecraft could not yet be, of the "fallen" nature of the male public sphere already discused and was one of the first to give woman the task of redeeming that sphere through her higher, less self-interested moral power. Fuller addressed the issue of man's shameless instrumental and expediency thinking and argued for woman taking issue with that men are doing, individually or in unity. What is interesting is her claim what, just because they are more distanced from the public sphere, women are able to see and judge society's errors. We will see how Stowe also showed this to be the case.

In this text, Fuller also anticipated Stowe and the second line of argument that 19th-century women were to make, namely that woman's special capacity for empathy gave her a distinct moral power (i.e., one different from men). In this discourse, far form moral action being the result of high-level abstract/principled thinking, woman's moral action arises first from "sympathy as to outward condition" of the slaves (i.e., women recognized their own oppression in that of the slaves, could identify personally with them, and then were moved to take moral action to remedy their plight). Second, moral action emerges from woman's desire to bring the world more in harmony with "her nature" (which is inherently self-sacrificing and caring.) (Fuller, 1845/1971, pp. 110-111-, 166-167).

Fuller took pains to reassure her readers that the changes she advocated would not affect established social institutions and arrangements. Nature and social need would ensure that women would continue to mother, so a few women should be able to do other things.

---

[2] As late as 1868, an issue of the influential *Lancet* magazine belittles the women who lay claim to doing serious intellectual work and asserts yet once more that woman is made for Motherhood and domesticity.

Fuller finally argued against the preconception that love is woman's whole existence: Once self-reliant, woman no more than man would be absorbed by love. But the constraints Fuller was under to keep intact woman's established familial duties and her "purity" is evident in her setting up the biblical Mary, Virgin Mother, as the Ideal Woman combining the Virgin Mind with "material wisdom and conjugal affections" (Fuller, p. 177).

Whereas both Wollstonecraft and Fuller prepared culture to accept woman's entry into the male public sphere, Harriet Beecher Stowe was primarily concerned with establishing the higher morality of woman's domestic realm. Working now in fictional form (as against the prose tracts of Fuller and Wollstonecraft), Stowe showed Mothers who exposed the instrumental thinking and immorality of men and their public sphere. Two scenes in her most famous novel, *Uncle Tom's Cabin,* reveal the "fallen" nature of the public sphere and woman's role in asserting a more humane and caring set of values with which to counter the corruption that undermines male social institutions.

In the first, Mrs. Shelby confronts her husband over his decision to sell their beloved slaves to a corrupt trader. Skilled in argument, Mrs. Shelby is described as a woman with "natural magnanimity and generosity of mind" to which was added "high moral and religious sensibility and principle, carried out with great energy and ability into practical results" (Stowe, 1860, 1966, p. 21). She puts the issue on the moral level of sacrificing not only *lives* for monetary gain, but also highly valued principles:

> I have told (Eliza that one soul is worth more than all the money in the world; and how will she believe me when she sees us turn around and sell her child?—sell him, perhaps to certain ruin of body and soul! (p. 45)

Mr. Shelby counters with expediency arguments, against which Mrs. Shelby raises the principled argument even higher, stating that "It is a sin to hold a slave under laws like ours" (p. 45). At this point, Mr. Shelby resorts to the inevitability of expediency thinking in the male sphere: "We men of the world must wink pretty hard at various things and get used to a deal that isn't the exact thing" (p. 46). But here, as earlier, he shows his dependence on the higher morality of woman. Men can disregard moral values in their daily dealings if they know that women (and usually ministers) uphold them.

In the second confrontation, this time between Senator and Mrs. Bird, we again see the woman move from empathic concern for individuals suffering under slavery to articulating general principles about the evils of slavery. Usually living only for her husband and children, Mrs. Bird is nevertheless outraged by cruelty and has taken in two of Shelby's runaway slaves, Eliza and her little son. On hearing that her husband has endorsed a new Senate Bill outlawing aid to slaves, Mrs. Bird is outraged:

> "You ought to be ashamed John! Poor, homeless, houseless creatures! It's a shameful, wicked, abominable law, and I'll break it for one, the first time I get a chance." (p. 92)

John Vird's reply examplifies abstract/instrumental moral thinking:

> "We mustn't suffer our *feelings* to run away with our *judgment.* You must consider that it's not a matter of private feeling... There is such a state of public agitations arising that we must put aside our *private* feelings." (p. 43)

Not to do so, he says, involves a "great public evil".

For Mrs. Bird, the is intellectual chicanery, a voiding the real issue, which is people's lives. She appeals to John's empathy for "poor, shivering, hungry creatures," trying to make him identify with them. Finally, she nails him by insisting that "political folks" have a way of "coming round and round a plain thing," which they wouldn't even put into practice themselves, exposing how the male public sphere is governed by expediency rather than by moral values. The principle of human justice is abandoned by the Senators in favor of winning votes. By contrast, like Mrs. Shelby, Mrs. Bird is firm in her abstract principle because she has arrived at it by way of empathic feeling for others.

Stowe's caring ethic ultimately relies on a model of Motherhood derived from Christ rather than from the Virgin Mary who is peripheral to the original Christ Story. Uncle Tom, in the Stowe novel, stands in for Christ making the supreme sacrifice of himself for the slaves around him. (It is one of the as yet unexplained puzzles of Western intellectual thought how and why the first cultural Mother Ideal was embodied in a male, only to be transferred to the female in 19th-century discourses.)

Stowe's moral thinking is limited in relation to theorizing social change just because of the Christian underpinning of her morality. Like Christ, Stowe believed in the individual change of heart that will prepare for the millenium (Tompkins, 1978). If Stowe seemed aware of the economic issues in her treatment of slavery as an institution, her work nevertheless pitted morality against capitalism. If capitalism can, by definition, never be moral, Stowe assumed we must throw out economic relations altogether. However, Stowe had no model of possible alternate economic relations that would be more humane and equitable. The Christian concept of the "change-of-heart" as the prerequisite for social change simply ignores the fact that there is no incentive for change as long as the system allows for profit to accrue from buying labor power. In relation to women, as long as they (like Stowe's women) have no economic independence, it is hard to see how their morally superior values can by themselves bring about liberation.

Charlotte Gilman Perkins, writing at the turn of the century, was one of the first women to theorize that a different social organization was essential for more humane interpersonal relations and to base the new ethic around specifically female qualities. Her revolutionary Utopian novel, *Herland* (1915), projects an all-female society based on a caring ethic premissed on women's mothering qualities. The loving Mother-daughter relationship provides the model for all the relationships among the women. Only a few women actually mother, while others pursue intellectual and physical tasks in an atmosphere of collectivity and democratic functioning. Morality is not an issue because there are no conflicts within a total caring ethic.

Gilman-Perkins again speculated, before Nel Noddings, that the cared for "glows" (sic) under the influence of the caring one; and that, in a mutually enhancing fashion, the caring one grows in the action of taking care. But Noddings does not project this onto an hypothetical social organization as does Gilman in *Herland*.

The political limitations of Gilman-Perkins' thinking are obvious, but it is imprtant to note a second limitation in the area of female sexuality. Perkins still could not free herself from the constraints of her period. Sexuality was omitted from *Herland* (reproduction is mysteriously self-generated), and in a sequal, Perkins subscribed to the eugenic theories fashionable at the time that were part of the drive for social purity, including race and sex.[3] Motherliness ("goodness") and sexuality were still polarized.

Writing as she was at the turn of the century, Gilman-Perkins' discourse is still essentially a 19th-century one. Freud was to revolutionize that discourse by his "discovery" and articulation of the psychoanalytic level of human existence hitherto not explicitly recognized. Freud's account of the processes within the nuclear family provides an explanation, on a level other than the social and economic, for the 19th-century discourses that insist on positioning woman as the idealized "Angel in the House," or, failing that, as the wicked witch or stepmother. The theory of the Oedipus complex suggests psychic origins for the polarized representations of the Mother but initiates an element not present in 19th-century discourses and only glimpsed in early 20th-century ones, like Gilman's. This element, linked to Freud's castration theory, has to do with conceiving the Mother as a threat, as endangering male autonomy and independence.

In Freud's theory, both the boy and the girl suffer a trauma on "discovering" the Mother's castration and turn away from her but for different reasons. The boy must eliminate the "feminine" castration and identify with his Father, whereas the girl must accept her "bleeding wound," her lack and remains angry with her mother whom she holds responsible.

---

[3] For a recent survey of the development of ideas about eugenices, cf. series of articles in The New Yorker, especially October 27, 1984 and October 29, 1984.

These insights are crucial for understanding that the child can only accomplish its separation from its Mother through constructing contrasting images of her. These symbolic mothers–one good, one bad–enable the child to cope with the *real* mother's alternate nurturing and punitive dimensions.

But Freud himself could not ultimately escape the heritage of the 19th-century sociological discourses about the Mother or prevent these from being laid over his completely different level of discourse. It is true that Freud paralleled earlier theories in looking from the child position, and then mainly from that of the *boy* child; Freud did not discuss the Mother's representations of the mother-child interaction or analyze the psychic consequences of mothering for the woman.

Nevertheless, it was later child psychiatrists and psychologists Bowlby (1951/1966), Winnicott (1971), and Fraiberg (1977) who drew inferences about the woman's social position from Freud's theories of the girl's unconscious processes, rather than Freud himself. These thinkers prescribed the self-denying, self-abasing behavior that in fact puts an intolerable burden on the mother as *woman;* and it was their neo-Freudian theories that gave new legitimacy to 18th- and 19th-century ideologies concerning women's proper functions and moral capacities.

There was, however, an important shift in the rationale offered for the mother's function that may have indirectly contributed to the oft-proclaimed decline in social morality, and the increase in moral relativism in our day. The mother is no longer to uphold traditional, agreed on *social* moral values but is now responsible for the child's *psychic* health. She is to reproduce in the girl her own nurturing qualities, to ensure the psychic health of the next generation, but to prepare the boy for his later functioning in an increasingly instrumental/expediency-oriented male public sphere.

Neo-Freudian work closed off the terrain that 19th-century women had opened up, so that it was left for later psychologists to recover it. Martin Hoffman was one of the first to research the links between morality and gender and to test long-established gender-role stereotypes. He has suggested that social-role conditioning may be responsible for the sex differences that he found. Hoffman discovered in girls "a more highly internalized humanistic moral orientation" (1975) than in males and suggested that this may result from the girl's receiving more affection from the mother, together with the mother using more induction-style discipline techniques with girls than with boys. Girls are socialized into the "expressive" role, "giving and receiving affection and being responsive to the feelings and needs of others" (p. 726) leading to a more humanistic morality. Boys are early on trained to be expressive, but this is soon replaced by the demand for "instrumental character traits and skills necessary for acting as a liaison between family and society, that is for occupational achievement and success" (p. 726). Achievement striving overrides sensitivity to others' feelings, and lessens the likelihood that males will suffer guilt on transgressing some social norm.

In a later article on "The Role of the Father in Moral Internalization," Hoffman implies that the male public sphere manifests at best amoral thinking and that it is women alone who continue to think morally (1981). And indeed one may ask where there is evidence of Kohlberg's projected highest level justice-thinking actually functioning.

Hoffman's discourse is similar to that in 19th-century women's thinking. His theory that female moral action has an empathic, as against purely cognitive base, fits in with 19th-century women's intuitive sense that this was the way things worked, and that women were more likely to be capable of empathic morality than men.

Carol Gilligan (1977) and Nel Noddings (1984) return to this terrain, now explicitly taking on Lawrence Kohlberg's theory of moral development because it is premissed on what has been considered desirable in male socialization, namely the creation of an autonomous self and the ability to reason out moral conflicts on the level of logic not feeling. Because he rates morality based on feeling as inferior, Kohlberg saw women as mainly functioning at a stage 3 moral level. Building on Hoffman's research, Gilligan argues that women have a different moral developmental pattern because of their different relationship to the Mother, and generally different socialization.

For Gilligan, as for Hoffman, women are socialized into an empathic morality. But Gilligan goes on to point out that the moral conflicts that confront women have specifically to do with the training toward the sacrifice ethic that I have traced historically. But what is interesting is how this discourse causes different problems for women today than for her 19th-century sisters.

Nineteenth-century women accepted the discourse of devotion to others at expense of self as defining their "natural" role. For this, they were, as we've seen, heralded as the saviors of civilization; they placed their caring morality as higher than that of men but experienced little conflict in acting in accordance with the ethic because this defined their domestic role.

Twentieth-century women, on the other hand, arguably face different conflicts because of the possibilities opened us as a result of recent economic, social, ane technological developments that I do not need to reiterate. The new possibilities for self-fulfillment and personal achievement conflict with the continued discourse of devotion to the other.

The dominant mass media form of the 20th-century (at least up until the invention of television), i.e., the Classical Hollywood Film, frequently presents the conflict between the heroine's needs and desires, and those of a loved one close to her. Two films by Dorothy Arnzer (one of the few female Hollywood directors in the sound period), *Christopher Strong* (1932) and *Dance Girl Dance* (1940), expose this sort of conflict, as do also films by male directors like Cukor's *Camille* (1932), Stahl's *Imitation of Life* (1934), Vidor's *Stella Dallas* (1937), or Rapper's *Now Voyager* (1942). Conflict between self-fulfillment (whether in the public sphere or through a relationship deemed "illicit" in one way or another by patriarchy) and the perceived needs of a loved one, is the paramount conflict in melodramas that address the female spectator (E. A. Kaplan, 1983b, 1986). Although in any one narrative the conflict is complex, the point of these films is to teach women the higher value of the sacrifice mode, and the putting aside of woman's own needs, desires, and wishes for self-fulfillment.

Movies produced on the brink of the women's movement (such as Douglas Sirk's remake of *Imitation of Life* (1959) increasingly showed the threat that any change in woman's moral system implied for the society as a whole. This was a theme recently revived at the very height of women's entry into the public sphere in films like *Kramer Versus Kramer* (1980) or *Ordinary People* (1981) pairing the old, cold, neglecting mother with the new nurturing father, or those like *Mommy Dearest* (1981) and *Frances* (1982) reinstating the 1940s cruel, sadistic mother.

Gilligan's discourse builds on and begins to alter the 19th-century female discourse of devotion to the other at expense of self. Her moral developmental pattern for women keeps intact Kohlberg's notion of preconventional, conventional, and postconventional morality but changes the content of the latter two stages. Girls, like boys, will begin with a preconventional "selfishness" orientation; but for women, this is then reversed at the conventional level, becoming the ethic of devotion to others over self. She suggests that in order to become fully autonomous, independent, and moral people, women must bring the self into the moral order. The postconventional morality of the good is still based on empathy rather than on a purely abstract logical reasoning, but it must include the right of the self to want things. The rights of the self have to be balanced against the rights of others, and the outcome depends on the particular context rather than on some principle that would apply in all cases (Gilligan, 1977, pp. 481-517).[4]

Obviously influenced by Gilligan's work, Nel Noddings picks up on the concept of women's empathic morality. Her theory, however, abandons the cognitive elements as she explores exactly what the caring ethic means and how it works. In this way, her discourse interestingly looks back to the kind of Christian-based caring ethic that we saw in Harriet Beecher Stowe, writing 100 years earlier. Noddings does not claim that only women are capable of the caring ethic, but merely that women have more access to it through their identification with the Mother. The Mother-child relationship provides, for Noddings, the model of the caring relating that should characterize all our social dealings (Noddings, 1984 pp. 30-31, 83, 99).

The empirically based reiteration of the 19th-century notion of the split between the male and female moral worlds is a fascinating aspect of the work of Hoffman, Gilligan, and Noddings. All three thinkers conceptualize woman's

---

[4] This article presents Gilligan's points far more concisely and coherently than the much longer and popularized version made into a book, *In A Different Voice: Psychological Theory and Women's Development*, Cambride, MA: Harvard University Press, 1982.

morality as more empathic, and as a model for improving moral relations in a society that apparently operates amorally. Woman's morality is thus, once again, reified as the desirable form.

This discourse finds itself up against (and is arguably re-evoked by) the increasingly individualistic and materialistic discourses of the postmodern, Reagan era. Hoffman, Noddings, and others only fantasize the possibility that women's caring ethic will be able to transform the male public sphere, shifting it in a humanistic direction. It is obvious that women alone cannot be expected to produce social change. Most discourses simply assume that, in order to survive, women will abandon the caring ethic to conform to dominant, amoral male functioning, or that, disillusioned with the amorality of the male public sphere, women will abandon *it*. Discourses favoring women's return to the home build on the notion of this sort of disillusionment.

The only way out seems the construction of a discourse that transcends the gender-based morality polarity so long a dominant feature of Western discourses. Obviously, neither cognitively arrived at moral principles nor empathic morality based on emotion will alone suffice. We need to develop a moral system that will combine the virtues of what the historical discourse has relegated to men on the one hand and to women on the other. We need to continue the demand for men to share the hitherto female-defined caring ethic, but we also need to argue for women developing the cognitive reasoning skills hitherto mainly assigned to men. Armed with such a discourse, we may be able to construct a socially shared humanitarian goal that would begin to reverse the negative social direction Western culture is currently embarked on.

REFERENCES

Bowlby, J. (1966). *Maternal care and mental health.* New York: Schocken Books.

Cott, N. (1977). *The bonds of womanhood: Women's sphere in New England, 1780–1835.* New Haven and London: Yale University Press.

Degler, C. N. (1980). *At odds: Women and family in America from the revolution to the present.* New York: Oxford University Press.

Fliegelman, J. (1982). *Prodigals and pilgrims: The American Revolution against patriarchal authority, 1750–1800.* Cambridge University Press.

Fraiberg, S. (1977). *Every child's birthright: In defense of mothering.* New York: Basic Books.

Fuller, M. (1845). *Woman in the nineteenth century.* Reprint New York: Norton, 1971.

Gilligan, C. (1977). In a different voice: Women's conception of the self and of morality. *Harvard Educational Review, 47* (4), 481-517.

Gilligan, C. (1982). *In a different voice: Psychological theory and women's development.* Cambridge, Mass: Harvard University Press.

Gledhill, C. (1978). Klute I: A contemporary film noir and feminist criticism. In E. A. Kaplan (Ed.), *Women in film noir.* London: The British Film Institute.

Hoffman, M. L. (1975). Sex differences in moral internalization and values. *Journal of Personality and Social Psychology, 32* (4).

Hoffman, M. L. (1981). The role of the father in moral internalization. In M. Lamb (Ed.), *The role of the father in child development.* Hillsdale, NJ: Lawrence Erlbaum Associates.

Kaplan, C. (1983). Wild nights: Pleasure/sexuality/feminism. In *Formations of pleasure* (pp. 15-30). London: Routledge & Kaplan.

Kaplan, E. A. (1983b). The case of the missing mother: Patriarchy and the maternal in Vidor's *Stella Dallas. Heresies, 4* (4), p. 81-85.

Kaplan, E. A. (1986). Mothering, feminism and representation: The maternal in Hollywood melodrama, 1910–1940. In C. Glendhill (Ed.), *Women and melodrama.* London: The British Film Institute.

Kerber, L. (1980). *Women of the republic: Intellect and ideology in revolutionary America.* Chapel Hill: University of North Carolina Press.

Leverenz, D. (1980). *The language of puritan feeling: An exploration in literature, psychology and social history.* New Brunswick, NJ: Rutgers University Press.

Marx, L. (1964). *The machine in the garden:* Technology and the pastoral ideal in America. New York: Oxford University Press.

Nietzsche, F. (1887/1954). *The genealogy of morals.* In *The philosophy of Nietzsche,* Modern Library Edition. New York: Random House.

Noddings, N. (1984). *Caring.* Berkeley: University of California Press.

Rousseau, J. J. (1762/1974). *Emile.* Foxley, trans.). London: Dent.

Sigourney, Mrs. Lydia Howard (1838). *Letters to mother.* New York: Harper & Bros.

Stowe, H. Beecher (1860/1966). *Uncle Tom's Cabin.* New York: Signet.

Tompkins, J. P. (1978). Sentimental power: *Uncle Tom's Cabin* and the politics of literary history. *Glyph 2.* Reprinted in E. Showalter (Ed.), *The new feminist criticism: Essays on women, literature and theory (pp. 81-104). Pantheon, 1985.*

Welter, B. (Summer 1966). The cult of true womanhood: 1820–1860. American Quarterly, XVIII.

Winnicott, D. W. (1971). *Playing and reality.* New York: Basic Books.

Wollstonecraft (1792). *A vindication of the rights of woman.* London: Dent (reprinted 1974).

Author Index

T

U-V

W

Y-Z

Subject Index